THE TIMUCUAN CHIEFDOMS OF SPANISH FLORIDA

Florida Museum of Natural History: Ripley P. Bullen Series

UNIVERSITY PRESS OF FLORIDA

Florida A&M University, Tallahassee
Florida Atlantic University, Boca Raton
Florida Gulf Coast University, Ft. Myers
Florida International University, Miami
Florida State University, Tallahassee
New College of Florida, Sarasota
University of Central Florida, Orlando
University of Florida, Gainesville
University of North Florida, Jacksonville
University of South Florida, Tampa
University of West Florida, Pensacola

The Timucuan Chiefdoms of Spanish Florida

VOLUME 2: RESISTANCE AND DESTRUCTION

John E. Worth

University Press of Florida
Gainesville · Tallahassee · Tampa · Boca Raton
Pensacola · Orlando · Miami · Jacksonville · Ft. Myers · Sarasota

Copyright 1998 by John E. Worth
Published in the United States of America
All rights reserved

First cloth printing, 1998
First paperback printing, 2020

25 24 23 22 21 20   6 5 4 3 2 1

Library of Congress Cataloging-in-Publication Data
Worth, John E.
The Timucuan chiefdoms of Spanish Florida / John E. Worth
p. cm.—(The Ripley P. Bullen series)
Includes bibliographical references and index.
Contents: v. 1. Assimilation.—v. 2. Resistance and destruction.
ISBN 978-0-8130-1574-3 (cloth: alk. paper).—ISBN 978-0-8130-1575-0 (cloth: alk. paper)
ISBN 978-0-8130-6840-4 (pbk)
1. Timucua Indians—Kings and rulers. 2. Timucua Indians—Government relations. 3. Timucua Indians—Missions. 4. Franciscans—Missions—Florida—History. 5. Florida—History—Spanish colony, 1565–1783. 6. Spain—Colonies—America—Administration. I. Title. II. Series.
E99.T55W67 1998   97-51442
975.9'01—dc21

The University Press of Florida is the scholarly publishing agency for the State University System of Florida, comprising Florida A&M University, Florida Atlantic University, Florida Gulf Coast University, Florida International University, Florida State University, New College of Florida, University of Central Florida, University of Florida, University of North Florida, University of South Florida, and University of West Florida.

University Press of Florida
2046 NE Waldo Road
Suite 2100
Gainesville, FL 32609
http://upress.ufl.edu

To Christopher

Contents

List of Figures and Tables xi
Foreword, by Jerald T. Milanich xii

Chapter 1: Demographic Collapse

The Flaw in the System 1
Baseline Population Levels 2
Seventeenth-Century Demographic Collapse 8
Epidemic Diseases 10
Stresses of the Colonial Labor System 13
Frontier Raiding 16
Reduced Population Growth 21
Out-Migration 22

Chapter 2: Repopulating Timucua

Countering Demographic Collapse 27
The Aggregation of Towns 27
Directed Resettlement 30
Out-Migration and *Reducción* 32
Population "Backflow" 35
The Impact of Depopulation 37

Chapter 3: The Timucuan Rebellion

Armed Resistance 38
Governor Diego de Rebolledo 39
The Immediate Cause 45
Buildup to Rebellion 50
Murders in Timucua 60

Chapter 4: The Pacification of Timucua

The Initial Response 66
The March to Ivitachuco 74

Negotiations at Machava 79
Punishment of the Timucuan Rebels 83

Chapter 5: The Transformation of Timucua

The Visitation of Apalachee 88
The Political Transformation of Timucua 89
The Geographic Transformation of Timucua 97

Chapter 6: Implementation and Resistance

Rebolledo vs. the Franciscans 106
Further Disputes 110
Military Presence in the Western Provinces 112
Persistence of the Rebolledo Plan 114

Chapter 7: Late Seventeenth-Century Timucua

A Transformed Interior 117
Unrest at San Martín 118
Continued Fugitivism 121
Junta in San Pedro 122
Timucua during the 1670s 124
New Spanish Haciendas 130
Immigrants to Ibiniuti 133
The Census of 1681 134
Leadership of the Timucua Province 135
Taking Stock 138

Chapter 8: The Destruction of Timucua

Slave-Raid at Santa Catalina 140
The Destruction of San Juan 141
Assault on Santa Fé 144
Siege on Apalachee 145
The Final Raids 146

Chapter 9: Remnants

Regrouping in St. Augustine 147
Exile 156

Appendix A: Mission Locations

Introduction 159
Missions of the Camino Real 165

Missions of the Northern Timucua Mission Province   182
Missions of the Upper St. Johns River Watershed   187
Missions of the St. Marys/Satilla River Watersheds   190

Appendix B: Translations of Selected Documents

Junta in San Pedro de Potohiriba, 1670   192
1682 Report by the Royal Officials   198
1740 Francisco de Castilla Relation   200

Notes   207
Bibliography   225
Index   251

Figures and Tables

Figures

1-1. Chronology of global population estimates for Florida missions   9
3-1. Early events in the Timucuan rebellion   53
4-1. Pacification and punishment of the Timucua rebels   76
5-1. The geographic transformation of Timucua after 1657   98
8-1. Timucua at the close of the seventeenth century   143
9-1. Refugee missions around St. Augustine, 1730s   154
A-1. Comparative distances between missions on the Camino Real   161
A-2. Reconstructed route of the 1655 Florida mission visitation   164

Tables

1-1. Documented numbers of communities and population estimates for interior Timucuan local chiefdoms, early mission period   3
1-2. Documented population estimates for interior Timucuan communities, early mission period   4
1-3. Selected documented expeditions to recover fugitives from mission provinces   23
4-1. Rebel and Spanish-allied caciques during the Timucuan rebellion   77
5-1. Timucuan leaders attending the Rebolledo visitation in San Pedro, February 13, 1657 (with the visitation of Asile, February 8)   91
7-1. Compiled mission lists for the Timucua province, 1675–98   125
7-2. Comparative demographic data for individual Timucuan missions, 1675–89   126
7-3. Demographic data from 1681 Florida mission census   136
9-1. Demographic data from the 1711 Florida mission census   148
9-2. Demographic data from the 1717 Florida mission census   150

9-3. Demographic data from the 1726 Florida mission census   151
9-4. Demographic data from the 1728 Florida mission census   152
9-5. Comparative demographic data from 1736–39 Florida mission lists   153
9-6. Franciscan *conventos*, 1735–36   155
A-1. Original order and spelling of all missions with missionaries listed on the 1655 list   163

Foreword

In the summer of 1539 the army of Hernando de Soto marched through northern Florida on its trek into the interior of the southeast United States. At the time, the northern portion of peninsula Florida, including the Atlantic coast, and southeastern Georgia were home to the Timucua Indians.

De Soto's march across northern Florida was the vanguard of a European invasion that sought to colonize the Timucua and incorporate them into Spain's rapidly expanding American empire. An integral part of the process of colonization was to turn the Timucua into loyal Catholic subjects of the Spanish crown, a peaceful population that would labor in support of La Florida, the Spanish name for the southeastern United States.

Subjugation would be accomplished not by the sword, but with the cross. Beginning in the 1580s, two decades after the founding of St. Augustine, Spanish Franciscan friars backed by the military might of Spain would venture into the villages of the Timucua to establish Catholic missions. For nearly two hundred years Indians and Spaniards would interact through the mission system.

In the end, the rigors of colonization would doom the Timucua. As a people they ceased to exist by the mid-eighteenth century. The Timucua and the other Indians of Georgia and Florida would be caught up in the rivalries of European monarchies, rivalries that spilled across the Atlantic Ocean into the Americas.

As a graduate student three decades ago, I was involved in the excavation of a colonial-period Timucua Indian archaeological site on the west side of Orange Lake in Alachua County, Florida. At the time, I believed that the history of those people derived from French and Spanish archives, that it was well understood, and that it would be archaeological research that would enhance what we knew about the Timucua. How wrong I was.

It would be anthropologist John Worth who initially turned my world upside down and made me realize that the story of the Timucua was quite different from that found in most books. As a part of his dissertation research carried out at the University of Florida, John found and interpreted a host of new documentary sources that literally rewrote our history of the Timucua and led to a reevaluation of much of what was known from archaeological research.

But he did not stop there. John has continued to discover and use additional Spanish documents, some never used previously by other investigators, to substantially revise our understanding of the Timucua Indians and the Spanish mission system. In this volume John integrates all of these new sources of information with past knowledge to offer a brilliant new interpretation of the colonial period in Spanish Florida.

The Timucuan Chiefdoms of Spanish Florida is a scholarly benchmark that will forever influence how we view our colonial history. The Florida Museum of Natural History and the University Press of Florida are very proud to publish these important volumes in the Ripley P. Bullen series.

Jerald T. Milanich
Series Editor

CHAPTER 1

Demographic Collapse

The Flaw in the System

As it developed during the initial phase of the primary Florida mission period (1587–1706), the colonial system of Spanish Florida came to be based fundamentally upon the maintenance of stable population reserves in strategic nodes in centers of agricultural production or along the primary transportation network of Spanish Florida. These reserves served not only as the primary labor pool for agricultural production in the Spanish fields around St. Augustine itself (as administered through the yearly *repartimiento*), but also as the resident labor force for the mission towns along the Camino Real, maintaining strategic way stations with food, shelter, and burden bearers for passing travelers, and supporting furthermore both the provincial garrisons and the individual Franciscan convents. The fatal flaw in this system was aboriginal depopulation; the integration of Indian chiefdoms into the colonial system simultaneously resulted in steep demographic collapse, not only from European-introduced epidemics but also exhaustion, exposure, and starvation in the context of the colonial labor system, as well as frontier raiding and even out-migration. The colonial system of Spanish Florida was thus characterized by an almost continual process of adaptation and change driven by rampant demographic collapse in the mission provinces.

The consequences for the missionized Timucuan chiefdoms of the interior were severe, falling within a landlocked mission province situated precisely along the primary transportation conduit between the Atlantic port city of St. Augustine and the populous Gulf province of Apalachee, which ultimately supplied the lion's share of both *repartimiento* laborers and locally produced corn. Although corn and other agricultural products were generally shipped to St. Augustine by sea, workers had to be transported over land. For this reason and many others, the strategic value of the interior Timucuan missions lay in their maintenance as way stations and river crossings. As a result, the depopulation of the Timucua mission province along the Camino Real effectively jeopardized the entire colonial system. Consequently, as population levels dropped in strategic missions, plans were formulated and implemented for the directed resettlement of Timucuan towns and villages, aggregating and relocating entire communities, including converted groups north and south of the primary transpeninsular road. As the strains of the system worsened, more and more fugitives fled the Timucuan missions, and Spanish efforts were increasingly directed toward the recovery of these fugitive *cimarrones*. Even the immigration of unconverted, non-Timucuan Indians was encouraged, ultimately resulting in disastrous consequences. The seventeenth century was thus characterized by increasingly substantial transformations to the social geography of the peninsular interior, resulting not only in a general decline in total population but also in the directed resettlement of surviving Timucuan communities. Even by midcentury, interior Spanish Florida was already a changed landscape, a fact not unnoticed by the Timucuan *caciques* who ultimately rose up in rebellion in the spring of 1656.

Baseline Population Levels

The question of pre-European population levels among the Timucuan chiefdoms in the interior of what would become Spanish Florida is extremely difficult to resolve.[1] Population estimates (on both a local and regional scale) by sixteenth-century European observers are virtually nonexistent, and would be highly suspect even if they existed due to the lack of direct and thorough European reconnaissance in most areas. Even prehistoric archaeology would seem to be largely ineffective in this regard, since even if all the habitation sites of the interior Timucuan chiefdoms were to be located and tested (an unlikely prospect, given the pace of site destruction), ceramic and radiocarbon chronologies will probably never be fine grained enough to permit the discrimination of precisely which sections of each and every archaeological site were occupied at precisely the same moment in time. Finally, even if this were to be possible, population estimates would have to be based on projected interpretations of the average number of inhabitants per aboriginal structure, making resultant population figures essentially wild guesses on a regional scale. More importantly, the impact of indirect European contact during the early and mid-sixteenth century, including not only undocumented epidemics but also Euro-Indian conflict (sparked between aboriginal chiefdoms as a result), is virtually impossible to gauge, but was undoubtedly substantial. By the time the first even

Table 1-1. Documented numbers of communities and population estimates for interior Timucuan local chiefdoms, early mission period

Local chiefdom	Communities	Population	Date	Source
Agua Dulce	6	200*	1602	Montes (1602)
Agua Dulce	5	225*	1606	Davila (1606)
Ibihica	5	7–800	1597	López (1602)
Potano	5	1,000+	1597	López (1602)
Potano	4	1,200	1606	Oré (1936)
Timucua/Ayacuto	5	1,500+	1597	López (1602)
Oconi	?	[2,000?]	1635	Ocaña (1635)
Tarihica	?	4,000 converted	1635	Ocaña (1635)

Note: Asterisks indicate severely depopulated areas.

vaguely reliable population estimates began to appear around the turn of the seventeenth century, pre-European population levels had undoubtedly changed (presumably declining) to varying degrees in most if not all regions of interior Florida, making it virtually impossible to extrapolate backward in time to the moment of initial European contact.

The cautious use of seventeenth-century demographic data, admittedly only fragmentary, in concert with information regarding Timucuan sociopolitical structure and settlement distribution on a local and regional scale, can provide comparatively sound evidence for interpretations regarding baseline population levels among the interior Timucuan chiefdoms at the dawn of the seventeenth-century mission period. An examination of population estimates for several local Timucuan chiefdoms during the late sixteenth and early seventeenth centuries suggests that these sociopolitical units ranged in size between perhaps 200 and 4,000 inhabitants, but were more commonly composed of between perhaps 750 and 1,500 inhabitants distributed in perhaps four to six communities prior to sustained direct European contact (table 1.1). Using these figures, the average community size might range widely between perhaps 125 and 375 people. Contemporaneous estimates of the actual populations of specific Timucuan communities within these local chiefdoms suggests a wide range of between 90 and 712, but more commonly ranging between 200 and 400 individuals (table 1.2). Using an average of about 300 individuals and five communities, the average local chiefdom might thus be projected to contain 1,500 people based on these figures (presuming considerable variation in actual figures for each group). The fact that Timucua's ranking principal town of San Martín de Ayacuto apparently administered a local chiefdom consisting of some 1,500 inhabitants distributed in five towns might provide further

Table 1-2. Documented population estimates for interior Timucuan communities, early mission period

Community	Local chiefdom	Population	Date	Source
Tocoy	Tocoy	90*	1606	Davila (1606)
San Martín de Ayacuto	Timucua/Ayacutu	100 children	1608	Oré (1936)
San Miguel	Potano	200	1606	Oré (1936)
San Buenaventura	Potano	[200]	1606	Oré (1936)
San Francisco	Potano	400	1606	Oré (1936)
Santa Ana	Potano	400	1606	Oré (1936)
Santa Cruz de Tarihica	Tarihica	712	1616	Oré (1936)

Note: Asterisks indicate severely depopulated areas.

support for using this figure as a rough upper limit (assuming that politically subordinate local chiefdoms in the region did not significantly exceed this number).[2]

These projected average figures are, of course, only conjectural; but if surviving documentation is any guide, they may provide some general sense of the "typical" local chiefdom of the Timucuan interior. Obviously, the actual populations of each separate local chiefdom would have varied widely from the projected average, but since individual documentation for each chiefdom is in large part lacking, projected averages must suffice. Using these figures to project regional population figures for the early seventeenth century is even less secure but nonetheless instructive. An examination of the sociopolitical structure of the Timucuan chiefdoms of interior Florida at the dawn of the Franciscan mission era, in combination with a review of the administrative structure of the Franciscan mission provinces, suggests that formal missions (*doctrinas* with convents) were, as a rule, established at the principal towns of local chiefdoms. Not only did this reflect the practical integration of local Franciscan jurisdictions into preexisting aboriginal political structures, but it also resulted in a more or less optimal distribution of individual friars with respect to the native populations to whom they ministered. Consequently, it is possible to roughly equate the number of resident mission stations established during the early seventeenth century with the number of local chiefdoms forming each broader mission province. Indeed, what little evidence that exists with respect to the number of satellite villages served by each Timucuan mission, and the local political structure of these site clusters, only confirms this supposition.

During the early stages of missionization (early to mid-seventeenth century), the two regional chiefdoms of Timucua and Yustaga were composed of a number of individual local chiefdoms, each of which seems to have possessed a Franciscan convent at its principal town. Although the precise number of local chiefdoms in the Yustaga region is less certain, a rough estimate of the projected regional population can be made using the figures for local chiefdoms discussed above. Based on this exercise, eight local Yustaga chiefdoms might have contained a total regional population ranging between perhaps 6,000 and 12,000, and the four Timucua chiefdoms and Potano might have contained between 3,750 and 7,500 people. While these numbers are only rough estimates, the figure of thirteen thousand conversions in the province of Cotocochuni (Yustaga) by 1635 might serve as independent confirmation that these projections are not too far from the mark.[3]

Whether or not the actual numbers above are accurate, later demographic data confirm the fact that the Yustaga region indeed contained roughly double the population of the Timucua/Potano region.[4] Following the resettlement and aggregation of the Timucuan missions after the 1656 rebellion, the four remaining principal missions of Yustaga nonetheless contained consistently larger populations than those of the Timucua regions to the east. Some evidence suggests that despite the forced relocation of many populations to the east, the inhabitants of at least some of the northernmost Yustagan missions (particularly Arapaja) ultimately seem to have remained in the Yustaga area during the late seventeenth century.[5] Furthermore, during the two decades following the geographic transformation of Timucua, and particularly the contraction of all mission populations along the Camino Real (with roughly equal exposure to disease), some degree of relative demographic equilibrium may have been reestablished, with resultant population levels broadly reflecting early-seventeenth-century regional distributions. One reason for this consistent demographic imbalance between Yustaga and Timucua seems apparent in the eighteenth-century description of these two regions by Francisco de Castilla. Castilla's text clearly implies a more widespread and continuous distribution of loamy agricultural soils in the Yustaga area in comparison to the patchy, discontinuous distribution of such soils in the sandy Timucua area, accounting for considerably less relative population density.[6]

If, as some authors have suggested,[7] neighboring societies characterized by extended hostility or warfare may be presumed to have been roughly parallel in terms of human resources (otherwise one or the other would quickly dominate the other), then a comparison between the populations of these two allied Timucuan regional chiefdoms with that of their long-time enemy—Apalachee—would be expected to reveal similar scales of overall population. Intriguingly, if we accept the upper limit on the range of projected populations of these two regional societies, then the combined Yustaga/Timucua/Potano total comes to just under 20,000, at least roughly approximating the pre-mission period population of Apalachee at between perhaps 24,000 and 30,000 individuals.[8] Whereas Yustaga's projected 12,000 and Timucua's 7,500 (with Potano) would have been dwarfed by the populous Apalachee chiefdom individually, together they presented a more even match. Indeed, this might even provide one possible explanation for the documented interregional alliance between Yustaga and Timucua, since neither chiefdom alone could effectively defend against the powerful Apalachee. Such speculations are of course virtually incapable of proof, but they nonetheless provide at least some support for the relative magnitude of the projected regional populations of these Timucuan areas.

The populations of other interior Timucuan chiefdoms are more difficult to project, largely due to limited documentation. The northern chiefdoms of Ibihica and Oconi—strongly suspected to have been local, simple chiefdoms—might be anticipated to possess perhaps between 1,500 and 3,000 individuals based on the "average" projections above. In 1602, Ibihica was described as a province containing five towns and between 700 and 800 inhabitants.[9] If the neighboring chiefdom of Oconi (which seems to have later become politically preeminent over Ibi), contained equal or slightly larger numbers of inhabitants, then these two chiefdoms might have reached perhaps 2,000 people. The 1635 Ocaña relation is a problem in this regard, for the printed transcription of his original text clearly states that by that date more than "twelve thousand [*doce mill*] souls" had been baptized in "only this nation [of Oconi]."[10] Based on what is known about the Oconi chiefdom, particularly its low historical visibility in comparison to other provinces, this figure seems severely exaggerated (indeed, putting the Oconi chiefdom on par with the regional province of Yustaga, with only thirteen thousand conversions). Unless Oconi was indeed thickly populated (which seems unlikely, if only for the fact that only a single mission was ever established there), the most likely explanation is a simple transcription error, either on the part of Fray Ocaña (or even the author of the data source he consulted in 1635) or a modern transcriber, replacing *doce* (twelve) for *dos* (two). If this is the explanation (which would be a supposition, though not at all unlikely), then the original figure might have been 2,000, a far more reasonable number given Oconi's near invisibility in the historical record for Spanish Florida.

Estimations of early-seventeenth-century populations along the middle St. Johns River are simultaneously easier and yet less reliable with respect to normal precontact levels. Based on figures provided in 1602 and 1606, the combined populations of the remnants of Tocoy and the Antonico chiefdom (later San Antonio) amounted to between perhaps 200 and 315 individuals distributed in just over half a dozen communities.[11] These figures seem quite reliable with respect to the first decade of the seventeenth century, but in fact they represent only the smallest fraction of the original population of this same area. Largely due to extensive early interaction between the towns and chiefdoms of the Outina confederacy and mid-sixteenth-century French and Spanish colonists along the Atlantic coast, aboriginal population levels along the middle St. Johns River seem to have plummeted during the last quarter of the sixteenth century, resulting in the reduction and fragmentation of the once-powerful society ruled by chief Outina. The end result was a region that had almost been completely depopulated by the beginning of the seventeenth century, as confirmed by the population estimates noted above. Nevertheless, the descendants of the two hundred or so individuals constituting the remnant Antonico chiefdom ultimately became the resident population of mission San Antonio de Enacape following the apparent succession of Antonico's heir between 1612 and 1616, and thus must be incorporated into the general estimate of the overall population of the interior Timucuan chiefdoms at this time.

One region remains to be examined: Acuera. As yet, no contemporaneous population estimates have been discovered regarding this remote southern province along the Oklawaha River. Therefore, only an educated guess may be offered here. A further complicating factor is that at least three mission convents (San Blas de Avino, San Luis de Eloquale, and Santa Lucia de Acuera) were apparently situated along this river valley, either as allied or nominally subordinate towns or local chiefdoms within the Acuera region (one of which could even have been a relocated town from the old Ocale chiefdom along the Withlacoochee River to the west). Regardless, employing the assumption offered above that resident Franciscan friars were generally distributed to the principal towns of individual local chiefdoms, and using the range of projected "average" population figures discussed above, the three missions in the Acuera region might be presumed to have originally served between 2,250 and 4,500 Indians. These figures may actually be somewhat large, for only slightly more than half a dozen named towns are actually known from this area, suggesting that its overall population may have been more on the order of a single "average" local chiefdom, despite its apparent political fragmentation.

Pushing these projections even farther into the realm of speculation, using the reconstructed figures discussed above for the local and regional chiefdoms of Antonico (and Tocoy), Acuera, Potano, Timucua, Yustaga, Oconi, and Ibihica, the projected total population for all the interior Timucuan chiefdoms examined in this book at the beginning of the seventeenth century would range between about 13,500 and 27,000 Indians—probably closer to the higher of the two figures. It must be emphasized that these figures reflect the results of extremely severe depopulation along the middle St. Johns River valley and possible late-sixteenth-century population decline in other areas (though probably not even remotely as devastating due to only limited European contact beyond the St. Johns valley). Nevertheless, based on what little direct documentation is available regarding interior Timucuan populations around A.D. 1600, these figures seem reasonable, at least in terms of the relative scale of magnitude (somewhere in the low tens of thousands). Though somewhat less than might be expected from other conservative estimates of overall Timucuan populations at the time of European contact (such as Jerald Milanich's recent figure of 150,000, including both interior and coastal Timucuan groups),[12] it must be remembered that the figures used as baseline populations in this chapter represent the interior Timucuans following more than half a century of sporadic European contact. The original populations of the prehistoric Timucuan chiefdoms of Florida's interior might well have exceeded 50,000 (particularly during chief Outina's tenure), suggesting that a 1492 Timucua-speaking population of 150,000 is probably a sound estimate.

Seventeenth-Century Demographic Collapse

That the populations of the missionized interior Timucuan chiefdoms declined rapidly within the context of the Spanish colonial system is beyond any doubt. Proof of this fact is demonstrated by the near-continual drop in global population figures of the Florida missions after the mid-seventeenth century. Following the consistent rise in the total number of Christian Indians as the conversion effort expanded to the north and west during the first half of the century, these numbers plummeted following the mid-century halt in further missionization (fig. 1.1). From 4,000 converted Indians in 1608, the number jumped to 8,000 in 1617, to 20,000 in 1630, and to 30,000 in 1635.[13] Nevertheless, despite the incorporation of perhaps 24,000 or more Apalachee Indians into the mission system soon after 1633, the total population of converted Indians in 1655 had dropped to only 26,000.[14] Later figures reveal even more severe decline. By 1675 the

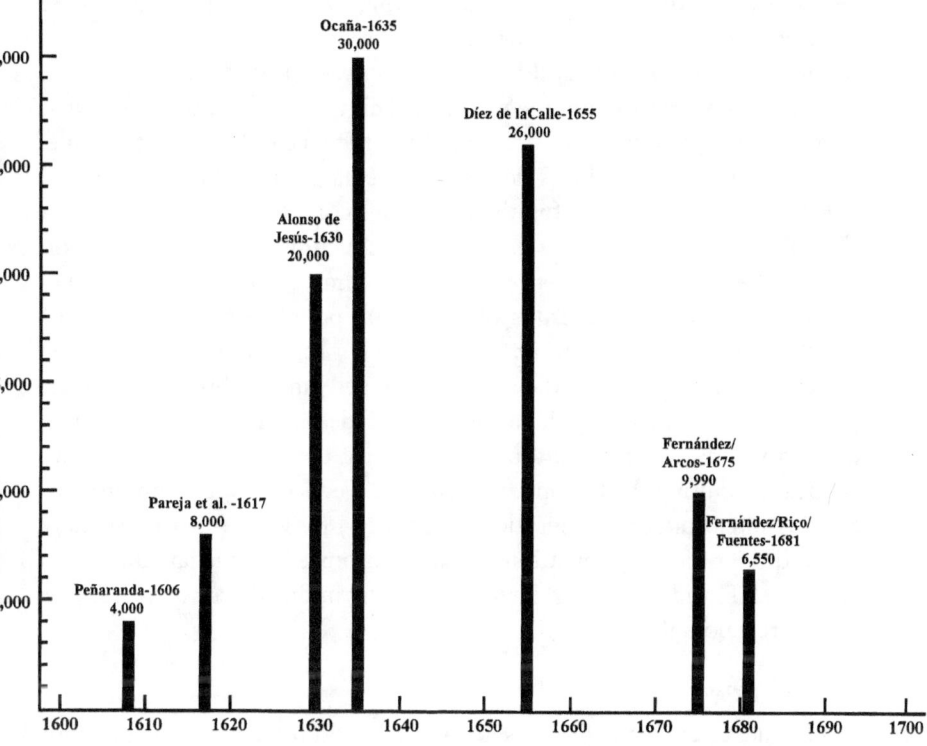

Figure 1-1. Chronology of global population estimates for Florida missions. Sources: Díez de la Calle 1655 (Díez de la Calle 1659).

total combined populations estimated by military authorities for the three districts of Apalachee, Timucua/Yustaga, and Guale/Mocama reached a grand total of only 10,666 Indians (possibly excluding young children in some provinces), despite the incorporation of nearly a thousand newly converted Indians, including Yamassee immigrants to Guale/Mocama and several recently established missions west of Apalachee. Six years later, the detailed 1681 census revealed only 7,364 adults (over eleven years old) remaining in all the Florida missions, including several hundred unconverted immigrants.[15]

Of these last two totals (for 1675 and 1681), the missions making up the Timucua mission province (representing the remaining remnants of all the interior Timucuan chiefdoms examined in this book) amounted to a grand total of only 1,370 and 998 inhabitants, respectively. Using the projected total populations for the chiefdoms ancestral to these missions (13,500–27,000), therefore, it is possible to estimate that in the space of roughly eighty years, population levels dropped to between 3 percent and 7 percent of their original levels. Even allowing for considerable error in the projected original population levels, there seems little doubt that the rate of Timucuan population decline roughly between 1600 and 1680 was in excess of 90 percent within the missions. This is not to say, of course, that catastrophic mortality rates accounted for the entire 90 percent decline. At least some portion of this demographic collapse was due to successful out-migration (specifically fugitives). Furthermore, there is some hint of a general decrease in birthrate, resulting in a reduction of natural population growth. Nevertheless, the net result was the same: the missionized Timucuan chiefdoms lost nine-tenths of their total population in the space of just three-quarters of a century. The reasons for this massive demographic collapse are numerous, but they may be grouped into five broad categories: (1) death resulting from epidemic diseases; (2) death resulting from exhaustion, exposure, or starvation in the context of the colonial labor system; (3) death resulting from frontier raiding; (4) reduced population growth; and (5) intentional out-migration. Ultimately, these five factors steadily reduced the resident populations of the missionized Timucuan chiefdoms of Spanish Florida's western interior, resulting in drastic consequences for the entire colonial system.

Epidemic Diseases

The impact of epidemic diseases introduced by European colonists cannot be overstated. As happened in every other part of the New World, from the very beginning of European contact, a host of virulent plagues rapidly took a tragic toll on the native inhabitants of colonial areas. Epidemic diseases ravaged aboriginal populations throughout the seventeenth century. Mortality due to these epidemics among the Indians in the Florida mission provinces was undoubtedly the single most significant factor in the documented demographic collapse within the colonial system. A great deal of research, both historical and archaeological, has been directed toward addressing various facets of the question of aboriginal depopulation due to epidemic disease in the broad region within and surrounding Spanish Florida.[16] Nevertheless, direct evidence for epidemic population loss within the interior Timucuan missions, or in other Florida mission provinces, remains elusive. Contemporaneous estimates of relative population losses, however, make it clear that the lion's share of demographic collapse among the Florida Indians was a direct result of disease.

Specific references to ongoing epidemics are rare. One of the earliest direct references was made by the Franciscans during their 1617 Chapter, when they noted "great plagues [*pestes*] and contagious sicknesses that the Indians have suffered," during which fully half of the converted Indians were calculated to have died in the previous four years.[17] While this report does not specify which mission provinces were affected by these epidemics, there are several clues that suggest the inhabitants of the recently established missions of Potano and Timucua were among the casualties. In describing Fray Antonio de Cuellar's early labors among the Indians of Tarihica, Fray Ocaña made specific note of a "plague" there (perhaps lasting as long as two years), during which Fray Cuellar was said to have "baptized more than eight hundred in the moment of death."[18] Fixing the date of the establishment of mission Santa Cruz de Tarihica in late 1612, this reference probably refers to the documented epidemics of 1613–17, indicating that the recent conversions in Timucua were affected.

It is important to realize that while there is no specific documentary evidence for epidemics among the interior Timucuans prior to those noted for the 1613–17 period, there is no way to gauge the degree of population decline that may have been going on in these interior provinces since the advent of more intensive contact with the Spanish during the late sixteenth and early seventeenth centuries. Indeed, the note in the 1617 Chapter report may only have been in response to a particularly steep population decline during the previous years, at which time the friars formally petitioned for permission to begin aggregating surviving communities. If their calculations of a 50-percent drop in population are even remotely accurate, the mortality rate due to disease in the existing mission provinces must have been extremely high during these years. Even if it is assumed that the available historical record is relatively complete (which is highly improbable), the nature of this documentary evidence is such that, in many cases, only the most extreme of circumstances prompted Spaniards to take up the pen in correspondence with the crown. Consequently, direct evidence for epidemics must be viewed as only a fragmentary representation of the potential scope of epidemic population decline.

Interestingly, the 1635 Ocaña relation provides indirect evidence for the widespread nature of epidemics in the Florida missions by making a specific statement relative to one province, Santiago de Oconi, "where the natives diverse times have seen the glorious apostle [Santiago] and the sacred angels above the crosses that the missionaries placed in the same town, which the divine Majesty has always preserved with these favors from all the contagions and sicknesses."[19] Fray Ocaña's comment suggests that the remote Oconi chiefdom, situated far off the primary road network of Spanish Florida, was somehow spared the worst effects of the plagues in Florida. This would seem to be no coincidence, given that due to its comparative lack of regular, direct contact with Spanish soldiers and other Indians in transit, Oconi was not generally exposed to the primary source of

European pathogens. If true, this 1635 statement implies that the severity of mission epidemics was influenced by physical location, particularly with respect to the primary transportation corridors of the Spanish colonial system.

The 1650s witnessed several major epidemics in Florida during which tens of thousands perished. One of the best-documented Florida epidemics occurred during 1649–51, coinciding with one of the worst epidemics ever to strike the Spanish colonial port city of Seville across the Atlantic. This plague ultimately resulted in the deaths of two Florida governors (Benito Ruíz de Salazar and his successor Nicolás Ponce de León) and the Franciscan provincial minister of Florida (Francisco Trebejo) in the year 1651 alone. The mission provinces were also hit hard; one contemporaneous report complained of "the new lack which there is of ministers, through many having died in the plague of the years of [sixteen] forty-nine and fifty."[20] Yet another epidemic struck in the winter of 1654–55; secondhand testimony made specific note of the fact that during this plague, "almost half of the people of the said province of Timucua had died."[21] Apalachee itself was unable to contribute to the yearly *repartimiento* draft that year due to the epidemic, which raged throughout 1655, and the governor was forced to draft unconverted and fugitive Indians from the southern Timucuan district of Ibiniuti to make up the shortfall.[22] The simultaneous effect of these epidemics on Guale was later confirmed by its caciques, who reported in 1657 that "we have had plague for two years, and this province of Guale has remained deprived of human forces on account of so many deaths." At the same time, Governor Rebolledo indicated that Guale and Timucua had comparatively few remaining inhabitants, noting that "many have died with the illnesses of plague [*peste*] and smallpox [*viruelas*] which have occurred these years, and they likewise continue dying in the [province] of Apalachee."[23] Rebolledo's successor Governor Alonso de Aranguiz y Cotes later reported that some ten thousand Indians had died in 1659 alone as a result of yet another epidemic.[24]

If direct documentary evidence for epidemics is rare, then archaeological evidence is virtually nonexistent, particularly for the interior Timucuan missions. Recent analyses of substantial burial populations from mission and pre-mission sites in the coastal Guale and Mocama provinces have provided clear support for a substantial increase in nonspecific infections in mission-period populations (as evidenced by visible reactions on preserved bones), mirroring a widespread deterioration in the health of mission communities.[25] Similar examination of a comparatively small sample of interments beneath the church floor at mission San Martín de Ayacuto in the

Timucua province (at the Fig Springs archaeological site) has demonstrated the predominance of multiple burials there, providing indirect support for the frequency of epidemic disease.[26] Unfortunately, the very nature of epidemic population decline, often involving rapid death, generally precludes the preservation of specific diagnostic evidence on skeletal remains.

Nevertheless, the overall picture provided by the available historical and archaeological data is one of dramatic demographic collapse in response to widespread epidemics in the missions of Spanish Florida, even if their occurrence was only sporadic. Limited direct historical evidence for specific epidemics combined with substantial indirect evidence in the form of global population data and contemporary commentary relative to the high rate of mortality among the mission Indians builds a sound case for the interpretation that diseases accounted for the majority of the demographic collapse within the mission provinces, including those of the interior Timucuan chiefdoms examined in this book.

Stresses of the Colonial Labor System

Though clearly important, epidemic disease was not the only cause for the overall increase in mortality among seventeenth-century mission Indians in Florida. As related again and again by contemporary observers, introduced stresses related to the draft labor system, particularly to travel and burden bearing along Spanish Florida's far-flung network of roads and trails, resulted in the deaths of many individuals, some of whom were said to die literally by the roadside. One recurring problem seems to have been the lack of provisions in the royal warehouses of St. Augustine for use in feeding *repartimiento* laborers, both during their stay and on their return journey. In July of 1654, for example, newly arrived Governor Don Diego de Rebolledo provided the following account regarding summer *repartimiento* laborers, many of whom were said to be sick upon his arrival in June:

> some of the said Indians, by it being during the rigurosity of the summer, frequently fall ill, and these are customarily given [food] and sustained on the account of His Majesty, because in lacking this recourse and charity they would die miserably from hunger, lying on the roads, as I am informed has happened some years when they lacked this aid on account of the royal warehouses not having enough to supply, and it has likewise happened that some Indians have died on the roads and in the uninhabited areas [*despoblados*] on account of the said lack, not having been able to dispatch them with sufficient food until entering in their lands.[27]

An example of the potential severity of this problem was provided by Fray Juan Gómez de Engraba, who in 1657 referred to an incident under Rebolledo's late predecessor (presumably Governor Ruíz, 1645–51) in which only ten of two hundred Indian laborers sent to St. Augustine lived to return to their lands (presumably Apalachee). The rest died from hunger on the trails.[28]

Burden bearing, both for soldiers and friars, involved similar risks. In 1630 Fray Alonso de Jesús made specific note of the severe impact of such burdens on the Indians of the interior Timucuan missions. In his longer petition, the friar requested

> that Your Majesty order that we be provided with the pack animals that seem to be necessary, from the horses that there are in the land, so that they might carry the hardtack, wine, and the rest of the things that Your Majesty gives us as charity for our sustenance, and I swear at present that six will be sufficient in the provinces of Timucua, inasmuch as the Indians that are occupied in the said ministry and service of carrying them have suffered and suffer grave disturbance and notable damages, by the distance of the road being so long and difficult, since the nearest *doctrina* to this presidio is more than thirty leagues from it, and the last more than seventy, for which the said Indians, with the burden, the ruggedness of the land, and their miserable condition, arrive so injured and disturbed that they usually remain unable to be able to work, and some lose their lives, for which cause many of the missionaries, their hearts distressed at seeing the children that they engendered in Jesus Christ, Our Lord, ruined and wounded with the toilsome burden, do not dare to send for all their provisions, from which results another, not lesser, damage, and it is that the said missionaries sicken and lose their health.[29]

A quarter century later, royal treasurer Don Joseph de Prado revealed that burden bearing continued to be a problem when he summarized the difficulties involved in land transport using Indian labor:

> for lack of pack animals, the said Indians bring on their back and transport the fruits and goods of the land which are bartered and traded, a hard thing, which they refuse and resent so much, since it is commonly said that for this cause some absent themselves from among the Christians, and many others leave it off and refuse to be [Christians] in order not to experience similar labor, from which it has resulted in some dying on the roads in times of cold [weather], and

there was a Christian Indian woman who, having had a male child, killed him without baptism in order not to see him made a slave.[30]

Not only did some Indians sicken and die as a consequence of burden bearing (some were even said to have been eaten by wolves),[31] but others chose to flee the missions in order to avoid such service. Although the Spanish crown repeatedly forbade the practice throughout the Indies and Florida governors issued specific orders that burden bearing for individual soldiers would only be permitted if it were both voluntary and paid,[32] Prado added to the above description that "very few times are they paid anything for this labor, and when they actually do so it is a hatchet [*achuela*] or things of this quantity, the value of which is up to eight *reales,* for fifty or eighty leagues of burden-bearing."

Death on the road from exhaustion, exposure, or starvation was but the most immediate and extreme consequence of the stresses of draft labor and burden bearing. Detailed analyses of the skeletons of Guale Indians provide ample proof of the long-term consequences of the colonial labor system as a whole.[33] In comparisons between pre-mission and mission-period populations, several trends were noted with respect to patterns of labor. Overall body size increased during the mission period, with greater weight relative to height, resulting from increased consumption of carbohydrates, specifically corn. Lower limbs among some males exhibited significant increases in size, undoubtedly reflecting long-distance travel associated with the labor draft and burden bearing. Evidence from upper limbs suggests that upper-body activity among males generally increased during the mission period, probably reflecting increased participation in agricultural activities, and perhaps burden bearing as well. Furthermore, skeletal evidence for degenerative joint disease (osteoarthritis) jumped from between 1 to 12 percent in pre-mission populations to between 58 and 65 percent in mission populations in Guale, demonstrating the cumulative effects of increased labor. Overall, however, skeletal changes resulting from activity, or labor, were found to affect males more than females during the mission period, precisely as would be expected from the Spanish documentary record.

Skeletal samples from Guale and Timucua also exhibit evidence for a general decrease in community health among mission Indians.[34] Evidence for increases in both the duration and severity of physiological stress during the mission period confirms that, in general, health was generally compromised within mission communities. Due in part to decreases in nutritional quality (if not quantity) and sanitation within the context of crowded mission villages consisting of many aggregated communities, as complicated by increased stress levels associated with labor demands, native resistance to introduced diseases may have been reduced, facilitating the spread of epidemics within the mission provinces. In sum, the general decline in community health among mission Indians in response to new stresses (including the colonial labor system) effectively served to augment and magnify the effects of ongoing epidemics. Disease and stress thus complemented each other, contributing further to the overall demographic collapse.

Frontier Raiding

In addition to the combined and interrelated effects of European-introduced diseases and the stresses of the colonial labor system (accounting for the majority of increased mortality among mission Indians), violent death also accounted for at least a portion of the overall population decline. Although individual murders are not at all uncommon in the Spanish documentary record,[35] organized group raiding along the mission frontier was a chronic problem that resulted in many deaths among the interior Timucua during the first half of the seventeenth century. It should be noted that similar raiding ultimately caused the destruction and final retreat of all the Florida missions during the late seventeenth and early eighteenth centuries (including Timucua, Apalachee, and Guale). These later assaults, beginning as early as 1661, were part of a relatively organized campaign by English settlers to the north, and they seem to have been motivated in large part by the Virginia and Carolina market for Indian slaves.[36]

Documentary evidence for frontier raiding is not uncommon but probably only reveals the most dramatic examples of what may have been a more common phenomenon. Curiously, the direct motivations for such armed incursions are rarely ever addressed in the early-seventeenth-century documentary record, but in most cases individual attacks were carried out by unconverted groups against Christian Indians living in the mission provinces. While some of these raids may have represented a directed attempt to halt the spread of Spanish influence, many others may simply have reflected preexisting patterns of intergroup hostility (such as the ongoing war between Apalachee and its Timucuan neighbors until 1608). Some attacks may even have served an internal function within the raiding group, consolidating and reinforcing the political power of its leadership. Regardless of the individual motivations for such attacks, frontier raiding was a chronic problem in Timucua and did contribute to the overall loss of population in the mission provinces.

Frontier raids against the missionized chiefdoms of the Timucuan interior seem to have occurred even during the earliest stages of missionization. In the summer of 1608, for example, seemingly during Fray Martín Prieto's trip to Apalachee, the newly converted Potano Indians were apparently threatened by an unidentified enemy force (perhaps the Pohoy). Complaining about the lack of soldiers in St. Augustine, Governor Ybarra reported in August that "I have news from the interior, from the province of Potano, that a great number of pagan Indians are coming upon the Christian natives to make war on them, and so that they will not understand the limited number of people I have, I will come to their rescue with all the best artifices that I can."[37] Although the resolution of this situation is not known, just three years later, in 1611, Governor Juan Fernández de Olivera was forced to retaliate against further depredations on the frontier of Potano and Timucua by Indians from the Tampa Bay region. In testimony dating some eighteen years after the fact, Capt. Alonso Díaz de Badajoz, the leader of this expedition, remembered that Governor Fernández "sent the said Captain Alonso Díaz with infantry from this presidio to punish the Indians of Pohoy for having killed seventeen Christian Indians who were coming by the river of Cofa with the food and clothing of a missionary. With the order which he carried to punish them, he killed them all."[38] While there is little contemporary documentation, this testimony suggests that the victims of the unconverted Tampa Bay Pohoy might have been a party of Indians from Potano or perhaps Timucua on their way to resupply the mission at Cofa.

Governor Fernández evidently ordered a "launch and canoes" to be built in the river of Cofa (the lower Suwannee) specifically for the 1611 retaliatory expedition, for these were subsequently used during the summer of 1612 to reconnoiter the newly discovered route to the Gulf of Mexico. Immediately prior to this expedition, the governor dispatched soldiers "to say to the heirs of the said *caciques* [of Pooy and Tocopaca] that from then onward they should not do damage to the towns of Christians, since that punishment was made for the [damage] which their predecessors had done. I also sent them some gifts, offering them peace and amity on the part of Your Majesty, with which, and with the fear of the past, they offered complete [peace and amity] on their part."[39] Ensign Juan Rodríguez de Cartaya carried further gifts for the heir of the executed cacique of Pohoy on his reconnaissance trip to visit the cacique of Carlos. Governor Fernández reported that fall that the new cacique "remained content and assured."[40] Despite this early success, in 1636 further raids by the Pohoy prompted the dispatch of soldiers to the Timucuan province of "Viniute"

(Ibiniuti) along the upper St. Johns River drainage to look for guides and make twenty canoes for a retaliatory expedition.[41]

While there is no evidence that the Pohoy ever directly troubled Potano or the neighboring Timucuan missions again, another unconverted group—the Amacano—ultimately raided both the Pohoy and the Christian Indians. The homeland of the Amacano is not known with certainty, but they seem to have been located along the Gulf coast, situated between the Tampa Bay Pohoy, the interior Timucuans of the Suwannee River valley, and the Apalachee province to the northwest. Warfare during the 1620s between the unconverted Pohoy and Amacano Indians might even have led to the abandonment of the Cofa mission at the mouth of the Suwannee River, which disappeared between 1616 and 1635.[42] Perhaps in response to the impact of their ongoing war, late in 1628 or early 1629 Governor Don Luis de Rojas y Borja sent soldiers who "brought the captain of that town [of Pohoy], who is the second person of the *cacique*, so that the señor governor might give him gifts, and negotiate peace between them and the Amacanos."[43] Although it is possible that Franciscan friars worked among the Amacano bordering the Apalachee province in 1633,[44] this group was later noted to be among three unconverted groups involved in warfare and raiding against the Christian Apalachee and Timucua. Late in 1638, outgoing Governor Luís Horruytiner dispatched Sgt. Maj. Antonio de Herrera, López, y Mesa to the western mission provinces in order to make peace between the leaders of the western mission provinces and the pagan Chacato (west of Apalachee), Apalachicola (northwest of Apalachee), and Amacano (probably southeast of Apalachee at this time).[45] During the fall of 1638, raiding parties had been sent from both the Apalachee and Timucua provinces in order to take vengeance for the earlier murders of Christian Indians in both provinces. Killing many of their enemies, the raiding parties brought back a number of prisoners, held at that time in Apalachee. In an attempt to halt the escalation of such warfare, Herrera was instructed to mediate in peace negotiations between the warring parties, returning the prisoners and convening a meeting of the leaders in order to facilitate the process. Later reports indicate that this effort was successful, and that all the groups remained in "agreement and amity."[46]

Yet another group that caused considerable problems on the mission frontier was the Chisca, who appear sporadically in seventeenth-century Spanish documentation as early as 1618. Although their ultimate origins are unclear, they may represent the relocated remnants of a warlike chiefdom by the same name in the Appalachian highlands of North Carolina, largely destroyed by Spanish soldiers during the Juan Pardo expeditions of 1566–68.[47] Sometime during the term of Governor Juan de Salinas (August 2, 1618–October 28, 1624), the Chisca made an appearance on the western mission frontier. Years later, Ensign Adrián de Cañizares y Osorio reported that he had been sent more than sixty leagues into the interior by Governor Salinas for "the punishment of the Chisca and Chichimeco Indians, ferocious people who were disturbing and robbing and killing the Christian Indians of the provinces of Timucua and Apalachee, who are subjects to the crown of His Majesty."[48] While no contemporaneous references either to the causes or results of this expedition have been discovered, later evidence indicates that the Chisca were at that time a nomadic group, apparently characterized by a sort of parasitic existence on the mission frontier, preying on the Christian Indians settled in the missions. In 1639, Gov. Damián de Vega, Castro, y Pardo referred to the Chiscas as "warlike people" who "walk freely through these provinces."[49] The governor's plans to settle them near St. Augustine, employing them in recovering fugitive Christian Indians, met with only mixed success, since their stay in peninsular Florida (and more specifically along the upper reaches of the St. Johns River) ultimately sparked the Apalachee rebellion of 1647 and was subsequently marred by increasingly severe raids against the Christian Timucua.

The role of the Chisca in the February 1647 Apalachee revolt has long been recognized, since contemporaneous sources attribute the prompting of the non-Christian Chisca (and their pledges of military support) as the primary reason for the uprising among the unconverted Apalachee.[50] What has remained poorly understood, however, is the effect of the Chisca presence on the interior Timucuans. Scattered documentation has recently been uncovered, however, that provides a number of important details. Immediately following the pacification of the Apalachee rebellion and the execution or imprisonment of its instigators, for example, the Chisca seemed to have turned their attention in early June to the Timucuan Yustaga region, where scattered groups of Chisca rebels were said to have stationed themselves along the roads and river crossings in order to ambush soldiers and Christian Indians.[51] In an effort to rid Yustaga of the remaining Chisca, acting co-governor Francisco Menéndez Márquez divided his troops in the Apalachee mission of Ivitachuco. He directed the troops to scour the roads between there and San Pedro in search of Chisca Indians, who were to be captured if possible, or killed if necessary.

At that time scattered throughout the southern Timucuan province of Ibiniuti along the upper St. Johns River drainage, the Chisca were ordered to leave Spanish Florida or settle down peaceably among the Christian Indians, probably as a direct response to their instigation of the Apalachee rebellion. Nevertheless, those who remained were in 1650 described as "rebellious and risen up" and were said to have "caused many deaths and scandals among the Christian Indians," frightening the Indian laborers.[52] In the spring of 1651, however, the Chisca embarked on several more ambitious raids within the heart of the Timucua mission province. April letters from two Spanish officers described three separate assaults to Governor Ruíz.[53] During a nighttime raid on the town Napufai within the jurisdiction of mission Santa Fé de Teleco, fourteen adults and children were killed, and thirty were also murdered in mission Santa Cruz de Tarihica. A third raid was carried out against the hacienda of La Chua, during which an Indian servant was killed and another Indian and a slave were wounded. Squad Leader Alonso de Argüelles was even struck in the shoulder with an ax during the raid on La Chua. A later account noted that during this period, "the Chisca nation [gave] assault to the province of Timucua, and killed and carried off many men, children, and women as captives."[54]

In response to these substantial assaults, Governor Ruíz ordered the Chisca to be "completely expelled and thrown out of all these provinces as people who are foreign, unsettled, and wicked," establishing the death penalty for any Christian cacique who provided refuge or harbor to the Chisca Indians. Furthermore, the governor offered a bounty of an ax and a hoe to any Indian killing a Chisca.[55] Shortly before his death in the epidemic, the governor dispatched then-adjutant Estévez de Carmenatis once again to the south, with a substantial troop of infantry instructed to scour the land from the coastal town of Nocoroco through Mayaca until arriving at the interior province of Ibiniuti, killing or capturing all the Chisca remaining in the land. Apparently at the same time, Ensign Juan Bauptista Terraza was sent "as a spy with six soldiers to extinguish and kill the Chiscas he found in the villages of the said province [of Timucua]."[56] The expulsion from Timucua was apparently successful; after the Spanish reprisals against the Chisca, "the rest fled, leaving the province free." Nevertheless, the Chisca soon appeared far to the north and were rumored to be preparing for new attacks against the coastal Guale.[57] In subsequent spring and summer expeditions in defense against the Chisca, the Spanish soldiers were warned that "they should not kill the Indian women and youth who might be with them, because it is understood that they will be Christians of those they have stolen and carried away from some missionaries' *doctrinas*, where they have given assaults and caused and made some deaths," indicating that in addition to the Christian Timucuans who were murdered, some were carried off as prisoners.[58] Based on the fragmentary documentary record, then, frontier raiding during the first half of the seventeenth century seems to have been only sporadic, particularly in comparison with the many slave raids of the late seventeenth century. Nevertheless, the murder or capture of Christian Indians as a result of such raids did contribute to the ongoing population decline among the inhabitants of the interior Timucuan missions. Fear of such raids might indeed have prompted out-migration in some instances.

Reduced Population Growth

Demographic collapse in the Florida missions was not only due to widespread increases in the death rate. Another factor seems to have been a general reduction in fertility or birthrate. The demographic profile of the excavated mission-period burials in mission Santa Catalina de Guale, for example, demonstrates an increase in age at death (with a higher percentage of adults in older age categories) during the mission period, which has been interpreted as a secondary indicator of a general reduction in fertility and birthrate.[59] That such a phenomenon must have indeed affected mission populations seems a likely conclusion, partly due to the overall decline in community health (possibly resulting in lower fertility), as well as the documented increase in the adult death rate (resulting in fewer births). Yet another factor—localized demographic imbalance—may have played a role. A clue was provided by the caciques of Guale in their 1657 petition to the Spanish king in which they commented that "there is one of our towns that does not have even sixteen Indian men, and more than sixty single women, unable to marry because all the single Indian men (outside of the married Indian men who serve the soldiers) are detained serving the Governor and Spaniards."[60] Also noting that even some married women lacked husbands during much of the year, the caciques requested the return of their vassals "so that some of so many single women and our daughters might be able to marry, and remake [rehacerse] our towns." The obvious implication of this passage is that the prolonged absence or disappearance of male Guale laborers (single and married) due to abuses in the colonial labor system left the mission communities abnormally imbalanced in favor of single women and caciques (exempt from the labor draft). The end result was that Guale towns were effectively incapable of reaching and maintaining normal population levels because of the reduction in birthrate caused by a lack of marriage partners. Mission Indians were thus unable to counter the prevailing trend of depopulation with an increased birthrate. This situation cannot have been unique to Guale.

Out-Migration

A final component of the demographic collapse within the mission provinces was out-migration. Spanish documents make it abundantly clear that not all the Indians who disappeared from the mission provinces were dead;

a substantial number simply left their homes and communities, fleeing the mission provinces as what the Spaniards called *cimarrones,* or fugitives. That such a phenomenon was common is clear from the many documentary references to such fugitives and from the Spanish attempts to return them to their homes. Less clear are their motivations for fleeing and their ultimate destination. Why did they become fugitives from the missions, and where did they go? Based on an examination of a wide variety of Spanish documentary accounts, it is possible to conclude that the primary reason for such expatriation was the colonial labor system.

Contemporaneous accounts occasionally make explicit reference to the labor system in connection with fugitives; in 1646, for example, Gov. Benito Ruíz de Salazar Vallecilla described the inhabitants of the Okefenokee Swamp mission of Oconi as "fugitive Indians from the towns of the province of Timucua and other places, in order not to work."[61] In this particular instance, the fact that there was a resident Franciscan friar in this remote mission provides indirect evidence that the fugitives living there were not fleeing the Spanish church, but rather the labor system, as noted by the governor. Most of the evidence for this conclusion is indeed indirect, centering on the fact that out-migration does not seem to have occurred in equal frequency in all missions, but instead was noticeably more common in mission towns exposed to greater Spanish demands for Indian labor. Judging from documentary references to fugitives (particularly attempts to recover them), out-migration seems to have been most common from the Timucua mission province of the peninsular interior and secondarily so from the Atlantic coast provinces of Mocama and Guale. References to fugitives from Apalachee are virtually unknown—although this may be more a result of the fact that there never seems to have been a shortage of labor in the populous Apalachee province rather than an indication that laborers did not run away from Apalachee. As seen in table 1.3, with the exception of the southern province of Mayaca, references to fugitives seem to be most common in connection with missions or mission provinces along the primary transportation corridors of Spanish Florida (through Timucua and Mocama). By far the most troublesome locations with respect to fugitives from the mission provinces seem to have been along strategic river crossings, where the inhabitants of mission towns were expected to remain available for ferrying duty. During the first half of the seventeenth century, these towns included Tocoy and its nearby successor, San Diego de Helaca, on the St. Johns River west of St. Augustine; Nombre de Dios and Tolomato along the Tolomato River just north of the city; and San Juan del Puerto at the mouth of the St. Johns River farther north. Interestingly, these towns were generally exempt from the yearly *repartimiento* labor

Table 1-3. Selected documented expeditions to recover fugitives from mission provinces

Date	Destination	Transport	Leader	Source
Early 1620s	Guale/San Pedro	land	Adrián de Cañizares y Osorio	Cañizares y Osorio (1635)
1622	San Pedro	sea	Pedro de San Martín	San Martín (1635)
August 1623	San Pedro	?	Pedro de San Martín	San Martín (1635)
1635	?	?	Diego de Trevijano	Trevijano (1643)
1638	Mayaca	land?	Diego de Trevijano	Trevijano (1643)
April 18, 1648	Helaca/Acuera	land	Juan Domínguez	Ruíz de Salazar Vallecilla (1648a)
July 20, 1648	Helaca	land	Juan Domínguez	Ruíz de Salazar Vallecilla (1648b)
1649?	Helaca	land	Martín Alcayde de Cordoba	Alcayde de Cordoba (1649)
December 23, 1649	Mayaca	land	Francisco de la Rocha	Rocha (1679)
January 19, 1654	Potano/Timucua	land	Ensign Pedro de Florencia	Florencia (1670)
November 19, 1659	Yustaga/Timucua	land	Capt. Juan Fernández de Florencia	Fernández de Florencia (1670)
April 18, 1665	Potano	land	Adj. Ysidro de Reynoso	Guerra y Vega (1665d)

draft, indicating either that ferrying duty was considered comparatively more onerous or that its strategic importance was such that special dispensations were made in order to maintain populations at river crossings—or (most likely) both. In this sense, the Spaniards seem to have considered it more important to maintain a reserve of Indians for periodic ferrying duty than to have that same community contribute a handful of laborers to the yearly draft. When, for example, the *mico* of the relocated Guale town of Tolomato in 1658 requested a royal decree that the governor of Florida excuse them from all additional tasks (such as loading ships and cutting wood and thatch) except ferrying soldiers and cargo between St. Augustine and San Juan del Puerto, his petition was granted.[62]

As traffic increased along the western mission chain after the 1633 missionization of Apalachee (and its 1647 incorporation into the *repartimiento* labor draft), and as populations diminished severely in the northern coastal provinces of Guale and Mocama (presumably reducing overall foot traffic), the St. Johns River crossing west of St. Augustine became easily the most strategically important location with respect to transpeninsular traffic and, simultaneously, the most difficult location in which to maintain native populations. Fugitives were apparently a nearly constant problem at this site. Indeed, that three separate towns served this function over the course of the seventeenth century provides eloquent testimony to this fact. On at least one occasion, for example, the entire population of San Diego risked a standing order for the execution of fugitives, fleeing southward with their cacique (who did apparently suffer the penalty of death).[63] Flight from this mission, and ultimately its successor (Salamototo), was chronic. Spanish attempts to resettle this strategic location were continual and sometimes drastic.

Fugitives are also documented for other specific locations within the Timucua province. In January of 1654, acting governor Don Pedro Benedit Horruytiner ordered Ensign Pedro de Florencia to search for the inhabitants of missions San Francisco de Potano and Santa Fé de Teleco, "for fear that they might become depopulated, from which would result great detriment to the service of His Majesty, through being the passage for the remaining provinces."[64] Although this expedition seems to have been successful, these missions and all those along the Camino Real were nearly depopulated as a consequence of the 1656 Timucuan rebellion. And, despite Spanish attempts to repopulate these missions, fugitives continued to leave them. In 1665, for example, mission San Francisco and its satellite Santa Ana seemed once again to have been in danger of depopulation due to flight. Yet another Spanish expedition was sent to round up the fugitives in some woods three leagues distant, bringing the leaders back for punishment.[65] Not a single reference, however, has been found either to fugitives from interior Timucuan missions located off the Camino Real or to the depopulation of such remote towns. While this may be in part a result of the fact that the Spanish military primarily focused their efforts on the maintenance or repopulation of towns along the primary road, it would seem to be no coincidence that all the Timucuan missions along the Camino Real participated in the 1656 rebellion, and that none of the northern Timucuan missions (distant from the Camino Real) sided with the rebels, instead aiding the Spanish during the revolt.

Given, then, that out-migration seems to have been in response to the stresses of the colonial labor system, and that it occurred most commonly in mission communities along primary transportation corridors, where exactly did the fugitives go? While this is a difficult question to answer, in part because completely successful fugitives would have vanished from the historical record (biasing the historical record in favor of fugitives who relocated to nearby and known locations), a clear pattern seems to emerge with respect to many fugitives from the interior Timucuan missions along the Camino Real. In the few instances that are documented, Timucuan *cimarrones* seem to have typically fled either northward to the Okefenokee Swamp (the Oconi province) or southward to the upper St. Johns River valley and its lake district (Acuera, San Antonio de Enacape, etc., collectively known as the Ibiniuti province). These regions shared two characteristics that undoubtedly made them attractive to fugitive Timucuan Indians: their indigenous inhabitants spoke the Timucuan language and they were remote and comparatively inaccessible, located off the main road in swampy, wet areas not generally visited by Spanish soldiers. In addition, the fertile environment was apparently rich enough to support populations using either wild resources or agricultural products such as corn.[66] Though Franciscan convents were apparently maintained in these areas through the mid-seventeenth century, they do not seem to have been normally incorporated into the yearly *repartimiento* labor draft at that time, and certainly they had almost no demand for burden bearers (and few transitory visitors to support). Consequently, many fugitive Christian Timucuans seem to have relocated to these out-of-the-way corners of Spanish Florida, maintaining at least marginal participation in the colonial system but remaining largely insulated against the worst effects of the labor system. Indeed, such areas might even have been known as havens from the seventeenth-century epidemics. As noted above, in 1635 mission Santiago de Oconi was protected from the worst of the plagues, indicating that the Okefenokee Swamp was sufficiently isolated to be beyond the reach of many infections more common among the well-traveled mission communities.

At least a few Timucuan fugitives seem to have fled westward to the Apalachee province prior to the institution of the *repartimiento* draft there following the rebellion of 1647. In 1645, Governor Ruíz promised the cacique of Asile that in return for the loan of a tract of land for his projected wheat farm, he would, among other things, "make the people who have gone away from here to Apalachee return here."[67] While the cacique Manuel later indicated that this promise was never fulfilled, the fact that some of his vassals had fled to Apalachee indicates that at least some Timucuan Indians expatriated themselves even beyond the Timucuan language area. Many fugitives from coastal Guale are known to have fled to the unconverted coastal province of Escamaçu or even to the deep interior province of Tama, and some interior Timucuans may indeed have opted for that destination.[68] Indeed, one of the most frequently repeated concerns of the Florida Franciscans was that fugitive Christian Indians should live among pagans, dying without the benefit of the sacraments.

Based on extant documentation, there is no way to even estimate the number of fugitive Timucuan cimarrones living in Oconi, Ibiniuti, or other more distant provinces at any given time during the seventeenth century. That at least a small number of Christian Indians fled the missions with some degree of regularity is certain, although the proportion who remained permanently beyond the realm of Spanish influence is unclear. Nevertheless, at least some of the overall demographic collapse of the mission provinces, particularly Timucua, resulted from out-migration. Inasmuch as fugitive Indians could be captured and forcibly resettled in their homes (in contrast to depopulation as a result of death), Spanish authorities seem to have dedicated much energy in this endeavor in an effort to stabilize the ongoing population loss. However, this was only one part of ongoing Spanish attempts to mitigate the effects of depopulation in the Timucuan interior. Given the rapid and massive decline in aboriginal populations throughout the seventeenth century, the very survival of the colonial system of Spanish Florida was largely dependent upon this effort.

CHAPTER 2

Repopulating Timucua

Countering Demographic Collapse

Spanish efforts to counter the ongoing demographic collapse in the interior began almost as soon as the Indians began to die or flee. Ultimately, a number of strategies would be employed in this plan, including the aggregation of subordinate communities within local chiefdoms, forming congregated mission towns, or *congregaciónes;* the intentional establishment or reestablishment of strategically placed towns using relocated populations; and the ongoing recovery and resettlement of fugitive *cimarrones*. In sum, as populations dwindled in the most strategically important mission towns, Indians were either voluntarily or forcibly resettled in an attempt to maintain the infrastructural base of the colonial system. Although at first this simply involved the aggregation of neighboring communities on a local scale (probably within each principal cacique's local chiefdom), by the second quarter of the seventeenth century, more drastic measures were introduced in heavily depopulated areas. The transformation of the social geography of the Timucuan interior was gradual at first; but it eventually resulted in the reduction of local chiefdoms into little more than a single community surrounding the Franciscan mission compound at the principal town, or in the relocation of individual communities to uninhabited sites along the transportation network. Ultimately, however, such alterations would pale in comparison to the sweeping resettlement plan initiated following the Timucuan rebellion of 1656. Nevertheless, the pattern for such resettlement was established long before the rebellion, as Timucuan populations dwindled to less than 50 percent of their original condition.

The Aggregation of Towns

Aggregation of outlying communities within local mission jurisdictions seems to have begun formally after 1617, although it was almost certainly practiced informally earlier than that. During the provincial Franciscan chapter in 1617, the Florida friars made specific note that "because of the great mortality which there has been among the Indians, there have remained some little villages [*lugarillos*] of little consideration with very few Indians, such as [villages] of ten or eight houses, and in others fewer or none."[1] In later comments relative to his own visitation at the same time, Fray Luís Gerónimo de Oré commented on the difficulties involved in ministering to such scattered and tiny communities, noting with regard to the Florida friars:

> the incredible labor and solicitude with which they attend in baptize and administer the sacraments to the sick, in six leagues more or less in distance that the little settlements [*poblezuelos*] of Christians that they visit are. If the governors would like to make reductions [*reducciones*] of three or four little villages in one, as was done in the reductions of Peru by the plan and resolution of the Viceroy Don Franciso de Toledo, the Indians would be better instructed and the ministers allieved of the excessive labor that they have now, with differences of weather, raining or snowing in winter, or burning up with heat in the summer.[2]

A formal proposal in this regard was indeed made by the friars in their 1617 letter to the king. At that time, prompted by an estimated 50 percent decline in population during the previous four years of epidemics, the Franciscans requested permission to resettle the Indians within their jurisdictions, asserting that:

> the Indians cannot be indoctrinated by the missionaries, and as Christians, they have little more than the name, on account of being very far from the missionary, from which it follows also that when they send news to the missionary to administer the sacraments to a sick person, when the minister arrives, [the person] is already dead, and for this cause the missionaries walk with extremely great labor day and night, very much at cost to their health. We request that Your Majesty would be served to command that, whenever these necessities occur, as long as the governors are advised by the [Franciscan] prelate, these disordered [settlements] should be drawn together [*compongan estos desordenes*], since there is not one inconvenience, through those that have to join together not being from different families or languages, but rather friends of friends, brothers of brothers, and relatives of relatives beforehand. It is an important and necessary thing for them, since the reason for which so many Indians die is customarily that being few, they cannot help each other in their labors, and thus it

burdens them so much from unavoidable services which they make use of among themselves, and from those who command them on the part of the presidio, like to row canoes [or] to carry burdens by land, that oppressed under so many labors they are consumed and die.[3]

The aggregation of dispersed and dwindling communities was thus seen as a solution both for the Franciscan friars, who tired in walking several leagues to administer sacraments to plague victims before their death, and for the Indians themselves, whose communities were in many cases so small that there were not enough people to attend to daily chores (or to the demands of the labor system).

That the above plan for *congregación* was indeed practiced in seventeenth-century Florida is evidenced clearly by the fact that by the end of the seventeenth century, each and every local Timucuan chiefdom within the Potano, Timucua, and Yustaga regions had been either reduced to a single mission village with no more than a few hundred inhabitants (and generally less than a hundred) or effectively aggregated or assimilated within another remnant local chiefdom. The disappearance of the numerous named subordinate communities within Timucuan chiefdoms during the seventeenth century, and the survival of only the principal town in each local chiefdom, is supplemented by at least a few specific examples of localized aggregation in the Timucua province, including the aggregation of Santa Ana to San Francisco de Potano and of Ajoica to Santa Catalina during the 1670s.[4] This same phenomenon of early-seventeenth-century *congregación* can be documented for the similarly devastated Guale and Mocama provinces during precisely the same period.[5] Indeed, the clearest demonstration of the dynamics of this phenomenon lies in the comparatively more detailed visitation records for the missions of these two coastal provinces between 1677 and 1701. An examination of four distinct visitations during that period makes it clear that although outlying towns and villages within original Guale and Mocama chiefdoms had been physically relocated to principal towns on a local scale, the chiefly matrilineages of these subordinate communities persisted throughout the mission period.[6] This remarkable persistence of internal sociopolitical structure under conditions of *congregación* was probably not unique to Guale and the Timucuan-speaking Mocama. Although largely undocumented, it may have characterized the interior Timucuans as well.

Directed Resettlement

On a local scale, the aggregation of satellite communities undoubtedly bolstered populations sufficiently within the principal town to maintain its viability in the short term. Among the many interior Timucuan chiefdoms missionized after 1606, Franciscan mission convents at only two (Cofa and Avino) seem to have been abandoned prior to 1656, despite severe demographic collapse on a local and regional scale and the aggregation of many subordinate communities to administrative centers across the interior. In most cases, the missions established between 1606 and 1630 seem to have survived until the Timucuan rebellion of 1656, even if severely reduced in both numbers of inhabitants and numbers of surrounding communities. In some areas, however, populations became too completely devastated to permit the survival of viable Indian communities using local residents alone. One such area in the interior Timucua region was the middle St. Johns River, precisely at the all-important river crossing of Tocoy.

Tocoy was the original town ruled by a Timucuan cacique who took the name Pedro Márquez upon his baptism.[7] Probably in order to elevate his own standing, during the late sixteenth century this chief relocated his primary town to a site dubbed San Sebastián just south of St. Augustine. Here, the cacique acted as the principal leader of both the new town of San Sebastián and his old town of Tocoy, still situated on the east bank of the St. Johns River. Although both of these towns survived until at least 1608, the 1606 visitation record of Bishop Juan de las Cavezas Altamirano revealed that Tocoy was a town in severe decline, evidently possessing only ninety Christian inhabitants.[8] By the time of the 1616 Franciscan visitation by Luís Gerónimo de Oré, both Tocoy and San Sebastián were gone, their surviving inhabitants perhaps having aggregated to neighboring Timucuan missions (perhaps Nombre de Dios).

Whether or not the increased level of activity in the interior Timucuan missions and the concurrent increase in ferrying traffic had anything to do with the abandonment of Tocoy is unknown. The site itself does not seem to have been reoccupied to any significant extent ever again, as demonstrated by the persistence of the geographic name Tocoi even to the present day. Nevertheless, by 1627 a completely new mission had appeared on the east bank of the St. Johns River, this time named San Diego de Helaca.[9] Apparently situated just slightly to the north of the site of Tocoy (see appendix A), San Diego served for the next three decades as the primary river crossing on the Camino Real extending from St. Augustine into the western interior.

The sudden appearance between 1616 and 1627 of a new mission under a totally distinct name in this abandoned region suggests that it was artificially created to serve Spanish interests at the strategic river crossing west of St. Augustine. Significantly, at precisely this same time Gov. Don Luís de Rojas y Borja relocated the entire Guale town of Tolomato from its original site in the coastal zone of present-day Georgia to a site three leagues north of St. Augustine "with the intention of making the passage continuous for Mocama, Guale, and the rest of the neighboring provinces."[10] Although the precise date of this move is not known, the relocation took place during Rojas y Borja's term in office (1624–30). The creation of a new mission town (Tolomato) three leagues north of St. Augustine for canoe passage to the northern provinces almost certainly coincided with the creation of another mission town (San Diego de Helaca) five leagues west of St. Augustine for canoe passage to the western provinces. Governor Rojas y Borja was probably responsible for both. Circumstantial evidence for this conclusion is provided by the coincidental appearance of the Timucuan name Utiaca, or Utiaco, in connection with both the inhabitants of mission San Diego and Governor Rojas y Borja. This name appeared first in a 1627 proposal by the governor regarding hemp production in Florida. In this proposal he noted three nearby towns situated along a river some forty leagues and four days in transit from St. Augustine.[11] One of these—Avino—had been the site of a mission named San Blas since before 1612. The other two—Tucuru and Utiaca—were situated nearby, since the governor placed them one and a half and two leagues apart from one another. These towns apparently comprised a minor chiefdom or cluster of towns within the broader Acuera region along the Oklawaha River (see appendix A). Nevertheless, the only other known appearance of the name Utiaco was in a 1648 gubernatorial order in which "Francisco, the *cacique* of the people of Utiaco" was said to have fled mission San Diego de Helaca with all his people toward Acuera, leaving San Diego depopulated.[12]

Based on this information, it seems likely that Governor Rojas y Borja established mission San Diego de Helaca between 1624 and 1627 as a part of a two-pronged effort to provide Indian labor for canoe traffic in the devastated regions west and north of St. Augustine. The town was almost certainly populated using Indians from the Acuera region, perhaps by relocating the entire cluster of towns surrounding mission San Blas de Avino to the middle St. Johns River region. That this town of Utiaca was ultimately relocated to San Diego before 1648 is certain, although it is possible that its relocation postdated the original establishment of the mission.[13] Nevertheless, neither mission San Blas nor the town of Tucuru were ever mentioned again in their original locations, suggesting that Utiaca was not alone in its relocation downriver. Indeed, based on later evidence it seems clear that throughout the rest of the seventeenth century, mission San Diego de Helaca and its successor San Diego de Salamototo (somewhat to the north) were almost entirely populated with Indians from the upper St. Johns River region. Beyond an explicit statement dating to 1682,[14] this fact is demonstrated by the apparent frequency with which fugitives from San Diego fled southward to the more remote missions of San Antonio de Enacape and the towns of the Acuera province during the mid-seventeenth century.

Interestingly, by the 1640s the remnants of at least three originally distinct chiefdoms, including the Timucuan chiefdoms of Antonico/Agua Dulce (mission San Antonio) and Acuera (missions Santa Lucia and San Luís) and the more distant Mayaca just south of Lake George, were apparently all included within the general designation of the province of Ibiniuti (also spelled as Diminiyuti), a Timucuan term apparently meaning "water land" (*ibineuti*).[15] Perhaps due to localized depopulation, or simply physical proximity, once disparate towns were by midcentury grouped into a new provincial designation. By the time of the official 1648 visitation of Timucua and Apalachee, the province of Ibiniuti was even included in visitor Juan Fernández de Florencia's route.[16] Although the designation of this broad district may have had more to do with the Spanish administrative structure than aboriginal political structure at a regional scale, the fact that the name used to designate this province was a Timucuan geographic term tends to imply that the administrative district of Ibiniuti may have at least partially reflected internal sociopolitical changes among the native populations along the upper St. Johns River. The "appearance" of the provincial designation Ibiniuti may have been in part a reflection of the comparative fluidity of social and political boundaries in the region resulting from the increasing movement of people and towns both in and out of this remote district.

Out-Migration and *Reducción*

That Indians living in mission San Diego along the Camino Real occasionally fled south into the Ibiniuti district is certain; in 1647, for example, when Ensign Nicolás Estévez de Carmenatis was ordered to lead troops into this region, he was secondarily instructed to "bring a married Indian called Lorenzo in the said town of Helaca, who is in the village of San Antonio de Enacape, to the said town of Helaca so that he makes a life with his wife and serves in it."[17] In this instance, a married male Indian living in San Diego had fled a short distance upriver to mission San Antonio, presumably in order to escape ferrying duties at San Diego. That this upper St. Johns region of Ibiniuti was indeed a haven for such fugitives is confirmed by a 1655 labor draft from this region (in response to epidemics in Apalachee and Timucua), in which "the province of Ybiniyutti, and the rest of that district" was noted to have not only unconverted Indians, but also "some fugitives [*cimarrones*] who have absented themselves from the evangelical word."[18]

Between 1646 and 1648 the problem of out-migration from mission San Diego to the province of Ibiniuti reached crisis proportions. As noted above, in 1646 Governor Ruíz developed a plan to resettle the inhabitants of the northern interior mission of Oconi (also inhabited by fugitives from Timucua) to mission San Diego de Helaca, noting that at that time it was "lacking in people," and had to be repopulated as "the principal gateway [*paso*] for the provinces of Timucua and Apalachee" through which soldiers "pass through the said *doctrina* every day."[19] Two years later, San Diego was largely depopulated (indicating that the resettlement of Oconi had not proceeded), and in April, Juan Domínguez was sent to the south in search of its cacique and his people. Domínguez instructed to come "from the town of Santa Lucia . . . gathering all the Indians from the stated town of Elaca and bring them and make them come to their town."[20] Following this resettlement, Governor Ruíz commanded that "on pain of their life no one should absent himself from the said town without my license."[21] Nevertheless, by mid-summer, the governor received word that "Francisco, the cacique of the people of Utiaco, who serves in the said town of Helaca" had violated this standing order, having "absented himself from the said town with all of his people, leaving it depopulated, causing much note and scandal, and taking away married women with force and violence." On July 20, Governor Ruíz condemned the cacique to death, dispatching Juan Domínguez a second time to the area of San Antonio and Santa Lucia with orders to find him and "garrotte him until he naturally dies," following confession, if possible.

During his visitation of the western mission provinces the following December, Capt. Juan Fernández de Florencia was apparently also sent to the province of Ibiniuti "on matters of royal service," perhaps in connection with the repopulation of San Diego.[22] Indeed, the fact that mission San Diego did survive through the late 1650s indicates that the repopulation of this crucial crossing was somehow successful following its 1648 abandonment. Regardless, these documents make it abundantly clear that the middle and upper St. Johns River were zones of considerable population movement, with the general trend being southward, away from the Camino Real. Perhaps for this very reason, Spanish authorities either invited or acquiesced to the presence of the nomadic Chisca Indians in this very region no later than the late 1640s.

The Chisca appeared along the western mission frontier at some point immediately prior to 1624, when they were described as "ferocious people" who robbed and killed Indians in both Timucua and Apalachee. Nevertheless, in 1639, Gov. Damián de Vega Castro y Pardo proposed that these nomadic and "warlike" people might be settled down in agricultural communities near St. Augustine in a program of *reducción*, noting that they would be useful in recovering Christian fugitives. Whether or not this plan proceeded at that time is unknown, but by the late 1640s, the Chisca were scattered throughout the upper St. Johns River region, among the Timucuans of the Ibiniuti district, suggesting that Governor Vega might have settled the Chisca along the St. Johns in an effort to curb the problem of out-migration from mission San Diego (either as fugitive-hunters or possibly even as replacements for the Timucuan fugitives). Documentation between 1639 and 1647 is lacking, but in 1647 the Chisca were implicated as the primary instigators of the Apalachee rebellion, implying that at least some Chisca Indians may have been living among the Apalachee at that time.

Nevertheless, when acting governors Menéndez Márquez and Horruytiner issued an ultimatum to them on September 5, 1647, ordering them to choose within two months between being ejected from Spanish Florida or settling down within the towns of the Christian caciques, the officer dispatched two months later in charge of a troop of soldiers was sent specifically to "the province of Ybineiute," indicating that the main body of the Chisca was definitely in the upper St. Johns River valley by that date (and very probably earlier).[23] The order detailing the planned 1647 resettlement of those Chisca caciques and *principales* who elected to settle among the Christian Timucua reveals that the process of *reducción* involved not only the willing participation of the immigrant group to be "reduced," but also required the "approval of the Christian *caciques*" in whose jurisdiction they were to settle, indicating that unconverted foreign Indians were incorporated as subordinate groups within the existing sociopolitical structure of the region's native inhabitants. This process is virtually identical to that later employed for the immigrant Yamassee Indians among the coastal Guale and Mocama during the 1660s and 1670s.[24] The reduced Chisca were instructed to "live quietly" in the mission towns of the Christian Indians, and "if they try to become Christians, they will be able to achieve it attending in the said towns were they will be catechized by the missionaries [*religiosos doctrineros*]."

Although the *reducción* of the Chisca after 1647 apparently proceeded, documents dating to 1650 and 1651 reveal that the Chisca had not effectively assimilated into the towns of the Christian Timucua, and were noted in 1650 to be "rebellious and risen up."[25] At that time occupying several encampments (*rancherías*) along the St. Johns River valley (including Santa Lucia in Acuera and the abandoned sites of Tocoy and Moloa along the middle and lower St. Johns River), the Chisca had continued preying upon the Christian Indians and, as discussed above, were ultimately expelled from peninsular Florida the following April in response to several ambitious raids against the Timucua province. Pushed out of their settlements to the south and west of St. Augustine, the Chisca fled briefly north to the frontier of Guale, and ultimately seem to have relocated to the far western panhandle region of Florida, where they continued their predation on the Apalachee missions well into the 1670s.[26]

Population "Backflow"

Spanish efforts to repopulate the devastated zone around the original riverside town of Tocoy began before 1627 and continued throughout the next quarter century and beyond. When the aggregation of satellite towns failed, leaving the St. Johns River crossing abandoned, entire towns of Christian Timucuans were intentionally resettled in this strategic location, including at least the Acuera town of Utiaca. A later attempt to resettle the northern town of Oconi failed. Finally, the immigrant Chisca Indians were permitted to settle in this zone around Tocoy, both as potential fugitive hunters to recover Timucuan *cimarrones* and as potential Christian converts who could take up permanent residence in the dwindling Timucuan mission towns. These three primary strategies—*congregación* on a local scale, long-distance town relocation, and *reducción* of immigrant groups—ultimately became fundamental components of the overall Spanish plan for directed resettlement in the Florida missions. In the peninsular interior of early-seventeenth-century Spanish Florida, these strategies minimally resulted in the directed "backflow" of Timucuan populations from distant regions (specifically that of Ibiniuti along the upper St. Johns River) toward more heavily depopulated regions in strategically important locations (such as the Camino Real). In the single well-documented case described above for mission San Diego de Helaca, directed resettlement resulted in the relocation of Timucuan populations from one aboriginal chiefly jurisdiction to another. Such a phenomenon was not necessarily an isolated case. At least two of the seven murders during the 1656 Timucuan rebellion were committed by Indians who had been born and baptized in the missions of the Acuera province but in 1656 seem to have been residing in the northern regions of Potano, Timucua, and Yustaga. That such immigration was not entirely restricted to provinces of the same language group is further demonstrated by the important Apalachee, Diego Salvador, a Timucua interpreter who was likewise born in the Ibiniuti district (in the town called Mocoso, apparently in the Acuera province) but raised in the Apalachee province.[27]

Directed resettlement within the Timucua mission province only increased in the latter half of the seventeenth century, beginning with the massive program initiated by Governor Rebolledo following the Timucuan rebellion. Nevertheless, archaeological evidence from the prerebellion mission sites of Timucua and Potano reveals that significant changes in aboriginal material culture (specifically domestic Indian pottery) occurred in these eastern regions between the time of their missionization and the Timucuan rebellion.[28] Though data are incomplete and difficult to interpret, a general trend of west-to-east ceramic transformation ultimately resulted in the apparent spread of Lamar-related ceramics (evidently in use within the Apalachee province by the beginning of the seventeenth century) into areas previously dominated by Suwannee Valley and Alachua ceramics upon missionization (specifically the Timucua and Potano regions within the broader Timucua mission province). This radical change in material culture evidently occurred within the space of the first fifty years following the establishment of missions in these Timucuan chiefdoms, and thus occurred within the context of the developing colonial system. Given the lack of archaeological data from the Yustaga region situated precisely in between Apalachee and Timucua/Potano, it is impossible to state with certainty whether this reflects a widespread "backflow" of Timucuan populations from Yustaga to Timucua and Potano (similar to that documented between the southern Ibiniuti province and mission San Diego de Helaca), or whether it simply resulted from some form of aboriginal cultural influence from Apalachee itself (perhaps simply related to methods of food preparation), facilitated by the tremendous amount of transpeninsular foot traffic that characterized the post-1633 era. A similar change in material culture has been documented for the coastal Timucuan Mocama province. Lamar-derived San Marcos/Altamaha ceramics originating among the Guale seem to have spread rapidly southward along the primary north-south transportation corridor to and from St. Augustine, blending with and replacing the local Savannah and St. Johns ceramics of the late prehistoric Mocama.[29] Given the similar increase in human traffic along this corridor during this same period, and the documented north-south trend of directed resettlement in Guale and Mocama, similar explanations for changes in material culture probably apply in both cases.[30]

The Impact of Depopulation

Ultimately, the pace of demographic collapse among the missionized Timucuan chiefdoms of interior Florida outstripped the pace of Spanish efforts to counter this trend. Over the course of the first half of the seventeenth century, as the Franciscan mission frontier expanded westward, the balance between increases in the number of converted Indians through new missionization and decreases in that number due to depopulation and out-migration gradually shifted, resulting in substantial rates of population loss within the developing colonial system of Spanish Florida. The effects of demographic collapse seem to have been most pronounced in precisely those areas of the greatest strategic importance to the continued viability of the entire system. For this reason, Spanish authorities directed considerable energy toward programs of directed resettlement in these locations. As individuals and towns were relocated, in some cases forcibly, old sociopolitical divisions lost their significance and new mission provinces largely replaced the local and regional chiefdoms of the early seventeenth century. By the midpoint of the seventeenth century, only two major administrative districts remained, each consisting of several previously autonomous units. The Ibiniuti province—comprising the towns and missions of the old Acuera, Agua Dulce, and even the neighboring Mayaca chiefdoms—was increasingly a haven for Timucuan fugitives from the Camino Real mission of San Diego. The Timucua mission province represented the aggregated missions of the local chiefdom of Potano and the regional chiefdoms of Timucua and Yustaga, perhaps half of which lay along the path of the Camino Real between St. Augustine and Apalachee. The remnants of the local Oconi and Ibihica chiefdoms along the northern frontier were considered at that time part of the coastal Mocama province and would shortly fall victim to forced resettlement. By the summer of 1654, the western interior was characterized by increasingly dysfunctional Timucuan societies, largely due to the combined effects of demographic collapse and the pressures of the colonial labor system. Into this scene stepped Gov. Don Diego de Rebolledo, whose term of office witnessed an armed rebellion by the Timucuan caciques and the complete restructuring of the mission frontier.

CHAPTER 3

The Timucuan Rebellion

Armed Resistance

Late in the spring of 1656, the Timucua mission province of Florida's interior erupted into a full-scale rebellion against the military government of St. Augustine. Ordering the immediate murder of all Spanish soldiers in the province (but specifically excepting the Franciscan friars), Lúcas Menéndez, cacique of mission San Martín and principal cacique of all Timucua, embarked on a desperate course of action designed to wrest political control of the Timucua province from hated Florida governor Don Diego de Rebolledo. The events of the next eight months would effectively seal the fate of the remnants of Spanish Florida's interior Timucuan chiefdoms, rapidly accelerating their full assimilation into the Spanish colonial system. Sweeping political and geographical transformations initiated after the rebellion would ultimately result in the reduction of Timucua's remaining inhabitants to a chain of populated way stations along the Camino Real, forever altering the face of Florida's transpeninsular interior. In the wake of the uprising, the widely dispersed towns of more than a dozen local Timucuan chiefdoms were forcibly resettled along the primary transportation corridor between St. Augustine and Apalachee, setting the stage for the final chapter in Timucua's existence before its inhabitants' retreat eastward as refugees.

Following nearly half a century of decline due to the effects of demographic collapse, the Timucuan rebellion was the watershed event in the assimilation of the interior Timucuan chiefdoms into the colonial system of Spanish Florida. An examination of the roots of this uprising, the spark which set it off, and the events of its course and aftermath, provides an object lesson in the internal stresses of the colonial system, specifically in the jurisdictional struggle between the Republic of Indians and the Republic of Spaniards. The assimilation of chiefdoms inevitably resulted in the erosion of chiefly power and the loss of political autonomy. The Timucuan rebellion represented armed resistance to that process, and as such marked a tragic consequence of the colonial experience. The following discussion focuses on the immediate causes for the rebellion, the important events that shaped its course, and the Spanish pacification of the Timucua mission province. The time period covered in this chapter and the following is thus quite small, extending only from mid-1654 to late 1656. In this sense, these chapters will present an extremely magnified view of a specific event in the history of the Timucuan chiefdoms, focusing more on the human rather than historical scale of analysis. Ultimately, the long-term impact of these events, including the complete reorganization of Timucua, will be addressed in the following chapters.

Governor Diego de Rebolledo

Don Diego de Rebolledo, son of the former royal treasurer of Cartagena, was granted the royal title to the governorship of Florida on March 24, 1653.[1] Just over a year later, on June 18, 1654, he arrived in St. Augustine to take formal possession of the government of Florida. By the time of his death five years later, he had earned a reputation that would prompt historians to characterize him as one of the most corrupt and controversial governors of colonial Spanish Florida. Although Timucua was indeed a province under considerable stress prior to his arrival, it was no coincidence that violence erupted during Rebolledo's term of office. The combination of these prior stresses with Rebolledo's personal exploitation of the colonial system, and his repeated failure to acknowledge and respect the privileged status of the caciques of Timucua as hereditary leaders and administrative intermediaries, brought the Timucua mission province to a previously unprecedented level of tension. In the end, all that was required for the uprising was a spark.

From the beginning of his term in office, Governor Rebolledo, later argued to be a "man of little experience,"[2] broke with prior tradition and practice regarding the uniform distribution of gifts and sustenance to all the mission caciques within his jurisdiction. Apparently in an effort to redirect expenses from the Indian fund toward more profitable endeavors (such as the amber trade), Rebolledo openly slighted the Timucuan caciques of Florida's interior by failing to present them with gifts and sustenance when they traveled to St. Augustine to render obedience to the new governor. Perhaps suspecting the new governor's intentions regarding the fund, and fearing considerable excesses, Royal Treasurer Joseph de Prado moved quickly to assert control over the Indian fund, which had by that time become a sort of discretionary account for Florida governors in relation to Indian affairs. Citing the limited wording of the 1593 and 1615 *cédulas* originally instituting the *gasto de indios*, Prado argued to the governor and subsequently the Spanish crown that the general distribution of gifts to caciques and common Indians from both converted and unconverted provinces throughout each gubernatorial term was not justified.[3] Regular disbursements from the Indian fund should be strictly limited to rations for visiting or sick Indians, and otherwise the letter of the *cédulas* should be followed with regard to gifts of clothing or iron tools only when caciques renewed their vows of obedience at the start of each gubernatorial term or when unconverted leaders provided intelligence regarding the frontier. In his December 1654 letter to the crown, Prado advised that the governor should be shut out of this process, and that the caciques' clothing "should come out of the royal munitions, and not as has been done in another government, with the governor running it, but rather that the Indians themselves should receive it from the hands of the quartermaster, without running in another [account], with which the bridge to many inconveniences will be closed, and a good account and copy will be had in the royal books."

Ironically, in his earlier reply Governor Rebolledo claimed that such limitations on the use of the Indian fund might provoke resentment or rebellion on the part of the Indians: "if this [expense] disappears because of the said contradiction to such an established custom, it would be in disservice to His Majesty, and of grave danger on account of the general protest that would be raised in all the land, and . . . a particular remedy should be devised in order not to motivate them to some disobedience, since from this could result unrest and disturbances, obligating that they be punished with military force."[4] In point of fact, however, both Prado and Rebolledo explicitly argued in favor of continuing the practice of gift-giving to Indian caciques; the 1654 dispute was one of control over the Indian fund. Prado argued that gifts should be distributed by the quartermaster out of the treasurer's account in order to control expenses, while Rebolledo argued that he as the governor should continue to control the distribution. By the time the *fiscal* of the Council of the Indies had rendered his decision in favor of Prado's request on July 3, 1656, however, the rebellion Governor Rebolledo had unwittingly predicted was already underway.

While Rebolledo publicly expressed concern that all mission caciques be provided gifts and food, he privately used the Indian fund selectively, offering gifts only to those caciques who were strategically positioned to foster the governor's personal trading activities. As later accusations asserted, and subsequent investigations during his *residencia* confirmed, Governor Rebolledo actively pursued the increase of his own personal wealth during his term, using a variety of illegal means to exploit both soldiers and Indians within his jurisdiction.[5] Beyond operating a store out of the house of his personal secretary, Ensign Francisco de Oria, and making personal profit using royal funds to buy goods from Havana, Rebolledo maintained illicit trading relations with the Indians of the unconverted Ais province along the Atlantic coast near Cape Canaveral. There he bartered iron tools and other goods for amber, which he then sold in Havana without paying royal taxes. This amber trade (which actually had long precedent in Florida),[6] along with the western trade for deerskins and other goods from the rich provinces of Apalachee and Apalachicola, forced the diversion of many items that otherwise could have been used as gifts to Timucuan caciques. Rebolledo was subsequently accused of having "melted down an anchor, cannons and their breeches, musket and arquebus barrels" to make sixty quintals (6,000 pounds) of iron for hoes and other tools as trade goods, leaving the fort and the garrison in poor condition.[7] Not only did this contribute to the eventual lack of military preparedness in St. Augustine in 1656, but it also left the Timucuan caciques with little or nothing in return for their pledge of continued allegiance. In this respect, the interior Timucuans were actually singled out for neglect; their neighbors in Apalachee were, in contrast, treated favorably by Governor Rebolledo. Don Luís, cacique of mission San Lorenzo de Yvitachuco and principal cacique of the entire Apalachee province, was evidently favored with a rich reception and gifts in St. Augustine, including a fine sword from Toledo.[8] Ignorant or oblivious to the potential consequences, Rebolledo evidently saw no immediate profit from maintaining good relations with Timucua, and thus broke with half a century of tradition in selectively failing to present its caciques with gifts and food.

Sgt. Maj. Pedro Benedit Horruytiner, son of former Florida governor Luís Horruytiner and acting governor of Florida immediately prior to Rebolledo's arrival, petitioned Governor Rebolledo several times with respect to this change in policy, arguing that the language of the two cited *cédulas* was out of date, having been issued during the early years of the colony.[9] Horruytiner argued that he understood the nature of the Indians, who he said responded not to reason but instead to charm and gifts, and thus he appealed that Rebolledo should give something to all the caciques and not simply "to the Indians of the coast because they brought amber." Although Horruytiner's later testimony belied his own failure to grasp the reason *why* such gifts were important to the caciques in maintaining internal chiefly rank within their own local and regional jurisdictions, he did nonetheless understand that they were indeed important, and apparently made a sincere effort to reverse Rebolledo's course of action (in so doing becoming a political enemy of the governor). Nevertheless, Horruytiner's advice was apparently ignored by Governor Rebolledo, laying the groundwork for unrest in Timucua.

In contrast to many years of excellent relations between Timucua's ranking cacique, Lúcas Menéndez, and the family of royal treasurer and one-time co-governor Francisco Menéndez Márquez, Governor Rebolledo's poor treatment of Lúcas and many other Timucuan caciques resulted in a general feeling of resentment and disgust. Ample testimony documents the fact that the cacique of San Martín was openly dissatisfied with his treatment at the hands of Rebolledo, and that such feelings were widespread among the chiefs of the Timucua mission province. Lúcas Menéndez and other caciques in Timucua openly complained on many occasions that Rebolledo failed to treat them with the proper respect that they were due. During Lúcas's visit to St. Augustine to render obedience to the newly installed Governor Rebolledo (presumably in 1654), Capt. Martín Alcayde de Cordoba found the cacique eating in the house of the soldier/interpreter Estéban Solana and questioned him why he was eating there. Responding that he had been hungry and that his "comrade" Solana had done him the mercy of feeding him, Lúcas revealed that Governor Rebolledo refused to give him food. The cacique revealed his awareness of Rebolledo's amber trade with the unconverted Indians along the southern coast, remarking that "if he were *cacique* of Ays, or another pagan, that the Governor would give it [food] to him"[10]

Sgt. Maj. Don Juan Menéndez Márquez, eldest son of Francisco and primary owner of the La Chua ranch at that time, reported that Lúcas stated that "now he was not *cacique* of Timucua, nor was attention paid to him, since having come to this city, in order to return he did not have food to carry for the road, nor [could he buy it?], the cost being barbarous, [and thus] he lacked wheat and corn."[11] Don Juan further reported that an Indian interpreter from the coastal Timucuan mission Nombre de Dios, Juan Menéndez, said that Lúcas Menéndez had not gone away content from this first meeting with Rebolledo, "but instead disgusted from the little reception that he had found in the Governor."[12] Having returned to mission San Martín, Lúcas later told Don Juan's brother Antonio, "After your father died, no attention is paid to us now," which Don Antonio understood to be a reference to Rebolledo's treatment of him in St. Augustine. While in San Francisco Potano, Don Antonio heard similar complaints from its cacique and the subordinate *caciquillo* of Namo regarding the lack of gifts from Rebolledo. Don Antonio furthermore reported that while in his house in St. Augustine, Sgt. Maj. Adrián de Cañizares had one day asked Benito Ruíz, the cacique of Santa Cruz de Tarihica, "How are you going, without carrying something for the road?," and the cacique had responded that in three or four visits to the city, he had never been given anything. He said "he would go running in order to arrive quickly at his land."[13] Several caciques of Guale complained similarly to another officer regarding Rebolledo's failure to distribute gifts, unlike his predecessors.[14]

Other statements made by Lúcas Menéndez and the caciques of Timucua are particularly telling, and tend to indict Rebolledo's unrelenting demands within the context of the existing *repartimiento* labor system as one component of the decision to rebel. Don Antonio also related that the cacique of San Martín "also complained that the year of [1655, the governor ordered that],[15] thirty-two Indian field hands [*indios de cava*] should come to this city for the labors, and afterwards there had been a plague and almost half of the people of the said province of Timucua had died, and that consecutive year he had ordered that fifty or sixty be drafted."[16] The cacique Lúcas was said to have retorted to Don Antonio that "the Indians died and the Spaniards will die," which the Spaniard understood to mean that "upon the Indians dying, the Spaniards would die." Another fragmentary statement related by a soldier demonstrates a similar sentiment, suggesting the Indians were of the opinion that "if they had to perish, it was better to rise up."[17] Rebolledo seems to have followed a similar policy in the province of Guale, which was evidently affected by simultaneous epidemics. In 1657, the caciques of Guale complained of the governor and his soldiers that "although we have had a plague for two years, and this province of Guale has been left deprived of human forces on account of so many deaths, as is on record, today they gather by force more people than ever."[18] This passage is remarkably similar to the quote from Lúcas Menéndez above, confirming that not only did Rebolledo fail to allow for depopulation in his yearly labor quotas, but he even increased the demand in the midst of a particularly harsh epidemic in both Timucua and Guale.

On another occasion, when the all-important Apalachee province was unable to provide the normal quotas due to epidemics, Governor Rebolledo forcibly extracted laborers from the towns of pagan and fugitive Christians along the upper St. Johns River watershed in the province of Ibiniuti. When Apalachee's provincial lieutenant Capt. Antonio de Sartucha and several missionaries wrote a letter to Rebolledo in March 1655, recounting the effects of "the great contagion of *peste* that there has been in [Apalachee], where a great sum of Indians have died and die, and many others sick, for which cause people cannot come for the [plantings and labor of the fields of the infantry]," the governor subsequently dispatched Capt. Antonio de Argüelles to the interior Timucuan province of "Ybiniyutti, and the rest of that district" for laborers to make up the shortfall in the yearly *repartimiento*.[19] Once there, Argüelles was to "enter in the villages of its pagans, and from each village he will gather the people that he sees can be taken from each one in conformity to the inhabitants that he sees in it, and he will likewise bring the *cimarrones* that he finds in them in his company." The fact that several prominent participants in the Timucuan rebellion the following year were natives of this southernmost Timucuan province may not be purely coincidental.

One particularly tragic example of Governor Rebolledo's heavy-handed dealings with the interior Timucuan caciques revolves around his subsequent 1656 attempt to repopulate the nearly unoccupied mission of Nombre de Dios just north of St. Augustine along the coast. In mid-January of that year, Rebolledo dispatched Ensign Juan Domínguez, an officer with considerable experience among the interior Timucuans, inland from St. Augustine to call upon "the *caciques* of the towns of Ybica and Oconi" in regard to unspecified matters "both for the service of His Majesty and for their own convenience," for which he and the caciques should return to the presence of the governor.[20] At the same time, Domínguez was to request that ten young, unmarried male Indians be sent to St. Augustine as a part of the yearly labor draft. Later testimony reveals that Rebolledo's intention was to resettle the inhabitants of these remote towns to the largely depopulated mission of Nombre de Dios, "which would be more among the Catholics, and at hand for the service of the King, for which he called the *caciques*."[21]

Traveling to St. Augustine as requested, the cacique of Santiago de Oconi (the largest town), who had come "as head of the rest," expressed his willingness to comply but requested that he and his vassals should be given time to harvest their current crops before moving. Rebolledo was said to have become "infuriated," and ordered the cacique to be imprisoned in the fort until his vassals and those of the other caciques moved to Nombre de Dios. The governor seems to have immediately dispatched Capt. Juan Fernández de Florencia in charge of a group of soldiers, with orders to force the Indians to come to St. Augustine by burning their houses.[22] The date of this second expedition is fixed by the simultaneous dispatch on February 15 of Ensign Domínguez to Guale for several large canoes and some corn in order to transport and feed "the Indians of the towns of Oconi and Ybica" during their assigned move to Nombre de Dios.[23] Domínguez was ordered to wait with the canoes at mission San Pedro at the mouth of the St. Marys River. This river flowed out of the Okefenokee Swamp, the home of the Oconi province.

Captain Fernández later recounted to another officer that following a meeting with all the Indians in the principal town of Santiago de Oconi, "the greater part of them fled to the forests, and most of them never again had recourse to the village, except for some who had gone to the village of San Pedro."[24] Presuming that the towns were indeed burned as the governor had instructed, the last remnants of two interior Timucuan chiefdoms, both previously missionized, were thus destroyed in the winter of 1656 and their inhabitants scattered, all at the hand of Gov. Don Diego de Rebolledo. With this tragic incident fresh in mind, it would seem no coincidence that just over two months later, the caciques of Timucua rose up in armed revolt in response to yet another affront to chiefly authority.

In sum, Governor Rebolledo displayed remarkable insensitivity to the nuances of maintaining good relations with the aboriginal leaders of the established mission provinces, particularly those of Timucua and other interior provinces. As discussed in previous chapters, Lúcas Menéndez and the other caciques of Timucua governed an aboriginal society that had been severely transformed by the process of assimilation into the Spanish colonial system, gradually usurping the political autonomy of the province. Largely as a result of massive demographic collapse in the context of the colonial system, the chiefdoms of the Timucua mission province represented increasingly dysfunctional societies during the second quarter of the seventeenth century. Into this clearly unstable situation stepped Gov. Don Diego de Rebolledo, whose ill-advised and occasionally brutal policies brought Timucua to the verge of rebellion.

The Immediate Cause

The event which ultimately provided the spark for the Timucuan rebellion occurred not in Florida, but some eight hundred miles to the south of St. Augustine in the Caribbean Sea. The British seizure of Jamaica in May 1655 was a severe blow to Spanish interests in the Indies, and it reinforced concerns regarding the defense of strategic ports across the Caribbean. Later that same year, intelligence gathered by the Spanish ambassador to England, Don Alonso de Cárdenas, revealed details of similar British designs on the port of St. Augustine. In a letter to the king in October of that year, Cárdenas reported a plan overheard by an imprisoned Spanish mariner who had just returned with the British armada. British intentions were reported to include:

> the conquest of the port of St. Augustine in Florida, judging it the most easy and suited for their intentions, since upon occupying it they would be left owners of all that country which includes the mainland and the Bahama Channel, with which it seems to them that they could impede the passage of the fleets and galleons. The mode of conquest of that fort would not be by entering through the river upon which it is

situated, because it does not have enough depth for the ships that they lead, but rather by placing people on land through another place near there in order to occupy it, being assured that they would be able to do so with facility, since that presidio has no more than three hundred men, and is deprived of munitions and lacks many other things.[25]

A plan of defensive action was soon formulated, and the governor of Florida was informed by a royal *cédula* dated November 16. The king feared that although the British armada had returned to England without accomplishing this goal, it could easily pursue such a course of action on its next voyage. Consequently, another royal *cédula* was dispatched simultaneously to the viceroy of New Spain instructing that he provide assistance in the form of soldiers, along with gunpowder and other munitions, to Florida. The viceroy was likewise to instruct the governors of Havana and Yucatan to provide further aid, being closer to St. Augustine. Timing was considered crucial, and the tone of the *cédula* directed to Rebolledo indicates that the threat to Florida was considered imminent. Unfortunately, due to the sluggish pace of communications between Europe and the New World during the seventeenth century, the *cédula* did not arrive in Florida until April of the following year. Adding to the urgency of this decree, another letter arrived at the same time from the governor of Havana, Don Juan Montano, relating information extracted from several prisoners from a British armada somewhere off the coast of Cuba at that time.[26] Their testimony confirmed the British intentions toward Florida and indeed suggested that the enemy fleet could descend upon St. Augustine within days or weeks.

There seems little doubt that Rebolledo was caught more or less completely unprepared for such an impending threat. In large part due to the chronic lack of soldiers and supplies in Florida, almost certainly augmented by the governor's diversion of funds and materials otherwise available for military expenses, St. Augustine seems to have been poorly equipped to deal with a frontal assault by an enemy armada at that time (as indeed the British seem to have been well aware). In Rebolledo's own words, "In that time this presidio found itself with the fort [largely] on the ground, with gates open, and with more than forty infantry less than the complement [of three hundred], and with no more sustenance than three-hundred *arrobas* of corn which there were at that time in the royal warehouses in order to give ration to the infantry."[27] Later testimony confirmed the governor's account, describing the pitiful state of military preparedness in St. Augustine. Capt. Alonso de Argüelles later recalled that "its fort was very ruined and collapsed to the ground in many places . . . [and] in that occasion this presidio was very lacking in provisions, since there was neither wheat nor considerable corn, and [it was decided] that the little that there was should be reserved for the occasion [of the British attack]."²⁸ Substantial testimony from Rebolledo's *residencia* confirms the above descriptions. As a result of these conditions, the arrival of the royal *cédula* and Governor Montano's letter in early April of 1656 initiated a series of events that would ultimately ignite the undercurrent of resentment and hostility within the Timucua mission province into murderous violence, threatening not only all previous Spanish expansion into the interior, but also the very existence of the colonial system upon which Spanish Florida was based.

In an effort to comply with the royal order to assure the defense of Florida, Governor Rebolledo was forced to embark on a course of action that would rapidly upgrade the defensive status of St. Augustine. His tasks were threefold: the crumbling fortifications around the city had to be repaired and expanded, the royal warehouses had to be restocked with additional food and supplies, and the number of infantry in the presidio had to be augmented. Furthermore, the perceived urgency of the situation demanded immediate solutions. While the British threat ultimately failed to materialize during this time, few options were available to Rebolledo based on the information in his possession that April. Not daring to wait for reinforcements from Cuba, Rebolledo quickly dispatched Capt. Francisco García de la Vera in the frigate *Nuestra Señora del Monte* to Havana to inform its governor of the extreme necessity in St. Augustine for men and supplies, and presumably to encourage the governor's immediate compliance with the royal order that he send aid to Florida. In St. Augustine, the repairs to the fort began almost immediately, along with the construction of new trench lines at the mouth of the port. The officers dispatched on this errand even brought the Indians they had in their service at the time, presumably including agricultural workers in St. Augustine as a part of the yearly *repartimiento* draft.²⁹

At the same time, the governor called a meeting of infantry officers and other officials in St. Augustine, during which he conferred with them regarding the best course of action.³⁰ Although the names of all those who attended are unknown, it was almost certainly at this meeting that Rebolledo's plan to draft Indians to make up the shortfall in troops was formulated. Following this meeting, and probably in an effort to forestall any later complaints by the Franciscans that they had not been consulted, Rebolledo next traveled to the nearby mission town of Tolomato just north of the city in the company of treasurer Don Joseph de Prado and several other officers and soldiers in order to confer with Franciscan provincial officials there.³¹ Present at this meeting were the Franciscan *comisario visitador* Fray Pedro Chacón (residing at Tolomato), Provincial Minister Fray Juan de Medina, and three other friars. During the meeting, Rebolledo informed the friars of the anticipated British assault on St. Augustine and discussed his plans to repair the fort, for which he requested the use of some wood that had been previously cut for the purpose of repairing the Franciscan convent. In addition, at this time he revealed the plan he had formulated in order to remedy the lack of infantry and supplies in the presidio.

Due to the imminent danger of attack from the enemy armada, compounded by the suspicion that this attack would come by land, Rebolledo realized that more infantry would be needed to fend off the British troops. Although he had reason to believe that more Spanish soldiers might eventually be sent from New Spain, Yucatan, or Cuba, this relief might arrive too late. Thus, Rebolledo decided upon the one course of action left to him: the immediate activation of the Indian militia throughout the mission provinces for service in St. Augustine. In his subsequent orders, the governor further stipulated that only the "most valorous" warriors were to be sent, and only those who could be spared from their agricultural fields, in recognition that it was planting time.[32] In this manner, Rebolledo would receive the supplemental infantry he needed, and the valuable agricultural crops in the mission provinces would not be threatened.

Rebolledo's strategy was simple. As later described by an officer under the governor's command:

> ordering the said principal Indians was necessary, in that there should not be doubt for the defense of this post if the English were coming, because the infantry, or at least the greater part of them, had to be in the fort, and there was no one who might make opposition to the enemy, and they could enter through the bar and other parts and seize the land, and the said Indians would be able to face up to them with some of the soldiers and not let them disembark on land, because unless there was someone who could do this, it would be unavoidable [for the English] to conquer the city and then the fort, having it besieged by land and by sea, with which it would be impossible to be able to sustain themselves in it, nor to have aid for it.[33]

Due to the lack of an effective force of Spanish infantry who could be spared from duty at the fort, Rebolledo planned to distribute Indian warriors on land and along the coast as a first line of defense to fend off the expected land assault by English troops. Citing several earlier occasions in which Indian warriors were used as complements to the Spanish infantry, Governor Rebolledo reasoned that he was simply following established precedent in augmenting his military reserves.

The problem with this strategy, however, was the lack of food in St. Augustine. If there was barely enough food for the Spanish soldiers and their dependents already in the city, then the addition of several hundred Indian warriors would surely devastate the food reserves in the royal warehouses.[34] The dilemma lay in the fact that Rebolledo had an urgent need for Indian warriors whom he could not feed. Consequently, the governor proposed that each Indian warrior be required to carry a quantity of corn with him to St. Augustine for his own sustenance. This corn was intended to suffice for the journey of some eight to ten days on the road and a one-month stay in the presidio, during which provisions would be brought from other locations.[35]

According to later witnesses called by Rebolledo in his own defense, the friars did not openly object to his plan, and the only discussion at this meeting related to the amount of corn that would be necessary. The Franciscans, on the other hand, argued in a separate letter of complaint that Rebolledo had not called the meeting for their advice, but instead to inform them of a decision already made, as was his usual practice.[36] Although it seems likely that the meeting at Tolomato was indeed an effort by Rebolledo to cover himself from anticipated criticism that he had not discussed the matter with the Franciscans, there is nevertheless no evidence that the friars mounted an active opposition to Rebolledo's plan until later learning of the first reaction of the caciques of Timucua.

The snag in Rebolledo's plan, which ultimately would provide the immediate reason for the Timucuan rebellion, was that the preexisting militia within the mission provinces consisted of the highest-ranking males in each chiefdom, including not only the warriors with achieved status but also the hereditary caciques and *principales*, who continued to serve as military leaders under the Spanish colonial system. Consequently, by activating the Indian militia, Rebolledo called up only the highest-ranking individuals in each province, leaving the bulk of the common laborers to tend the fields (excluding, of course, the *repartimiento* laborers already in St. Augustine). It was Rebolledo's insistence that each warrior carry his own food, however, that created the problem, for such tasks were never delegated to caciques and *principales* within Indian society. In a culture with sharp distinctions of rank and privilege, low-ranking Indians from non-noble matrilineages were given tasks of manual labor, such as that associated with the *repartimiento* draft. Thus, Rebolledo's command violated long-standing institutions within aboriginal society. Given the governor's situation, however, there was little else that he could do in order to immediately supplement the Spanish infantry with the Indian militia. Every individual who came to the city had to carry enough food to sustain himself. There could be no provision for leaders who brought burden bearers to carry their food, since each servant would also be required to carry enough food for himself.

Although Rebolledo correctly noted that at least two of his predecessors had similarly called upon the Indians of Timucua during their terms of office, these earlier instances were different in significant ways from Rebolledo's quandary. Governor Rojas y Borja had indeed drafted Indian warriors for service in St. Augustine, and Governor Vega Castro y Pardo had drafted burden bearers to transport corn to the city, but no governor had ever combined these two orders, commanding that high-ranking Indian warriors should literally stoop to carry their own provisions to St. Augustine. Under normal circumstances, such an unprecedented request might not have resulted in bloodshed, but Rebolledo's 1656 order, and his unyielding posture in response to subsequent protests, was only the governor's latest affront to the chiefly authority of the caciques of Timucua. The end result was disaster.

Buildup to Rebellion

Following the meeting at Tolomato, Rebolledo's party returned to St. Augustine. Soon thereafter, the governor set his plan in motion, drafting appropriate orders on April 19 and 20.[37] The first order was directed to the western mission provinces of Timucua and Apalachee, and the second went to the northern province of Guale. Close examination of the text of these orders implies different expectations from the coastal Guale province than from the two interior provinces of Timucua and Apalachee. The orders for the latter two provinces emphasized a specified number of warriors who would carry their own food. This contrasts explicitly with the request from Guale for an unspecified number of warriors, especially those bearing firearms, and for the immediate purchase of corn on credit. This distinction in wording presumably reflected Guale's comparative accessibility to ships for the rapid transport of corn to St. Augustine and its substantially depleted population levels in comparison with the western missions. Nevertheless, the wording of the order to Timucua and Apalachee seems potentially more inflammatory, especially considering the explicit mention of each Indian warrior carrying his own food. Furthermore, Rebolledo's request for five hundred Indian warriors was essentially twice the size of the standard yearly labor draft from these two provinces, which would have made it the largest simultaneous mobilization of native labor in the history of Spanish Florida. With perhaps three hundred Apalachee, Guale, and Timucua laborers already working the agricultural fields in St. Augustine, Rebolledo's mobilization would have placed some eight hundred male

Indians in and around the city, including effectively all the most important aboriginal leaders and warriors in both western provinces (not including additional warriors from Guale). The order to Guale resulted in almost immediate compliance, although Rebolledo's subsequent treatment of the caciques of Guale during their stay in St. Augustine and his delays in paying for the corn bought on credit that year eventually resulted in a formal complaint to the Spanish crown.[38] The reaction of the Timucuan caciques to the governor's order, however, was far more negative, and nearly immediate. Even as the order was being hand delivered to the principal towns of the Timucua mission province, the ranking regional caciques of both Timucua and Yustaga convened secret meetings, planning their strategy for armed resistance.

On August 19, Capt. Agustín Pérez de Villa Real left St. Augustine in the company of Estéban Solana, a soldier who was to serve as *atiqui*, or interpreter, during the delivery of Rebolledo's orders to Timucua and Apalachee. Pérez was a forty-five- to fifty-year-old soldier with considerable experience among the Timucua, including several years managing the *hacienda* of Asile, and perhaps also serving simultaneously as the acting provincial lieutenant for Apalachee. The two embarked on a journey that would ultimately take them through most of the important missions in the Timucua province. While the duration of this expedition is not known, they apparently spent several weeks in transit, including travel time and meetings with local caciques. The day following their departure from St. Augustine, however, another letter was dispatched by Governor Rebolledo, apparently directed to his current lieutenant in the Apalachee province, Capt. Antonio de Sartucha. The original dispatch, written and signed in Rebolledo's hand, survived to be entered as evidence in Rebolledo's later *residencia*.[39] The communication, while only fragmentary due to the twentieth-century fire that charred these papers, reveals the governor's increasing concern for the urgency of his situation. Capt. García de la Vera had apparently returned unfortunate news: reinforcements could not be expected from Havana, and although Rebolledo commented that "they remain owing us for another occasion," the governor's immediate situation remained unchanged. Faced with potentially long delays in receiving additional men and supplies from other locations, Rebolledo emphasized to Sartucha the immediate dispatch of all five hundred warriors from the western missions. This letter, however, was far more specific than the April 19 order already in the hands of Captain Pérez, urging Sartucha to command Pérez to "immediately and without one delay send five hundred men—*caciques, norocos,* and *principales*—who would not be needed for cultivation, with all the firearms, many bows and arrows, [and] food for the road and for sustenance during one month in this presidio, and that he should place himself immediately on the road with them." Furthermore, Governor Rebolledo explicitly noted that "these Indians should not bring me one hen [*gallina*], nor any other thing than the corn that I refer to for their sustenance," presumably referring to the practice of bringing gifts of food (perhaps turkeys?) to audiences with the governor. Rebolledo further specified that one of Captain Sartucha's horses should be sold to Pérez for use during his return journey.

Presumably designed to arrive in Sartucha's post at the Apalachee capital in Ivitachuco prior to Pérez and Solana, this direct communiqué (or another like it) may have been intercepted in transit. Based on later events, it seems likely that Timucua's principal cacique, Lúcas Menéndez, had somehow received news of Rebolledo's plan prior to the arrival of Pérez and Solana and had already left mission San Martín. One of two explanations seem likely: either messengers had been sent from San Francisco de Potano or Santa Fé (presumably visited first by Pérez and Solana) to inform the cacique of the governor's plan, or Lúcas intercepted a written communication from the governor, learning of the details of the plan prior to reading the formal gubernatorial order. The fact that the April 20 letter above was the only original document from the rebellion period included in the Rebolledo *residencia* suggests that it might even have been the original intercepted letter.[40] Regardless, the absence of Lúcas Menéndez from San Martín does not seem to have been a coincidence. Later events make it clear that he had gone to San Pedro for consultation with the cacique of San Pedro, named Diego, who was his ranking counterpart in the Yustaga region.

Details regarding the expedition of Pérez and Solana are known only from the later testimony of Pérez (fig. 3.1).[41] This testimony begins upon their arrival at the mission of San Martín, whose cacique was absent, as noted above. Passing through San Martín, Pérez and Solana next traveled northward along the upper Camino Real to mission Santa Cruz de Tarihica, presenting Rebolledo's order to its cacique Benito Ruíz. Although the cacique responded that he would comply with the order and would send the warriors that were asked of him, Benito Ruíz would later be revealed as one of the ringleaders of the rebellion, suggesting that his initial positive response was feigned. The next stop along the road was Niahica (probably identical to San Agustín de Urihica, but with a female leader—*nia* + *hica*), where the *cacica* responded similarly that she would prepare the people that she could in order to comply with the order. Once again, this leader was later found to be involved in the rebellion. From Niahica, Pérez dispatched the interpreter Solana along the primary Camino Real to go to

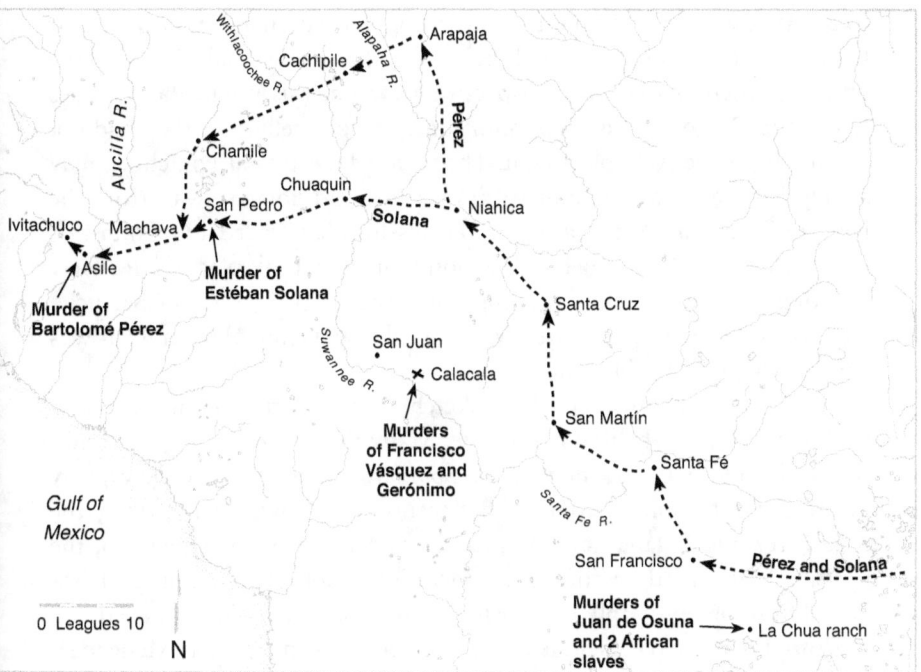

Figure 3-1. Early events in the Timucuan rebellion. Routes of Agustín Pérez de Villa Real and Estéban Solana shown.

the mission of San Pedro de Potohiriba, where he had been informed he could find the caciques of San Martín and San Pedro. Solana presumably crossed the northwestern curve of the Suwannee River below the mouth of the Alapaha River, descending along the main upper trail to mission San Pedro west of the river, where he was to deliver Rebolledo's order to both caciques and then proceed to Santa Elena de Machava and await the arrival of Pérez. In the meantime, Pérez traveled north along the spur trail to the distant mission of Arapaja, where he relayed Rebolledo's order to its cacique Pastrana, who responded that he and his vassals would comply and come to St. Augustine immediately. As Pastrana was very old (and indeed died within four years), Pérez convinced him to name a subordinate to lead the warriors from Arapaja. This done, the entire group proceeded to Machava.

At Machava, Pérez rejoined Solana, the latter apparently having succeeded in sending a message to the caciques of San Martín and San Pedro. In response, Lúcas and Diego sent word that they would meet Pérez and Solana in the principal Apalachee border town of Ivitachuco, where all the warriors and supplies would have to be gathered before the journey to St. Augustine. This request is interesting, considering in hindsight that the rebels of Timucua ultimately endeavored to draw Apalachee into the uprising. There is reason to suspect that even at this point, the caciques Lúcas and Diego were at minimum considering rebellion, if they had not already begun actively plotting it. The planned meeting at Ivitachuco may simply have been an attempt to draw Pérez and Solana away from the heart of Timucua's Yustaga region (at missions San Pedro and Santa Elena, where most of the rebellion's action ultimately took place), effectively isolating the two Spaniards (along with Apalachee Lieutenant Sartucha and his two-man garrison already stationed in Ivitachuco) from what was about to happen in Timucua.

While details of this period are sketchy, a reconstruction of the events leading up to the rebellion is possible. Many things were going on simultaneously, and it is evident that the Spaniards were at first only vaguely aware of the trouble to come. What seems clear, however, is that by the time Pérez and Solana actually met the two caciques in Ivitachuco, the uprising was already a foregone conclusion. Soon after learning of Rebolledo's order (probably even before Pérez and Solana had reached San Martín), the principal cacique of the Timucua province, Lúcas Menéndez, apparently began to garner support for a stand against the governor. While the cacique of Santa Cruz de Tarihica, Benito Ruíz, was one of the first mentioned by Pérez to have verbally agreed to comply with the order, Fray Juan Gómez de Engraba asserted that he was also among the first to call it into question, implying that his initial acquiescence to Pérez may have been a stalling measure.[42] In any case, when Estéban Solana passed through San Pedro, he apparently left word for the two absent caciques regarding Rebolledo's order before moving on to Santa Elena to await the arrival of Captain Pérez. This may have been in the form of a letter from Pérez to the cacique of San Pedro, in which he requested that he go to Apalachee with his people in order to get the corn they would need to bring to St. Augustine.[43]

However the order was formally delivered, the two caciques of San Martín and San Pedro soon dispatched a letter from mission San Pedro to Governor Rebolledo. At the same time, the resident friar at San Pedro, Fray Alonso Escudero, sent a second letter to Rebolledo. While the specific contents of these letters are unknown, later testimony suggests that each attempted to persuade the governor to drop his request that the caciques be required to carry their own corn. Fray Escudero's letter, probably written after he had spoken with Lúcas and Diego, evidently represented an attempt to forestall what Escudero probably suspected could happen (and which eventually did happen), requesting that Rebolledo suspend the order.⁴⁴ Escudero apparently dispatched a similar warning to Provincial Minister Fray Juan de Medina at that time, but this letter was not sent with the first. The contents of the letter from the caciques of San Martín and San Pedro are more difficult to judge, although the message probably ranged between a polite request to suspend the order and outright refusal on the part of the caciques to comply with the letter of the order.⁴⁵ In light of the fact that the two apparently did not wait for a response, the latter seems more likely. The letter from Fray Escudero evidently stated flatly that although the caciques had agreed to come to St. Augustine, they would not bring corn on their backs.⁴⁶

The two letters to Rebolledo, one from the friar and the other from the two caciques, were sent on foot to St. Augustine via two Indians—Juan Alejo, a native of the Acuera mission of Santa Lucia in the province then called "Diminiyuti" (Ibiniuti), and Antonio, son of the Yustagan cacique Lazaro of San Ildefonso de Chamile.⁴⁷ Both of these messengers would later play important roles in the rebellion itself. Departing from San Pedro, the two traveled to St. Augustine and delivered the letters to Rebolledo. Unmoved by the petitions, Governor Rebolledo immediately wrote in response that the caciques should come burdened despite their objections, for "in the Spanish militia, not one [person] is exempt in an occasion to come to the aid of the [presidio] and to carry that which is necessary." He added that "on a similar occasion, the sergeant majors and captains also carried burdens."⁴⁸ From Rebolledo's perspective, all members of the standing Indian militia, including noble caciques and *principales,* were acting as military officers and soldiers under his direct command as Florida's royal governor captain general. Although Rebolledo's actions must be viewed within the context of a trained military officer under pressure to prepare for an imminent enemy assault, the governor's original order and his subsequent refusal to grant an exception reveal a fundamental lack of understanding with regard to the culture and sociopolitical structure of Florida's native peoples. In a very real way, this misunderstanding was emblematic of the jurisdictional struggle that finally erupted into open hostilities in the Timucua province. As the Franciscans later explained in their formal complaint against Rebolledo, "it is a very different matter to give orders to a Spaniard, who knows what it is to obey, than [to give them] to one who does not know how to accept such orders."⁴⁹ In openly subordinating the Timucuan caciques beneath his direct command, stripping them of their aboriginal birthright and privilege, Governor Rebolledo committed the final act that pushed the Timucua mission province into open rebellion.

The governor dispatched two letters of response with the Indian couriers. The first was for Captain Pérez and the second for the cacique of San

Pedro.⁵⁰ Franciscan officials later concluded that these two Indians had been instructed by the Timucuan caciques prior to their initial departure to kill any Spaniard they encountered upon their return if the governor's response was negative.⁵¹ However, based on the testimony of Juan Alejo himself (still imprisoned in the *castillo* in St. Augustine four years later), a different sequence of events seems likely. Alejo testified that the two letters from Rebolledo were sealed, and that he and Antonio were unaware of their contents when they departed from St. Augustine. On their return journey, however, they encountered five Indians on the road just past mission San Martín. From this group they learned of the first murder of the rebellion and were informed of the general command by Lúcas Menéndez to kill all Spaniards.⁵² Consequently, it seems probable that the final decision to rebel was made sometime during the journey of these couriers, and that the two letters they carried from Rebolledo ultimately played no direct role in the actual initiation of violence.

It is intriguing to note that Fray Alonso Escudero was later implicated as having supported, if not encouraged, the rebellion. Rumor among the soldiers held that a friar had told the cacique Lúcas Menéndez that Rebolledo wished to make slaves of the Indians, and that he should rise up against the Spaniards. Even a fellow friar named José de Urrutia, later openly criticized by the Franciscans, asserted that the rebellion had been caused by the friar who wrote Rebolledo a letter of warning.⁵³ While these were clearly exaggerated charges, there is reason to suspect that Escudero did unwittingly ally himself with Lúcas Menéndez against Rebolledo's order, perhaps even supporting disobedience, not suspecting that murder and rebellion would be the outcome. Escudero was, after all, the resident friar at San Pedro, where the rebellion took shape. And, his letter to the governor actually accompanied that of the caciques of San Martín and San Pedro.⁵⁴ In retrospect, then, Fray Alonso Escudero may indeed have played some supporting role in the refusal of the caciques of Timucua to comply with Rebolledo's order, but the events set in motion by this stand soon spun out of control.

Some time after the letters were dispatched (and perhaps even before Captain Pérez and Solana had rejoined in Santa Elena), the cacique of San Martín called a meeting of all the caciques of the Timucua province in the regional council house at San Pedro.⁵⁵ Here Lúcas Menéndez made his case against Governor Rebolledo and in favor of rebellion. The details of this historic meeting of the leaders of Timucua may never be fully known, but based on the scattered evidence from second- and thirdhand testimony, it is possible to go beyond the more simplistic explanations for the rebellion and reconstruct the factors considered by the cacique of San Martín. As discussed above, Lúcas Menéndez took particular offense to Governor Rebolledo's persistent refusal to accord him the customary respect he felt he was due. Rebolledo consciously failed to distribute the appropriate gifts and food for the caciques of Timucua during their stays in St. Augustine. Furthermore, he seemed determined to extract more yearly laborers, despite raging epidemics. Even the slightest resistance to Rebolledo's plans by the cacique of Oconi resulted in the cacique's immediate imprisonment and the immolation of his town just two months earlier. Nevertheless, although the decision to rebel was specifically directed against the authority of the hated Governor Rebolledo, Lúcas Menéndez was acting within the context of a major jurisdictional struggle that had been building for years. The abuses of Rebolledo, including his order to draft the Indian militia, were only symptoms of a broader phenomenon relating to the structural assimilation of Timucua into the colonial system of Spanish Florida.

One statement made by a high-ranking Timucuan Indian mirrors what is argued here to have been a fundamental reason behind the decision to rebel. Capt. Alonso de Argüelles reported that a principal Indian, also the *sacristan* of his town in Timucua, had told him one day in his house in St. Augustine that the instigator of the Timucuan rebellion had been "the said *cacique* of San Martín, named Lúcas Menéndez, who was principal *cacique* and did not have vassals, and through that course [the rebellion] would have them."[56] This statement, along with Lúcas's earlier assertion that he was no longer cacique of Timucua, reveals a decline in chiefly authority, at least as perceived by Lúcas Menéndez, and suggests that the rebellion was a directed attempt to regain internal political power. Governor Rebolledo had effectively robbed him of his own Indian vassals, usurping his chiefly authority by circumventing his role in the aboriginal political structure. The governor's 1656 order was simply the last blow to chiefly authority that Lúcas would tolerate.

It is of course also possible that the assertion that Lúcas Menéndez did not have vassals was a literal statement, referring to the ongoing depopulation of the Timucua province. Following nearly half a century of demographic collapse, San Martín's cacique governed only a fraction of the original population of Timucua. Using the figure of 26,000 converted Indians cited for 1655, if Timucua and Yustaga contained a roughly similar share (about 15 percent) of the overall mission population documented between 1675 and 1689, Lúcas Menéndez may have literally had only around 4,000 "vassals" within his traditional jurisdiction.[57] Furthermore, mission San Martín was situated precisely on the Camino Real. Thus, it was presumably exposed to some of the worst effects of the colonial system, including a nearly constant stream of travelers, many of whom were housed at no charge and provided burden bearers on a regular basis (some of whom undoubtedly introduced further epidemic diseases). Those who survived under such circumstances may have been strongly motivated to flee the mission system. Furthermore, as was the case in Guale, abuses of the *repartimiento* labor system may have left Timucua a largely dysfunctional society consisting mainly of caciques and male *principales,* women, and young children, with very few males typically living under the direct authority of the aboriginal leaders throughout much of the year.[58]

The only direct reference to the arguments Lúcas Menéndez used to convince the remaining caciques of Timucua to rebel comes from the testimony of two interpreters during the later trial of the rebels. Both indicated that the cacique of San Martín had argued that Rebolledo's order had not been issued because there was a threat of enemies, but rather because the Spaniards "wished to ship them out for sale, so that they should be slaves, and to present most of them to the King so that they might be his slaves."[59] One soldier later reported having heard it said among the soldiers that "a missionary had said to [?] of the said province [?] that they were going to look for slaves, and that they should rise up," implying that a friar (probably referring to Alonso Escudero) had given this idea to Lúcas Menéndez.[60] Such assertions, certainly based on misinterpreted information, undoubtedly contributed to the rumor that Fray Escudero had sided with the Indians.

The argument that Rebolledo intended to enslave the Indians seems to have been somewhat of a rallying cry for the rebels, for not only was this ultimately given as a reason by the murderers at the La Chua ranch, but the Timucuan rebels also used this rumor in their efforts to draw the Apalachee province into the rebellion. Nevertheless, this reason was probably no more than a rationale provided in order to garner widespread support among the common Indians. In this connection, it is important to note that the Timucuan rebellion only began after the caciques and other ranking members of noble lineages in the province were ordered to carry burdens personally. Decades of participation in the *repartimiento* labor system had not pushed the Indians of Timucua to rebel; quite to the contrary, as long as the caciques themselves administered the draft (and were also exempt), no significant protests by the caciques themselves seem to have surfaced. The only reason universally given for the rebellion after the fact was the section of Rebolledo's order that explicitly mandated caciques and *principales* to carry corn on their own backs. The order's activation of the standing militia was not disputed, and even the requested contribution of corn was never contested.

The crucial point was that after so many assaults to their traditional authority, the aboriginal leaders were finally ordered to subject themselves to manual labor at the direct bidding of the Spanish governor of St. Augustine. Had Lúcas Menéndez and the caciques of Timucua submitted to this command, they would have been openly relinquishing their position as independent leaders of their own societies. Hereditary rank distinctions would have dissolved among common Indians who viewed their caciques doubled over with sacks of corn on their backs, effectively delegitimizing the hereditary birthright that the Timucuan chiefs spent so much energy maintaining. In sum, what the Timucuan rebellion ultimately boiled down to was a jurisdictional struggle between the Republic of Indians and the Republic of Spaniards in which the caciques of Timucua resisted the final assimilation of their chiefdoms into the colonial system of Spanish Florida. The results of this battle would decide the position of Timucua within the political structure of that colonial system.

The decision to rebel was agreed upon by the caciques of Timucua soon after news of Rebolledo's order had been received. While it is unclear whether the cacique of San Martín issued the command at that time or following the first murder of the rebellion, Lúcas Menéndez ultimately issued a general order that all secular Spaniards in the Timucua province were to be killed on sight. Franciscan friars were specifically exempted from this order. At the same time, Lúcas personally took steps to ensure that his godfather's (Francisco) eldest son, Don Juan Menéndez Márquez, would not be killed in the violence about to be unleashed. The Timucuan rebellion had been set in motion.

Murders in Timucua

The decision to stand up to Rebolledo's order had almost certainly been made before the caciques of San Martín and San Pedro dispatched a response to Agustín Pérez's request for a meeting, which had been delivered by Estéban Solana while in San Pedro. As the two highest-ranking caciques in the Timucua province, Lúcas Menéndez and Diego sent word to Pérez in mission Santa Elena de Machava that they would meet them in the principal Apalachee town of Ivitachuco on the western frontier of the Timucua province.[61] After marching on to Ivitachuco, where the provincial lieutenant Antonio de Sartucha was stationed with a two-man garrison, the two soldiers finally met the two caciques face to face. Through the interpreter, Solana, the order was formally delivered. According to Pérez, the caciques immediately agreed to comply with the order. After the supplies were arranged, all the Indians to be sent from Timucua were dispatched ahead with Estéban Solana, who was to accompany the group to St. Augustine. Pérez remained behind with the Apalachee contingent at the urging of Captain Sartucha, who argued that the two groups should be kept separate in order to avoid trouble. Readying his group for departure in the afternoon of the following day, Pérez sent one of Sartucha's garrison soldiers, Bartolomé Pérez, ahead to the neighboring Timucuan border town of Asile in order to gather some corn there for the journey. All seemed calm, but later that afternoon the storm would break (fig. 3.1).

At about two o'clock in the afternoon, either on the very day of Solana's departure with the Indians from Timucua or on the following day, Fray Joseph Bamba galloped on a horse into Ivitachuco at high speed, bringing news of two murders. Upon his arrival in the Yustagan town of San Pedro de Potohiriba, Estéban Solana had been murdered by the Timucuan Indians whom he led. Soon thereafter, when Bartolomé Pérez arrived in San Miguel de Asile, where Fray Bamba resided, an Indian from San Pedro entered the council house where the soldier was and killed him with a hatchet blow to the back of the head. The province of Timucua had risen up, refusing to comply with Rebolledo's order and killing the soldiers sent for its execution. With this news, Captains Pérez and Sartucha immediately sent all the Apalachee Indians already gathered in Ivitachuco back to their homes. The two were left in an unenviable position, having been stranded on the western edge of the rebellious Timucua province, guarding the gateway into Apalachee. Deciding to remain in Ivitachuco, they posted guards (presumably Apalachee Indians) and dispatched the one remaining Spanish soldier, Bartolomé Francisco, to bring word of the rebellion to Governor Rebolledo in St. Augustine. Francisco was cautioned to travel off the main road, skirting Timucua, in order to protect his life and ensure the safe passage of the letters.[62]

Interestingly, although the first two murders in San Pedro and Asile clearly occurred within the context of the general uprising among the Timucua, there is some reason to suspect that the victims had personally antagonized their murderers. Juan Alejo later testified that he had heard it said that Estéban Solana made disparaging remarks during his journey from Ivitachuco back to San Pedro, stating that "there did not have to be any more caciques than him," suggesting that Solana may have unwittingly brought on his own murder.[63] Furthermore, the later confession of the Indian who murdered Bartolomé Pérez revealed that this was partly a crime of personal revenge. Pérez had once offended the Indian, entering the council house [*buhio*] where the Indian was beside the fire, kicking him and saying "Go away, dog! Get up from there!"[64] Upon learning from several caciques in San Pedro of the command to kill all Spaniards, this Indian left immediately and traveled as far as Asile, where he met Bartolomé Pérez and killed him with a hatchet. Dragging the corpse outside, he scalped the soldier. Later, after his capture, he confessed everything to the Spaniards, saying that "he knew well that he had to pay later, but that up to then, he had not been a man, and with that action he was a *noroco* of God and of the King, and that he was very content."[65] This statement is important in several ways, for it demonstrates an intriguing blend of cultural norms. By killing and scalping his enemy, the Indian fulfilled (indeed exceeded) his traditional right for revenge, advancing to the warrior rank of *noroco*. Yet he claimed further that he was a *noroco* for the Spanish god and king. Nevertheless, the murder of Bartolomé Pérez seems to have been motivated primarily by personal goals, with the standing order to kill all Spaniards serving more as an excuse than a direct reason.

Regardless of the specific motivations that led to each individual murder, there seems little doubt that the general order for the murder of all Spaniards was issued very early during the rebellion. Clearly, the fact that all the caciques of Timucua openly professed compliance to the order to Agustín Pérez, while Lúcas and Diego simultaneously dispatched a letter of apparent refusal to Rebolledo, suggests that some degree of planning was involved. It seems probable that the murders were a calculated part of the uprising. Indeed, Captain Pérez later asserted that he was completely unaware of any resistance to the order; otherwise, he would not have proceeded with its execution without consulting the governor.[66] Furthermore, later testimony revealed that Lúcas Menéndez had very early on dispatched a letter to Don Juan Menéndez Márquez in St. Augustine, evidently warning him not to come to his hacienda.[67] Receiving the letter at the moment of his departure, Don Juan was unable to read it (since the letter had been written in the Timucuan language). Thus, he proceeded with his twenty-four-league journey to La Chua, unaware of the danger that awaited.[68] Nevertheless, the fact that the cacique Lúcas was able to send a letter of warning prior to the later murders at La Chua further reinforces the conclusion that bloodshed had been plotted from the very beginning.

In the meantime, however, violence was rapidly spreading to the eastern reaches of the Timucua province (fig. 3.1). A group of five Indians, two men named Lorenzo and a woman, all natives of mission Santa Fé, and two men native to San Martín, departed the town of San Pedro as soon as Estéban Solana had been killed (prior to learning of the subsequent murder of Bartolomé Pérez). During their journey to San Martín, the group met the two Indian messengers, Juan Alejo and Antonio, themselves returning from St. Augustine with Governor Rebolledo's responses. The group told them of having killed Solana in San Pedro, and they reported that "the *cacique* of San Martín said that upon meeting Spaniards, they should kill them."[69] Each group proceeding on its way, Juan Alejo and Antonio soon arrived after nightfall at a place called Calacala (probably on the banks of the modern Suwannee River at or near Royal Springs).[70] Here they encountered a pair of servants from the hacienda of La Chua: Francisco Vásquez, a Spaniard, and Gerónimo, an Indian from the province of Tabasco in New Spain. Returning from Apalachee with corn for the hacienda, the two had already gone to bed and were talking about the evening when Juan Alejo and Antonio approached the two and struck them in the head with a stick or club they carried. They followed this with a second blow, which killed the two servants. According to Alejo, his companion Antonio then took out a knife and scalped the Mexican Indian Gerónimo, placing the scalp in a cloth.[71]

Continuing on their journey back to San Pedro, the pair met another group of Indians after having crossed the river of San Juan de Guacara. This group of five included Timucua's principal cacique, Lúcas Menéndez; his *mandador,* Lorenzo; another principal Indian who was also sacristan; and another two Indians. Lúcas asked them for news from St. Augustine and inquired what the governor had said. In response, the two Indian messengers turned over both letters. After reading one, the cacique placed them both in a pocket or pouch (*faldriquera*). While one of these was addressed to the cacique of San Pedro, presumably in response to the letter he and Lúcas had jointly authored, the second was intended for Captain Pérez. Thus, Lúcas Menéndez did intercept at least one of Rebolledo's personal communications to Pérez.

The two Indian messengers told the cacique of the murders of the two Spanish servants, and Antonio showed him the scalp. Interestingly, while Lúcas praised the two for a job well done, he added that "although he had commanded that they should kill all the Spaniards, he had not commanded that they should scalp them, and he commanded him to bury it, and he did so at one side of the road."[72] This event seems to underline a basic feature of the Timucuan rebellion, at least as envisioned by its principal leader. The uprising does not seem to have reflected an attempt to return to precontact cultural norms, with a subsequent rejection of everything Spanish. Instead, it seems to have centered on a political power struggle between the remaining Timucuan chiefdoms of Florida's interior and the Spanish military government in St. Augustine. Indeed, Lúcas Menéndez later explained to a friar that the rebellion did not signify that the Timucuans were "abandoning the law of God, nor refusing to be obedient to [His] Majesty"; their actions were instead designed to "liberate themselves from the offenses and continuous injuries."[73]

Following the burial of the scalp, the cacique Lúcas wrote a letter to Diego, the cacique of San Pedro, and sent it with the two messengers to San Pedro. They were instructed to tell the cacique what they had done, to inform him that Lúcas was headed for the hacienda of La Chua to find out if there were any Spaniards he could kill and to request that he send more of his vassals to assist. Juan Alejo and Antonio carried out their instructions, and the cacique of San Pedro apparently dispatched several more Indians in search of Lúcas Menéndez. In the meantime, Don Juan Menéndez Márquez, senior owner of his late father's ranch, arrived at La Chua in the company of the soldier Juan de Osuna. Don Juan evidently had the letter from the cacique Lúcas read to him by an Indian working at the hacienda.[74] As was later testified, this Indian lied regarding the contents of the letter, and Don Juan remained at La Chua in ignorance of the rebellion.

The testimony regarding the subsequent murders at the La Chua ranch represents a moving and tragic tale. Early one night, Don Juan was visited at his house on the hacienda by the cacique Lúcas Menéndez, along with the caciques of San Francisco de Potano (Juan Bauptista) and Santa Fé de Teleco and some fourteen to twenty Indians.[75] Assuming that they had come on their way to St. Augustine in compliance to Pérez's order, Don Juan asked, "So quickly have you attended to going to the presidio?" Surprised at Don Juan's presence despite his warning, Lúcas Menéndez quickly seized the Spaniard by the arm and pulled him outside the house, saying "Don Juan, come here!"[76] The Spaniard watched helplessly as the rest of the Indians entered the house, and he heard the screams of his companions as they were murdered within; one or two were killed outside as they fled. Ultimately, the soldier Juan de Osuna and the two black slaves at the hacienda were murdered, while two Indians in Don Juan's employ successfully fled the carnage. Testimony from Juan Pasqua, later imprisoned in the fort at St. Augustine for one of the murders, detailed that he had been dismissed early from *repartimiento* duties in St. Augustine. Upon his arrival in San Francisco Potano, he had been commanded by the cacique Lúcas Menéndez, under penalty of punishment, to accompany him to La Chua. There he had ordered him to go to a hut outside the main house of the hacienda to which one of the slaves had fled and kill him. After the raid, not a single person was left alive in the hacienda beyond Don Juan; even the cattle had been killed by the Indians.[77]

Don Juan had been taken completely by surprise. He initially presumed that he would be killed with the rest.[78] Asking, "What is this?," the Indians told him it was in response to the Spaniards' wish to make slaves of them and said, "Now the Spaniards die!." Don Juan told the cacique, "If you have to kill me, let me go to a village, if you have left a missionary alive, in order to confess." He was assured by Lúcas that he should have no fear, saying that he alone would be spared "because of the benefits that they had received from him and his father."[79] Don Juan inquired about the safety of the friars, asking "if they had killed the fathers, and they had responded no, that [they had killed] the Spaniards who were in Apalachee and Timucua and no more." Given a horse and some of his clothes, Don Juan was instructed by Lúcas to return to St. Augustine and then Spain. He was told that "he might return within six years, for then they would be of good heart," although "until then they had to be of an evil heart for the evil which had been done with them." The Spaniard was accompanied as far as the village of San Francisco, three leagues away, by two Indians instructed by the cacique to protect him from harm. He returned from there alone.[80]

The murders at La Chua were the last of the Timucuan rebellion. In all, seven individuals had been killed over the course of just a few days: three Spanish soldiers, a Spanish servant, two African slaves, and a Mexican Indian. In retrospect, this seems a remarkably limited loss of life, considering the importance that this uprising would ultimately assume. Nevertheless, with these deaths, the only Spanish military presence in the whole of interior Florida was reduced to the two soldiers stranded in Ivitachuco (having dispatched the only remaining member of Sartucha's garrison to St. Augustine). Of considerable importance is the fact that not a single Franciscan friar was killed, either during this initial wave of violence or during the weeks and months that followed. In this, the Timucuan rebellion departs from the other major uprisings in the mission provinces of Florida. The 1597 Guale rebellion left five friars dead, and three more lost their lives in the Apalachee rebellion of 1647. In each of these cases, the friars seem to have been singled out as targets of aggression, whereas during the Timucuan rebellion not only were the friars spared but one (Escudero) was openly implicated as a conspirator in the uprising. Another unnamed friar even managed to arrange a meeting under cover of night with Lúcas Menéndez in Machava, endeavoring to convince the rebels of the rashness of their actions.[81]

In fact, the Timucuan rebellion displayed a number of qualities that set it apart from superficially similar events. The key lies in the fact that the rebellion seems to have been an outgrowth of the complex set of relationships that developed as an inherent part of the colonial system of Spanish Florida. What makes this event so difficult to disentangle is the presence of several factions, and factions within factions, in both the Spanish and Timucuan societies. The rebellion cannot simply be boiled down to the standard Spanish/Indian or religious/military dichotomies; nor can the often repeated explanation involving Rebolledo's order that the leaders carry corn be taken only at face value. All of these explanations form a part of the picture, but to gloss over the intricate complexities of the Timucuan rebellion is to ignore a golden opportunity to examine in detail the catastrophic consequences of contact and colonization in this corner of the European colonial world.

CHAPTER 4

The Pacification of Timucua

The Initial Response

If the story of the beginning of the Timucuan rebellion during the spring of 1656 reveals myriad complexities, the details of events during the subsequent months of 1656 complicate the picture considerably. News of the uprising in Timucua province arrived in St. Augustine within a few days after the initial wave of murders, probably in May. Governor Rebolledo, at that time unaware of any trouble in the frontier, was busy attending to repairs to the fort, having gone about a league from St. Augustine with a group of soldiers to investigate the condition of some wood for use in the fort. On the return journey, they were overtaken by Don Juan Menéndez Márquez on his horse, where he related the news about the murders at his hacienda of La Chua.[1] Returning to St. Augustine, Rebolledo ordered a cannon to be fired, calling all the soldiers in the fort to hear the report. This news was soon followed by further developments, for within a few days Bartolomé Francisco and a pair of Indians arrived with the letter from Captain Pérez and Lieutenant Sartucha, detailing the murders of the two soldiers Solana and Pérez.[2] There is no clear indication that Rebolledo was aware of the murders of the two servants from La Chua (Vásquez and Tabasco) at this stage, unless the cacique of San Martín had informed Don Juan.

The details of the summer of 1656 are sketchy and vague, but based on the timing of the well-documented retaliatory expedition in September, it seems evident that some three months passed before Rebolledo was able to organize an effective response to the rebellion. Although this might appear illogical, Rebolledo was in fact under direct orders from the king to be prepared for an English land assault during this period, and thus his actions must be viewed within a broader context. With the news of the uprising in Timucua, Rebolledo instantly knew that he could expect no reinforcements of Indian militia from Timucua and Apalachee without dispatching a force of Spanish infantry from St. Augustine, where they were thought to be needed for the very preservation of the city. In an effort to cut his losses, Rebolledo apparently decided that to quell the rebellion immediately would leave St. Augustine open to imminent attack. Thus, his measures reflect the cautious and calculated attempt to contain the uprising until soldiers could be spared after the danger of the English fleet had lessened in the fall hurricane season. Indeed, during this time, one of the officers working on the trenches remarked to another that "they did not have to have fear of the enemy which was to come by sea, but rather those on land, because the Indians of Timucua, according to what he understood, had not been sure for many days."[3]

During this period, the actions of both the rebel Timucua caciques and Governor Rebolledo revolved around the all-important province of Apalachee. Once news of the rebellion had reached St. Augustine, Rebolledo dispatched instructions to Pérez and Sartucha, commanding them to remain in Ivitachuco until assistance could be sent.[4] This order was evidently carried by several soldiers, including Bartolomé Francisco, who had returned alone from Apalachee with the initial news of the rebellion. Rebolledo dispatched these four soldiers off road, hoping to avoid their capture (and the interception of the orders) in Timucua.[5] The soldiers were also sent to reinforce Pérez and Sartucha, at that time alone in Ivitachuco. Letters were additionally carried for several friars. Testimony from the later service record of a member of this group, Ensign Juan Bauptista Terraza, described the journey: "off the road without passing through Timucua . . . he went across uninhabited land and woods until arriving and fulfilling with many hardships the order and [delivering the] news which he was given."[6] Given the northern distribution of the Timucuan missions in the Yustaga region, this party probably followed the southern border of Timucua, traversing modern San Pedro Bay before arriving at Ivitachuco just west of the Aucilla (Asile) River.

About this same time, several Indians arrived in St. Augustine from Apalachee, bringing notice of rumors in Apalachee that the principal cacique of Ivitachuco, Don Luís, and the *repartimiento* laborers from Apalachee, all of whom were at that time in St. Augustine, had been imprisoned by Rebolledo in the city, and that he intended to enslave them. The governor acted quickly to counter this rumor, writing to Lieutenant Sartucha and informing Don Luís personally. The cacique immediately dispatched his heir and several *principales,* among whom was his *iniha,* giving them instructions to reveal the rumor as a lie fabricated by the Timucuans and commanding that the province remain quiet.[7] This group of Apalachee Indians accompanied the four soldiers noted above to Ivitachuco. Some time later, another Indian messenger returned to St. Augustine, reporting that all the soldiers had arrived safely in Apalachee and their orders had been delivered.[8]

As Governor Rebolledo endeavored to formulate a response to the uprising, the Indians of Timucua were busily working to reinforce their position. During the weeks and months following the murders that plunged the province into revolt, the leaders of the Timucua province made rapid preparations for the Spanish military response that they knew would eventually come. While the details of these activities are poorly documented, it is possible to assemble a picture of the overall strategy put into effect during the summer of 1656. What becomes evident is that the Timucuans intended to make a stand in their own territory, and that a major component of their plan was the anticipated support of the Apalachee province. What had become the normal routine of daily life after nearly half a century of missionization came to an abrupt end in Timucua during the rebellion. As related by the Franciscans the following year, the resident friars in Timucua "found themselves reviled by the majority of the Indians, deprived of the necessary provisions, and many times forsaken and alone in their convents, because the Indians gave their attention solely to their dances and preparations for war to which they devoted their time, living like pagans during that period."[9] These preparations resulted in a substantial disturbance to the yearly crop in Timucua, for there were "many fewer plantings as a result of the forays that the unruly mob made." Most of the Indians at that time seem to have largely abandoned their normal residences in the mission villages, looting food stores for immediate use and "roaming through the woods with their wives."

As noted above, the meeting at which the decision to rebel was formally made was held in San Pedro de Potohiriba, the administrative center for the Yustaga region within the broader Timucua mission province. This fact alone is notable, considering that the paramount cacique of the entire province resided at San Martín, far to the east of San Pedro. The murders that started the uprising occurred in four separate locations across the Timucua province, essentially dictated by where the Spaniards happened to be at the time. Interestingly, however, immediately following the murders at La Chua, most of the rebels seem to have gone to mission Santa Elena de Machava (west of San Pedro), and virtually all of the subsequent events in the rebellion took place in this immediate vicinity.[10] A closer examination of this fact reveals a great deal about the strategic planning of the rebel leaders of Timucua.

Santa Elena de Machava was apparently located along the Camino Real leading toward Apalachee from the Timucua province. With mission San Pedro, the two constituted the demographic center of the Yustaga region.

The nearest Yustagan mission to the west was the border town of San Miguel de Asile, located just across the Aucilla River only two leagues east of Ivitachuco and the Apalachee province. Perhaps based in part on its more remote location, and the fact that it seems to have been severely depopulated even as early as 1651,[11] Asile apparently did not occupy a prominent position in regional politics. The resident friar in Santa Elena, Joseph Bamba, evidently also ministered to the neighboring town of Asile, supporting the interpretation that this westernmost town was relatively less populous than Machava. Although the subordinate cacique of San Lúcas, most likely within Asile's local jurisdiction, was eventually hanged as a participant in the rebellion, Asile's principal cacique was not mentioned even a single time in all the *residencia* testimony about the rebellion, suggesting either that Asile's chief held comparatively little regional import among the Yustaga or perhaps that he remained either neutral or even pro-Spanish due to the proximity and apparent social connections between Asile and Ivitachuco. In either case, mission Santa Elena de Machava seems to have been the westernmost town of regional importance in the entire Timucua mission province, a conclusion that is reinforced by the fact that the first resident provincial lieutenant of Timucua was stationed there in 1649. This possibility is significant, for it was at Santa Elena that the rebel caciques decided to make a stand, not at another, more centrally located town. In a forest next to the town, just half a league away, the rebels constructed a palisade using thick poles and fortified themselves within this structure. While the palisade was located within the jurisdiction of the village of San Juan Ebangelista, a satellite community subordinate to Santa Elena de Machava, it was evidently a new construction, hastily built in a defensible position away from the villages (and possibly on one of the prominent and isolated hillocks in this locality; see appendix A).[12] Here the Timucuan rebels gathered during the summer and fall of 1656.

Why did the rebel caciques choose to construct a military fortification so close to Apalachee and so far from the political center of the province at San Martín? The reasons for this decision may never be known with certainty, but based on the actions of these rebels that summer, it is probable that the Timucuan caciques had high hopes that they would be joined in their stand by the Apalachee province. Apart from the probability that the Yustaga region was generally more densely populated, the location of the Timucuan palisade so near to Apalachee and directly on the Camino Real presumably facilitated communication and negotiation with the caciques of Apalachee during the weeks and months following the initial murders of the rebellion that spring. Indeed, this is precisely what occurred during this period, for, as noted above, very early in the rebellion Governor Rebolledo received reports that the Timucuans were endeavoring to draw the Apalachee into the uprising, sending letters to argue their case.[13]

The rumors regarding the enslavement of Don Luís and the Apalachee *repartimiento* laborers in St. Augustine only serve as an example of the attempts by the rebels of the Timucua province to turn the Apalachee caciques against the Spaniards. It seems evident that a primary goal of the Timucuans was not only to consolidate their own internal support for the rebellion but also to garner support from Apalachee, which they realized was the key to its success. The Franciscans later concluded that had it not been for the prudence of one Apalachee cacique (presumably Don Luís, or the subordinate cacique who decided to verify the Timucuan rumor before acting), the Apalachee province would also have rebelled.[14] This would appear to be the reason behind the strategy adopted by the rebels, for there seems no other logical explanation for the actions taken that summer.

First, and perhaps most significantly, the very decision to make a stand within a fortified palisade constructed specifically for this purpose appears flawed unless the importance of Apalachee is considered. The Timucua caciques must have known that the construction of a fort would not fend off the Spanish infantry forever; sooner or later, the palisade would have been breached under assault. With all the rebel leaders inside, this would signal the end of the rebellion. The palisade would thus seem to have been constructed not for the permanent defense of the rebel forces, but rather to buy time for the consolidation of support noted above. The caciques must have hoped that with the construction of a fortified stockade, they could fend off a small Spanish force (such as the handful of soldiers in Ivitachuco), delaying the success of any Spanish response. Indeed, the very location of the Timucua palisade reveals much regarding its purpose. Had the purpose of such a fortification been to somehow keep the Spanish infantry in St. Augustine from entering the Timucua mission province, it would have been far more effectively located in the easternmost reaches of the province, along the Camino Real as it entered the interior (perhaps in the Potano district, or even at the St. Johns River crossing at mission San Diego). The fort's location on the western edge of the Timucua province gave the Spaniards free access to virtually the entire province, essentially sandwiching the bulk of the rebel force between the Spaniards, who would eventually come from the east, and the Apalachee Indians situated to the west.

The Timucua palisade was actually situated in an ideal location to potentially monitor (and perhaps hinder) the entrance of Spanish infantry into the Apalachee province. One possible goal might have been to isolate Apalachee from St. Augustine. The fort, therefore, might have theoretically slowed or blocked communications between Apalachee and the Spaniards, permitting the Timucua caciques time to win the support of this western province. Furthermore, in the eventuality that Apalachee should fail to stand with Timucua, the fort was well placed to repel a joint Apalachee/Spanish military raid along the Camino Real from the west. One significant factor in the planning of the Timucua caciques was almost certainly the failed Apalachee rebellion of 1647, only nine years earlier. Following the murders initiating that uprising, the Spanish infantry was augmented by a significant force of Indian warriors from the Timucua province, a fact which may well have made the difference in the infamous battle fought against the Apalachee and Chisca rebels on the eastern border of the Apalachee province. The Timucua leaders must have known that if they could not count on the support of the Apalachee, the Spaniards would certainly use the Apalachee against them.

Intriguingly, the very idea of a fort may have been inspired through earlier contact with the Spanish, for the Timucua caciques, *principales,* and other warriors had been schooled in Spanish tactics as a part of the developing Indian militia beginning at least as early as 1649. The construction of a palisade away from occupied villages appears atypical of aboriginal strategy, which in the prehistoric period generally focused on the fortification of the villages themselves. The Timucua fort's location half a league away from Santa Elena de Machava forms an interesting parallel with St. Augustine and its fort, particularly since one function of aboriginal labor in the *repartimiento* system of colonial Florida involved the occasional maintenance of the Spanish fort. The statement of one eyewitness, describing the stronghold as a "palisade in the form of a fort," might even imply that the Timucua palisade was modeled after the Spanish fort.[15] In retrospect, however, the fort was a flawed tactic. Despite the presence of at least a small number of Spanish firearms among the Timucuans, the rebels barricaded themselves within a stockade, abandoning a major advantage over the Spaniards: mobility. Although the palisade would ultimately never be tested in battle, there seems little doubt as to the outcome of a Spanish siege against the fort.

While the Timucua rebels prepared their fortification and attempted to win the Apalachee over to their cause, Governor Rebolledo pursued his own plan of action in response to the rebellion. Having sent the four soldiers noted above to Ivitachuco with orders to prevent the Timucuans from making inroads into Apalachee, Rebolledo made preparations for a major military expedition into the interior. Apart from assembling a body of Spanish reserve officers and soldiers for this force, the governor dispatched a new order to the leaders of the Guale province, requesting their assistance with warriors and arms (presuming that the original April order had been suspended with the uprising). On July 11, Rebolledo noted that he had "determined to send infantry to the provinces of Timucua for its pacification, and the punishment of its rebel *caciques*." He dispatched Capt. Matheo Pacheco y Salgado to Guale to request that "the *caciques* and *micos* aid me for this task with some arquebusier Indians, and with some bows and arrows in order to arm some [Indians] who find themselves without them in this presidio."[16] Although the Guale leaders readily complied, the following year the caciques protested to the Spanish crown regarding their month-long stay in St. Augustine:

> the Governor advising us of the uprising and how, determining to dispatch infantry, we should help him as loyal vassals of Your Majesty with some arquebuses, quivers of arrows, and bows, in order to arm the Indians of St. Augustine, all of our towns helped with all the quivers full of arrows that we could, and beyond this, as true vassals of Your Majesty, we offered to leave our towns, wives, children, and fields, and die with all our vassals at the side of the Spaniards. All of us *micos* and *caciques* left our houses from this province of Guale with all the best of our vassals, and presenting ourselves to the Governor, we offered to die in his defense, and telling us to wait eight or ten days, while the infantry was prepared, giving us only a little rotted hardtack to eat. Notwithstanding, we were waiting more than thirty days, and having seen that there was no order, nor were the people being dispatched, as they were not dispatched until three months from then, many of our vassals and some of us fell ill because of the poor treatment and rigor which was had with us.[17]

The caciques further indicated that during their stay in St. Augustine, news arrived "that the Timucuan enemy was trying to enter our villages and burn them, because of knowing that we, their inhabitants, were in St. Augustine," for which the leaders requested permission to return in defense their villages.

Treating the Guale leaders with considerable disrespect, Governor Rebolledo was later rumored to have "said some insolent words to a *cacique* of the province of Guale, which among others was to tell him to kiss him in the behind, and that the *cacique* had gone away very upset from it."[18] The governor subsequently ordered all the weapons the Guale warriors had brought to be confiscated before their return to Guale, asserting that he had need of the weapons due to the rebellion in Timucua, and that he intended to pay for them when royal funds arrived.[19] Later testimony indicated that there was a lack of arquebuses in St. Augustine at that time, and Rebolledo intended to arm the Apalachee Indians in St. Augustine using the firearms from Guale. While Rebolledo's stated excuse that the weapons were badly needed may have been true, it seems likely that the governor also hoped to avoid similar trouble in Guale by disarming the Indians. The Guale caciques were evidently offended by the confiscation, perhaps guessing Rebolledo's reasons, and although they complied, they returned in disgust with the governor.[20] Payment for the corn and confiscated weapons was ultimately delayed for years. The caciques even reported that during their stay, "in all this time he did not have to give us one thread of clothing of that which Your Majesty commands given to us as alms," incidentally demonstrating the preeminent value of Spanish clothing as gifts to Florida chiefs.[21] Later, it was rumored in St. Augustine that the Indians of the Guale province were watching the events in Timucua very carefully. Had the Timucuan rebellion succeeded, Guale would almost certainly have risen up as well.

Governor Rebolledo was thus not only faced with an existing rebellion in Timucua but also had good reason to fear that the uprising might spread to the remaining provinces of Apalachee and Guale. For whatever reason, Rebolledo did not employ Guale Indians in quelling the Timucuan rebellion, perhaps judging it best to isolate those Indians not already affected by the uprising. The Apalachee, on the other hand, had already been enticed to join the Timucua. Beyond this, their support and assistance in putting down the rebellion was crucial. As a consequence, Rebolledo made arrangements for all the Apalachee laborers in St. Augustine to accompany the planned military expedition into the interior, along with the principal cacique of the Apalachee province, Don Luís. At least some of these warriors were presumably supplied with the firearms and bows and arrows confiscated from the Guale. By the end of August, Governor Rebolledo was evidently sure enough of the safety of St. Augustine from the English threat that he could proceed with his planned military expedition into the interior. The rebel leaders of Timucua had finished their palisade by this time and were still actively involved in consolidating their support. The anticipated confrontation with the Spanish infantry was about to become a reality, and in early September of 1656, Rebolledo signed an order that could potentially decide the fate of all of Spanish Florida, dispatching troops for the pacification of the Timucuan rebellion.

The March to Ivitachuco

On September 4, 1656, Gov. Don Diego de Rebolledo issued an order and accompanying instruction to the sergeant major of the two companies of infantry in St. Augustine, Adrián de Cañizares y Osorio.[22] An officer with lifelong experience among Florida's mission Indians, Cañizares was directed to serve as the leader of a force of sixty Spanish soldiers charged with the task of pacifying the rebellious Timucua province. While the original order evidently did not survive, copies in the office of government in St. Augustine were transcribed during the Rebolledo *residencia*. This charred manuscript contains the only extant version of these important documents. Instructions to the sergeant major were quite explicit and conform to the later recollections of the original order by a number of soldiers who participated in the expedition. What seems clear from the text of the order is that Governor Rebolledo's explicit intention in dispatching troops under Cañizares's command was not to crush the rebellion by force of arms, but rather to endeavor to convince the rebels to return to their villages peacefully. Failing this, Sergeant Major Cañizares was instructed to round up the rebel Indians under command of the caciques without resorting to force, leaving the leaders of the Timucuan rebellion alone and helpless. Finally, the rebel caciques and the individuals responsible for the seven murders of the rebellion were to be apprehended and imprisoned in Apalachee, pending a decision on their fate by Rebolledo himself. Throughout the text of the order and instruction are statements that force was to be employed only as a last resort. This was indeed the perception of the soldiers after they learned of the order. Cañizares followed both the letter and spirit of these instructions in all of his subsequent actions, successfully achieving the stated goals of the order without spilling a single drop of blood in combat.[23]

The troops under Cañizares's command must have departed the city of St. Augustine soon after the issuance of Rebolledo's order. The sergeant major led a force of sixty Spanish soldiers, including a wide range of *reformados* and soldiers. Many of these officers possessed long experience in the frontier of Florida. Cañizares himself, later described as "a wise person of more than sixty years of age," was a veteran of numerous expeditions into the interior. He had been sent into the Timucua province on a military expedition to punish the raiding Chisca Indians before 1624.[24] Based on later testimony, he seems to have known many of the Timucua caciques personally. Don Juan Menéndez Márquez, Cañizares's second in command, along with his younger brother Don Antonio, were co-owners with their younger brothers of the La Chua ranch within the Timucua province. They were personal acquaintances, if not friends, of Lúcas Menéndez and other Timucua caciques. Many of the other officers and soldiers possessed similarly long experience in Florida Indian affairs. These infantrymen, constituting one of the largest mobilizations of Spanish troops ever sent from St. Augustine into the interior of Florida, were accompanied by the principal cacique of the Apalachee province, Don Luís of Ivitachuco, and all the

Apalachee Indians who had been in St. Augustine during the summer as a part of the yearly labor draft (perhaps as many as 200). At least some of these Indians presumably carried the arquebuses turned over by the Guale caciques.[25]

The force marched into the interior, presumably along the Camino Real, as far as the mission San Martín. Having passed this town, the group arrived at a lake (possibly present-day Blue Hole or the Ichetucknee headspring), where Cañizares assembled the troops and had the appointed notary, Ensign Don Juan Joseph de Sotomayor, read Rebolledo's order in front of all the men (fig. 4.1).[26] Continuing their journey to the west, the army seems to have stayed off the main route, marching across an uninhabited region (probably south of the Yustaga region) to arrive at the town of Ivitachuco on the eastern boundary of Apalachee province.[27] In this manner, Cañizares circumvented the Timucua rebels (probably known to be largely in Yustaga by that time) and joined the six Spanish soldiers already in Ivitachuco, additionally bringing the Apalachee Indians under the cacique Don Luís to their home territory. At Ivitachuco, the expedition found a considerable force of Indians assembled, including between 500 and 2,000 Apalachee Indians.[28] In addition to the soldiers sent from St. Augustine to Ivitachuco, one witness also reported the presence of Spaniards from a ship from Havana, presumably having been recruited by Lieutenant Sartucha from a trading expedition to the Apalachee port.

During subsequent days, the army rested and made preparations. Cañizares held a meeting with the caciques of Apalachee who had assembled in Ivitachuco and with several leaders from the Timucua province who were not among the rebels, including, curiously, Diego Heva, the cacique of Santa Catalina de Ayepacano, a satellite village of mission San Pedro de Potohiriba. While there, a Timucuan Indian named Francisco Hiriba, *mandador* of the northern Yustagan town of Chamile, arrived in Ivitachuco with a pledge of assistance from Lazaro, the cacique of that town.[29] The fact that not all of the caciques of Timucua chose to follow the rebels is an intriguing and extremely important facet of the rebellion. While it is clear that the majority of the caciques rebelled, including all of the most powerful regional leaders, a number of subordinate local chiefs chose to side with the Spanish (table 4.1). Their allegiance played an important, if not essential, role in the pacification of the province, and all would ultimately be rewarded by the Spanish for their stand. Significantly, virtually all of the Spanish-allied caciques were from towns not situated along the Camino Real, including those of Chamile, Cachipile, and Arapaja, all of which seem to have been located in the northern reaches of the Yustaga region (although Chamile was only four leagues from the rebel stronghold at

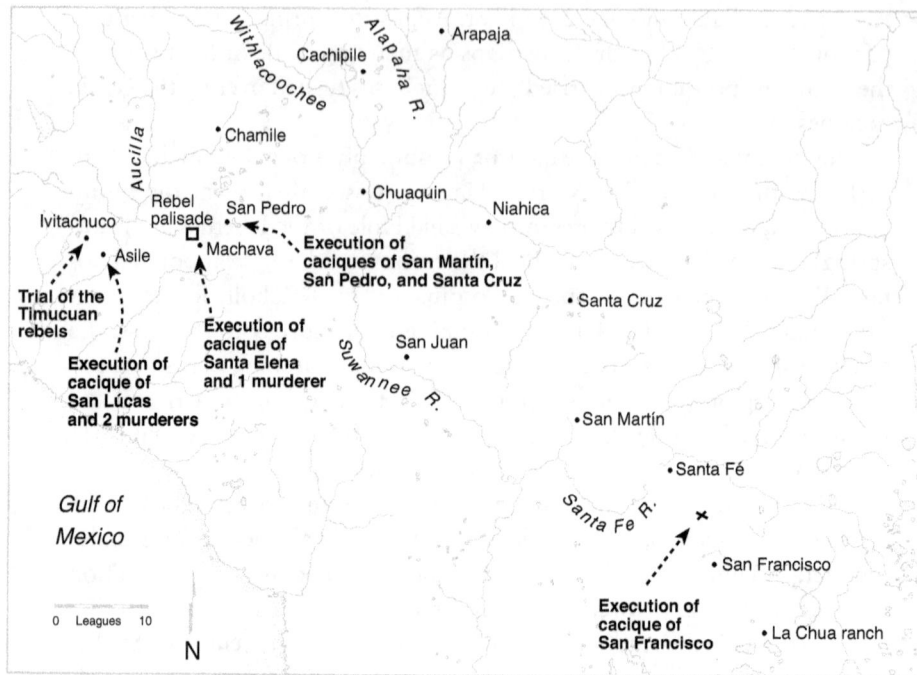

Figure 4-1. Pacification and punishment of the Timucua rebels.

Machava; see appendix A). The little-known unconverted town of Pachala, also near Machava, remained loyal to the Spaniards, as did Ayepacano, a subordinate community within the local chiefdom of San Pedro de Potohiriba.

The decision of the caciques of these towns not to stand with the regional chieftains and most of the rest of the local chiefs, but instead with the Spanish military, may well represent a political power play, for in failing to support the rebellion, their own individual standing with the Spaniards was increased considerably. This decision ultimately permitted these once-subordinate caciques to advance to more central positions within the Spanish-administered chiefly hierarchy of the Timucua mission province, and it is not unlikely that this was a factor in their decision to ally themselves with the Spaniards. Another probable explanation is the fact that most of these towns were not situated along the primary Spanish transportation conduit through the Timucua province, and thus their exposure to the worst abuses of the colonial labor system (in particular burden bearing) may have been only minimal prior to the rebellion. In this regard, it is notable that without exception, the principal caciques of every documented

Table 4-1. Rebel and Spanish-allied caciques during the Timucuan rebellion

Jurisdictional capital	Satellites	Chieftain	Allegiance	Fate
San Francisco Potano		Juan Bauptista, cacique	Rebel	Garroted
	Santa Ana	cacique	Rebel	Imprisoned
	Namo	cacique	Rebel	Imprisoned
Santa F		cacique	Rebel	Imprisoned
San Martín		Lú-cas Menéndez, cacique	Rebel	Garroted
Santa Cruz de Tarihica		Benito Ruíz, cacique	Rebel	Garroted
San Juan de Guacara		Molina, *cacica*	Rebel	Imprisoned
Niahica		*cacica*	Rebel	Imprisoned
Arapaja		Pastrana, cacique	Spanish	Promoted/Relocated
	3–4 villages	caciques [?]	Spanish (?)	Relocated
San Pedro de Potohiriba		Diego, cacique	Rebel	Garroted
	Santa Catalina de Ayepacano	Diego Heva, cacique	Spanish	Promoted
	San Pablo (?)	Pedro, cacique	Rebel	Imprisoned
Santa Elena de Machava		Dionicio, cacique	Rebel	Garroted
	San Juan Ebangelista	María, *cacica*	Rebel	Imprisoned
	San Lorenzo	cacique	Rebel	Imprisoned
	Pachala (?)	cacique	Spanish	?
San Ildefonso de Chamile		Lazaro, cacique	Spanish	Promoted/Relocated
Cachipile		Francisco, cacique	Spanish	Relocated
Chuaquin		cacique	Rebel	Imprisoned
Asile		(Gaspar??), cacique	?	Annexed (?)
	San Lúcas (?)	Juan Ebangelista, cacique	Rebel	Garroted

local chiefdom located on the primary northern and southern branches Camino Real took part in the rebellion.

It was only in Ivitachuco that Cañizares became aware of the rebel stronghold near Machava, having been informed by Chamile's cacique Lazaro (through Francisco Hiriba), and several friars who had taken refuge in his town, as well as others who were not involved in the rebellion.[30] Using his two interpreters, the Timucuan Indian Diego Salvador (born in the Ibiniuti district) and Spanish soldier Juan Bauptista de la Cruz (also known as "Namo" by the Timucuans), Cañizares learned from the *mandador* Francisco Hiriba that Lazaro had remained in his town of Chamile awaiting the arrival of the Spanish infantry, fearing reprisals from the rebel caciques. Now that Cañizares had arrived, Lazaro pledged his support and asked what he should do to assist him.[31] Cañizares sent Hiriba back to Chamile with the reply that Lazaro should send word to the rebel caciques in the palisade near Machava, informing them that the Spanish soldiers did not intend to make war on them, but rather to return the province to peace and investigate the causes of the uprising. The *mandador* did not return for several days to Ivitachuco. When he finally arrived, he brought word from the cacique Lazaro, who said that he had done as much as he could, conveying the requested message, but that he had not yet received a reply from the rebels.[32] Returning to Chamile, Hiriba related that Cañizares had not received any reply either, and that brevity was important since the sergeant major needed to inform Governor Rebolledo of his progress.

In the meantime, Cañizares seems to have sent two or three messages from Ivitachuco directly to the rebel caciques in the palisade, probably hoping to establish some sort of direct communication with them. All witnesses later stated that replies were received from the rebels, but there is some confusion in this testimony as to who wrote and sent the messages, and what the reply was. One testified that the messages were written by Fray Manuel Umanes, who had been the friar at San Martín before the rebellion, but who had fled to Apalachee after the violence.[33] This seems likely, based on the fact that one of Cañizares's regular interpreters, Juan Bauptista de la Cruz, made no mention of direct contact with the rebels from Ivitachuco.[34] All witnesses indicated that the messages were also dispatched with Indians, but it is evident that the response Cañizares received was either negative or equivocal. At least some of the replies indicated that the rebels were willing to leave the palisade and return to their villages in peace, but this was later concluded to have been a ploy designed to permit the rebels to summon further assistance for their cause.[35] Indeed, the rebels apparently used this time to spread rumors among the Spanish-allied Indians of Timucua, much in the same manner as had been done earlier in the summer with the Indians of Apalachee. Ultimately, Cañizares was forced to come to the palisade in person.

Negotiations at Machava

Seeing that he could accomplish no more from Ivitachuco, Cañizares ordered the army to prepare to march for the Timucua palisade (fig. 4.1). Before leaving Ivitachuco, the *mandador* Francisco Hiriba arrived, saying that he carried no message from his cacique, Lazaro, but had returned of his own volition in order to be with the Spaniards.[36] The army departed Ivitachuco and marched eastward along the Camino Real, ultimately arriving in the vicinity of the town of Santa Elena de Machava. Along with Cañizares's original force of sixty Spanish infantry came the rest of the soldiers at Ivitachuco and as many as five hundred Apalachee Indian warriors.[37] The long-anticipated confrontation had arrived.

Only half a league from Machava, the army came upon the Timucua stronghold in a forest within the jurisdiction of Santa Elena's satellite village of San Juan Ebangelista. If the location of Machava was indeed northwest of present-day Moseley Hall, then the rebel fort might have been situated on the isolated hill just northeast of the modern community of Ebb (see appendix A). The rebels had constructed a palisade, or stockade, using thick, stout poles, and they had heavily fortified the interior. Within were assembled a large number of Indians, including most of the rebel Timucua caciques. Upon seeing the Spanish army, the call to arms was sounded. Cañizares divided his army in two, sending one group ahead under the command of Sgt. Maj. Don Juan Menéndez Márquez, while the other group remained under his own leadership, effectively surrounding the palisade and sealing off the entrances.[38] Remaining at the distance of a single arquebus shot in front of the wall, Cañizares dispatched Francisco Hiriba to the palisade with the same message as before, requesting that they come out to speak with him, and further threatening to assault the palisade if they refused.[39] Two caciques emerged from the palisade; in the lead was María, the subordinate *cacica* of San Juan Ebangelista, on whose territory the palisade had been built. Following her was Dionicio, the principal cacique of Santa Elena de Machava. The pair approached Cañizares and told him that the rebel caciques were prepared to comply with his requests, but that they could not leave that day. They would meet him the following day in the council house (*buxio principal*) of Machava, promising to send Indians who would bring them firewood there.[40] Cañizares agreed, and the caciques returned to the palisade.

Encouraged, Cañizares ordered his army to withdraw from the forest, marching for Machava. Having arrived at the town, the soldiers quartered themselves in expectation of the arrival of the rebel caciques the next day. Late that same night, a group of Indians from the nearby town of Pachala, unconverted but nonetheless loyal to the Spaniards, brought firewood and water for the soldiers, the rebel caciques having failed to fulfill their earlier promise. During this same visit, these Indians from Pachala evidently turned over two Indians whom they said were among the murderers, probably wishing to cement their loyalty to the soldiers.[41] The rebel caciques did not remain idle during the withdrawal of Cañizares's forces from the palisade, however, apparently sending messengers to Chamile saying that "they should not trust the Spaniards, and that they were deceiving them, and in order to verify what they said, they advised them that [the Spaniards] had imprisoned the said Indians of Pachala." The rebels furthermore requested immediate aid from Lazaro and the other caciques, reporting that "the Spaniards had made war on them and had killed many people."[42] Late that same night, an Indian messenger dispatched by Lazaro arrived in Machava to investigate these rumors, noting that many of the inhabitants of the towns of Chamile and Arapaja wished to answer this call and rush to the aid of the rebels, since they had many relatives within the palisade, but that those of Chamile wished to confirm this news before acting.

In fact, neither of the rumors was accurate, but the rebels clearly wished to shatter the alliance between the soldiers and the Indians of these northern towns, drawing the rest of the Timucua province into the uprising and augmenting their own forces. As in the case of their earlier overtures to the Apalachee province, however, the rebel strategy backfired, for the exposure of these rumors as lies only served to cement the Spanish/Indian alliance. Indeed, the more the rebel Timucuans attempted to convert others to their cause, the more well-defined their opposition became. Cañizares openly invited the messenger from Chamile to personally confirm that neither of the rumors was true, and sent him back to his cacique to report his findings and invite Lazaro to come to Machava himself.[43] The following day, Lazaro arrived in Machava, bringing with him Francisco, the cacique of Cachipile, and Pastrana, the cacique of Arapaja. Confirming that the rumors were false, Lazaro agreed to take a message personally from Cañizares to the rebel Timucua caciques in the palisade. Lazaro stated that Cañizares still awaited them and that unless they left as they agreed, the consequences would be drastic.[44] After delivering the message, Lazaro returned that same day with the reply that the rebels had agreed to leave the palisade and come to Machava. Among the soldiers and Spanish-allied Indians at Machava, however, it was suspected that this was yet another ploy designed to delude the Spaniards into permitting their Indian allies to return home, leaving the soldiers open to assault by the rebel forces in the palisade. Taking no chances, Cañizares advised caution on the part of the soldiers and instructed each of the Apalachee caciques present in Machava to greet one of the arriving Timucua caciques with an embrace. The Apalachee caciques were then to sit next to the Timucua caciques in order to be ready to apprehend them.[45] A sign was decided upon which Cañizares would signal the Apalachee *norocos* to capture the rebels.

The next day, Lazaro went to the Timucua palisade a second time, and he finally returned leading the long-awaited rebel caciques. Among their number were Diego, cacique of San Pedro de Potohiriba; Dionicio, cacique of Santa Elena de Machava; Benito Ruíz, cacique of Santa Cruz de Tarihica; Molina, *cacica* of San Juan de Guacara; Pedro, cacique of San Pablo; Juan Ebangelista, cacique of San Lucas; María, *cacica* of San Juan Ebangelista; and the caciques of San Francisco de Chuaquin, San Lorenzo, Santa Ana, Namo, and the *cacica* of Niayca.[46] Other *principales* may also have come, along with at least two Indians who served the caciques. The rebel leaders entered the council house with Lazaro and were greeted and embraced by Cañizares, who instructed them to sit on the *barbacoas* beside him. Through his two interpreters, Diego Salvador and Juan Bauptista de la Cruz, Cañizares addressed the caciques, saying, "Come here, my sons. What has this uprising been about?" Considering the fact that they had been Christians and such loyal vassals to the Spanish crown for so many years, why had they risen up and killed the Spaniards?[47] According to all but one of the witnesses present, the caciques only spoke among themselves, failing to respond to the question although Cañizares asked them a second and third time. Admonishing the caciques that if they did not respond, he would be forced to imprison them in order to investigate the matter, Cañizares gave the prearranged sign to the Apalachee Indians in the council house, and the rebels were captured and thrown in chains.[48] Loyal cacique Diego Heva was dispatched to bring the murderers from the palisade, carrying the sergeant major's message that the remaining rebels in the palisade should return to their homes, for the Spaniards intended no reprisals against them. The cacique soon returned, bringing two Indians who had been handed over by those in the palisade, whom they said were responsible for the murders of Bartolomé Pérez and one of the African slaves in La Chua.[49]

Sergeant Major Cañizares had essentially achieved his goal: the apprehension of the rebel leaders and murderers. Only the principal cacique, Lúcas Menéndez, and the caciques of San Francisco and Santa Fé remained at large, and the rebel forces had retreated from their stronghold. A later reconnaissance of the palisade by Captain Argüelles confirmed that the Timucua palisade had indeed been abandoned.[50] Whether or not the majority of the rebels had returned to their towns and villages, or had fled for the woods, is unknown. Nonetheless, Cañizares succeeded in defusing the Timucuan rebellion, and without resorting to force of arms. What could have turned into a bloody slaughter at the palisade was instead solved using skillful negotiation. The immediate threat posed by the uprising was over, leaving the Timucua province effectively pacified for the time being. The only remaining question was the disposition of the prisoners and the location of Lúcas Menéndez and the other two rebel caciques.

The success of Cañizares's expedition was due in large part to Indians loyal to the Spanish. Beyond the fact that the bulk of his military force seems to have been composed of Apalachee warriors, the allegiance and assistance of the Spanish-allied Timucuan caciques was of critical importance. Not only did these caciques exercise considerable prudence in attempting to independently verify the rumors spread by the rebels, they eventually became directly involved in the negotiations between Cañizares and the rebel caciques. Indeed, it seems unlikely that the sergeant major would have been able to arrange a face-to-face meeting with the rebel leaders without the entreaties of the cacique Lazaro and his *mandador*, Francisco Hiriba. A large portion of the credit must indeed be given to Cañizares himself for his restraint and moderation in the command of his military force and his wise decision to use all the resources at hand, namely the Spanish-allied Timucuans. The old soldier lived up to his recommendation as "a person of all satisfaction, skill, and experience" and proved a wise choice to lead the expedition to pacify Timucua.[51] In this sense, Cañizares has been given an unjustified reputation in modern historical literature (based principally on sources other than the Rebolledo *residencia*), accused of having "quelled the rebellion with undue severity" or having "put down the revolt ... with such extreme cruelty."[52] This portrait largely resulted from the subsequent statements of Franciscan friars, whose letters have long dominated the documentary record of the Timucuan rebellion. Indeed, the cruelties yet to come were actually the product of Governor Rebolledo's hand, not that of his sergeant major.

Punishment of the Timucuan Rebels

Having imprisoned the caciques of the Timucua palisade, Cañizares made preparations for the army to march to Ivitachuco with their prisoners. In the meantime, one of the two Indian prisoners brought by Diego Heva was put on trial within the council house at Machava, having openly confessed to the murder of Bartolomé Pérez.[53] Recording his confession using the two interpreters (Salvador and Cruz) and appointed notary Don Juan Joseph de Sotomayor, the Indian declared that he had indeed killed Pérez in the

Asile council house, striking him with a hatchet in the back of the head and scalping him outside. Citing the earlier incident in Apalachee in which Pérez had kicked and insulted him as one reason for the murder, the Indian stated furthermore that he had killed the soldier in order to become a *noroco* of God and the king, and that he was content with his actions. Faced with the public confession of one of the murderers, and the fact that the Indian did not regret his actions, Cañizares had him garroted in public.[54] Although punishment was swift and brutal in this case, the execution of a confessed criminal for murder must be viewed as the only legal recourse available to the sergeant major; it was carried out in accordance with the law, taking his confession in writing before the execution (even though these papers were never found during the 1660 Rebolledo *residencia*).[55] Cañizares took no action against the rebel caciques or the other murderers, deciding instead to transport them to the relative security of the Apalachee province and await further instructions from the governor.

The day following the imprisonment of the caciques and the subsequent execution, Cañizares set out for Ivitachuco with his forces, leading the imprisoned Timucuans in chains. After their arrival, the rebels were placed in the council house at Ivitachuco and guards were posted.[56] A message was dispatched by Cañizares informing Governor Rebolledo of the expedition's progress. The most significant (and disturbing) news was that Lúcas Menéndez, the principal leader of the rebellion, remained at large. Ultimately, this would spur the governor to personal action. In the meantime, Cañizares took steps to capture the cacique of San Martín. Leaving the rebels under guard, Cañizares departed Ivitachuco in search of Lúcas Menéndez, bringing with him a contingent of soldiers and some Indians from Apalachee.[57] In their company came several friars on their way to St. Augustine, who had not dared to make the journey without an escort of soldiers following the rebellion. During this journey, Cañizares additionally saw to the peaceful status of the remaining Indians across the province.[58] Failing to come across the missing cacique in the town of San Pedro, the party continued eastward. They arrived at camp (*rancheria*) in a place called Aramuqua, a settlement next to the river of San Juan de Guacara, where a number of other Indians were rumored to be.[59] Once again, Lúcas was not found, and Cañizares dispatched a party of seven soldiers under his second in command, Sgt. Maj. Don Juan Menéndez Márquez, to return to St. Augustine with the friars, bringing news to the governor.[60]

Proceeding onward to the town of San Martín, Cañizares yet again failed to apprehend its cacique. Despairing of finding Lúcas Menéndez, and running out of provisions, Cañizares decided to give up the search and return to Ivitachuco. After sending Capt. Augustín Pérez de Villa Real to St. Augustine with several more soldiers, Cañizares returned the eighteen leagues to San Pedro, where he seems to have dispatched yet another party of eleven soldiers with Adj. Francisco de Monzon, carrying a letter for the governor. Returning finally to Ivitachuco, Cañizares sent Adj. Don Antonio Menéndez Márquez with other soldiers to accompany more friars going to an upcoming Franciscan chapter in St. Augustine.[61] It was during this time that Cañizares received news of the capture of the cacique of San Martín. Francisco Hiriba had been sent by Diego Heva, the cacique of San Pedro's satellite Santa Catalina, to report that he had captured Lúcas Menéndez and was sending him to the soldiers in Ivitachuco. The cacique requested a dozen soldiers to meet the party and escort him the rest of the way to Ivitachuco. The sergeant major quickly dispatched Captain Argüelles with six soldiers, who met the imprisoned cacique of San Martín on the road between Asile and Ivitachuco. They brought him to Ivitachuco and placed him in the council house with the rest of the rebels.[62]

By this time, the date was late November of 1656. Governor Rebolledo had received several successive messages from Cañizares, and while the news of the apprehension of the rebel caciques was encouraging, the fact that the instigator of the uprising, and the principal cacique of the entire province, had yet to be captured was undoubtedly disturbing to the governor.[63] Rebolledo would have to go personally to Ivitachuco in order to wrap up loose ends. He sent word to Cañizares of his plans and immediately began preparing for his journey. Clemente Bernal, the cacique of San Juan del Puerto and principal cacique of the coastal Mocama province, was informed of the rebellion and summoned to serve as a high-ranking Timucuan interpreter for the expedition. Also accompanying Rebolledo were several officials from St. Augustine, including the royal treasurer, two notaries, several military officers, and a Franciscan definitor. Several other soldiers were also brought, including some who had recently returned from the interior with reports from Cañizares, such as Capt. Augustín Pérez.[64]

Governor Rebolledo left St. Augustine on November 27, 1656, leaving behind Capt. Juan Ruíz Maroto as the interim lieutenant governor during his absence.[65] Ultimately, he would spend well over two months in the interior, during which time he evidently supported all the members of his expedition at his own expense.[66] The group marched west along the Camino Real, and Rebolledo was fortunate enough to capture the cacique Juan Bauptista in his own town of San Francisco de Potano. He followed this success with the apprehension of the cacique of Santa Fé in his town.[67] Meanwhile, having received word of the governor's departure, Cañizares was marching east from Ivitachuco to meet his party with a group of soldiers. The groups met in Santa Fé, where Governor Rebolledo ordered a group of soldiers under the command of Capt. Alonso de Argüelles to descend upon the Potano villages of San Francisco and Santa Ana in order to capture some of the Indians involved with the murders at the nearby hacienda of La Chua.[68] Although this detachment ultimately returned to St. Augustine without having achieved its goal, Cañizares and Rebolledo proceeded west to Apalachee, adding the caciques of San Francisco and Santa Fé to the group of prisoners in the Ivitachuco council house.

During the month of December, Governor Rebolledo put the rebel caciques of Timucua on trial in the council house at Ivitachuco. The original record of these proceedings, entitled "Criminal case against the *caciques* and remaining rebels [*tumultuarios*] of the provinces of Timucua and Ustaca," has not yet been located, even though a copy was definitely sent to Spain in 1657 with the completed *residencia* of Rebolledo's predecessor, Gov. Benito Ruíz de Salazar Vallecilla, and was still there as late as May 7, 1660.[69] Although details are scarce based on secondhand testimony, Rebolledo undoubtedly held a formal criminal trial, presumably employing Clemente Bernal, Diego Salvador, and Juan Bauptista de la Cruz as interpreters to take the confessions of the caciques and murderers, with Juan Moreno y Segovia as the notary. The only direct testimony relative to the course of this trial was provided by the Mocama cacique Clemente Bernal, who summarized the confession of the rebels.[70] According to Bernal, the rebels confessed that Lúcas Menéndez, the cacique of San Martín, had intercepted a letter from Governor Rebolledo. Based on its contents, he had convened a meeting of the caciques of Timucua in San Pedro de Potohiriba. In this meeting, Lúcas argued that Rebolledo was summoning them not because there were rumors of enemies, but rather in order to make them slaves. The text of these confessions were recorded by the notary, and Rebolledo, as judge, subsequently pronounced sentence.

In all, at least fifteen rebel caciques were put on trial and perhaps six of the murderers. After considering all the testimony, Governor Rebolledo sentenced six caciques to death by garrote, along with four of the murderers. In a later letter to the Spanish crown, Rebolledo reported that the caciques had been condemned as a result of "being the principal [Indians] who occasioned the rebellion, and for the forceful endeavors which they made so that the remaining provinces would follow their uprising."[71] Their corpses were apparently strung up at strategic points across the Timucua province, presumably as an example to the rest of the Indians (fig. 4.1).[72] All the major locations where some action occurred during the Timucuan rebellion were represented, including San Pedro, Asile, La Chua, and the palisade at Machava. The three principal architects of the rebellion—Lúcas Menéndez, cacique of San Martín; Diego, cacique of San Pedro; and Benito

Ruíz, cacique of Santa Cruz de Tarihica—were all hung in the town of San Pedro de Potohiriba, where the rebellion began. Dionicio, cacique of Santa Elena, was hung on the road leading to his town of Machava. Juan Ebangelista, cacique of San Lucas, was hung in the town of Asile, along with two of the murderers. Finally, Juan Bauptista, cacique of San Francisco de Potano, was hung on the road to his town of San Francisco, along with the remaining two murderers. The charges for Governor Rebolledo's subsequent *residencia* reveal the names of two of these executed murderers as Antonio García Martín Xinija (perhaps the son of Chamile's Lazaro) and Juan Bauptista Xiriva.[73]

The specific fate of the remaining rebel caciques and murderers is unspecified, but it seems likely that all were among those sentenced to varying terms of imprisonment at forced labor in St. Augustine.[74] This supposition is supported by the fact that none of the named rebel caciques were in power the following February during Rebolledo's visitation. Two of the Timucuan murderers, Juan Alejo and Francisco Pasqua, were still serving in the *castillo* at St. Augustine in 1660 during the Rebolledo *residencia*, and it seems likely that the remaining nine rebel caciques suffered similar fates. A later recounting of the forced labor pool in St. Augustine during the 1650s revealed that between 1655 and 1657, the number of Indians at forced labor jumped from only three to eighteen. Ten alone were added in 1657, "the year of the punishment of the Timucuan Indians."[75]

During the trial in Ivitachuco, Governor Rebolledo also seems to have formally convicted the Spanish-allied Timucuan caciques, subsequently granting them pardons due to mitigating circumstances (presumably their assistance in rounding up the rebels). Regarding Chamile's cacique Lazaro, Rebolledo noted the following year that "having found the said *cacique* guilty, and an accomplice with the rest, as is on record from the summary [of the case], on account of some requests and decisions, I was moved to pardon him of the crime which he was accused of."[76] This leader and the other Spanish-allied caciques were subsequently "promoted" to principal political offices within the Timucua mission province, agreeing to relocate their towns to the depopulated missions of the Camino Real. Whether or not Lazaro and the others were actually demonstrated during the trial to have been early accomplices in the planning for the rebellion, Governor Rebolledo probably used the formal convictions and pardons as leverage in forcing these northern caciques to comply with his plans for the restructure of the Timucua province.

With the execution or imprisonment of all the most important caciques in the Timucua mission province, the Timucuan rebellion was finished. As an aboriginal society within the Spanish colonial system, Timucua was politically decapitated, leaving in power only those caciques who had seen fit to ally themselves with the Spaniards. In many ways, however, this event initiated what would become the final phase in the assimilation of the remaining interior Timucuan chiefdoms into the developing colonial system of Spanish Florida. Governor Rebolledo did not leave the province in a state of disarray. The subsequent political and geographical restructuring of the Timucua province swept away many of the last vestiges of its previously aboriginal character and created a more or less fully integrated and functional component of the Spanish colonial society in Florida.

CHAPTER 5

The Transformation of Timucua

The Visitation of Apalachee

With the execution and imprisonment of the rebel caciques, the Timucua mission province was politically decapitated. All major leaders, including the regional caciques of San Martín and San Pedro, as well as the important cacique of Santa Cruz de Tarihica and virtually every other local chieftain throughout the southern Yustaga and Timucua regions, had either been killed or removed from power, effectively leaving the province in a state of anarchy. For this very reason, Governor Rebolledo could not leave the interior without attempting to repair what he had undone. Not surprisingly, Rebolledo's first action was to conduct a systematic visitation of the Apalachee province, presumably in an effort to ensure the stability of that all-important province following the Timucuan rebellion. During this visitation, which lasted from January 16 until February 8, the governor took steps both to ingratiate himself with the Apalachee caciques and simultaneously establish a considerably larger resident military presence within the province. Both of these actions were taken at the expense of the friars in Apalachee, for Rebolledo seems to have actively undermined the Franciscans during his visitation, soliciting or coercing complaints and negative testimony against them from the Apalachee caciques at each mission in an effort to provide further justification for a garrison in Apalachee.[1]

During the course of the governor's visitation, Sgt. Maj. Adrián de Cañizares y Osorio was named the new provincial lieutenant in Apalachee. He was given charge of an expanded garrison of twelve soldiers to be stationed in the Apalachee mission town of San Luís, variously referred to at this time as San Luís de Xinayca, Nixaxica, or Niayca.[2] Though not the political capital of the Apalachee chiefdom, the site of mission San Luís was chosen because it was "the closest to the sea," and because the "fort and settlement" were said to have been specifically requested during the visitation by "the *cacique* and the rest of the *principales* of this town."[3] Furthermore, at the start of the Apalachee visitation, Governor Rebolledo issued a new code of regulations to be posted in the council house of each Indian town throughout Apalachee and subsequently Timucua. This code nominally addressed a variety of contentious issues such as burden bearing, provisions for passing soldiers, free trade and price controls, native dances and games, and the punishment of native leaders, but the wording of these provisions is clearly a thinly veiled attempt by Rebolledo to exert stronger gubernatorial control over the mission provinces.[4] Without explicit written orders from the governor, for example, the friars were effectively prohibited from a variety of activities, including using Indians as burden bearers, conducting independent trading activities or restricting trade with soldiers, altering standing prices for goods, prohibiting "decent" native dances and games, and punishing any Indian cacique or *principal*. Based on the subsequent visitation record, these rules were apparently designed to accommodate the individual grievances of the Apalachee chiefs, inasmuch as their complaints largely mirror the regulatory code issued prior to the official visitation. Importantly, however, none of the regulatory code's six points addressed the root causes of the Timucuan rebellion, such as the treatment of Indian chiefs and nobles in the Indian militia or the inflexible demands of the *repartimiento* labor draft. In this sense, Rebolledo's orders appear to have primarily served the dual purpose of both rewarding the Apalachee leaders for their support during the Timucuan rebellion and ensuring their acquiescence to the new garrison post in San Luís. Only during his subsequent one-stop visitation of the Timucua province did the governor turn his attention to the consequences of the rebellion and its aftermath.

The Political Transformation of Timucua

By the time of Governor Rebolledo's mid-February visitation of the Timucuan leadership in mission San Pedro, many of the decisions regarding the political and geographic restructure of the Timucua mission province had already been made. Later evidence suggests, in fact, that the governor's master plan was actually set in motion during the criminal trial of the rebel caciques. Granting pardons to the Spanish-allied Timucuan caciques after having previously convicted them as accomplices, Rebolledo was able to force these leaders to relocate far south and east from their homeland, effectively repopulating the largely devastated mission towns of the eastern Camino Real (and not accidentally making them more accessible to the Spanish military). Furthermore, once-subordinate local chiefs and even village headmen were "promoted" to fill the positions left vacant by the most powerful regional caciques, establishing a new political order across the western interior.[5]

The general visitation held by Governor Rebolledo on February 13,

1657, in the council house of San Pedro seems to have been the first formal regional council convened after the formal political realignment of the province. The final list of caciques attending the meeting represented a radical change from the leadership of Timucua at the dawn of the rebellion less than a year previously. The caciques of Timucua were called to the *junta* by Capt. Matheo Luís de Florencia, dispatched by the governor from Apalachee with orders to convene the Timucuan leaders for the upcoming visitation.[6] As related in Florencia's later service record, Rebolledo sent him "to the most remote villages of [the province of Timucua] to convene its *caciques* so that they should go to negotiate different matters convenient to royal service and to peace, by having done justice to the *caciques*, their relatives, who were the prime movers [*motores*] of the uprising." Asserting that he was pressed for time and needed to return to St. Augustine following his visitation of Apalachee, Rebolledo decided not to attempt a personal visitation of each Timucuan mission, on account of "the villages of this said province of Timucua being separated from one another and on crosswise roads [*caminos trabexsales*], and not on the Camino Real, and having to go to all of them would be a delay in time." When the council was convened on the thirteenth, a list of caciques and *principales* attending the meeting was prepared, revealing the new political structure of the Timucua province.

Fortunately, the short visitation record was structured so that it is easy to associate subordinate caciques with their appropriate local political jurisdictions, at least as originally envisioned by Governor Rebolledo. In listing the twenty-seven Timucuan caciques who eventually attended, Rebolledo's notary Juan Moreno y Segovia typically placed higher ranking principal caciques first, followed by lower ranking caciques within their jurisdiction, noting other unnamed subordinate *principales* within each jurisdiction last. In the case of one of the new combined aboriginal jurisdictions, for example, the notary listed "Alonso Pastrana, principal *cacique* of the village of Arapaja and Santa Fé; Domingo *cacique* of San Francisco Potano; Francisco Alonso, *cacique* of San Pablo; Juan Bauptista, *cacique* of San Juan of the said jurisdiction of Arapaja, and others of its *principales*."[7] Ultimately, the new Timucua mission province was divided into seven major local jurisdictions, corresponding in most cases to preexisting local chiefdoms to which had been aggregated other towns and local chiefdoms from the northern Yustaga region off the primary Camino Real. The absence of a leader from mission San Juan de Guacara during the 1657 visitation almost certainly reflected its severely depopulated condition at that time (and the presumed imprisonment of its rebel *cacica*, Molina), but the fact that San Juan was later reestablished and survived until 1691 suggests that it should probably be considered an eighth local Timucuan

Table 5-1. Timucuan leaders attending the Rebolledo visitation in San Pedro, February 13, 1657 (with the visitation of Asile, February 8)

Jurisdictional capital	Satellites	Chieftain in attendance
San Pedro		Diego Heva, principal cacique
	Santa Ana	Maria Meléndez, *cacica*
Chamile/San Martín		Lazaro, principal cacique
	Cachipile	Francisco, cacique
	Chuaquin	Lorenzo, cacique
Arapaja/Santa Fé		Alonso Pastrana, principal cacique
	San Francisco Potano	Domingo, cacique
	San Pablo	Francisco Alonso, cacique
	San Juan	Juan Bauptista, cacique
Santa Elena de Machava		Pedro Meléndez, principal cacique
	San Joseph	Sebastián, cacique
	San Lorenzo	Dionicio, cacique
San Matheo		Sebastián, principal cacique
	San Francisco	Francisco, cacique
	San Miguel	Francisco Alonso, cacique
	Santa Lucia	Francisco, cacique
	San Diego	Francisco, cacique
	Santa Fé	Antonio, cacique
	San Pablo	Bernabé, cacique
	San Francisco	Francisco, cacique
	San Lúcas	Lúcas, cacique
	San Matheo	Santiago, cacique
	San Agustín	Domingo, cacique
Niahica		Lucia, principal *cacica*
Tari		Martín, governor
	San Pedro de Aqualiro	Martín, cacique
	Santa Maria	Alexo, cacique
Asile (Apalachee jurisdiction)		Gaspar, principal cacique
	?	Lúcas, cacique

Source: Rebolledo (1657a).

jurisdiction.[8] Regardless, as can be seen by comparing table 5.1 in volume 1 and table 5.1 in this volume, major changes had been instituted following the rebellion, revealing the fundamental elements of Rebolledo's plan for the political restructure of Timucua.

The most obvious difference was the replacement of executed or imprisoned caciques with new leaders. All of the rebel caciques for whom names are known were replaced by different caciques following the rebellion. It is quite probable that this was the case for each town involved in the uprising. Many of the names of these new caciques, such as those of Niahica, San Lorenzo, San Lúcas, Santa Elena de Machava, San Francisco Potano, and probably Santa Cruz de Tarihica, do not appear in the records of the rebellion, but most were probably the hereditary heirs of executed or imprisoned rebel caciques (or at least those who had not played important roles in the rebellion). This conclusion is supported by the fact that the new leaders gathered by Captain Florencia were later said to have been relatives of the rebel caciques. It is also supported by the fact that Machava's new cacique, Pedro Meléndez, was later indicated during the 1670 Horruytiner visitation to have been the hereditary heir of a cacique (presumably Dionicio) whose matrilineage had usurped the Machava chiefdom in 1633.[9] In several other cases, however, Governor Rebolledo seems to have emplaced completely new aboriginal leaders who, although they were from noble matrilineages in their own communities, were not the designated heirs of the executed caciques.

Diego Heva, formerly the subordinate cacique, or headman, of San Pedro's satellite village of Santa Catalina de Ayepacano, rose to fill the position vacated by his former superior, Diego, the principal cacique of Potohiriba who had been garroted for his principal role in the uprising. Diego Heva was in fact one of the first Timucua caciques to stand on the side of the Spaniards during the rebellion. He provided considerable assistance during the Cañizares expedition, personally turning over not only two of the murderers from the palisade, but also apprehending the paramount cacique of the entire Timucua province, Lúcas Menéndez, who was the last to evade Spanish capture. The fact that Diego Heva committed this final act of betrayal against his superior in the aboriginal sociopolitical hierarchy seems ultimately to have served him well within the Spanish colonial system, for by the time of the Rebolledo visitation, he had advanced to the central position at San Pedro as the regional center for Yustaga. Whether or not such an increase in political status and power was originally intended, Diego Heva was ultimately rewarded for his allegiance.

Lazaro, the other principal Spanish ally during the Cañizares expedition and the principal cacique of the local Yustagan chiefdom of Chamile, experienced a similar rise in political status, having been "promoted" by Rebolledo following his pardon during the trial.[10] Lazaro replaced the executed Lúcas Menéndez, consenting to move his entire village to the site of San Martín. In so doing, he acquired the paramount status of the former principal cacique of San Martín, a town described by Rebolledo as "the most principal of Timucua." This central rank may be confirmed by the fact that he was the only Timucuan leader to actually sign the visitation record in San Pedro, using the name "Lazaro Chamile Holatama."[11] Furthermore, the Yustagan mission towns of Cachipile and Chuaquin were simultaneously subordinated both politically and geographically within Lazaro's local jurisdiction, apparently having also agreed to relocate to the vicinity of mission San Martín along the Camino Real. That these two missions had previously been independent and autonomous with respect to Chamile is suggested by their relative distance from it (apparently some ten leagues), as well as the original establishment of distinct Franciscan *conventos* at each town. Thus, the subordination of both to Chamile's cacique Lazaro would seem to represent the aggregation of three local Yustagan chiefdoms into a single local administrative district around San Martín.

Another ally of the Spanish during the rebellion—the cacique of Arapaja—was also rewarded for his loyalty; in the 1657 visitation, Alonso Pastrana (probably the same Pastrana visited by Captain Pérez)[12] was listed as the cacique of both Arapaja and Santa Fé on the eastern Camino Real, having agreed to relocate his town far to the south of its original location in the northern reaches of the Suwannee watershed. Arapaja's cacique was furthermore given political preeminence over the previously independent mission town of San Francisco de Potano some three leagues distant. He was also given preeminence over at least two other local satellite communities that probably represented aggregated populations from the three to four villages noted to be subject to Arapaja before the rebellion. In this move, Governor Rebolledo artificially created a multicommunity political jurisdiction encompassing the entire eastern fringe of the interior Timucua province.

The substantial cluster of ten satellite communities under the principal mission town of San Matheo (later situated between Asile and Machava) remains difficult to explain with existing documentation. As yet, not a single documentary reference to a Timucuan mission called San Matheo has been discovered prior to the 1657 Rebolledo visitation. In contrast, one of the towns listed in 1657 as a subordinate member of San Matheo's local jurisdiction—San Lúcas—appears to have played a somewhat prominent role in the 1656 uprising, as its cacique Juan Ebangelista was hanged in mission San Miguel de Asile with two of the convicted Timucuan murderers.[13] Nevertheless, in recounting the Timucuan rebel leaders executed after the uprising, Timucuan interpreter Juan Bauptista de la Cruz specifically denoted the chief of San Lúcas as a *caciquillo*, in contrast to all others, strongly implying that he was a local village headman within some other chiefly jurisdiction. Unfortunately, no contemporaneous testimony identifies that jurisdiction. Several other clues, however, suggest that this jurisdiction was associated with the previously unmentioned San Matheo (somehow ignored in all the *residencia* testimony, perhaps because of subordinate status), and that both these communities may have been satellites of the nearby mission San Miguel de Asile.

During the 1660 oral testimony of Ensign Manuel Calderón, the name

San Matheo was originally written as the home of one of the hanged rebel caciques, but it was subsequently crossed out by the notary and replaced with San Lúcas, corresponding to all other contemporaneous testimony regarding the rebellion.[14] This error almost certainly represents Calderón's immediate correction of a misstatement and implies that the two *doctrinas* could be confounded. Furthermore, in his 1657 complaint regarding Governor Rebolledo's punishments, Fray Juan Gómez de Engraba erroneously included the cacique of San Matheo in his partial list of the rebel leaders (he could not remember the rest), suggesting that he, too, might have confounded San Lúcas with San Matheo.[15] Finally, the fact that the cacique of San Lúcas was executed and displayed in Asile might imply that his town was situated near Asile (like mission San Matheo later), or was even subordinate to that of Asile. Indeed, all testimony from the Rebolledo *residencia* states clearly and explicitly that Asile was the last major Timucuan town on the border with the Apalachee province, and that mission Santa Elena de Machava was the next primary town toward the east on the Camino Real, followed by the town of San Pedro.[16] This, in fact, corresponds precisely to the 1655 mission list apparently transcribed by Juan Díez de la Calle from the Franciscan visitation that year by Fray Pedro Chacón. In this list, Santa Elena was followed immediately by San Miguel de Asile, leaving out both San Lúcas and San Matheo. The simple proximity of the later mission San Matheo to Asile, consistently noted to be only two to two and a half leagues apart across the Aucilla River during the 1670s and 1680s, might provide further support for its political association with Asile (especially given the former's documentary invisibility prior to 1657).[17] Given all this evidence, it seems likely that the rebellion-era town of San Lúcas was directly subordinate to the local chiefdom of Asile, and that San Matheo (presuming it existed at the time) was also an Asile satellite.

The rise of San Matheo de Tolapatafi to local preeminence almost certainly relates to the broader context of Governor Rebolledo's 1657 political reorganization of the entire Timucua province. In this context, Rebolledo's simultaneous administrative realignment of the Asile mission within the Apalachee province undoubtedly played a role in this process. During his 1657 visitation of the Apalachee province, the governor included "the village of San Miguel de Azile" in the "jurisdiction of Apalachee" along with the other Apalachee missions. He did not include it within his visitation of the Timucua province, contrasting with virtually all previous documentation regarding that westernmost Timucuan mission town.[18] Perhaps in justification of this placement, Don Luís, the principal cacique of Ivitachuco and of all Apalachee, indicated during the visitation of his town that he had heard rumors about the conduct of Asile's friar "on account of the nearness [*cercania*] that [Ivitachuco] has to the town of Azile, and the [*cacique*] of the said village [of Asile] being the uncle of this principal *cacique* [of Ivitachuco]." Two explanations for this family relationship seem possible: either the father of Ivitachuco's chief Don Luís (about forty years old in 1658)[19] was a younger brother of the Timucuan heir to Asile's previous cacique, Manuel (making Asile's 1657 cacique, Gaspar, a paternal uncle from a distinct Timucuan matrilineage), or Governor Rebolledo had forcibly emplaced an Apalachee uncle of Ivitachuco's chief Don Luís as the cacique of Asile following the rebellion (presumably replacing the ruling Timucuan cacique or his heir). The former possibility seems more likely, since Don Luís used the fact that Asile's cacique was his uncle to demonstrate that he had direct access to information about Asile's resident friar during the 1655 landing of an English ship in Apalachee and the dispatch of a troop of soldiers under Gregorio Bravo to eject them, implying that his uncle Gaspar had been Asile's cacique prior to the 1656 rebellion.[20] Regardless, following the uprising, Rebolledo appears to have intentionally transferred the Timucuan town of Asile from Yustagan to Apalachee political jurisdiction. While this may have been simply in recognition of the proximity of Asile to Ivitachuco during that period (Governor Ruíz's hacienda was located only half a league from each town), Rebolledo may well have intended the move as a sort of annexation, expanding the territory of Apalachee's principal chief, Don Luís, all the way to the west bank of the Aucilla River as a reward for his support during the Timucuan rebellion.

In this context, although the principal town (San Miguel) of the local Timucuan chiefdom of Asile was thus apparently annexed within the Apalachee province after of Rebolledo's 1657 visitation, its (presumed) subordinate satellite town of Tolapatafi, located nearby on the eastern side of the Aucilla River, seems to have been upgraded at the same time to the status of a full-fledged mission *convento* named San Matheo, while another previously subordinate Asile satellite—San Lúcas—was placed within its local jurisdiction. Whether the previously unmentioned San Matheo was given preeminence over San Lúcas because of the participation of San Lúcas's cacique in the rebellion (and his execution in San Miguel de Asile), or perhaps because of San Matheo's more direct location on the subsequent route of the Camino Real (see appendix A), may never be known. Nevertheless, the appearance of some nine additional satellite towns within San Matheo's new local jurisdiction might suggest a substantial influx of new population after 1656, especially given Asile's low population levels in 1651.[21] Some of these towns, for example, may have been relocated from other areas of the Timucua province (perhaps even including Timucuan fugitives or refugees ordered out of Apalachee by Governor Rebolledo),[22] aggregating to the cluster of small communities apparently surrounding San Matheo. The later appearance of caciques from some four distinct communities bearing the name Arapaja during the regional Yustagan council of 1670 might indeed imply that populations from that northernmost chiefdom did in fact relocate to the vicinity of San Mateo and did not all settle around Santa Fé.[23] Furthermore, the 1681 inclusion of the Timucuan town of Pachala among the missions whose inhabitants had aggregated to the missions of the Camino Real might account for at least some of the population surrounding San Mateo. Virtually nothing is known about Pachala (pagans were said to have inhabited it in 1656), but the fact that during the rebellion it was located "very near [*cerquita*]" to San Mateo's neighbor Machava might support this interpretation.[24]

In sum, by the time of the February 1657 visitations in Asile and San Pedro, Governor Diego de Rebolledo had effectively accomplished a substantial transformation of the internal political structure of the Timucua mission province. Previously secondary caciques who allied themselves to the Spanish during the closing weeks of the rebellion were placed in the two primary seats of regional political power—San Martín de Ayacuto and San Pedro de Potohiriba—and in other strategic locations across Timucua (such as Santa Fé de Teleco). They either replaced or were subordinate to existing chiefly matrilineages on a local level. The border chiefdom of Asile was split in two along the Aucilla River, resulting in the administrative subordination of mission San Miguel de Asile within the Apalachee province and the appearance of the newly autonomous mission San Mateo de Tolapatafi on the eastern side of the provincial divide. All other rebel Timucuan caciques had apparently been replaced with their appropriate heirs. Over the course of a single winter, virtually the entire primary aboriginal leadership of the Timucua mission province had been replaced and reshuffled. The end result was a curious mix of native Timucuan and imposed Spanish administrative structures.

If there was initial resistance to the governor's political transformation, the documentary record is silent in that regard. The only record of any open complaints regarding chiefly successions administered by Governor Rebolledo was that of Dionicio, the new cacique of Machava's satellite San Lorenzo. Dionicio refused to obey Santa Elena de Machava's new principal cacique, Pedro Meléndez, on the grounds that he outranked him.[25] Presuming that Meléndez was the legitimate heir to Machava's rebel cacique, Dionicio, the complaint by San Lorenzo's cacique may have had more to do with the 1633 usurpation of Machava's original chiefly matrilineage than with any of Rebolledo's machinations. The governor addressed that question by ordering the village of San Lorenzo to be relocated closer to Santa Elena, although it would be thirteen years before the broader question of rival chiefly matrilineages would be settled definitively.

The Geographic Transformation of Timucua

If the political changes instituted by Governor Rebolledo resulted in significant alterations to the existing aboriginal sociopolitical structure among these regional Timucuan chiefdoms, the concurrent geographic transformations represented a complete overhaul of the social geography of interior Spanish Florida. On a broad scale, Rebolledo's resettlement policy may be summed up in a single statement: the reorganization of a geographically dispersed and demographically imbalanced aboriginal society into a more or less linear series of populated way stations along the Camino Real between St. Augustine and Apalachee. Initiated as a direct result of the Timucuan rebellion, the fundamental features of Rebolledo's plan seem to have largely persisted throughout the final decades of the seventeenth century. A detailed examination of the first years following the rebellion reveals the massive scope of this geographic transformation and provides the benchmark for any subsequent examination of the Timucua mission province.

Governor Diego de Rebolledo's geographic overhaul of the Timucua province centered on two primary directives: the abandonment and relocation of all mission towns off the primary southern corridor of the Camino Real and the carefully planned establishment, reestablishment, repopulation or relocation of mission towns to strategically positioned locations along that route (fig. 5.1). Not only were previous Timucuan political relationships rearranged, but the physical locations of local chiefdoms and the communities within them were also subjected to parallel changes. Whole towns and villages were uprooted from their traditional territories and relocated in some cases dozens of Spanish leagues from their homes. With respect to the primary east-west corridor of colonial traffic, these moves included a number of lateral (north-south) relocations designed not only to eliminate the need for side trails and spurs off the main Camino Real but also to augment faltering populations in the largely decimated missions in the eastern Timucua province. Other relocations represented simple east-west adjustments along the Camino Real, presumably designed to more evenly distribute the mission towns along particularly desolate stretches of road.

Central to Rebolledo's plan was the apparent designation of the southern branch of the original Camino Real as the primary route of colonial traffic across interior Spanish Florida. This route, running west from mission San Martín to intersect mission San Juan before crossing the Suwannee River along its largely uninhabited southwestern curve, effectively replaced the more northerly route originally followed by Hernando de Soto's army in 1539 between the later locations of missions San Martín and San Pedro.[26]

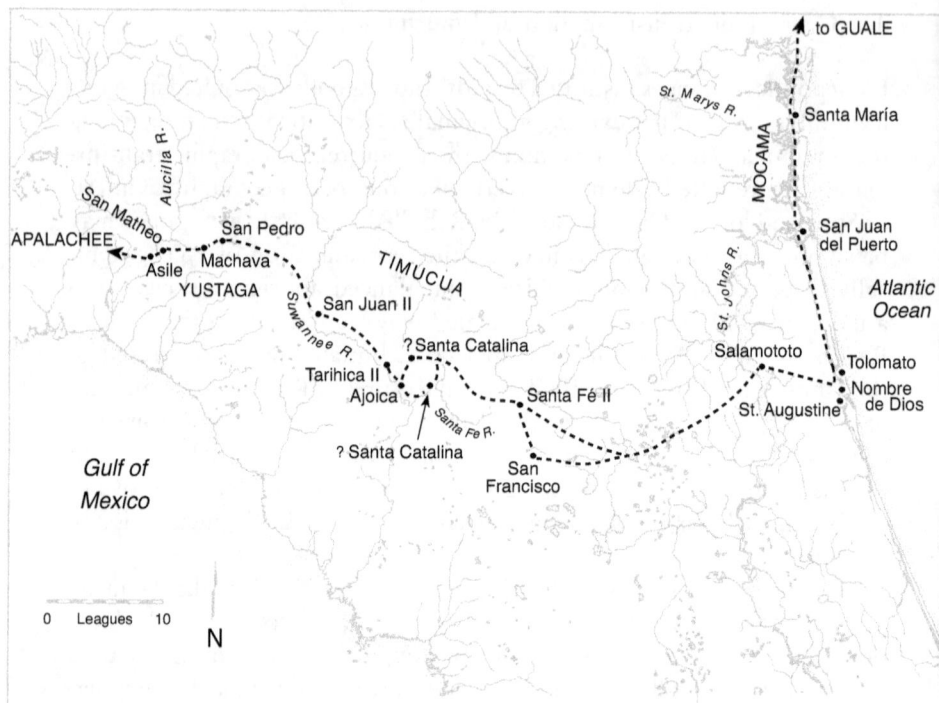

Figure 5-1. The geographic transformation of Timucua after 1657. Alternative locations for Santa Catalina shown.

Concurrent to the abandonment of this northern branch of the old Camino Real, all mission communities along its primary route (for example, Tarihica and Urihica/Niahica) were simultaneously relocated southward in an effort to consolidate aboriginal populations along the southern corridor. Representing a fundamental transformation of transportation patterns in the Florida interior, Rebolledo's newly consolidated Camino Real ultimately became one of his most successful and lasting contributions to Spanish Florida, since this same route eventually formed the basis for the famous Bellamy Road of the nineteenth century (portions of which remain today).

The most dramatic example of Rebolledo's overall resettlement policy was the relocation of all the most distant mission towns in northern Yustaga to sites along the new primary Camino Real. The governor's observation that Timucua's missions were "separated from one another and on crosswise roads [caminos trabexsales], and not on the Camino Real" was used in 1657 to justify the convocation of only a single visitation meeting in the centrally placed mission San Pedro. Brief testimony during the course of that visitation reveal elements of Rebolledo's initial plan to remedy the situation. Decisions seem to have been made immediately after the pacification of the province and perhaps during or immediately following the trial and execution of the rebel leaders, for by the time of the February 13 visitation, Chamile's cacique Lazaro indicated that he was "leaving his lands to go settle those of San Martín on the Camino Real from the presidio of St. Augustine."[27] The allied cacique's promotion had a price: the complete relocation of his town to the site of the executed Lúcas Menéndez's town at San Martín. Importantly, during the visitation Lazaro requested that Governor Rebolledo ensure that "no Indian from the rest of the villages should dare to cut down [*talar*] the woods that he is leaving, killing the game and gathering the fruits that he reserves for his sustenance and that of his vassals." Seconded in his request by Alonso Pastrana, the newly promoted cacique of Arapaja and Santa Fé (also relocating his town), the governor acquiesced, issuing a general order with respect to "all the lands of the remaining *caciques*." Though he could force the relocation of entire towns and their inhabitants, Rebolledo was evidently not willing to challenge the ownership of traditional lands.

In fact, based on the political realignments revealed during the 1657 visitation, the caciques of all the northernmost Yustagan towns, including Chamile, Cachipile, Chuaquine, and Arapaja, had already been induced to relocate to sites along the eastern Camino Real. Later evidence reveals, however, that this was only part of the governor's overarching plan. In October of that same year, a number of witnesses presented testimony regarding these resettlements as part of Rebolledo's effort to protect himself from a wide range of accusations by the Franciscans.[28] All the statements reveal that the primary intent of the governor's relocation policy was to repopulate the Camino Real. Rebolledo's notary, Juan Moreno y Segovia, stated that the governor "commanded [the Indians] to repopulate [*reparar de gente*] some villages which were dismantled, settling them on the Camino Real which goes to the said provinces, for the good government of this said city and of its natives, all with the willingness and liking of the *caciques*."[29] Capt. Augustín Pérez de Villa Real elaborated that Rebolledo "placed [the Timucua province] in good form and government, populating some villages on the Camino Real, with the agreement and consent of the *caciques*, for what might happen in the service of His Majesty . . . for the journeys . . . and so that there is commerce and easy dispatch in this presidio."[30] Other witnesses summarized, reporting that Governor Rebolledo "left the Camino Real populated."[31] The general agreement among all the witnesses was that the purpose of Rebolledo's policy of resettlement was to ensure that the Camino Real was populated with Indians.

Using a combination of contemporary testimony and subsequent evidence regarding mission locations, it is possible to re-create most or all of the range of town relocations evidently carried out during Governor Rebolledo's term (fig. 5.1). As noted above, all of the northern Yustagan missions originally located along spur trails off the primary northern branch of the old Camino Real were forcibly resettled under the Rebolledo administration, either repopulating or aggregating to surviving populations in mission towns along the eastern reaches of the Camino Real, many of which had apparently been largely abandoned following the rebellion. These long-distance moves were actually connected with the governor's political facelift of Timucua and involved the "promotion" of Chamile's cacique Lazaro to the ranking chiefly position as the new cacique of San Martín and of Arapaja's cacique Alonso Pastrana to the important position of cacique of Santa Fé. The towns of Cachipile and Chuaquin were similarly relocated southeastward, subsequently occupying a subordinate position within Lazaro's local jurisdiction around mission San Martín.

In addition to these aggregations or repopulations of existing town sites, a number of towns in the eastern reaches of Timucua were also physically relocated at this time. Beginning on the eastern terminus of the Camino Real, as a part of his overall restructure of the interior, Governor Rebolledo appears to have supervised the establishment of a new mission town in a place called Salamototo on the eastern bank of the St. Johns River. This town was probably populated at least in part using the remaining residents of mission San Diego de Helaca, inasmuch as the new mission was given the name San Diego de Salamototo precisely at the same moment that Helaca effectively vanished from the documentary record. Continuity is further demonstrated by the use of the original conventual name of San Diego de [He]laca in association with Salamototo in a list constructed by Bishop Diego Ebelino de Compostela in 1689.[32] Moreover, just like Helaca during the decades before the 1656 rebellion, Salamototo was later explicitly identified in Spanish documents to have been occupied by interior Timucuan populations aggregated from all the abandoned mission towns on the upper St. Johns watershed.[33] Interestingly, most or all of these remaining mission *conventos*, which included Santa Lucia and San Luís in the Acuera region, San Antonio de Enacape, and even the non-Timucuan San Salvador de Mayaca, seem to have been abandoned by the Franciscans shortly after the 1656 rebellion. This is not to say that the towns or regions themselves were entirely depopulated at this time, however, for the Acuera district is well documented to have supported unconverted and fugitive Timucuan populations for many decades to follow. Nevertheless, certainly by the mid-1670s, and most likely earlier, all four of these southern mission stations were abandoned by their resident missionaries, perhaps in an overall effort to consolidate remaining Christian populations at the newly established *convento* at San Diego de Salamototo.

The as yet undiscovered site of the Salamototo town was probably located somewhere at or near the mouth of Kendall Creek (west of present-day Orangedale), which as late as the latter half of the eighteenth century was still called "Salamototo" creek by Spanish authorities and was located within the "royal lands of the town of Salamototo" on a land-grant map of that period (see appendix A).[34] This location was some two or three leagues north of the abandoned site of Helaca, which was either at or just north of the site of present-day Picolata "directly opposite to" the known location of Pupo within Salamototo's local jurisdiction.[35] As a consequence, Governor Rebolledo gave orders "to open the new road that was made in order to go to the village of Salamototo, which is the village through which one passes in order to go to the provinces of Timucua and Apalachee."[36] Despite the slightly increased travel distance between the city of St. Augustine and this western St. Johns River crossing (from seven to ten leagues),[37] Salamototo remained unchanged here as the primary ferry town until the English-sponsored raids of the early eighteenth century.

A second mission apparently relocated by Rebolledo was that of the easternmost Timucuan mission of Santa Fé de Teleco, which was shifted approximately one and a half leagues to the southeast following the rebellion.[38] This move apparently coincided with the 1657 resettlement of Santa Fé by the cacique and inhabitants of Arapaja and the simultaneous political subordination of mission San Francisco de Potano within Santa Fé's local jurisdiction. Archaeological evidence confirms the abandonment of the original site of Santa Fé during this period.[39] Many subsequent documentary references to this mission use the name "Santo Thomás de Santa Fé," including a 1676 Franciscan chapter list and the 1689 mission list by Bishop Diego Ebelino de Compostela,[40] suggesting a sort of rededication of the convent upon its move to a new site. A similar dual name was originally given to the relocated Mocama mission of San Buenaventura de Guadalquini after its 1685 relocation, but the name "Santa Cruz de San Buenaventura de Guadalquini" was eventually dropped in favor of Santa Cruz in that instance.[41] In the case of Santa Fé, however, its original Christian name persisted in common usage.

As a result of its post-1656 relocation, mission Santa Fé II was not only closer to its newly subordinate southern neighbor, San Francisco (moving from about five leagues to roughly three or four leagues),[42] but it was also virtually on a north-south line with San Francisco, making it just as close to St. Augustine as San Francisco. Probably in direct response to this fact, the old course of the primary eastern Camino Real in this area seems to have shifted north, leaving San Francisco on a southern spur of the primary road leading directly between the relocated Santa Fé mission and Salamototo. Prior to the rebellion, westbound travelers seem to have frequently passed through San Francisco on their way to Santa Fé (or vice versa), making mission San Francisco de Potano the easternmost town in the Timucua mission province along the Camino Real.[43] Indeed, both San Francisco and Santa Fé were described as "the passage for the remaining provinces" in 1654, when Ensign Pedro de Florencia was dispatched on a military expedition to recover fugitives in an effort to avoid the depopulation of these towns.[44] Nevertheless, after the rebellion era and throughout the late seventeenth and early eighteenth centuries, the site of mission San Francisco was clearly located off the primary course of the eastern Camino Real, which ran directly between Santa Fé and Salamototo (excepting visitations or lists that incorporated all missions).[45] The branch trails leading to San Francisco seem to have forked south from the primary Camino Real at Santa Fé and at the southernmost bend of the road's course around the headwaters of the Santa Fe River (fig. 5.1).

Presuming that Governor Rebolledo's overarching plan was to consolidate all missions along the primary route of the Camino Real, why then did he leave mission San Francisco in its original location, despite the fact that the relocation of Santa Fé shifted the Camino Real's route to the north, relegating San Francisco to a southern branch trail off the new primary road? The reason for this decision was almost certainly based on the location of San Francisco so close to the only major private hacienda in the western interior at that time—the Menéndez Márquez cattle ranch at La Chua. Probably in an effort to foster the reconstruction and operation of the important hacienda (assaulted during the rebellion), mission San Francisco was evidently permitted to remain in its original location only three leagues distant from La Chua as a nearby source of labor or surplus foodstuffs (presumably bartered for trade goods).[46] Furthermore, the regular presence of Spanish soldiers and workers so near to the San Francisco mission community ultimately contributed to the mutual defense of both locations toward the end of the century.

Yet another major town relocation was that of the important mission of Santa Cruz de Tarihica, which was shifted from its inter-riverine location due north of mission San Martín and placed directly on the old southern branch of the Camino Real at a point virtually equidistant between missions San Martín and the newly relocated San Juan de Guacara (some seven to eight leagues distant from each; see appendix A). That its original location at the Indian Pond site was abandoned after 1656 is confirmed by archaeological evidence.[47] Although the relocated Santa Cruz has yet to be discovered, its situation along or adjacent to the new southern road by no later than 1674 is unquestionable based on the documentary evidence.[48] That the actual site of Santa Cruz II may not have been located precisely on the primary course of the Camino Real was flatly stated in the 1740 description of this region by Francisco de Castilla, and its absence on several Rebolledo-era lists of the principal towns along the main road might also confirm this possibility.⁴⁹ Nevertheless, its placement between San Martín and San Juan almost certainly formed part of Governor Rebolledo's post-rebellion transformation of the Timucua province. Based on distances alone, the site may have been at or near present-day Little River Springs on the north bank of the Suwannee River (see appendix A).

Mission San Agustín, originally located along the northern branch Camino Real several leagues west-northwest of Santa Cruz, was also relocated southward during this period, although the details of this relocation are somewhat difficult to sort out. Apparently known as San Agustín de Urica or Urihica in 1630 and 1655, this native name had apparently disappeared by the spring of 1656, when its seems to have been replaced by Niahica, perhaps in consequence of the appearance of a female *cacica*. Both Urihica and Niahica were apparently the only mission towns listed on the original trail between Tarihica and Arapaja in separate documents dating to 1655 and 1656, supporting the conclusion that they were in fact one and the same.⁵⁰ Still referred to as Niahica during the 1657 visitation at San Pedro (its new *cacica* was named Lucía, perhaps replacing an imprisoned older sister), this name in turn seems to have disappeared following this date and was replaced by a third native name, San Agustín de Axoyca. At this time, mission San Agustín was listed along with San Francisco, Santa Fé, San Martín, and San Juan as one of the primary missions repopulated by Timucua's new provincial lieutenant, Capt. Martín Alcayde de Cordoba, after January 1658 using populations from far northern Yustaga. The town of Ajoica was later confirmed to have been located only two to three leagues to the east of the relocated Santa Cruz until the circa 1675 aggregation of Ajoica with San Martín's successor, Santa Catalina.⁵¹ The short-lived archaeological site of the relocated Ajoica might possibly be located somewhere along the course of the Suwannee River between present-day Branford and the river's confluence with the Santa Fe River, although this conclusion is speculative and remains contingent upon the undiscovered locations of Santa Cruz II and Santa Catalina.

During this same period, mission San Juan de Guacara was similarly relocated from its original Baptizing Spring site to a location some two leagues west along the Camino Real, where the town was set up on the eastern bank of the Suwannee River at or near Charles Spring. Not only did this move shorten the unoccupied distance between San Juan and San Pedro (from eleven to nine leagues), but it also placed an occupied mission town at the crucial Suwannee River crossing along the primary Camino Real.⁵² Archaeological work at the original site confirms its abandonment following the 1656 rebellion, and while the second location has almost certainly been discovered near Charles Spring, further analysis will be necessary to confirm its late seventeenth-century date.⁵³ As noted above, the general lack of references to the original San Juan de Guacara from rebellion-period documents, and its notable absence during the 1657 Rebolledo visitation, suggests that its rebel *cacica,* Molina, ruled a substantially depopulated mission town even prior to the 1656 uprising. Nevertheless, the fact that San Juan (probably in its new location) had been reestablished as early as 1658 is indicated by Guacara's appearance in an August letter by San Pedro's friar, but the precise identity of its inhabitants remains somewhat unclear. Although San Juan II was clearly ruled and inhabited by Timucuan speakers throughout its 1657–91 existence, the remarkably detailed 1682 overview of past and present missions by then-royal officials Antonio Menéndez Márquez and Francisco de Rocha specifically stated that San Juan de Guacara was one of two villages in the Timucua province that had been "newly settled and made," in contrast to other towns to which other Timucuan villages had been aggregated.[54] Since the only other mission mentioned in this same context—Ivitanayo—is known from the 1677–78 visitation of Timucua to have been artificially formed using families from several populous Yustagan missions, this 1682 document may well indicate that San Juan II was actually a completely new community formed artificially under Governor Rebolledo's guidance. This would of course imply that the remaining inhabitants of Molina's rebellion-era San Juan had largely dispersed after 1656, and that the relocated San Juan incorporated few if any of the original Baptizing Spring town's native residents. Further documentary and archaeological studies will be needed to clarify this possibility.

As a part of his overall physical realignment of both the Camino Real and the missions along it, Governor Rebolledo also provided for improvements and routine maintenance along the Camino Real itself. As ordered in his 1657 visitation of Timucua, the governor "commanded that the bad roads be opened, and that a crossing or bridge of poles be made at the creeks or bad passages so that one can pass from some villages to others, and so that the couriers can go and come, and likewise the missionaries who serve them."[55] In later testimony relative to Rebolledo's *residencia,* witnesses confirmed that "in these roads he commanded to repair [*aderezar*] the bad crossings, and that in the rivers there should be canoes for their passage."[56] To this end, Adj. Francisco Sánchez and soldier Matheo Hernández were ordered by Rebolledo to make two or three canoes for these river crossings.[57] Other tasks were presumably carried out by soldiers and Indians along the entire length of the newly consolidated Camino Real, all in an effort to facilitate travel, transport, and communication across the interior.

Ultimately, the plan set in motion by Governor Rebolledo resulted in the rapid and effectively permanent transformation of a geographically dispersed and demographically imbalanced aboriginal landscape into a compact, linear chain of populated way stations along the Camino Real between St. Augustine and Apalachee. Principal towns and surviving satellites of some thirteen local Timucuan chiefdoms scattered across much of the Suwannee River watershed and adjacent zones were ultimately restructured and consolidated to form a line of ten more evenly spaced aggregate mission towns with outlying satellites. For the Franciscans, this consolidation and contraction of the Timucua mission province actually occurred at an opportune moment, for by the summer of 1657 only twenty-eight Franciscan friars remained alive in Florida after the death of six in a shipwreck between Apalachee and Havana.[58] In broader perspective, however, Rebolledo's reorganization of Timucua had more far-reaching implications.

Following half a century of demographic collapse within the context of the developing colonial system, and the near-complete depopulation of many missions in the comparatively sparsely populated eastern reaches of the Timucua province, mid-seventeenth-century Spanish officials were only barely able to maintain sufficient populations to support transpeninsular land traffic across these devastated zones. Despite the frequent dispatch of small military expeditions on fugitive-hunting missions, inconsistent programs of directed settlement *congregación,* occasional forced town relocation, and even *reducción,* it was only with the pacification of the Timucuan rebellion that Governor Diego de Rebolledo was provided with a unique opportunity to solve these recurrent problems in a more comprehensive and permanent fashion. Following the execution or imprisonment of virtually the entire aboriginal leadership of the Timucua province, Rebolledo was in a position to completely restructure the province in a form more suitable for the Spanish colonial system. By replacing ousted leaders with others loyal to the Spanish, and by repopulating the eastern portion of the Timucua mission province with the inhabitants of forcibly dismantled missions in the northern reaches of Yustaga, Rebolledo not only crushed aboriginal resistance by dividing and restructuring (both politically and geographically) the old sociopolitical order, but he also achieved a more comprehensive integration of Timucua into the colonial system of Spanish Florida. In this sense, Timucua was no longer a truly aboriginal society, but was finally transformed into a functional component of the colonial system as a series of populated way stations along the Camino Real that were inhabited by the surviving Indians of the Timucuan chiefdoms of Spanish Florida's western interior.

CHAPTER 6

Implementation and Resistance

Rebolledo vs. the Franciscans

Governor Diego de Rebolledo's ambitious plan for the political and geographic restructuring of the entire Timucua mission province was actually implemented under the supervision and guidance of reserve officers and soldiers stationed in the western interior after the governor's 1657 visitation. In addition to Apalachee's provincial lieutenant Sgt. Maj. Adrián de Cañizares y Osorio, who was stationed in mission San Luís with a dozen garrisoned soldiers, Rebolledo also left Capt. Martín Alcayde de Cordoba as the acting provincial lieutenant of Timucua, where he was definitely stationed at mission San Martín as early as December of 1657.[1] Whether or not Alcayde was given the title of lieutenant at that time or later,[2] his orders clearly centered on the physical implementation of the governor's resettlement program. As later recounted by Alcayde himself during testimony for Rebolledo's *residencia* (partially charred and thus only fragmentary):

> By order of the said Diego Rebolledo, this witness . . . [?] . . . and dismantle . . . [?] . . . Indians of the villages of Arapaja and its jurisdiction, which are three or four little villages of few people, and the village of San Yldefonso de Chamile, and the village of Cachipile, and [the village] of Choaquine, all of the said province of Timucua, in order that they should settle in the villages of San Francisco, Santa Fé, San Martín, San Juan de Guacara, and San Augustín de Axoyca, all of the said province of Timucua, which were depopulated, through some having died, and others having absented themselves, from which the said Indians formed a great complaint, even though it was suitable that these villages of San Francisco and the rest that they were ordered to settle should be populated, and in the service of His Majesty by being in the commerce and passage from Apalachee, and those that they were commanded to depopulate very astray [*muy extraviados*].[3]

Alcayde's testimony makes it abundantly clear that Rebolledo's resettlement policy was indeed a forced one, and that some of the relocated caciques were not willing participants in the geographic reorganization of Timucua. Indeed, almost as soon as these initial moves were carried out, resistance surfaced at the highest level of Timucua's new political structure.

The recent discovery of a gubernatorial order issued on December 21, 1657, preserved only as a result of its inclusion in the military service record of its recipient, reveals the extent of resentment felt by Timucua's newly promoted provincial cacique following the relocation of his town under the supervision of Lieutenant Alcayde. The text of Governor Rebolledo's order reveals both the roots of the disturbance and his initial corrective measures:

> through letters and news that I have had from the province of Timucua, it has come to my attention that Lasaro, *cacique* of the village of Chamile, who I promoted as [cacique] of San Martín so that with his vassals and people they might settle the said village, by being the most principal of Timucua, and by having found it dismantled of people when I passed through it last year to the punishment of the rebellion that the *caciques* of that province had, and having found the said *cacique* guilty, and an accomplice with the rest, as is on record from the summary [of the case] by some requests and decisions, with respect to which I was moved to pardon him of the crime which he was accused of, and in spite of the aforementioned he has wished to make understood in all the land the disgust with which he finds himself in the said village, not obeying or fulfilling my orders, while the rest of the *caciques* whom I promoted to other villages in the same manner have observed them, and inasmuch as some alleged and bad sounding words have occurred, calling together his vassals and others of that province so that they might prepare themselves with weapons, all indicating that they may come to new disturbances and dissentions among all the rest of the natives, and because I have made an investigation in virtue of the *auto* that I decreed for the said effect against the said *cacique* of Chamile, and there he is on record as being guilty as the cause of disturbances, and because it is suitable to emplace a remedy with all caution and to head off such depraved designs like those the said *cacique* is attempting, and to bring him to this presidio to my presence in order to proceed in the said case that I have substantiated against him, . . . [I order that] Ensign Juan Domínguez, *reformado* of this presidio . . . should leave this presidio, carrying in his company the infantry that I have commanded to be

loaned to him, with all the preparations that might be necessary, and he will go in pursuit of his journey until arriving at the village of San Martín, without revealing to any person the reason for which he goes, and having arrived, Captain Martín Alcayde being in the said village, with his intervention he will ask for the aid that might be necessary, and together they will endeavor to apprehend Lazaro, *cacique* of the said village of Chamile, and if Francisco, *cacique* of San Joseph, finds himself in the said town, they will do the same with him, and in case he is not there and is absent, he will endeavor not to move away to another village in his pursuit, and with the greatest brevity that is possible the said Ensign Juan Domínguez should return to this presidio, bringing in his company with all caution the said *cacique* Lazaro, by thus being suitable to the service of His Majesty, and to the peace of all those provinces.[4]

While the precise resolution of this case is not known with certainty, other testimony during the governor's 1660 *residencia* revealed that Chamile's Lazaro was still cacique of San Martín at that time,[5] indicating that he had not been deposed as a result of Rebolledo's 1657 order. Thus, he was presumably reinstated in 1658 after having professed renewed compliance with the governor's plan. However, Lazaro was destined for another confrontation with Spanish authorities several years later.

Lazaro's discontent was actually only one facet of a widespread pattern of increased tension across the western mission frontier, and indeed all of Florida, during 1657. Much of this tension revolved around the growing dispute between Governor Rebolledo and the Franciscans, centering on the Indians of the western mission provinces. Almost as soon as Rebolledo had returned from the interior, recently elected Franciscan provincial minister Fray Francisco de San Antonio seems to have set out on his own visitation of the Franciscan convents of Apalachee, returning on horseback in mid-May.[6] Either at that time or later, San Antonio also conducted a Franciscan visitation of Guale, reportedly returning "very disconsolate."[7] Based on Fray San Antonio's subsequent efforts to undermine Governor Rebolledo's governorship, Adj. Pedro de la Puerta was probably correct in his July 12 correspondence to Rebolledo, asserting that as a result of his on-site investigation of the matter in Apalachee, "the visitation of our provincial father does not seem to me to have been to visit the convents of the missionaries, but rather to make an inquiry of the life of the sergeant major and of the soldiers, pressing the *caciques* to testify against them."[8] Indeed, based on a substantial amount of documentation generated by both the Franciscans and Governor Rebolledo that year, mutual recriminations regarding the Timucuan rebellion and Franciscan resistance to the newly expanded Apalachee garrison quickly blossomed into a firestorm of open accusations and secret machinations played out in St. Augustine and across the western mission frontier.

In response to the combined effect of Governor Rebolledo's earlier attempts to shift the blame for the rebellion to San Pedro's former friar, Alonso Escudero (subsequently moved to Asile),[9] and his none-too-subtle attempt to exaggerate native grievances against the friars in the official record of his Apalachee visitation, along with the abrupt placement of a substantial garrison in their midst, the Franciscans mounted a concerted offense against the governor, gathering information and support for an all-out effort to have both Rebolledo and his Apalachee garrison removed.[10] While the lengthy petition eventually dispatched to Spain arrived after Rebolledo had been officially deposed and replaced on July 6, 1656 (a decision that would not actually be implemented until 1659),[11] second-hand information regarding Franciscan activities during the spring and summer of 1657 suggests that a substantial amount of effort was directed toward gathering native support against the new garrison. In a May letter to Governor Rebolledo, Apalachee's new lieutenant sarcastically accused "the blessed fathers" of "hiding their actions from Your Grace," asserting that they were "soliciting these *caciques* to say and demand that it not be consented that this [town of San Luís] be settled by Spaniards, nor any other [town] in Apalachee."[12] Although the friars were unable to convince the Apalachee caciques to openly oppose the placement of the garrison, they seem to have either encouraged or made use of existing factional divisions among both the Apalachee and Timucua chiefs in their effort to counter the new alliance between the Spanish military and Francisco Luís, the cacique of mission San Luís.

Lieutenant Cañizares reported in his letter that the Franciscan provincial had received letters from a friar and an Indian in the Timucua province. He refused to reveal their contents to the lieutenant, nonetheless hinting that the soldiers should be very careful on account of unrest among the Indians.[13] Following his own conversations with Apalachee leaders, however, Cañizares concluded that "everything has been a plot and trick of the Ustacanos [Yustagans], and it is to put this *cacique* of San Luís in a bad [light] because he does not welcome them, and so that the Spaniards should have ill will against him, because it would seem that even the *caciques* of Apalachee are jealous that he welcomes the Spaniards and is esteemed by them."[14] After a subsequent investigation ordered by the governor that summer, Adj. Pedro de la Puerta concurred that the rumors of an Apalachee uprising had been concocted by a small number of friars

(Frays Alonso del Moral and Miguel Garzón de los Cobos in Apalachee and Fray Joseph Bamba in Santa Elena de Machava), sarcastically remarking that "these saints aim to insure that Your Grace's good successes are not achieved at all."[15] Based on comments in a final letter by Lieutenant Cañizares, the friars appear to have been acting on the basis of the false assumption by "the gossipy Timucuans" that the Apalachee chiefs wished to rebel because of a request made during a junta with the Spaniards.[16] Whether or not the friars actively encouraged such Timucuan rumors in order to force a withdrawal of the garrison, they clearly used such aboriginal factionalism to their own advantage.

Even as the Franciscans gathered evidence against Rebolledo, in the spring of 1657 the governor himself embarked on a lengthy judicial review, or *residencia,* of the term of previous royal governor Benito Ruíz de Salazar Vallecilla and his interim successors.[17] Simultaneously, Rebolledo conducted an official "investigation" of his own actions between the time he received the 1655 royal *cédula* regarding the threat from an English fleet and the start of the Timucuan rebellion.[18] As correctly interpreted by the Franciscans, testimony gathered for this April investigation was in actuality an attempt by the governor to escape culpability by implicating the friars in his decision to order the members of the Indian militia to carry their own provisions.[19] In October, just a month after the Franciscans completed their barrage of accusations against Rebolledo in a petition to the Spanish crown, the governor assembled yet another group of nine witnesses to respond to many of the Franciscan charges against him.[20] Neither of these investigations were sent to Spain, but ironically both were used as evidence in Rebolledo's own posthumous *residencia* in 1660. The 1657 visitation record, however, was transcribed in September for inclusion with the *residencia* papers of Governor Ruíz.

Further Disputes

Irrespective of his ongoing battle with the Florida Franciscans, Governor Rebolledo's transformation of Timucua continued in the interior. Only two days after the December order to apprehend chief Lazaro was issued in St. Augustine, Apalachee's lieutenant Adrián de Cañizares died in mission San Luís after a long illness.[21] Only a month later, on January 23, 1658, Capt. Augustín Pérez de Villa Real was dispatched again into the interior as Cañizares's replacement "lieutenant and *justicia mayor.*" At that time, Governor Rebolledo took the opportunity to issue yet another mandate prohibiting the continued use of Indians as burden bearers, directing his order specifically to the caciques of what he referred to as "the towns of the Camino Real, which are those of Salamototo, San Francisco, Santa Fé,

San Martín, San Juan de Guacara, and San Pedro."[22] Only those Timucuan towns evidently located directly on the Camino Real itself were mentioned in this order. Left out were several others perhaps situated slightly off the main road. Nonetheless, the governor's mention of virtually all of the towns noted to have been repopulated by Lieutenant Alcayde using the former inhabitants of Arapaja, Chamile, Cachipile, and Chuaquin, as well as the new ferry town of Salamototo, indicates that Rebolledo's plan was well underway by this time and that all these towns were inhabited as of January 1658.

That same fall, less than two years after the initiation of Governor Rebolledo's transformation of the Timucua province, a dispute erupted in which both of the governor's provincial lieutenants were recalled and imprisoned during an investigation of Franciscan suggestions that they were conspiring against the governor. While both officers were eventually cleared of wrongdoing and reinstated in their posts, documentation assembled for the case provides many details regarding ongoing factional disputes in the western frontier.[23] The letter that sparked the controversy was written by native Floridian Fray Antonio de la Cruz, who had replaced Alonso Escudero as the resident missionary at San Pedro de Potohiriba. As a side note to his descriptions of an ongoing local jurisdictional dispute with San Pedro's cacique Diego Heva, the friar commented that captains Pérez and Alcayde had conspired with Sergeant Manuel Gómez to intoxicate the Timucuan Indian interpreter Diego Salvador in order to find out why he had been delayed in St. Augustine with the caciques and *repartimiento* laborers from Apalachee that summer. Cruz intimated that the officers suspected Governor Rebolledo was planning to lay the blame for the Timucuan rebellion on Lieutenant Pérez, and for this reason had delayed Diego Salvador and the Apalachee Indians in St. Augustine.

With this news, Rebolledo immediately withdrew the three officers from the interior, imprisoning them in St. Augustine "for having been involved in inquiring and investigating judicially the designs of what His Grace is carrying out in the service of His Majesty, and for the good of these provinces, interpreting them in conformity with their opinions and harmful intentions." Viewing the officers' alleged inquiries as meddling in the affairs of his government, Rebolledo not only interrogated Diego Salvador and the three officers but also commanded acting lieutenant Pedro de la Puerta to take the testimony of the Apalachee caciques themselves. In the course of this testimony, however, not only were the officers cleared of Fray Cruz's accusations, but it was also made clear that the Apalachee caciques had actually been delayed in St. Augustine that year for "the payment and satisfaction which was given to them for the corn which they gave on the account of His Majesty for the expenses of the war and pacification of Timucua at the time of its tumult."[24] Both lieutenants were subsequently reinstated and apparently served until the official end of the governor's term the following February.

This brief incident provides an instructive example of the continuing degree of internal factionalization present in the western mission provinces during the initial years following the Timucuan rebellion and the initiation of Governor Rebolledo's sweeping transformations. Cacique Diego Heva's personal quarrel with Fray Cruz's *sacristan* quickly blossomed into a jurisdictional dispute over the authority of caciques over mission church officials. This dispute subsequently reignited earlier disputes between the Franciscans and Florida military, since both provincial lieutenants sided with the cacique, whom Sergeant Gómez called "a man fit for the government of his town."[25] This, in turn, prompted San Pedro's friar to make exaggerated accusations regarding the officers, which resulted in a temporary rift between Rebolledo and his own provincial lieutenants. While the only real consequence to this episode was a formal charge against Rebolledo two years later for false imprisonment, it nonetheless illustrates the extent to which the mission Indians often served as pawns in jurisdictional spats between Spanish secular and ecclesiastical authorities.

Military Presence in the Western Provinces

Despite the brief interruption occasioned by the imprisonment of Rebolledo's provincial lieutenants, the ongoing physical transformation of Timucua evidently continued throughout the rest of Governor Rebolledo's term, which ended on February 20, 1659, with the installment of the new royally appointed governor Alonso de Aranguiz y Cotes. Little is known of the early months of Governor Aranguiz's term, but the general Franciscan chapter held late that fall seems to have provided an opportunity for the new governor to garner mutual support for new fortifications in the Apalachee province. Having received news from Apalachee's provincial lieutenant (apparently still Augustín Pérez de Villa Real) regarding the appearance of an as yet anonymous group of foreign Indian warriors bearing firearms, and rumored to be accompanied by white people (suspected at that time to be Englishmen from Jacán, or Virginia), Governor Aranguiz formally approached the Franciscans on October 21, 1659, during their chapter meeting for support in expanding the Apalachee garrison to thirty or forty men.[26] As would soon be discovered, these northern warriors were none other than the slave-raiding Chichimeco, who ultimately laid waste to the Guale mission of Santo Domingo de Talaje in the summer of 1661 and who plagued the northern interior through the early 1680s.[27]

Probably occasioned by the very real threat represented by the arrival of these gun-bearing warriors, in an almost unprecedented accord Franciscan officials joined ex-governor Rebolledo, the royal officials, and a long list of active and reserve officers in openly supporting Aranguiz's proposal. Franciscan signatories to the governor's October proposal included the newly elected provincial minister Fray Sebastián Martínez, both of his immediate predecessors (*padres de provincia*), all four provincial definitors, the president of the chapter, and four missionaries from Apalachee (including the controversial Fray Miguel Garzón de los Cobos). By early November, Governor Aranguiz y Cotes reported that he had already placed "up to 30 men" in the garrison in Apalachee.[28]

If there was resistance to Governor Aranguiz's proposal to expand the Apalachee garrison, it does not appear in the documents. Curiously, in September of that same year, an Indian leader named Pedro Miguel, cacique of a village called Oyubel (apparently within the jurisdiction of mission Santa Fé), seems to have robbed several Franciscan friars during their journey to St. Augustine for the chapter meeting, additionally destroying "the canoes of Zalamototo" used in crossing the St. Johns River.[29] By gubernatorial order dated September 18, he and his accomplices were to be arrested in mission Santa Fé and brought to the *castillo* in St. Augustine for criminal prosecution. It is unknown whether or not this action was in any way related to the proposed expansion of the Apalachee garrison and the eventual support provided by the Franciscan friars on their way to the chapter. At about this same time, Governor Aranguiz y Cotes ordered Capt. Matheo Luís de Florencia, returning from a mission to deliver defensive munitions to Apalachee, to remain as "leader at the post of Zalamototo, the general passage for all those provinces," probably in response to both external and internal threats.[30] Furthermore, within two months of the Salamototo/Santa Fé incident, the governor formally named a new provincial lieutenant for the Timucua mission province, including both of its constituent subregions, Timucua and Yustaga.

On November 19, 1659, nearly three weeks after Rebolledo's own death due to illness, Capt. Juan Fernández de Florencia, who had been the first lieutenant of Timucua a decade earlier, was dispatched once again with orders largely paralleling those of his immediate predecessor Martín Alcayde de Cordoba. In a later summary of his military service, the original commission was presumably quoted, in which Fernández was specifically ordered:

> go to the provinces of Ustaqua and Timuqua to populate and rebuild the villages of San Francisco, Santa Fé, San Martín, and San Juan de

Guacara, which had been depopulated by having died in the plagues which some natives have had, and others having fled to the woods, by these villages being the passage and communication to the said provinces from the presidio of St. Augustine, and it being adviseable to the service of His Majesty to deal with its remedy immediately, and for its better achievement he named him in his place as lieutenant of the governor and captain general of the said provinces of Ustaca and Timuqua so that he should govern them and arrange the aforementioned, as was entrusted to him.[31]

Clearly, Rebolledo's resettlement policy did not end with his death, for the ongoing effort to repopulate the devastated eastern missions of the Camino Real continued under the subsequent governor. Fernández's 1659 commission bears substantial similarity to the testimony of Rebolledo's lieutenant, listing precisely the same missions noted by Captain Alcayde to have been the subject of his own repopulation efforts following the 1656 rebellion (excepting only Ajoica). Although by this time the northern missions had already been formally dismantled, Captain Fernández presumably occupied himself in resettling fugitives from these eastern missions and might even have transferred populations from other more populous towns along the western Camino Real in Yustaga (although this is not specified).

Persistence of the Rebolledo Plan

In April and May of 1660, Royal Inquisitor Don Diego Ranjel conducted the posthumous *residencia* of Governor Diego de Rebolledo, during which notary Francisco de Rueda recorded lengthy secret testimony from nearly seventy-five witnesses called to respond to a long list of standard questions regarding the Rebolledo governorship.[32] Testimony from this massive document not only provides fundamental information regarding the Timucuan rebellion and its aftermath but also makes it clear that both Lazaro, the new cacique of San Martín, and Diego Heva, the new cacique of San Pedro, remained in power under succeeding Governor Aranguiz y Cotes, indicating that the basic elements of Rebolledo's political transformation of Timucua were successful, at least in the short term.[33] Furthermore, subsequent documentary evidence affirms that none of the dismantled Timucuan missions originally located off the newly consolidated Camino Real were ever reestablished, and that the vast majority of Timucuan missions either established, repopulated, or moved under Governor Rebolledo's direction survived until the last decade of the seventeenth century or later. In 1682, for example, the royal officials made specific note that "forty years ago there were many more villages to be found, as there were in the said province of Timucua: Arapaha, San Martín, Cachipile, Chamile, Pachala, Niahica, and Choaquine, these find themselves depopulated, and their inhabitants aggregated to the villages of the said province."[34] Their comprehensive list included each and every mission town known to have been dismantled after the rebellion, excepting only San Martín, the demise of which appears to date to the mid-1660s. In sum, Governor Rebolledo's plan was a near-complete success, inasmuch as most of the fundamental elements of both his political and geographic rearrangement of Timucua were never reversed, and in fact endured largely intact for another quarter century.[35]

Nevertheless, as might be expected, there is clear evidence that out-migration and fugitivism significantly increased among populations relocated to town sites along the primary Camino Real. This fact, and the concurrent wave of epidemics that seems to have ignited among newly congregated (and previously isolated) Timucuan populations, soon prompted the Franciscans to mount what would be a final organized effort to reverse Governor Rebolledo's policy. During their next provincial chapter meeting of 1662, almost six years after Governor Rebolledo's master plan had been set in motion, Franciscan officials drafted a formal complaint to the Spanish crown regarding the negative impact of wide-reaching geographic changes implemented and enforced under both Rebolledo and his successor. Forming one part of a long letter dated December 21, 1662, the friars petitioned that Rebolledo's original policy be reversed:

> Governor Don Diego de Rebolledo, when he went to the reduction of the province of Timucua and the punishment of the principal heads of the uprising, resolved that some towns of the said province should be dismantled, and that their people should aggregate to the [towns] which there are on the Camino Real from this presidio to the province of Apalachee, and although the goal could be good, experience shows that it has only served that almost all of the people, by having drawn them out of their native lands, walk as fugitives in the woods, and live among pagans as they do, and die in their apostasy, as in effect happens thus. I find that for reparation of this grave damage, and so that so many souls are not lost, Your Majesty has no other means than to command that the governor should effectively endeavor with all the gentleness and good treatment possible to reduce them to the villages of their native lands, so loved by these Indians, since to draw them out of them reduces them to rigorous slavery.[36]

This final passage is an obvious reference to the colonial labor system and confirms that Rebolledo's relocation of the more remote northern Yustagan towns to the Camino Real resulted in greater exposure to military demands on native labor (particularly burden bearing), which in turn resulted in an increase in fugitivism. While none of the towns established or repopulated by Rebolledo seem to have actually disappeared as a result of out-migration, dwindling populations in the surviving post-rebellion missions undoubtedly prompted the Franciscan friars to request permission to return them to their remote and protected homelands. Ironically, when the contents of their long 1662 petition were finally reviewed and acted upon by the Council of the Indies, the issue of Timucuan resettlement was not addressed. Thus, the governor of Florida was given no direct instruction in that regard. Rebolledo's vision for Timucua remained largely intact, persisting throughout the final decades of the province's existence in the interior of Spanish Florida.

CHAPTER 7

Late Seventeenth-Century Timucua

A Transformed Interior

In the aftermath of the post-rebellion transformation of the Timucua mission province, the western interior settled into its new configuration. In the space of a few short years under Diego de Rebolledo's governorship, the entire social geography of Florida's peninsular interior had been transfigured from a landscape dotted by the scattered remnants of local Timucuan chiefdoms into a consolidated chain of mission communities on or adjacent to the Camino Real. The towns of Oconi and Ibihica in the southeastern Georgia Coastal Plain had been destroyed, most of their surviving inhabitants apparently relocating beyond the Spanish realm. The mission convents of the upper St. Johns River valley seem also to have been abandoned shortly after the rebellion (certainly by the mid-1670s), with many of their Christian inhabitants aggregating to the new ferry town of San Diego de Salamototo.[1] This southern region, which had been known collectively as the province of Ibiniuti as early as the 1640s, continued to harbor Indian populations, however, and ultimately remained a haven for unconverted and fugitive Christian Timucuans. Nevertheless, Spanish military officials still considered this region within their political jurisdiction, including it on at least one occasion (1668) in the yearly *repartimiento* labor draft from the western mission provinces.[2]

The new Timucua mission province, extending from Salamototo to Asile along the Camino Real, represented the next incarnation of Florida's now fully assimilated interior Timucuan chiefdoms. Throughout the remaining decades of the seventeenth century, Spanish authorities concentrated their efforts on preserving the remaining Timucuan missions along this all-important corridor across Florida, largely abandoning the depopulated regions immediately north and south of the primary Camino Real. In this sense, the new Timucua was for the first time literally a mission chain.

Just as a chain is only as strong as its weakest link, none of the Timucuan missions could be allowed to drop below viable population levels without threatening the stability of the entire system. Nevertheless, several threats emerged during the 1660s that severely challenged Spanish officials in their efforts to preserve this western mission chain.

Unrest at San Martín

Early in 1664, mission San Martín once again revealed itself to be a center of unrest when its cacique was suspected of somewhat extreme abuses of power. Following is a summary from the service record of the officer dispatched to remedy the disturbance on his way to Apalachee to arrange a corn shipment:

> On the 24th of March of the year 1664, the interim governor of Florida [Nicolás Ponce de León] ordered [Capt. Antonio Menéndez Márquez] to go to the village of San Martín de Ayacuto in the province of Timucua to investigate the proceedings of the *cacique* of the same village, on account of having notice that he had made an extraordinary punishment on the *principales* of the village of Santa Cruz de Tarihica, for which cause it was depopulated, and the greater part of its residents went to the woods, and on account of being afraid that the said *cacique* had killed the missionary of [the Order of] San Francisco who was *doctrinero* of the village of San Martín, and from this all the province was disturbed, and that he should make a summary investigation of everything.[3]

Along the way, the officer was specifically empowered to "settle any discords that might have occurred among their natives, endeavoring that those who might have absented themselves and taken up residence in other [towns] should reduce themselves to their towns, acting in this with the greatest prudence he could," suggesting that illegal migration between mission communities was a continuing problem with regard to the towns of the Camino Real.

Given the earlier difficulties between San Martín's newly installed cacique, Lazaro of Chamile, and Governor Rebolledo late in 1657, and the fact that Lazaro was still in power as late as 1660, the unnamed cacique of San Martín mentioned in the 1664 order was probably Lazaro himself. Although the rumor of his having murdered San Martín's friar was certainly false (such an event would definitely appear elsewhere in the historical record), his punishment of the Tarihica *principales* apparently resulted in Lazaro's removal from office and imprisonment. In two 1667 letters complaining about the poor treatment of Florida Indians and the need for a public defender to be appointed on their behalf, Antonio's older brother Juan Menéndez Márquez made reference to an important unnamed cacique who had apparently been imprisoned in 1664 by acting governor Ponce de León. In his earlier correspondence, the royal accountant explained that Florida governors were

> depriving some *caciques* from their chiefdoms [*cacicados*] and reducing them to a very miserable state, as has been experienced today with one, the most principal of all the land, whom they have had here for more than three years without letting him go to govern his vassals and possess his lands, from which one might expect some inquietude among them, which would be in disservice to Your Majesty, and although it was brought up in the *residencia* that was taken about four months ago of the sergeant major of this post [Nicolás Ponce de León] for the time that he governed it on account of the death of Governor Don Alonso de Cotes, for having brought [the cacique] in his [governorship], this case was never sentenced, against what Your Majesty has commanded, and the poor *cacique* has remained as before and his justice has been obscured on account of not having a person who would come forth to defend him in his name.[4]

That this cacique was identical with the unnamed cacique mentioned in the 1664 order is highly probable (no other ranking aboriginal leaders are known to have been involved in criminal proceedings that year), prompting the conclusion that chief Lazaro of Chamile/San Martín was arrested and imprisoned between at least 1664 and late 1667, and perhaps longer.

The 1664 order to Captain Menéndez Márquez is the last known reference to mission San Martín de Ayacutu as an occupied aboriginal town. By the time the numerous Spanish mission lists and visitations dating to the years between 1674 and 1681 were drafted, San Martín had completely vanished from the documentary record, apart from a few later references to the abandoned site of the town. In its place, however, had emerged a completely new mission convent—Santa Catalina—in a town evidently situated some two leagues to the west of San Martín along the Camino Real. It hardly seems coincidental that San Martín vanished and Santa Catalina appeared just two leagues distant during the same decade between the 1664 arrest of San Martín's cacique and the 1674 visitation of Bishop Gabriel Díaz Vara Calderón. The most likely explanation is that the primary mission town at San Martín de Ayacuto was relocated to a nearby site within the former local jurisdiction of mission San Martín, which, like nearby Santa Cruz de Tarihica and San Agustín de Ajoica, was apparently slightly off the actual trail of the Camino Real.[5] This new site, called Santa Catalina, might even have been an as yet undocumented secondary *doctrina* within the original mission circuit of the friar at San Martín. That the abandoned site of San Martín was indeed within the local jurisdiction of the new mission Santa Catalina was subsequently indicated in a 1690 letter by Timucua's provincial lieutenant Diego de los Ríos Enríquez. The lieutenant indicated that Santa Catalina's resident friar was upset that the governor had ordered the church, council house, and chief's house at San Martín to be cleaned, implying that the lieutenant had once again been issued an order to move the town of Santa Catalina (perhaps back to San Martín?).[6] Though evidence is admittedly sparse, it is not unreasonable to hypothesize that mission San Martín was abandoned, its inhabitants relocating to Santa Catalina, as a direct or indirect result of chief Lazaro's arrest and lengthy imprisonment. Based on the limited number of suitable sites with fresh water in the barren region just west of San Martín (in the forest called Ayeheriva in Timucuan),[7] Santa Catalina was probably located either at the confluence of the Ichetucknee and Santa Fe Rivers (on the northwest bank) or somewhere in the cluster of sinkhole lakes due west of the Ichetucknee headsprings (appendix A).

Despite the apparent abandonment of mission San Martín in favor of a new site at Santa Catalina after the imprisonment of chief Lazaro in 1664, mission Santa Cruz de Tarihica appears to have survived its near depopulation that year more or less intact, appearing on all subsequent mission lists until the 1690s. The mechanisms employed to resettle this town are unknown, but perhaps the arrest of Lazaro encouraged Tarihica's fugitive populations to return to their homes. During that same period, however, Santa Cruz's neighbor San Agustín de Ajoica seems to have been the site of some sort of disturbance relative to the slave-raiding Chichimecos, at that time probably based on the middle Savannah River.[8] In November of 1665, Governor Francisco de Guerra y Vega dispatched Adj. Francisco Sánchez "to go to the province of Timucua to the village of Ajoica to inquire and find out about certain inquietudes which there have been in that province about some pagan Indians called the Chichimecos."[9] Sánchez was ordered to investigate the state of the villages in the province of Timucua and report to the governor so that he might "emplace the remedy suitable to the peace and quietude of the natives." While the comparative lack of urgency in this order would seem to rule out a major Chichimeco assault comparable to that which destroyed the Guale town of Talaje just four years earlier, this incident revealed the continuing exposure of the Timucuan missions to external raiders. Curiously, precisely twenty years later, the inhabitants of Ajoica would also become the first major victims of the onslaught of other English-allied raiders in Timucua.

Continued Fugitivism

Out-migration also continued to plague the missions of eastern Timucua. In April of 1665, for example, Governor Guerra y Vega reported the existence of a band of fugitive *cimarrones* along the margins of the old Potano district, said to be living "in some forests [*montes*] which are about three leagues from the villages of San Francisco and Santa Ana in the province of Timucua."[10] Because of its proximity to mission San Francisco de Potano and its sole surviving satellite community, Santa Ana, and the fact that many of them were relatives and former associates, this band was the cause for an ongoing drain on mission populations, representing a threat to the survival of both towns. At that time, the governor dispatched Adj. Ysidro de Reynoso with a troop of infantry to "go to the said place and the rest [of the places] in that district in which he has notice that there are fugitive Indians, to whom as soon as he runs across them he will endeavor with the best means that he can to attract them violently or amicably," bringing them for punishment to St. Augustine, "serving as a warning for the rest." That not all these fugitives were resettled in 1665 is demonstrated by the 1678 trial record of a fugitive Christian Potano woman from mission San Francisco named Maria Jacoba. This woman was said to have been a runaway for fourteen or fifteen years by that date, and she might have been part of the group mentioned in 1665.[11] By that date (and presumably earlier), fugitives from Potano seem to have commonly fled southward to the Acuera district, where unconverted Timucuans were still living in towns called Piriaco (Piliuco), Alisa, and Biro Zebano. From this southern district, pagan and fugitive Christian Timucuans alike apparently wandered far and wide in the eastern regions of Spanish Florida—including La Chua, Salamototo, and the lower course of the St. Johns River—occasionally resulting in hostile encounters between mission and non-mission groups. The 1678 arrest and prosecution of an unconverted Acuera Indian called Calesa, aptly described as "a seventeenth-century Native American serial killer," provides eloquent testimony to the fragility of actual Spanish control over the transpeninsular mission corridor.

Primarily due to the internal threat of fugitivism, and perhaps also due to external threats from enemy raiders such as the Chichimeco, in 1665 a permanent Spanish garrison post was formally established in the Timucuan ferry town of San Diego de Salamototo. On December 22, 1665, reserve officer Adj. Manuel de Torres was stationed in Salamototo with a small garrison of soldiers instructed to ensure that the town's residents did not absent themselves, since the town was "the principal gateway of all the land, including Timucua and Apalachee."[12] Following the apparently temporary placement of Matheo Luís de Florencia at Salamototo late in 1659,[13] the later Salamototo garrison, normally consisting of only two or three soldiers under an officer, would ultimately persist throughout the remaining decades of the seventeenth century. It effectively represented the final solution to the nearly continual difficulty experienced by seventeenth-century Spanish authorities in maintaining aboriginal populations at this crucial river crossing along the St. Johns River. Not only did this garrison presumably reduce the degree of out-migration simply by its presence, but these resident soldiers also represented a quick-response team for the recovery of any fugitives.

Despite continued fugitivism, Timucua remained an important part of the colonial labor system. The preservation of summaries and transcripts of several orders by Governors Aranguiz y Cotes and Guerra y Vega between 1663 and 1669 indicates that the new Timucua province remained a consistent contributor to the *repartimiento* labor draft during this period, along with the Apalachee and Guale provinces. Retrospective comments by Guerra y Vega in 1673 reveal that between fifty and fifty-five Indians were normally drafted each year from the missions of Timucua during this period. Unfortunately, a precise breakdown of individual town quotas has yet to be discovered.[14] Beyond these generally brief and indirect mentions of Timucua, there is little other extant documentation relating to the province during this period. Fortunately, however, the preservation of transcripts from the regional Yustagan council meeting convened in mission San Pedro during the 1670 visitation of the western provinces by Sgt. Maj. Pedro Benedit Horruytiner provides a detailed glimpse of the internal composition of that portion of the broader Timucua mission province.[15]

Junta in San Pedro

The 1670 Yustagan junta was convened at the request of an Indian named Benito, who claimed to be the legitimate heir to the chiefdom of Machava. Control of the chiefdom had apparently been wrested from his matrilineage in the 1630s as a result of the death of his great uncle Lorenzo, the previous cacique of Santa Elena. Following deliberations in the council house at San Pedro, during which a long list of Timucuan chiefs and nobles finally admitted that Benito was the legitimate heir, Horruytiner officially deposed the current cacique of Machava Pedro Meléndez and installed

Benito as the new chief. Meléndez, who had succeeded his executed predecessor, Dionicio, in the aftermath of the 1656 rebellion, was nonetheless ordered to be treated with chiefly privilege and respect during the rest of his lifetime, including the contribution of public labor for his fields, house, and granary. That this chiefly deposition was actually met with some degree of internal resistance is confirmed by the cacique Benito's 1674 petition for royal confirmation and protection for him and his heirs from future offenses by the family of Pedro Meléndez.[16] The 1676 royal *cédula* dispatched to this effect seems to have prompted further Spanish involvement in this case, for Sgt. Maj. Domingo de Leturiondo was dispatched on March 5, 1677, to remedy the continuing "discords" in the village of Machava.[17] The eventual disposition of this case is unknown, but of greater significance to the present discussion is the list of Yustagan leaders attending the 1670 council meeting. The list reveals several important details regarding the status of this region after the rebellion era.

Importantly, the 1670 list reveals that the internal political organization of the Yustaga region remained largely intact following the transformations implemented by Governor Rebolledo; San Pedro was still the regional capital, and Santa Elena and San Matheo remained as important secondary centers. That satellite communities to these central mission towns may still have been in existence in 1670 is suggested by the appearance of caciques from two previously unknown communities within Machava's jurisdiction—Ybiuro and Ybichua. The absence of a leader from San Miguel de Asile in the junta record was presumably due to its location on the opposite side of the Aucilla River, and does not seem to represent a persistence of Rebolledo's brief annexation of that mission within the Apalachee province (Asile was specifically included in the 1666 *repartimiento* draft for "Timucua and Ostaca,"[18] and was always included in the Timucua province after 1674). Of considerable note, however, is the appearance of caciques from four separate towns bearing the native name of "Arapaxa." Since only one of these names (San Juan) corresponds to the satellite villages within Arapaja's relocated jurisdiction at Santa Fé after the rebellion, and since none correspond to the original principal town of Santa María de los Angeles de Arapaja of the prerebellion era, it seems unlikely that these towns reflect a wholesale migration of Arapaja populations from eastern Timucua to the Yustaga region after the 1657 visitation (although this is a possibility). Given, however, that the Arapaja caciques were listed immediately after mission San Matheo in the 1670 junta, these towns may in fact have formed part of the large cluster of satellite villages listed within San Matheo's local jurisdiction in 1657, although once again, only one of the town names corresponds (San Francisco). Regardless of the precise explanation, however, the 1670 junta in San Pedro indicates that at least some chiefly lineages from the former Arapaja chiefdom did persist within the Yustaga subregion of the Timucua mission province.

Timucua during the 1670s

Although the period between 1657 and 1674 is only sparsely documented for the new Timucua, the subsequent two decades are blessed by a comparative wealth of historical documentation. Numerous mission lists, visitations, and a single detailed census dating to the period between 1674 and 1698 provide crucial information regarding the final decades of Timucua's existence in the interior of Spanish Florida. As can be seen in table 7.1, a simple presence-absence chart based on these data traces the emergence, persistence, relocation, and disappearance of the primary mission towns along the Camino Real during this final period. These lists, supplemented by a wide variety of textual descriptions of Timucua during this time, permit an overview of the degree to which the transformation of Timucua engineered by Governor Rebolledo persisted until its destruction by English-allied Indians after 1685, and they provide important evidence for the daily life of the inhabitants of the Timucuan missions as the assimilated remnants of the interior Timucuan chiefdoms.

Demographic collapse continued to plague the eastern reaches of the Timucua mission province during the decades after Governor Rebolledo's transformations. Data from three separate mission lists between 1675 and 1689 provide an overview of the continuing effect of depopulation, detailing the relative populations of specific mission towns within the Timucua chain (table 7.2).[19] Unquestionably, the 1681 census is by far the most reliable of the three, although two missions—Salamototo and Santa Catalina—were not included in the lieutenant's enumeration. The 1675 list is less specific, but probably reliable in intervals of ten persons. The 1689 list, based on secondhand data reported to the bishop of Cuba, seems least reliable, if for no other reason than the fact that the size of each family is not individually specified. Uniformly clear from all three lists, however, is the fact that Yustaga's three principal mission towns—San Pedro, Santa Elena, and San Matheo—constituted the demographic core of the Timucua mission province. Together these towns possessed more people than all the other missions in Timucua combined. The missions of eastern Timucua, extending from San Juan to Salamototo, were thinly populated in comparison, comprising numbers not exceeding a hundred persons, except in the case of the regional capital at Santa Fé.

Table 7-1. Compiled mission lists for the Timucua province, 1675–98

Mission site	1674a	1674b	1675	1678	1679	1680	1681a	1681b	1681c	1682	1683	1687	1689	1694	1697	1698
Salamototo	x	x	x	x	x	x	?	x	?	x	x	x	x	x	x	x
Ivitanayo										x	x	x	x			
San Francisco	x	x	x	x	x	x	x	x	x	x	x	x	x	x	x	x
Santa Fé II	x	x	x	x	x	x	x	x	x	x	x	x	x	x	x	x
Santa Catalina	x	x	x	x	x	x	x	?	x	x	x	x	x			
Ajoica	x	x														
Santa Cruz II	x	x	x	x	x	x	x	x	x	x	x	x	x			
San Juan II	x	?	x	x	x	x	x	x	x	x	x	x	x			
San Pedro	x	?	x	x	x	x	x	x	x	x	x	x	x			
San Pedro II												x		x	x	x
Santa Elena	x	?	x	x	x	x	x	x	x	x	x	x	x			
San Matheo	x	?	x	x	x	x	x	x	x	x	x	?		x	x	x
Santa Elena II														x	x	x
Asile	x	?	x	x	x	x	x	x	x	x	x	x	x	x	x	x

Sources: 1674a (Díaz Vara Calderón 1675); 1674b (Palacios 1675); 1675 (Fernández de Florencia 1675); 1678 (Leturiondo 1678); 1679 (Barreda 1680); 1680 (Márquez Cabrera 1680); 1681a (Cárdenas 1681); 1681b (Riço 1681); 1681c (Cárdenas 1682); 1682 (Menéndez Márquez and Rocha 1682); 1683 (Solana 1683); 1687 (Reyes 1687); 1689 (Ebelino de Compostela 1689); 1694 (Florencia 1695); 1697 Menéndez Márquez and Florencia 1697); 1698 (Ayala Escobar 1698).

Table 7-2. Comparative demographic data for individual Timucuan missions, 1675–89

Mission list	1675 list	1681 census	1689
Salamototo	40 persons	?	40 families
Santa Rosa de Ivitanayo	-	-	20 families
San Francisco	60 persons	54 persons	25 families
Santa Fé de Teleco	110 persons	108 persons	36 families
Santa Catalina	60 persons	?	40 families
Santa Cruz de Tarihica	80 persons	32 persons	20 families
San Juan de Guacara	80 persons	56 persons	30 families
San Pedro de Potohiriba	300+ persons	217 persons	150 families
Santa Elena de Machava	300 persons	186 persons	100 families
San Matheo de Tolapatafi	300 persons	240 persons	50 families
San Miguel de Asile	40 persons	105 persons	30 families

Sources: Fernández de Florencia (1675, 1681); Riço (1681); Ebelino de Compostela (1689).

Perhaps for this reason more than any other, Timucua's provincial lieutenants seem to have been routinely based in Yustaga during this period. The original site of mission Santa Elena de Machava was stated to be the primary garrison post for lieutenants Andrés Pérez in 1678 and Joseph de Cárdenas in 1681, and this same site was lieutenant Andrés García's residence with his family in 1698, despite the relocation of mission San Pedro to that location after Santa Elena's move westward.[20] In eastern Timucua, however, an apparently secondary garrison post was mission Santa Fé, where provincial lieutenants appear to have been at least occasionally stationed during the late 1680s.[21] During this period, however, the Timucua garrison, like that of Salamototo, never comprised more than a few soldiers under the command of the resident provincial lieutenant, and as such it paled in comparison with the dozens of soldiers living in and around mission San Luís de Talimali in the Apalachee province at the same time.[22]

The consequences of continued depopulation in Timucua were perhaps most severe in the two important ferry towns of San Diego de Salamototo and San Juan de Guacara. During the 1678 visitation of Timucua's missions by Sgt. Maj. Domingo de Leturiondo, both towns requested assistance with the fabrication and maintenance of canoes for the river crossings. In San Juan the Indians elaborated, complaining to Leturiondo about the immense workload involved in ferrying travelers, "for which cause the Indians deserted the said village, as His Grace would recognize at present, since there have only remained twenty persons in it including old and young."²³ In the subsequent visitation of Salamototo, the leaders requested that "the six men who effectively serve in the said crossing" be given rations at royal expense, and that the fugitives from the town be sought out and returned to help in the chores. Importantly, Leturiondo noted that "in attention to there being so few people, and many *caciques,* most of them without vassals, His Grace admonished them that all [the caciques] should help with the cultivation of their fields, each one working for himself, without relying on their vassals, who are bothered for this reason." In the end, Timucuan caciques whose predecessors had risen in revolt at the idea of performing manual labor were forced through pure necessity to assist in growing their own food for lack of sufficient subordinates.

This phenomenon was not unique to Timucua during the closing decades of the seventeenth century; Christian Guale and Mocama mission towns on the Georgia and Florida coast were characterized by considerable numbers of caciques and *principales,* who made up an average of nearly 25 percent (43 out of 177) of the adult male population in each of seven enumerated missions, and 11 percent of their total population.²⁴ As noble and non-noble matrilineages alike were gradually extinguished through disease, chiefly offices such as that of the cacique and his *principales* were always filled under strict aboriginal rules of inheritance, meaning that no matter how severe depopulation became on a local level, appropriate heirs to the principal chiefly offices were always found. In the long run, as death and reduced health and fertility due to disease and overwork reduced mission populations, supplemented by occasional out-migration by non-noble laborers and their families, mission towns were frequently inhabited by literally too many chiefs and not enough Indians. Regardless of long-standing traditions, there simply were not enough subordinate laborers to carry out all the tasks in each community. Caciques eventually found themselves relinquishing some of the privileges of rank in order to maintain what little real power and respect remained for them.

As was the case before the rebellion, settlement aggregation was a common solution to the difficulties involved in maintaining viable population levels in individual towns. By the mid-1670s, depopulation had reached a sufficiently critical level to prompt several significant alterations to the existing distribution of settlements in eastern Timucua. One move was the circa 1673 aggregation of the sole surviving subordinate Potano *doctrina* of Santa Ana to its nearby neighbor San Francisco de Potano, which had become severely depopulated by that time. The mission's leadership later made reference to this aggregation, complaining about the impact of even this short move to San Francisco; the *cacica* and *principales* noted that "in only moving from one league from here they had found themselves on another occasion without people because they regretted moving from one place to another."[25] Interestingly, later documentation reveals that although the principal *cacica* of San Francisco, María de Jesús (married to Spanish soldier Bartolomé Francisco), seems to have maintained her preeminent rank over Marzela, the relocated *cacica* of Santa Ana, her actual political control in the newly aggregated community was eventually limited by the fact that she possessed extremely few direct "vassals" of her own, since most of the population comprised the former residents of Santa Ana.[26] At that time (early 1678), Santa Ana's *cacica* blocked María's proposal to relocate the town to Ivitanayo. This decision was supported by Spanish authorities. Regardless of this fact, however, it was María's half-Spanish son Miguel who inherited the office of principal cacique in San Francisco when she renounced the position in 1678, governing through the 1694 and 1698 visitations until the final retreat of Timucua in 1706.[27]

Apparently sometime in early 1675, mission San Agustín de Ajoica was relocated once again and aggregated to its nearby neighbor Santa Catalina, presumably under similar circumstances to those described above. Although on November 1, 1674, both towns were visited individually by Bishop Gabriel Díaz Vara Calderón and his secretary Pedro Palacios, by the following summer, on July 15, 1675, Apalachee's lieutenant Capt. Juan Fernández de Florencia listed only Santa Catalina with sixty residents in his comprehensive enumeration of the western missions.[28] Just over two years later, during the January 1678 visitation of mission Santa Catalina, Ajoica's cacique Lúcas revealed that his town had previously been "aggregated in this said village," revealing that he had recently struck a deal with the soldier Nicolás Suárez to set up a new cattle ranch between "the old village of Ajoyca, which is depopulated" and that of Santa Catalina.[29] The newly aggregated mission town was subsequently referred to as Santa Catalina de Ajoica (though in at least one instance the original conventual name of San Agustín was used),[30] suggesting that most of its inhabitants may have been from the original town of Ajoica. Indeed, by 1680 Ajoica's cacique Lúcas had evidently assumed the principal position in mission Santa Catalina, occupying a captain's rank within the aboriginal militia structure (evidently second only to Santa Fé's principal cacique Don Thomás de Medina with the rank of sergeant major).

Just two years after the fusion of Santa Catalina and Ajoica, a plan was developed to establish a completely new mission community on the Camino Real in the uninhabited inland district extending for roughly twenty leagues between Salamototo and Santa Fé. In early November of 1677, Spanish soldier Bartolomé Francisco proposed on behalf of his Timucuan wife María de Jesús, the principal *cacica* of mission San Francisco de Potano, that the Indian inhabitants of that town be permitted by Gov. Pablo de Hita Salazar to relocate "to the woods of Bitanayo, which are in the uninhabited zone [*despoblado*] in the halfway point between the river of Salamototo and Santa Fé." His stated reasons were two: "the one [reason] by of being more convenient to the Indians to have more at hand the sustenance that could be acquired with less difficulty, and by being closer to this city, and the other [reason] because in that place being settled it would result in greater convenience for the infantry, couriers, and passersby, and for the Indians of Salamototo and Santa Fé." The opinion of the royal officials was mixed; Bartolomé Francisco and his wife could not speak for the majority of San Francisco's inhabitants, because the *cacica* María "does not have any vassals to establish the lands that he asks for, because those who live in the said village of San Francisco are vassals of the *cacica* of Santa Ana." If, however, Santa Ana's *cacica* and her vassals were willing to move, the only difficulty noted was that of providing a new missionary, since mission San Francisco was at that time served by the resident friar at Santa Fé. The issue was turned over to Sgt. Maj. Domingo de Leturiondo, soon to depart on his formal visitation of the western provinces.

By the time the visitor began making his way east from Apalachee in January of the following year, he seemed to have already established that Santa Ana's *cacica* opposed the move to Ivitanayo, for Leturiondo openly requested volunteers for such a move during the general visitation of Yustaga long before arriving at mission San Francisco. In her formal refusal on January 25, the *cacica* Marzela referred to difficulties during the 1673 move of Santa Ana to San Francisco and predicted that "if they were to do the same at present, everyone would go away to live in other villages." Earlier, however, during the January 15 junta of the caciques of Yustaga at mission San Pedro, Leturiondo had asked "if there were some *caciquillo* who would like to go to settle with some families to the place called Hivitanayo, by being as it is for their own good and for that of those who go and come to these provinces." The following day, Antonio, described as a "*cacique* of those of the village of San Matheo*," offered that "he would go with some relatives of his and with the eight families that had been proposed to be gathered from the towns of San Pedro, Machava, and San Matheo, and give a beginning to the said settlement." Presumably a secondary cacique within the local jurisdiction of San Matheo, Antonio may have been identical with the cacique of the same name associated with San Antonio de Arapaja (a probable satellite of San Matheo) in 1670.[31] The cacique was promised assistance in transporting the corn and other belongings of the settlers, which would be brought by canoe up the River of San Martín (the lower Suwannee) and from the landing at Pulilica by horse to Ivitanayo under the cacique of Santa Fé's supervision. Axes were to be given to them for clearing roads and fields, and "until the town was in [good] form and with enough people, no field hands [*yndios de cava*] would be drafted for some years." Though a Franciscan minister was not available at that time, one was promised in short order. Furthermore, in the final instructions left for the Timucua province by the visitor, the new town of Ivitanayo was specifically excepted from the rule against inter-village migration in order to encourage immigrants, and the provincial lieutenant was directed to selectively exile Timucuans violating minor laws to Ivitanayo. Despite the 1678 agreement to establish this new mission, however, it was not until after 1681 that the mission Santa Rosa de Ivitanayo was actually established. It first appeared in the October 1682 list of active mission stations in Florida and on the June 1683 Alonso Solana map of Florida.[32] The town eventually persisted into the early 1690s, albeit with at least one additional infusion of external populations from the Acuera district.

New Spanish Haciendas

With declining population levels and resultant settlement aggregations, abandoned Timucuan lands in the interior became increasingly available for private Spanish enterprise in the form of haciendas. The ranch at La Chua was but the first of several Spanish haciendas ultimately established in the interior Timucuan region. By the end of the seventeenth century, some twenty-five individual haciendas had been established across eastern Spanish Florida, extending from the Atlantic coastline north and south of St. Augustine to the St. Johns river and westward to the Potano district.[33] Nine haciendas had even been established within the Apalachee province far to the west by that time. The vast majority of the eastern haciendas were situated in the considerable area of land bounded by the Atlantic Ocean on the east and the full course of the St. Johns River on the west. That most of these lands were granted during the last half of the seventeenth century is confirmed by the fact that the names of most original landowners indicated on hereditary haciendas shown on several late eighteenth-century maps were actually prominent officials and soldiers from the mid- to late-seventeenth century, such as the rebellion-era Martín Alcayde de Cordoba, Augustín Pérez de Villa Real, Antonio de Argüelles, and Lorenzo Joseph de

León. Indeed, by 1700 essentially all lands in this region surrounding the city of St. Augustine had either been designated as royal lands pertaining to past and present Indian towns (Salamototo and San Antonio) or had been granted to Spanish entrepreneurs. Only a few haciendas, however, were established on lands west of the middle St. Johns River, and these were largely restricted to the region immediately north and south of the Camino Real between the Salamototo ferry and the easternmost interior Timucuan missions of San Francisco and Santa Fé. Most of these, moreover, were either established or subsequently purchased by Thomás Menéndez Márquez and his son Francisco, the hereditary owners of the original La Chua hacienda established by Thomás's father, Francisco, before 1630. Nevertheless, at least one hacienda was proposed to be established even farther west during the 1670s.

At least as early as the mid-1670s, some land grants had been recorded for the uninhabited district between Salamototo and Santa Fé. When Gov. Pablo de Hita Salazar decided to move forward with the plan to establish a new town equidistant between these two missions, he was obligated to confiscate lands that had been granted at some earlier date to Spanish soldier Nicolás Suárez. Sergeant Major Leturiondo noted in his 1678 visitation record that "the lands that he possessed of Hivitanayo, which had been conceded by the *señores* governors, were being taken away from Nicolás Suárez on this occasion in order to found on them a settlement of natives of this province."[34] Perhaps in compensation, Suárez was at that time granted permission to proceed with the deal he had negotiated with the cacique of Ajoica to establish a new hacienda between the abandoned site of his town and mission Santa Catalina. Leturiondo confirmed the contract, noting it to be "of common utility and benefit for all the land to proceed introducing cattle, since their increase could be to the advantage of the royal treasury." Despite the apparent success of these negotiations and land deals, however, there is no evidence that this hacienda was ever actually established. Even if it was, it did not survive until the 1694 visitation of Timucua.[35] The fact that Santa Rosa de Ivitanayo does not appear to have been established until 1682 might suggest that Nicolás Suárez's planned "land swap" did not actually take place as outlined in the 1678 visitation.

Other haciendas were clearly established in the region around the important ranch of La Chua during the closing decades of the seventeenth century, however, including one named Santa Cruz, which had been founded before 1694 by the governor's son Capt. Juan Antonio de Hita Salazar, and another named Santa Catalina (commonly called Chicharro), established by Capt. Francisco Romo de Uriza along the southern margin of the *nayoa,* or savannah, of La Chua (present-day Payne's Prairie) prior to 1703.[36] All three of these were in operation in 1703 during the trial of one of Santa Catalina's African slaves, accused of murdering an Apalachee Indian worker. Additional haciendas were established in the immediate environs of Salamototo on the east bank of the St. Johns River during the late seventeenth century, including that of San Joseph de Puibeta founded only a league from Salamototo by Capt. Juan de Pueyo, and another on the riverbank called Piquilaco (probably Picolata), owned by Bentura González as early as 1685 and operating in 1694.[37] Nevertheless, if other individual ranches were in operation in the Timucua province west of the St. Johns River during the last quarter of the seventeenth century, specific documentation regarding their existence has yet to be discovered.

Based on the 1700 list of tithes contributed from Florida cattle ranches during 1698 and 1699, Capt. Thomás Menéndez Márquez clearly dominated the relative productivity of all other landowners in Spanish Florida. Registering an impressive seventy-seven calves tithed during this two-year period, Menéndez far exceeded all other tithes, alone contributing 42 percent of the entire number of calves tithed from all twenty-five east Florida ranches combined. The only ranches that even came close were those of Capt. Francisco Romo de Uriza at his nearby hacienda, Chicharro (thirteen and a half calves), and two Apalachee haciendas owned by adjutants Diego Jiménez and Joseph Salinas (fifteen and thirteen calves, respectively).[38] Although it is possible that the well-established Menéndez Márquez hacienda at La Chua was sufficiently productive to account for the seventy-seven tithed calves, a late eighteenth-century Spanish land-grant map reveals that Thomás and his son Francisco ultimately owned immense tracts of land stretching across much of the interior region between La Chua and the St. Johns River, including "the *haciendas* of La Rosa del Diablo and Acuitasique" situated in the lake district northwest of Ivitanayo and its lands, and a vast tract to the southeast of La Chua called the Abosaya hacienda, apparently including the site settled by the refugees from Apalachee after its destruction in 1704. Other lands to the south and northwest of La Chua on the map, referred to as the lands of "[Ab]losuro" and Hamaca, may also have been ranches owned by the Menéndez Márquez clan, although this is not indicated. That the lake called Amaca (Sunshine Lake north of present-day Gainesville) was once the seat of a Spanish cattle ranch was confirmed in 1740 by Francisco de Castilla in his description of the Camino Real, but the date of its establishment, and its owner, is unknown.[39] While it is unclear when these individual Timucuan ranches were originally established (some might postdate the abandonment of the interior missions), they might help account for the tremendous number of cattle tithed by Thomás Menéndez Márquez in the years preceding 1700.

Immigrants to Ibiniuti

Although the abandonment of Franciscan *conventos* in the chiefdoms of the upper St. Johns River valley after the 1656 rebellion left the southern district of Ibiniuti largely beyond the scope of effective Spanish control for many years, the region upriver from Salamototo was eventually resettled by immigrant populations from the deep frontier of Spanish Florida. Despite the survival of pagan and fugitive Christian Timucuan populations in the Acuera region of the far southwestern St. Johns River watershed until well into the 1670s and 1680s, the abandoned sites of missions San Antonio de Enacape and San Salvador de Mayaca farther upriver eventually became havens for aboriginal refugees from the northern interior. These refugees were part of a nascent confederacy of unconverted Indians forced out of their homelands in central Georgia and coastal South Carolina by repeated assaults from English-allied Chichimeco slave raiders, also known as the Westo Indians.[40] Already distributed in a number of newly established towns and villages across the Guale and Mocama mission provinces by 1675, a small number of these Indians, collectively called Yamassees, had established small settlements at Mayaca and Enacape by the end of 1679.[41]

Although no friars appear to have been stationed in either of these refugee communities during the following winter (they do not appear on the Franciscan patent remitted to all Florida missions between December 1679 and January 1680), by the end of 1680 both San Salvador and San Antonio were described as "new conversions" by Gov. Juan Márquez Cabrera in his comprehensive mission list.[42] Later evidence indicates that two recently arrived friars (both from the 1678 Franciscan expedition to Florida)[43] were dispatched to these renewed mission towns, where they apparently served episodically between 1680 and 1682. Neither Yamassee mission was mentioned in April, July, or December visitations by the provincial lieutenants of Timucua, including the 1681 census by Manuel Riço, but this probably reflects the separate administrative jurisdiction of Salamototo's lieutenant over all towns on the St. Johns River.[44] Populations at both these missions were quite minimal; Fray Juan Miguel de Villa Real complained in a June 1681 letter to the governor that Enacape had fewer than thirty inhabitants (only five of which were men who could work), and that several Yamassees from San Antonio had recently relocated to be with other Yamassees living in the abandoned Mocama towns of Santa María and San Pedro and in a small Yamassee community near the relocated Guale mission of San Phelipe on Cumberland Island.[45] By the spring of 1682, Enacape possessed only twenty-one residents, whereas Mayaca held seventy-nine, despite the impetuous 1681 departure of Fray Bartolomé de Quiñones with two mission bells and the church furnishings, which he left in Salamototo. Nevertheless, neither San Antonio or Mayaca were included in the list of active mission *conventos* compiled by Florida's royal officials in October 1682. Both were stated to have been abandoned in previous decades.[46] Regardless, both Yamassee missions were shown on the 1683 Alonso Solana map of Florida missions. In 1689, mission "San Antonio de Mayaca" was enumerated with thirty families.[47] These new conversions ultimately became staging grounds for the eventual establishment of new missions among the Jororo and other southern Florida groups.[48]

The Census of 1681

Despite the resettlement of the long-abandoned southern Timucuan town at San Antonio de Enacape by immigrant Yamassees during the early 1680s, Salamototo, Ivitanayo, and the rest of the surviving interior Timucuan missions endured for at least another decade, and in some cases longer. In this context, the recently discovered global mission census of 1681 provides a pivotal benchmark relative to the demographic profile of Florida's indigenous and immigrant mission populations shortly before their final destruction and retreat to the environs of St. Augustine (table 7.3).[49] Placing the Timucua province in the context of the entire mission system, the census reveals that Timucua, like Guale and Mocama, was heavily depopulated by 1681, containing only slightly more inhabitants throughout its entire extent than Apalachee's most populous mission town at San Luís de Talimali (both with roughly 1,000 people). The coastal provinces of Guale and Mocama were even more severely depopulated, containing only 420 Christian Indians distributed in eight missions. These predominantly indigenous populations were supplemented by some 322 immigrant Yamassees living in a handful of distinct villages and hamlets scattered among the congregated Guale and Mocama missions (43 percent of the total population, contributing some 50 percent of the yearly *repartimiento* draft).[50] Even including the pagan Yamassees, however, the entire resident population of the northern coastal provinces reached only 742 individuals, well below Timucua's more than 998 (not including perhaps 100 or so omitted residents from Salamototo and Santa Catalina).

Of considerable note is the fact that Timucua apparently contained no non-Timucuan immigrants within its provincial jurisdiction. Excepting the perhaps 100 Yamassees living in the St. Johns River missions of Enacape and Mayaca, the Timucua province appears to have comprised only Timucuan populations in 1681, albeit drawn from a number of congregated Timucuan chiefdoms from across the interior. Even the populous Apalachee province contained 82 unconverted immigrant Yamassees, Chacatos, Chines, Pacaras, and Amacanos distributed among recent converts in three mission communities, together comprising a total population of 579 individuals (or about 10 percent of the entire provincial Apalachee population). The interior Timucua region appears to have somehow remained unaffected by the increasing flow of immigrant populations from distant regions, despite the perpetual complaints of underpopulation.

Leadership of the Timucua Province

The internal political structure of postrebellion Timucua seems to have largely reflected a continuation of precolonial aboriginal norms, although the transformations instituted by Governor Rebolledo were ultimately marked by several changes in leadership resulting from a variety of natural and imposed circumstances, including at least two major instances of prosecution of caciques within the context of the Spanish colonial legal system. The arrest and long-term imprisonment of chief Lazaro, Rebolledo's chosen successor to San Martín's cacique Lúcas Menéndez, for severe abuses of power seem to have had long-term implications for the regional political structure of Timucua. At some point after the physical abandonment of Timucua's former regional capital at San Martín de Ayacutu, and the probable relocation of its inhabitants to Santa Catalina between 1664 and 1674, nearby mission Santa Fé seems to have assumed the central role in the native administration of the province. While the fate of Spanish-allied cacique Alonso Pastrana of Arapaja at his new home in the relocated Santa Fé is unknown, a subsequent cacique at mission Santa Fé clearly occupied the ranking aboriginal position within the Timucua region (and indeed all of the Timucua mission province) during the mid- to late 1670s. During the November 1674 visitation of the bishop of Cuba, secretary Pedro Palacios noted that mission Santa Fé was the home of "Sergeant Major Don Thomás de Medina, *cacique mayor* of all that Timucuan province, alias Usta[c]a," an evaluation confirmed by the bishop himself.[51] Don Thomás ultimately became a strong ally of Gov. Pablo de Hita Salazar. In 1678, he recruited the cacique to capture a pagan Acuera cacique named Jabajica in the town of Alisa, and in 1679 he accompanied Spanish soldier Juan Bauptista de la Cruz on an officially sanctioned expedition to ransom Spanish captives from the Calusa on Florida's southern Gulf coast.[52] As late

Table 7-3. Demographic data from 1681 Florida mission census (unconverted Indians in parentheses)

Community	Males		Females		Total	Comments
	Married	Single	Married	Single		
San Lorenzo de Ivitachuco	193	107	193	112	605	Fray Bartolomé de Ayala; head principal town
N. S. de la Concepción de Ayubale	200	80	200	102	582	Fray Marçelo de San Joseph
San Francisco de Oconi	80	46	80	49	255	Fray Juan Arias
San Juan de Aspalaga	104	42	104	56	306	Fray Miguel de Valverde
San Joseph de Ocuya	183	109	183	122	597	Fray Francisco de San Joseph; a principal town
San Pablo/Pedro de Patale	147	56	147	65	415	Fray Juan de Ocon
San Antonio de Bacua	55	19	55	23	152	Principal town
San Damián de Escambi	150	109	150	123	532	Fray Francisco de Vega
San Carlos de los Chacatos	63	48 (7)	63	26 (9)	200 (16)	Fray Juan de Mercado; Chacatos
San Luís de Talimali	302	168	302	196	968	Fray Francisco Blanco; a principal town
San Pedro de Medellín	45	15 (14)	45	8 (31)	113 (45)	Fray Juan de Lem; Chines, Pacaras, Amacanos
N.S. de la Candelaria de la Tama	74	20 (14)	74	16 (7)	184 (21)	Fray Juan Angel; Guale and Yamassa language
Tomole	194	84	194	77	549	Fray Miguel Martorel; Guale language
Santa Cruz de Ychutafum	25	20	25	14	84	cacique is brother/heir of Ivitachuco cacique
Apalachee subtotals	1815	923 (35)	1815	989 (47)	5542 (82)	
[Salamototo]	?	?	?	?	?	
San Francisco Potano	19	9	19	7	54	3 firearms
Santa Fé	26	29	26	27	108	3 firearms
[Santa Catalina]	?	?	?	?	?	
Santa Cruz de Tarijica	13	4	13	2	32	2 firearms
San Juan de Guacara	19	11	19	7	56	
San Pedro de Potogeriba	83	23	83	28	217	4 firearms

Santa Elena de Machava	72	22	72	20	186	5 firearms
San Matheo	87	27	87	39	240	2 firearms
Asile	43	13	43	6	105	1 firearms
Timucua subtotals	362	138	362	136	998	
Tupiqui	19	4	19	6	48	Fray Simón Martínez de Sala
Sapala	10	5	10	9	34	" " "
Satuache	18	3	18	8	47	" " "
Santa Catalina	21	7	21	8	57	" " "
Yamazes	-	(44)	-	(23)	(67)	
Asajo	13	4	13	9	39	Fray Domingo Santos
Colones	-	(9)	-	(8)	(17)	
Yamazes	-	(50)	-	(23)	(73)	
Guadalquini	28	17	28	14	87	Fray Francisco García
San Phelipe	23	5	23	20	71	Fray Juan Bauptista Campaña
Yamazes	-	?	-	?	(11)	
San Pedro	-	(36)	-	(17)	(53)	
Santa Maria	-	(72)	-	(29)	(101)	
San Juan del Puerto	14	3	14	6	37	Fray Francisco de la Cruz
Guale/Mocama subtotals	146	48 (211)	146	80 (100)	420 (322)	
Grand subtotals	2,323	1,109 (246)	2,323	1,205 (147)	6,960 (404)[a]	

Grand totals: males 3,678; females 3,675; total mission population 7,364

Sources: Fernández de Florencia (1681); Riço (1681); Fuentes (1681).

a. Includes 11 Yamazes not specified by gender.

as the summer of 1680, the governor called Medina to St. Augustine along with other Timucua caciques for a consultation regarding the ejection of the Chichimeco Indians.[53] Although at one point the governor even described him as "the most prestigious defender of the evangelical law and of all those things that pertain to the service of His Majesty,"[54] at some point in 1680 Don Thomás was also arrested and criminally prosecuted by outgoing Gov. Hita Salazar. During the term of his successor, Juan Márquez Cabrera, the cacique was condemned on September 13, 1681, by Havana judge Juan Díaz de León to torture and execution by garrote. Although the case was appealed in 1682, its ultimate disposition is unknown, though Don Thomás vanished from the documentary record after that date.[55] Medina's successor as cacique of Santa Fé was Don Francisco Riço, who was probably the Timucuan godson of Adj. Manuel Riço, one of Timucua's lieutenants during that period. Don Francisco ultimately presided over the rapid contraction of eastern Timucua's remaining missions during the 1690s, and, together with San Francisco's cacique Miguel, retreated to St. Augustine with the last remnants of Timucua in 1706.

Taking Stock

By 1682, when Florida's royal officials composed a short overview of the occupied and abandoned missions of Spanish Florida, the Timucua mission province was but a shadowy reflection of the numerous missionized chiefdoms that once stretched across the interior.[56] Noting that "forty years ago there were many more villages to be found," they began their listing of abandoned missions with Timucua, including the towns that "find themselves depopulated, and their inhabitants aggregated to the villages of the said province." The missions of the Ibiniuti district were next. They were said to be entirely depopulated, with the survivors either aggregated to Salamototo or scattered in the frontier in small settlements called *rancherías*. Last on the royal officials' list were the abandoned missions of Guale, which had retreated southward and seaward over the previous two decades in the face of nearly constant English-supported raids.[57]

The roughly 1,000 people living in the ten surviving missions of late seventeenth-century Timucua were very nearly the last remnants of perhaps as many as eighteen individual Timucuan chiefdoms, once boasting combined populations probably exceeding 20,000 people at the beginning of the seventeenth century. Despite long precedent, however, their final years in the interior would not ultimately be characterized by the gradual, lingering effects of demographic collapse in the context of the Spanish colonial system. With the final retreat of the northern coastal missions of Guale and Mocama following a disastrous pirate raid during the fall of

1684, English-allied Indians quickly turned their attention to the south and west. The fragile chain of Timucuan missions stretching from St. Augustine to Apalachee would soon be subjected to armed invasion by Indian slavers bearing English muskets, accelerating the collapse and ultimate demise of Timucua to a space of only a few short years. The twenty guns listed for the Timucuan towns during the 1681 census would ultimately prove futile in the face of the coming juggernaut of Carolina aggression.

CHAPTER 8

The Destruction of Timucua

Slave Raid at Santa Catalina

Between 1685 and 1706, a series of slave raids by Yamassee and Apalachicola Indians under English influence repeatedly pounded the missions of the Timucua province, ultimately resulting in the retreat of all surviving Christian Timucua to the protection of Spanish guns in the Castillo de San Marcos just north of the city of St. Augustine. The first major assault occurred in February 1685, when a group of some fifty to sixty Yamassee warriors led by chief Altamaha and armed with English shotguns and cutlasses descended upon mission Santa Catalina de Ajoica during the night.[1] Approaching from both directions along the Camino Real (from Tarihica to the west and Santa Fé to the east), the Yamassees razed the town, looted and burned its mission church and convent, and killed eighteen people, capturing twenty-one others to be sold as slaves in the newly established Scottish colony of Stuart's Town. An undetermined number were sold to a merchant from Charles Town, and the rest embarked on an Irish ship carrying new settlers for the town.[2] Only a handful of residents survived, including the cacique and sixteen warriors, who set out in a fruitless pursuit of the raiders. Despite the assault, however, the visitation of mission Santa Catalina that same fall revealed that the town had survived, presumably having been reconstructed around the ten houses that endured the assault.[3] The mission was listed under its conventual name, San Agustín de Ajoica, in the 1689 list constructed for Bishop Diego Ebelino de Compostela. The appearance of what was said to be some forty families in the town suggests that external populations had settled there since the 1685 attack.[4]

Five years later, in the fall and winter of 1690–91, internal disputes in mission Santa Catalina seem to have prompted Timucua's provincial lieutenant Capt. Diego de los Ríos Enríquez to make arrangements for the aggregation of its inhabitants and those of Santa Cruz de Tarihica (nearby or already aggregated to Santa Catalina) to his garrison headquarters at mission Santa Fé. In a September letter, the lieutenant made reference to earlier difficulties between Santa Catalina's friar, Pedro de la Lastra, and at least some of the mission's former inhabitants, said to be "Ocochunos" under the leadership of a cacique named Marcos.[5] While their identity remains a mystery (they might be immigrant Yamassees or possibly even Timucuans), this group may have constituted most or all of Ajoica's revitalized population levels in the 1689 list. They were indeed later listed as one of the towns of the old Timucua province in a 1736 overview of past provinces in Florida.[6] Having left the mission at some point because of Fray Lastra's brutality, the cacique of the Ocochunos evidently returned in August 1690 to find out whether the friar had been transferred yet. He was advised at that time to bring all of his people to Santa Fé, where the cacique Riço had offered to help and feed them. A November letter from the lieutenant revealed that the relocation of Ajoica's inhabitants within Santa Fé's jurisdiction (either to the *ycapacha,* or abandoned site, of Santa Fé I, or to the new site of Santa Fé II) had been approved by the governor, despite anticipated objections from Santa Catalina's friar. In January 1691, Lieutenant Ríos accompanied Santa Fé's cacique Riço and his people to assist in the move of not only Santa Catalina but also Santa Cruz de Tarihica, whose inhabitants pleaded that Fray Lastra be replaced with another missionary. The fact that neither town appeared on the later 1694 visitation record or on subsequent mission lists dating to 1697 and 1698 suggests that this move was indeed carried out,[7] and that both Santa Catalina and Santa Cruz were aggregated to mission Santa Fé during 1691. If these aggregated populations remained long at the abandoned site of the original mission Santa Fé, however, evidence for their late seventeenth-century stay has yet to be identified at the Shealy archaeological site.[8] Most or all of these immigrants probably merged with existing populations in Santa Fé's postrebellion site, as yet undiscovered (Santa Fé II).

The Destruction of San Juan

The abandonment of Santa Catalina and Santa Cruz left mission San Juan de Guacara in a remote and isolated position along the middle stretches of the Camino Real. On August 30, 1691, San Juan was destroyed in an assault by Uchise and Yamassee Indians, who burned the mission and village, killing and capturing many of the town's inhabitants.[9] Attempts by Governor Quiroga y Losada to reconstruct the town do not appear to have been successful, since the mission did not reappear on any subsequent list or visitation record; by the mid-1690s San Juan was described as "dismantled" on account of a lack of residents.[10] Probably in direct response to their obviously vulnerable military position, at that time or soon thereafter Guacara's nearest Yustagan neighbors—San Pedro and Santa Elena—seem to have relocated their towns westward toward the more well-defended Apalachee province (see table 7.1). Santa Elena de Machava was apparently reestablished along the eastern side of the Aucilla River, placing it roughly between the towns of Asile and San Matheo, while San Pedro de Potohiriba apparently moved just over two leagues to the west to the then-abandoned site of Machava (see appendix A). Although currently undocumented, apart from the change in mission order, these moves almost certainly were defensive in nature, serving to lessen the distance between Yustaga's remaining missions and the populous Apalachee province.

By the time of Joachín de Florencia's visitation of the western mission provinces during the winter of 1694–95, Timucua consisted of only seven principal mission towns distributed into two widely separated clusters, including only Salamototo, Santa Fé, and San Francisco on the east, and San Pedro, San Matheo, Machava, and Asile on the west (fig. 8.1).[11] Despite an earlier attempt to revitalize its population with pagan Acuera and Ayapaja Indians from central Florida during the term of Gov. Diego de Quiroga y Losada (1687–93), the short-lived mission town of Santa Rosa de Ivitanayo had already been abandoned by that date and was evidently never reestablished. As later described by the governor, the town had become "dismantled, and the Indians in the woods on account of the little care that has been taken to aid and favor them."[12] While on his visitation route, Captain Florencia dispatched an order to San Francisco's cacique Miguel instructing him to gather all the fugitives he could find for resettlement either in San Francisco or Salamototo. During this same visitation, Florencia also included individual visitations for the owners and overseers of several Spanish haciendas bordering Timucuan missions, including those of La Chua and Santa Cruz near mission San Francisco (owned by Thomás Menéndez Márquez and Juan Antonio de Hita Salazar), and San Joseph de Puibeta and Piquilaco near mission San Diego de Salamototo (owned by Juan de Pueyo and Bentura González). Despite the fact that at least a few Timucuan Indians were employed at these haciendas, unmarried Apalachees also seem to have been routinely employed. During the visitation, ranch owners were instructed by Florencia to ensure that no married Apalachee Indians be consented on their haciendas and that other Apalachee workers attended Mass regularly, returning to Apalachee for confession each Lent. The haciendas bordering Salamototo were furthermore ordered to fence in their cattle to prevent damage to Indian crops and to permit Salamototo's residents to gather acorns and other wild foods from the nearby woods.

Of particular interest, in the list of instructions left for the Timucua province, Captain Florencia directed that no Indians from the mission towns of

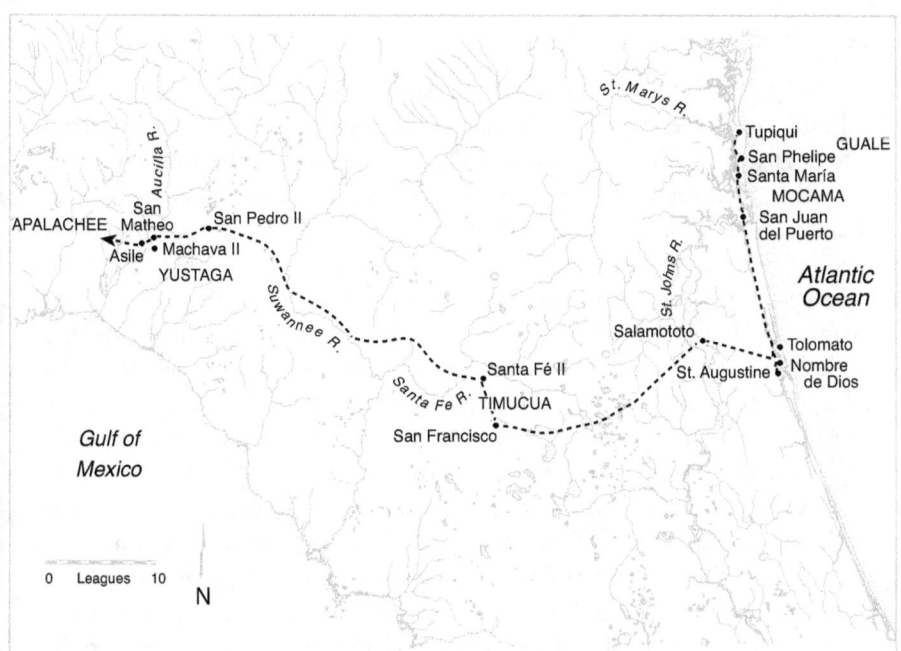

Figure 8-1. Timucua at the close of the seventeenth century.

San Francisco, Santa Fé, and particularly San Pedro (where the lieutenant resided with his family) were to be permitted to leave their homes and migrate to other villages. The residents of San Matheo and Machava were specifically excluded from this rule, however, and were almost encouraged to relocate to one of the aforementioned three villages. Clearly, maintaining population levels in the more isolated Camino Real mission towns of San Francisco, Santa Fé, and San Pedro was of considerable importance to the Spanish (San Francisco's residents were even permitted at that time to shift their entire village to a more fertile spot half a league to the south, where the mission church and convent were already located). In contrast, San Matheo and the relocated Santa Elena de Machava were close enough to the Aucilla River and the towns of Asile and Ivitachuco just beyond it that population levels were less critical in these towns (appendix A). A subsequent 1697 mission list by Florida's royal officials, as well as a brief 1698 visitation by Capt. Juan de Ayala Escobar, revealed that all seven of the Timucuan missions visited in 1694 survived through the dawn of the eighteenth century.[13]

Assault on Santa Fé

On May 20, 1702, the garrisoned mission of Santa Fé was itself assaulted and nearly destroyed by Apalachicola (Lower Creek) warriors from the English-allied town of Achito (Hitchiti).[14] Although the attackers were forced to withdraw after a three-hour battle, Timucua's lieutenant Adj. Juan Ruíz de Cañizares pursued them with a small force for six leagues before being ambushed and killed along with another soldier and ten Timucuan warriors. A massive retaliatory strike led by Capt. Francisco Romo de Uriza that fall resulted in the deaths of more than half of his eight hundred Apalachee, Timucua, and Chacato warriors along the banks of the lower Flint River in an ambush staged by English-allied Apalachicola Indians.[15] Compounding this blow, early in November allied English and Indian forces under Carolina's governor Col. James Moore swept across the last remnants of Guale and Mocama, destroying the three surviving Guale missions of Santa María, San Phelipe, and Tupiqui on Amelia Island.[16] The last remaining Mocama mission of San Juan del Puerto was soon abandoned, and the provincial lieutenant and friars there were captured by the English before proceeding southward to lay siege to St. Augustine. Despite the near-complete destruction of the city, however, the fort was never breached, and St. Augustine and Spanish Florida survived to rebuild. Guale and Mocama refugees soon banded together into two camps around a newly fortified location called Pilijiriba on the south bank of the St. Johns River north of St. Augustine, although by 1704 renewed enemy attacks forced yet another retreat southward.

Despite the 1702 assault, the interior Timucuan mission of Santa Fé evidently remained a distinct settlement at least until August 1703, when it was still the primary garrison post for Timucua's subsequent lieutenant, Adj. Diego de Xaen, when he investigated murder charges against a slave working in a nearby hacienda.[17] At that time, the eastern Timucua province west of Salamototo on the St. Johns River still consisted of only the two remaining mission towns of Santa Fé and San Francisco along with three Spanish ranches in the immediate vicinity—La Chua, Santa Catalina (or Chicharro), and Santa Cruz. At some point during late 1703 or early 1704, however, Santa Fé was formally aggregated to mission San Francisco, which subsequently became the principal Timucua garrison post with a fortified stockade.[18] La Chua was also fortified and seems to have become a secondary military post about three leagues from San Francisco.

Siege on Apalachee

The first half of 1704 witnessed the total annihilation of the once-vaunted Apalachee mission province just west of Timucua's Yustaga region. Beginning with a frontal assault on the Apalachee mission of La Concepción de Ayubale, later called the "war of Ayubale," Carolina's Governor Moore once again led English-allied Indians in a massive January raid upon the missions of the Apalachee province.[19] Upon his departure, Moore led perhaps more than one thousand Apalachee slaves, along with the inhabitants of several other Apalachee towns who had agreed to relocate to English Carolina in return for their freedom. In subsequent June attacks most of the remaining villages were assaulted and destroyed, with many more slaves led off to Carolina. In the end, only missions San Luís and Ivitachuco remained intact. Slaves were not the only casualties; during the two attacks, Apalachees and Spaniards alike were maimed, mutilated, or killed outright. Dozens of mission Indians were skinned or burned alive, and one murdered Spanish soldier in the Apalachee garrison was brutally mutilated before having burning splinters placed in his wounds. Fray Juan de Parga was killed in a battle between Spanish and English forces on a road outside Ayubale, his body beheaded and left to rot in a canebrake and his head brought to the council house by English-allied warriors. Fray Manuel de Mendoza was shot and killed upon opening the door of his convent; his half-charred corpse was found later beneath a collapsed wall. In the aftermath, the aboriginal leadership of San Luís confessed total disillusionment with efforts at Spanish protection; if they remained, they would side with the English attackers in the anticipated next assault. In the aftermath, some eight hundred Apalachees from San Luís and Escambé, as well as a few Chacatos and Yamassees, led a caravan westward to the Spanish outpost at Pensacola and ultimately joined the French at their newly established colony in Mobile. Only the remaining inhabitants of Ivitachuco under the cacique Don Patricio de Hinachuba retreated eastward when the Spaniards finally withdrew from Apalachee, burning the fort at San Luís.

At some point in August, English-allied Indians overran the remaining Yustagan missions, newly exposed after the collapse of Apalachee. Timucua's lieutenant reported to the governor in early September that "the enemies from Apalachee had laid waste to the land and district of San Pedro and San Matheo, and had burned alive the *caciques* of [that district] and their vassals."[20] The nearby Santa Elena presumably suffered a similar fate during the same period. Any survivors who were not killed or enslaved might subsequently have retreated to eastern Timucua, although the only evidence to support this conclusion is the persistence of the mission convent named in Latin S. Petri de Potohiriba well into the eighteenth century. At the same time, the enemies pushed far to the east, "dismembering" a captured black slave from the La Chua ranch only four leagues from San Francisco. After the final withdrawal from Apalachee province, all the remaining survivors who did not migrate to Pensacola aggregated to the only surviving Apalachee town at Ivitachuco, where under the leadership of cacique Don Patricio they finally left their homeland and moved east in a caravan of more than four hundred Indians and Spaniards to the relative safety of eastern Timucua. The remnants of the Apalachee province eventually settled "in a place called Abosaia, one day by road from the garrison of San Francisco, a land of many wild fruits and roots with which they will have to sustain themselves until they can form their seed beds next year, and in the meantime they will proceed in making a *corral* in which to defend themselves from the enemies, who will not stop pursuing them."[21] There, in the environs of the old Potano district, the surviving remnants of both the Apalachee and Timucua provinces made what would be their last stand in the interior. Consolidated into only two fortified mission communities—Abosaya and San Francisco—flanking the La Chua hacienda, their combined populations probably did not exceed six hundred Indians. These towns, supplemented by the few Timucuans still living at Salamototo next to the Spanish stockade there, would not survive even two years before the final retreat to St. Augustine.

The Final Raids

The attacks resumed in August and September of 1705, during which time Abosaya, San Francisco, La Chua, and Salamototo were all assaulted by waves of English-allied Indians.[22] Apalachee refugees under cacique Don Patricio de Hinachuba soon abandoned their fortified village at Abosaya, retreating south of St. Augustine in an ultimately futile effort to find protection; the cacique himself and most of his people were killed in subsequent raids. After additional raids in the spring of 1706, field master Don Francisco Riço, the cacique of Santa Fé, and Capt. Don Miguel, the cacique of San Francisco, finally consented to incoming governor Francisco de Córcoles y Martínez's plan to relocate their aggregate town to the nearby garrison community at Salamototo east of the St. Johns River. Falling back to Salamototo by early May, Santa Fé/San Francisco soon joined Salamototo's residents in yet another retreat, this time to St. Augustine itself. By the end of May 1706, the Timucuan interior had effectively become an uninhabited war zone, and the surviving residents of Santa Fé/San Francisco and Salamototo prepared to begin a new life among the Spaniards.

CHAPTER 9

Remnants

Regrouping in St. Augustine

The retreat from the Timucuan interior had been tumultuous and rapid; by May 19, 1706, Royal Treasurer Francisco de Florencia reported that "now I have gathered in the patios of my house, and within it, more than one hundred fifty persons, men, women, and children, from the towns of Santa Fé and San Francisco while their *caciques* establish settlements [*rancherías*] adjacent to this presidio."[1] By the end of the year, the new village of San Francisco had been established under the shelter of the guns of the fort. The remnants of Florida's once-extensive mission system had been reduced to only five towns located along a defensive line just north of St. Augustine, along with the old mission Nombre de Dios immediately north of the city. Among these new towns, or more accurately refugee camps, were the ruins of the old Guale province in Santa María and Tolomato, the remnants of Apalachee in Abosaya, and the two towns of San Francisco and Salamototo, representing the final remnants of the interior Timucuan chiefdoms.[2] Based on later evidence, Yustagan refugees may well have been living in mission Nombre de Dios as well. Early in 1707, when the *residencia* of ex-governor Joseph de Zuñiga y Cerda was published in each town, San Francisco was the only community distinguished by the presence of "the *caciques* and *principales* of this village, and those of the villages aggregated to it," suggesting that other Timucuan refugees had joined with those in San Francisco. Apart from the recently aggregated mission Santa Fé, these may have included the remnants of the Mocama province (later to appear as a distinct community) or even other refugees from the destroyed Yustagan missions.

Four years later, a census of these surviving towns revealed the magnitude of the destruction wrought by English aggression.[3] As shown in table 9.1, the entire population of all the remaining missions of Spanish Florida

Table 9-1. Demographic data from the 1711 Florida mission census

Town	Men	Boys	Women	Girls	Total
San Luís de Talimali, alias Abosaya	31	3	11	3	48
Santa Catharina de Guale	27	4	22	8	61
Santo Thomás de Santa Fé	16	5	19	11	51
Salamototo	5	-	7	-	12
San Juan del Puerto	11	6	14	9	40
Nombre de Dios	15	5	11	7	38
Tolomato	9	15	14	7	45
La Costa	5(51)	7(12)	(20)	(4)	12(87)
Ais	(1)	(7)	(8)	(6)	(22)
Total	171	64	126	55	416

Source: Córcoles y Martínez (1711).

was slightly more than 400 people, including a number of recent converts from the coastal groups south of St. Augustine. A comparison between tables 7.3 and 9.1 reveals that in the three decades between 1681 and 1711, the massive Apalachee province (including native Apalachees and other immigrants) had been reduced from a population of 5,542 people in fourteen towns to only 48 people in a single town (San Luís/Abosaya), comprising the largest drop in population across all of Florida's seventeenth-century mission provinces. Guale had dropped from 296 people in six towns to only 61 people in one town (Santa Catalina), not including the relocated Guale town of Tolomato, for which no data are available in 1681. The coastal Timucuan Mocama province had similarly dropped from 124 people in two towns to only 40 people in a single town (San Juan). Most importantly, however, interior Timucua had plummeted from a total population of more than 1,000 people (including two missions not enumerated) distributed in ten primary mission towns to a total population of no more than 101 people living in three separate communities.

In 1711, these communities included Salamototo, still separate from other interior Timucuan towns but comprising only twelve adult Timucuan Indians; mission Santo Thomás de Santa Fé (the former aggregate town of San Francisco/Santa Fé under its primary conventual name), with fifty-one Timucuan residents; and evidently at least a few Yustagan refugees from mission San Pedro among the thirty-eight inhabitants of the coastal Timucuan mission of Nombre de Dios.[4] Although Salamototo was still ruled by the cacique Don Alonso of the 1698 visitation, both Santa Fé's former cacique Francisco Riço and San Francisco's cacique Miguel had evidently died by this date. The principal cacique of mission Santa Fé in 1711 was Juan

Arucatesa, who had in 1701 appeared as a secondary leader in mission San Francisco.[5]

The 1715 Yamassee war resulted in a substantial flood of Yamassee refugees from lower Carolina into the mission communities around St. Augustine.[6] By the time of another detailed mission census dating to 1717, three entirely new aggregate Yamassee towns (each incorporating several distinct political/ethnic units) had emerged among the surviving mission communities listed in 1711 (table 9.1).[7] All but one of the earlier mission towns was still in existence (though in some cases under different conventual names), including Santa Fé/San Francisco under the name Nuestra Señora de los Dolores (with seventy-two Timucuan inhabitants) and Nombre de Dios (with forty-seven Timucuan inhabitants). The tiny community of Salamototo had apparently dispersed by 1717, with its inhabitants attaching themselves to the Mocama town of San Buenaventura de Palica (the old San Juan del Puerto) and Nombre de Dios, with some fifteen and four Salamototo residents, respectively. Interestingly, although Don Juan de Arucatesa remained cacique of the interior Timucuans at Santa Fé/San Francisco in 1717, the new cacique of Nombre de Dios was named Don Juan Alonso, a name not directly matched by any of that town's residents six years earlier. Given that a few of Salamototo's former inhabitants are listed within Nombre de Dios, however, this individual might in fact be identical with Salamototo's earlier cacique, Don Alonso.

Of considerable significance, the 1717 census reveals that the inhabitants of the newly aggregated refugee communities around St. Augustine were beginning to mix and intermarry, as demonstrated by the presence of multiple linguistic and ethnic backgrounds within most of the established mission villages (table 9.2). The Mocama/Salamototo town at Palica was also inhabited by Yamassee and Chachise (apparently a branch of Yamassee) Indians, for example, and Apalachee Indians were living in both Timucuan towns of Nuestra Señora de los Dolores and Nombre de Dios. This phenomenon was presumably a natural result of the fact that individual refugee villages did not offer enough marriage partners to maintain the viability of each community. In the crowded siege environment around early eighteenth-century St. Augustine, multi-ethnic intermarriage was an obvious solution to minimal population levels.

By the late 1720s, the two towns constituting the remnants of interior Timucua had been aggregated together at Nombre de Dios, also known as Macaríz. Although in late 1726 the town of Santa Fé included twenty recently converted Pojoy immigrants along with twenty-five "old Christians" (Timucuans), it was noted at that time to be aggregated to mission Nombre de Dios with fifty-five "old Christians" and seven recent converts

Table 9-2. Demographic data from the 1717 Florida mission census (unconverted Indians in parentheses)

Town	Language	Cacique	Men	Boys	Women	Girls	Village Total
Santa Catharina de Guale	Ybaja	Don Alonso de la Cruz	42	13	40	11	125
Aggregated pagans	?		(6)	(5)	(6)	(1)	
San Buenaventura de Palica	Timucuan	Juan Ximenez	26	11	27	11	132
Aggregated from Salamototo	Timucuan		9		4	2	
Aggregated Chachises	?		(19)	(5)	(14)	(3)	
Aggregated Yamassee	Yamassee		—	—	—	(1)	
Nuestra Señora de la Candelaria de la Tamaja	Yamassee	Don Antonio de Ayala	16 (13)	—	9 (16)	5 (13)	162
Aggregated Yamassees under cacique Jospo	Yamassee	Jospo	1(23)	(7)	(23)	(7)	
Aggregated Yamassees under cacique of Ocute	Yamassee	Alonso Ocute	2 (7)	(2)	—	(1)	
San Joseph de Jororo	Mayaca	Don Juan Romo	7 (9)	(2)	3 (10)	1(1)	33
Nuestra Señora de los Dolores	Timucuan	Don Juan de Arucatesa	26	11	23	12	74
Aggregated Apalachees	Apalachee		2	—	—	—	
Pocosapa	Yamassee	Langne Chapqui	2 (40)	1 (12)	31 (10)	5 (14)	172
Aggregated Apalachees and Timucuans	Ap./Tim.		11	—	?	—	
Aggregated Casapuia	Casapuia		16	7	14	9	
Nuestra Señora del Rosario de Abosaya	Apalachee	Don Pedro Osunaca	14	3	12	4	34
Aggregated Chasta	Chasta		—	—	2	—	
Pocotalaca	Yamassee	Don Francisco Yaquisca	3 (35)	12	6 (25)	13	96
Aggregated Ybaja	Ybaja		4	—	—	—	
Tholomato	Ybaja	Don Francisco Martín	18	16	21	9	64
Nombre de Dios	Timucuan	Don Juan Alonso	12	10	12	9	50
Aggregated Apalachees	Apalachee		3	—	—	—	
Aggregated from Salamototo	Timucuan		—	—	4	—	
Totals			214(152)	84(33)	208(104)	91(41)	942

Source: Primo de Ribera (1717).

Table 9-3. Demographic data from the 1726 Florida mission census

Doctrina	Nation	Men	Women	Children	Total
San Antonio	Yamassee	22	16	11	49
San Antonio	Yamassee	21	12	16	49
Aggregated pagans					4
San Diego	Yamassee	26	27	12	65
Santa Cathalina	Yguaja	35	47	22	104
Nuestra Señora de Guadalupe	Yguaja	11	16	18	45
Aggregated new converts	?				6
San Joseph, aggregated	Yguaja	15	18	5	38
San Buenaventura	Chiluca	19	24	27	70
Aggregated Macapiras	Macapiras	17	6	1	24
Nombre de Dios	Chiluca	19	23	20	62
Santa Fé, aggregated	Timucua/Pojoy	20	17	8	45
San Luís	Apalachee	36	27	24	87
San Antonio	Cosapuya	24	13	18	55
San Antonio	Costas	55	13	20	88
Carlos (no church)	Piaja	17	6	1	24
San Antonio	Yamassee in Apalachee	66	51	29	146
San Juan	Apalachee/Yamassee	16	17	13	46
Totals		419	333	245	1,007

Source: Benavides (1726).

(table 9.3).[8] Just over a year later (early 1728), Nombre de Dios itself held only forty-three inhabitants (four new Christians), including only one man actually native to the mission. The aggregated "town of Timuca" had only fifteen inhabitants, including two new converts (table 9.4).[9] By the time of a 1736 roster, however, Nombre de Dios, called at that time the "village of Timucua," held a total of only sixteen adult male inhabitants, including the cacique Alucatesa.[10] The list's author, Havana engineer Antonio de Arredondo, lamented at that time that the total of 417 mission Indians were the "remains of nearly thirty thousand which there were between the jurisdiction of Apalachee and St. Augustine, Florida." Due to rapidly changing circumstances in the context of raids and epidemics, however, cited population levels fluctuated during this period almost on a monthly basis. During 1738 and 1739 alone, for example, the total recorded population of "Nombre de Dios Macaríz" ranged from a low of twenty-three to a high of fifty-two residents in four separate census lists (table 9.5). By this period, however, mission locations seem to have largely stabilized in specific locations surrounding St. Augustine (fig. 9.1).

Table 9-4. Demographic data from the 1728 Florida mission census

Doctrina	Site	Men	Women	Children	Total
Nuestra Señora de Guadalupe	Ayachin	11	17	20	48
Aggregated Ybaja town		10	12	7	29
San Antonio de Pocotalaca	Esperanza	22	19	14	55
Pagan					1
Nombre de Dios	?	14	17	12	43
Aggregated town of Timucua		7	7	1	15
San Buenaventura de Palica	El Muelle	13	19	28	60
Nuestra Señora del Rosario	Moze				
Padre San Francisco de los Corrales		7(14)	8(9)	7(7)	22(30)
San Luís/Antonio de la Tama		6(9)	7(8)	5(5)	18(22)
Santa Catharina de Gualecita					
incl. 12 Ybaja and 13 Yamassee	N.D. Chiquito	25	23	23	71
San Antonio de la Costa	?	33	14	18	65
Totals		148(158)	143(145)	135	427(439)

Source: Castillo (1728).

Despite the dwindling populations of Florida's congregated eighteenth-century missions, detailed Franciscan records from the 1730s reveal the apparent persistence of seventeenth-century convent names associated with missions long-since destroyed and depopulated. In 1736, a detailed list of the convents and friars in the Franciscan province of Santa Elena de la Florida included the primary convents in Cuba and St. Augustine, but listed eight lesser convents in Florida, including all the most important late seventeenth-century missions of the western and northern mission provinces (table 9.6). This list is confirmed by Latin records from the 1735 Franciscan chapter meeting in St. Augustine.[11] Surviving convents included San Lorenzo and San Luís from the Apalachee province; Santa Catalina from the Guale province; San Juan del Puerto from Mocama and both Santo Thomás de Santa Fé and San Pedro. Only San Antonio de la Tama and Santa María de Galves de Pensacola represented eighteenth-century formations. A comparison between the secular lists of actual mission communities during this period (table 9.5) and Franciscan lists of convents and mission posts (table 9.6) reveals that most conventual names actually corresponded to extant communities, though in some cases aggregated. The convents of Santo Thomás de Santa Fé and San Pedro de Potohiriba represent the fused Timucuan towns in mission Nombre de Dios. The substitution of San Pedro de Nombre de Dios in the 1736 list at least

Table 9-5. Comparative demographic data from 1736–39 Florida mission lists

Mission town	Common name	1736	1737	4/1738	6/1738	12/1738	3/1739
Nombre de Dios de Macaríz	Macaríz	17 warriors	17 m/26 wc	49 (15 war.)	46	43 (13 fam.)	52
San Antonio de la Costa	La Costa	10 warriors	8 m/14 wc	6 or 7	19	23 (7 fam.)	14
N.S. de Guadalupe de Tolomato	Tolomato	13 warriors	14 m/33 wc	64 (14 war.)	30	29 (8 fam.)	36
N.S. de la Asumpción/San Juan del Puerto de Palica	Palica	18 warriors	18 m/47 wc	61 (17 war.)	53	48 (11 fam.)	56
N.S. de la Concepción de Pocotalaca	Pocotalaca	23 warriors	23 m/44 wc	62 (23 war.)	47	44 (14 fam.)	54
N.S. del Rosario de la Punta	La Punta	17 warriors	17 m/17 wc	41 (15 war.)	43	51 (14 fam.)	26
Santo Domingo de/Nombre de Dios Chiquito	Chiquito	15 warriors	?	56 (16 war.)	40	55 (18 fam.)	51
San Nicolás de Casapuyas	San Nicolás	10 warriors	?	? (9 war.)	32	61 (19 fam.)	47

Key: m = men; wc = women and children; war. = warriors; fam. = families.

Sources: Arredondo (1736; 1737); Benavides (1738); Montiano (1738); Güemes y Horcasitas (1739); Torres (1739).

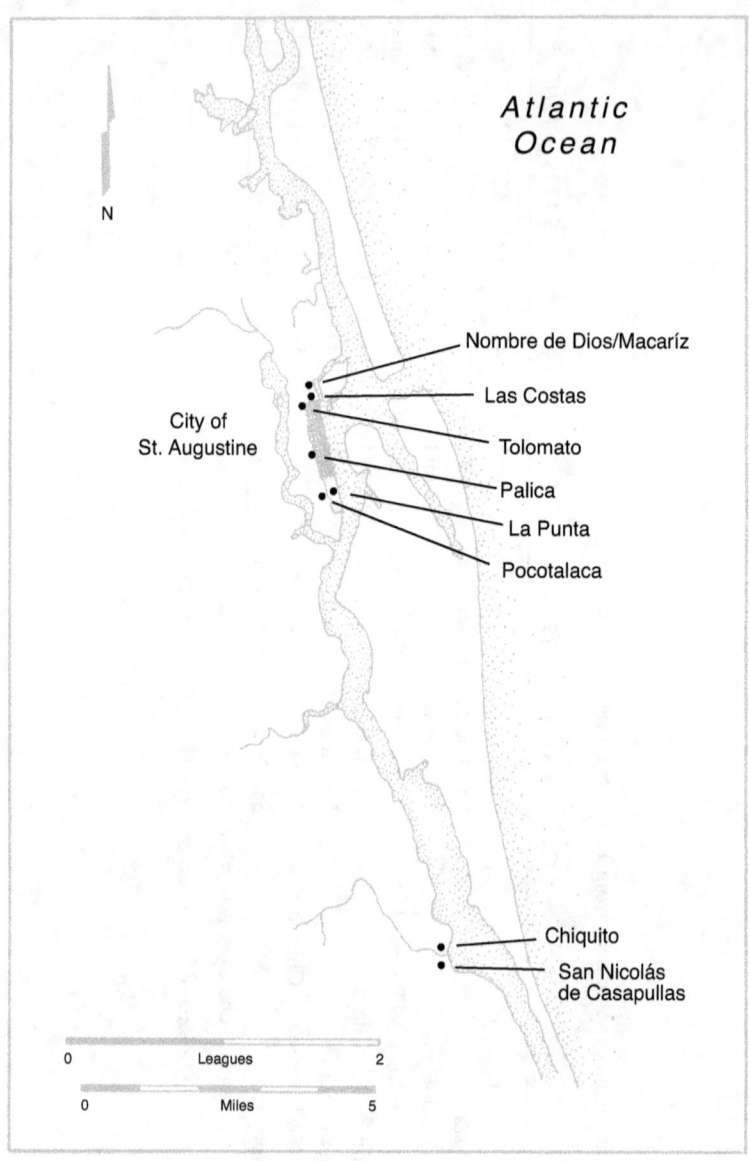

Figure 9-1. Refugee missions around St. Augustine, 1730s.

Table 9-6. Franciscan *conventos*, 1735–36

1735 chapter list	1736 minor convent list
Santa Catharina de Guale	Santa Catarina de Guale
San Thomás de Santa Fé	Santo Thomás de Santa Fé
San Petri de Potohiriba/Pothoxiriba	San Pedro de Nombre de Dios
San Laurentis de Hibitaquu	San Lorenzo de Hibitachucu
San Ludovici de Hinataxum/Hinathaphum	San Luís de Hinataphum
San Joannis del Puerto	San Juan del Puerto
Santa María de Galves de Pansacola	Santa María de Galves
San Antonij de la Tama	San Antonio de la Tama

Sources: Morales et al. (1735); Ojitos (1736).

implies that Nombre de Dios's predominant early eighteenth-century population may have been from Yustaga, while that of the aggregated town of Timucua (Santa Fé) represented the congregated remnants of the eastern Timucua province. Harder to reconcile is the presence of two Apalachee mission convents for only a single surviving Apalachee community at La Punta. To greater or lesser extents, these Franciscan lists probably reflect a combination of simple administrative inertia with a desire on the part of the Franciscans to maintain as many official posts on the roster as possible (in order to avoid reductions in external funding).

Following further contractions and aggregations, by 1752 only five missions remained north of St. Augustine, not including Nombre de Dios.[12] This number dropped to four by 1754, leaving only the predominantly Guale town of Tolomato, the Mocama town of Palica, the predominantly Yamassee towns of Pocotalaca and Punta (the latter perhaps with remnant Apalachee), and the Timucuan town of Nombre de Dios.[13] Ultimately, however, only Nombre de Dios and Tolomato remained by the end of the decade as the two final aggregation points for the mission Indians of Spanish Florida (see fig. 9.1). By the time of a 1759 census, only six "Timucua" Indians were listed for Nombre de Dios (also known as Nuestra Señora de la Leche), by that time governed by a Christian Yamassee cacique named Juan Sánchez.[14] All but one of the thirteen Indians identified as Chiluque (Mocama) were living in the nearby mission of Tolomato, indicating that the last Mocama mission at Palica had aggregated to the surviving Guale at Tolomato. Furthermore, at least one of the individuals identified as "Timucua" in Nombre de Dios (Juan Puje) had been living in Palica as a teenager in 1736.[15] Ultimately, then, only a handful of interior Timucuans survived until 1759, including the ninety-year-old Manuel Riço, probably a younger relative (son or nephew) of mission Santa Fé's cacique between 1680 and 1706 (Don Francisco Riço), and the fifty-year-old Juan Alonso Cavale.

Exile

In the end, mission Nombre de Dios would be the last home for the few remaining interior Timucuans before their 1763 departure from Florida. In 1763, the Florida colony was turned over to the British crown in exchange for the captured city of Havana in a diplomatic deal ending the Seven Years' War. What more than a century of skirmishes and open battles had failed to achieve was accomplished with the signature of a treaty; Spain surrendered Florida without bloodshed, evacuating its remaining inhabitants to Cuba. With them went some eighty-nine native Florida Indians, who willingly chose to expatriate themselves along with their Spanish neighbors.[16] By the beginning of 1763, a small community of Florida Indians emerged in Guanabacoa, near Havana. Among their number were the last surviving interior Timucuans. In a comprehensive census taken in early April 1764, sixty Florida Indians were listed, including many of those Timucuans listed in 1759.[17] The elderly Manuel Riço evidently died on the voyage or shortly thereafter, and other names are absent, probably resulting from rapid mortality in Cuba. Based on a comparison between the 1764 census and recently obtained death records from the church of Nuestra Señora de la Asunción in Guanabacoa, at least 25 percent of the Florida Indian immigrants alive in early 1764 are known with certainty to have died within five years of their arrival in Cuba.[18] These deaths included a man named Juan Alonso Cavale, who appears to have been the last living full-blooded Timucuan whose parents were born in the interior of Spanish Florida.[19] Evidently born in the aggregate mission town of Santa Fé/San Francisco during the first years after the 1706 retreat from the interior, young Juan Alonso first appeared in the documentary record among the children listed for Santo Thomás de Santa Fé in the 1711 census. The adult Pedro Cavale listed in the same village might possibly have been a father or uncle.[20] Appearing once again in the 1759 census of mission Nombre de Dios, Cavale was by that time married to a Yamassee woman named María Rosa Culiparca, and had two sons. Cavale's entire family survived the voyage to Cuba to appear in the 1764 census for Guanabacoa, although his wife died in March of the following year. Juan Alonso Cavale himself died on November 14, 1767.[21] Although the fate of his half-Timucuan sons, Juan Joseph and Francisco, is unknown, Cavale's death represented the end of the last surviving bloodline of the interior Timucuans and symbolized the final assimilation of the missionized remnants of the chiefdoms that once inhabited the lakes and river valleys of interior Florida.

In a curious postscript to this tragic story, two maps drawn up by Juan Joseph Elixio de la Puente shortly after the evacuation of Florida hint that a few of Florida's native Timucuan Indians still lived in the remotest reaches of the Okefenokee Swamp, still known at that time as the Lake of Oconi. As stated in the key to one of these 1768 maps:

> In the said lake of Ocone there are also pearls, and on its island a town of Indians of the Timucuan nation, who were all Christians, and in the first year of the present century they lived as faithful vassals of the Spanish crown in the village of Salamototo, 8 leagues distant from St. Augustine, and with the motive of the siege that the English then placed, taking the city and burning the houses, the aforementioned Indians withdrew there, where (based on intelligence that the British forces forced the said St. Augustine to surrender, and remained in possession of it) they remained without any communication, and it is only known that they preserve the Catholic religion, because they conserve at their necks the rosaries of large beads that they wore, and they have been heard to pray in their language.[22]

The map's author went on to note that "it is very difficult to enter in the cited island, there being people to hinder [entrance] on part of it, because the shores of the lake that surrounds it are on both sides [*ambas margenes*], and for more than half a quarter league a terrible swamp." In part for this very reason, Spaniards seem never to have returned to the Okefenokee after the English conquest of the northern interior, undoubtedly fostering rumors of a hidden Timucuan town in the heart of the vast swamp.

While the mission town of Salamototo, inhabited by the remnants of Timucua and Mayaca Indians from the upper St. Johns River drainage, actually survived the 1702 Moore raid to be withdrawn and reestablished just north of St. Augustine, it might indeed be possible that a few fugitive *cimarrones* fled during that period to the haven of the old Oconi province in the remote reaches of the Okefenokee. Nevertheless, even if a band of Christian Timucuans somehow survived there in total isolation as the new English colony of Georgia emerged and grew along the Atlantic coast to their east, any surviving remnants would undoubtedly have either been replaced, or perhaps even assimilated, during the eighteenth century by immigrant aboriginal groups eventually known as Seminoles. If true, then at least one small remnant of the interior Timucuan bloodline might actually have survived the Spanish withdrawal from Florida, blending with other peoples originating far to the north. Regardless of these faint genetic traces, certainly in Cuba and possibly in Florida, the culture shared by the Timucuan chiefdoms of Florida's prehistoric interior ultimately became an early victim of the European colonial era. All that remains today of the chiefdoms examined in this volume are the historical accounts of their last decades in the Timucuan homeland and the physical remains of their communities beneath modern Florida soil.

APPENDIX A

Mission Locations

Introduction

This appendix provides locational information relative to all the principal documented seventeenth-century interior Timucuan mission and village sites discussed in the text, including those associated with specific and known archaeological sites and those yet to be discovered. These entries are divided into sections based on geographic location, including (1) sites on or immediately adjacent to the well-documented southern Camino Real of the postrebellion era; (2) sites located north of the Camino Real in the northern Yustaga region within the broader Timucua mission province; (3) sites located in the upper St. Johns River drainage (including the Agua Dulce and Acuera regions); and (4) sites located in and around the Okefenokee Swamp (Oconi/Ibihica).

Documentary evidence used to identify either a specific archaeological site or a location where one should exist includes data from contemporaneous descriptions of active missions (seventeenth century), as well as data from later descriptions or maps of the former sites of abandoned missions (primarily eighteenth century). Perhaps the most important source of information is a wide range of lists and documentary references to distances between active and former mission towns, and particularly so for the missions of the primary Camino Real through Timucua. Many of these lists were generated during seventeenth-century ecclesiastical or secular visitations of inhabited missions, or eighteenth-century travel across this same region, while others were reconstructed secondarily based on recollections or existing records in either Franciscan or governmental archives.[1] Although the precision and accuracy of reported distances varied considerably with individual judgment and memory, these lists form the primary documentary basis for reconstructing the locations of Florida missions. The key to making effective use of the many and varied mission lists available for the Timucua province, however, is using them all in concert to create a comprehensive portrait of relative stated distances between distinct sites of individual missions, some of which are known to have relocated at least once. As illustrated in the diagram in figure A.1, focusing on the missions of the Camino Real, comparative analysis demonstrates that such mission lists are collectively more instructive than they are individually.

Another important source of evidence regarding mission locations in the Florida interior is a limited number of hand-drawn maps detailing specific locations of missions or abandoned town sites ("old fields"), as well as other geographic names or features relating to the seventeenth-century mission period. For the interior Timucuan missions, these maps include the contemporaneous 1683 Alonso Solana map, which lacks detail but provides a rough overview of mission locations, and several important eighteenth-century maps drafted by both Spanish and English authors.[2] Spanish maps include two 1768 Florida maps by Juan Joseph Elixio de la Puente, displaying several important details regarding sites along the St. Johns River valley, and an anonymous Spanish land-grant map detailing the boundaries and owners of all the hereditary estates corresponding to seventeenth- and early eighteenth-century haciendas across eastern Florida, particularly along the St. Johns River.[3] Although thought to date to circa 1785, an English-language version of what was obviously this same map (or its source) was drawn by James Moncrief in 1764 from an original plan by John Gordons, suggesting that at least the information represented on the Spanish map actually derives from the circa 1764 period following the transfer of Spanish Florida to English control.[4] Indeed, the Spanish map contains much more detailed information than the Moncrief map, which therefore might actually be a copy of an undiscovered original Spanish map (circa 1760s) on which the circa 1785 Spanish manuscript is drawn (unless it actually dates to this earlier period). Another important English map is the extremely detailed 1778 map of the road between St. Augustine and Pensacola, commissioned by George Stuart and penned by Joseph Purcell (commonly known as the Stuart-Purcell map).[5] Additional eighteenth- and even nineteenth-century maps provide additional clues to these early sites and the roads connecting them.[6]

A few preliminary comments are necessary regarding one of the most important sources of evidence used in locating the interior Timucuan missions prior to the widespread destruction wrought in 1656 and afterward. The 1655 mission list provides the earliest comprehensive overview of the seventeenth-century missions of Spanish Florida. Outside of the 1616 Oré visitation record, it is the only systematic description of the Timucua mission province and the rest of the western interior prior to the 1656

MISSION SITE	DISTANCE	MISSION LISTS								
		Oré 1616	Díez 1655	Ranj. 1660	Díaz 1674	Palac. 1674	Flor. 1675	Riço 1681	M.yF. 1697	Peña 1716	Cast. 1740
San Diego de Salamototo	18-21 leagues				20	19	20	18	21	21	18
Santa Fé II	1.5-2 leagues				?					2	1.5
Santa Fé I	4-5 leagues		4		9	7	9	8		4	5
San Martín	2 leagues				?						
Santa Catalina	3 leagues				3	2					
Ajoica	2-3 leagues	8		18	2	3	5	4	22		12
Santa Cruz de Tarihica	5-6 leagues					3					
San Juan de Guacara I	2 leagues				7		8	7		2	2
San Juan de Guacara II	8-10 leagues				10		9	9		8	9
San Pedro I	1.5-4 leagues		4		2		1.5	2	5	2	2.5
Santa Elena de Machava I/San Pedro II	3.5-5 leagues				4		3.5	4		<5	4
San Matheo de Tolapatafi	1 league								<1		1
Santa Elena de Machava II	1 league				2		2.5	3		2	
San Miguel de Asile	1 league								1		1

Figure A-1. Comparative distances between missions on the Camino Real. Sources: Oré 1616 (Oré 1936); Díez 1655 (Díez de la Calle 1659); Ranjel 1660 (Ranjel 1660); Díaz 1674 (Díaz Vara Calderón 1675); Palacios 1674 (Palacios 1675); Florencia 1675 (Fernández de Florencia 1675); Riço 1681 (Riço 1681); Menéndez Márquez and Florencia 1697 (Menéndez Márquez and Florencia 1697; Peña 1616 (Peña 1617); Castilla 1740 (Castilla 1740).

rebellion (table A.1).⁷ This list was originally published in 1659 by royal secretary Juan Díez de la Calle, who served thirty-eight continuous years in Madrid as a secondary and later the principal official of the royal secretariat for the district of the viceroyalty of New Spain (including Florida), managing the voluminous correspondence with the Council of the Indies, the House of Trade, and the Junta de Guerra.⁸ This important official personally compiled an immense collection of transcripts and original documents extracted from the tremendous volume of correspondence that crossed his desk in Madrid. These collections and several books on Spanish colonial government that he published (including the 1659 volume) are still stored in the manuscript collections of the Biblioteca Nacionál in Madrid. Given these facts, then, the 1655 mission list in his 1659 book was certainly transcribed from an original manuscript report from Florida (as yet undiscovered) that he processed in the secretariat's office in Madrid. Furthermore, based on internal clues such as the order and internal groupings, as well as the stated cumulative distances of the missions in this list, the 1655 list was almost certainly derived from an actual visitation of all the missions of Florida in 1655.⁹ Given that the official gubernatorial visitations of the mission provinces were conducted in 1657 and 1658,¹⁰ this earlier visitation was most likely carried out by Fray Pedro Chacón, who was noted to be the official *comisario visitador* for Florida in April 1656, a temporary Franciscan office occasionally assigned for the purpose of conducting a formal visitation and review of each Franciscan province.¹¹

The ultimate consequence of this conclusion is that the distances stated in the 1655 list cannot be employed uncritically as simple straight-line measurements from St. Augustine (most of which would be quite inaccurate), but must be used in coordination with a variety of other sources of evidence to interpret the relative distances (subsequently summed) between missions along a precise visitation route. This route led north from St. Augustine as far as the Guale mission of San Diego de Satuache. It then crossed the western interior (presumably from San Pedro de Mocama) past the Okefenokee Swamp mission of Santiago de Ocone and then wound through the northernmost missions of the Yustaga region within the Timucua province to end up in Apalachee (figure A.2). The route then swung to the southeast, passing the southernmost missions of the eastern Timucua province (including Potano) to arrive at the Acuera province, from which the visitor descended the Oklawaha River to San Antonio de Enacape, visiting the more southerly Mayaca province upriver before finally descending the St. Johns River to Helaca and St. Augustine. Future research may eventually result in the discovery of the original document

Table A-1. Original order and spelling of all missions with missionaries listed on the 1655 list

Doctrinas	Stated distance (in leagues) from St. Augustine	Comments
St. Augustine, Florida (1st)	-	Chapter convent
Nombre de Dios (2nd)	1/4	
Nuestra Señora de Guadalupe (3rd)	3	
San Juan del Puerto (4th)	12	On the seacoast
San Pedro de Mocamo (5th)	20	
San Buena de Boadalquibi (6th)	32	
Santo Domingo de Talege (7th)	40	
San Joseph de Zapala (8th)	45	
San Phelipe (9th)	54	
Santa Cathalina de Guale (10th)	50	Principal Guale town
Chatuache (11th)	60	Last on northern coast
Santiago de Ocone (12th)	30	On an island
Santa Cruz de Tarica	54	
San Agustín de Urica	60	
Santa María de los Angeles de Arapaja	70	
Santa Cruz de Cachipile	70	
San Yldefonso de Chamini	70	
San Francisco de Chuaquin	60	
San Pedro y San Pablo de Potuhiriba	60	
Santa Elena de Machaba	64	
San Miguel de Asile	75	
San Lorenzo de Apalache	75	2,500 *doctrina* Indians
San Francisco de Apalache	77	
La Concepción de Apalache	77	
San Joseph de Apalache	84	
San Juan de Apalache	86	
San Pedro y San Pablo de Apalache	87	
San Cosme y San Damián de Apalache	90	
San Luís de Apalache	88	
San Martín de Apalache	87	
San Martín de Ayaocuto	34	
Santa Fé de Toloco	30	
San Francisco de Patano	25	
San Luís de la provincia de Acuera	32	To the south
Santa Lucia de Acuera	34	
San Antonio de Nacape	20	
San Salbador de Mayaca	36	
San Diego de Laca	7	

Source: Díez de la Calle (1659).

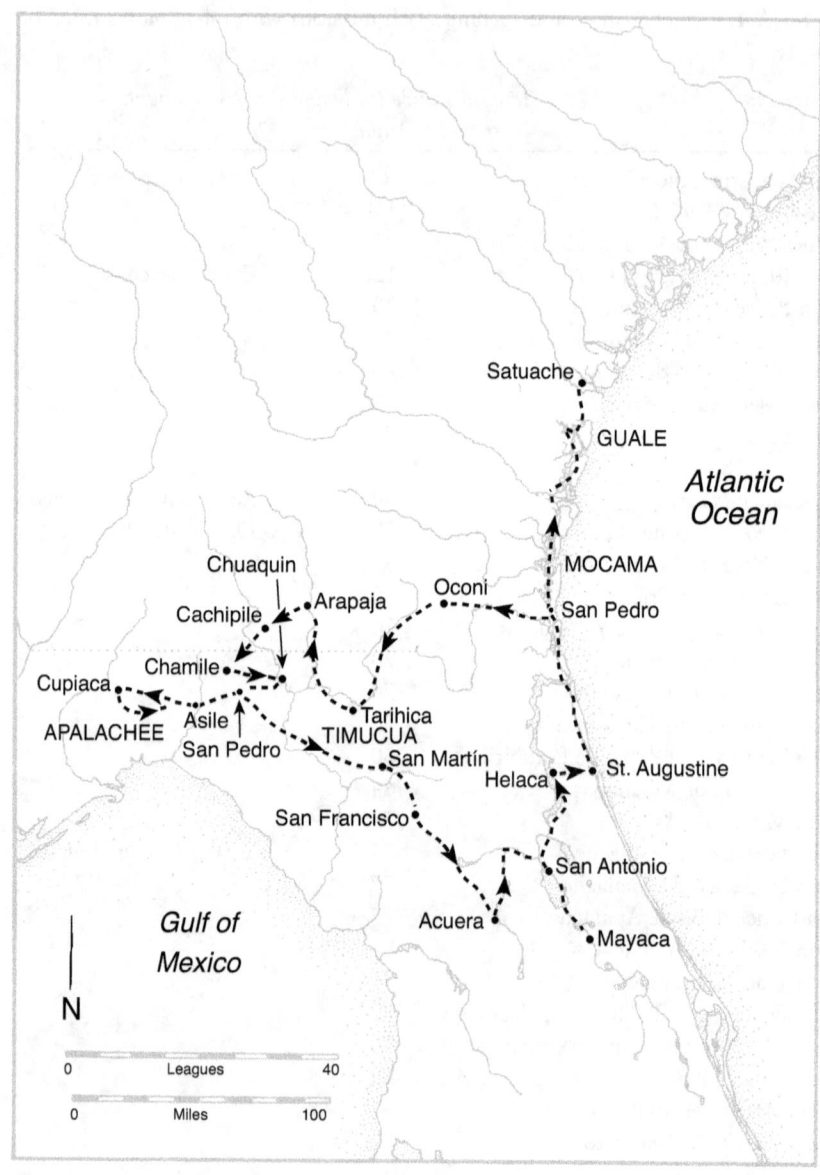

Figure A-2. Reconstructed route of the 1655 Florida mission visitation. Selected missions shown.

(or transcript) used by Juan Díez de la Calle in compiling this list for his book.

Missions of the Camino Real

Tocoy (1587–circa 1610s)

The early mission of Tocoy was certainly located at or near the modern community of the same name (Tocoi) on the east bank of the St. Johns River west of St. Augustine.[12] Despite the early disappearance of this mission, the persistence of its name until the present day is undoubtedly due to the establishment here of a Spanish hacienda by the same name during the seventeenth century. Late eighteenth century land-grant maps clearly show that the Tocoy hacienda was immediately south of the Picolata hacienda along the middle St. Johns River almost due west of St. Augustine. This placement additionally conforms to the five-league distance between St. Augustine and Tocoy recorded during the 1606 visitation of Bishop Juan de las Cavezas Altamirano.[13] The town of Tocoy vanished at some point during the decade between 1606 and 1616, when a second visitation by Fray Luís Gerónimo de Oré failed to note any town in this same vicinity.[14] That neither of the subsequent middle–St. Johns River missions (Helaca or Salamototo) was located on the original site of Tocoy is strongly indicated by the persistence of its name throughout this period.

San Diego de Helaca (circa 1624–1657)

This mission town, apparently artificially established by Governor Luís de Rojas y Borja using upper St. Johns River populations, was located on the east bank of the St. Johns River directly across from the known site called Pupo, where an eighteenth-century Spanish fortification was later placed.[15] One possible site for Helaca is thus the location later known as Piquilaco during the late seventeenth century (where a Spanish hacienda was established), and as Picolata during the eighteenth century (where yet another eighteenth-century fort was placed as a companion to Pupo).[16] If Helaca was not identical with the later site of Picolata, however, the most likely location for Helaca would be the point of land just north of Picolata and southwest of the modern community of Palmo. The 1655 mission list placed Helaca seven leagues from St. Augustine, corresponding to its somewhat more northerly and westerly location in comparison to Tocoy and the consequent increase in travel distance from the city.[17] In addition, in 1678 the site of "Geraca" (Helaca) was said to be within the local administrative jurisdiction of Helaca's successor San Diego de Salamototo, now recognized to have been located just two to three leagues even farther to the north, possibly supporting Helaca's more northerly location.

San Diego de Salamototo (circa 1657–1706)

This mission site was first established at the direction of Governor Diego de Rebolledo as a part of his planned restructure of the Timucua mission province and realignment of the Camino Real following the Timucuan rebellion of 1656. Probably representing the relocated mission San Diego de Helaca, which effectively vanished from the documentary record after Rebolledo's term, Salamototo became the new primary crossing of the St. Johns River between St. Augustine and the western interior. Salamototo was located on the east bank of the St. Johns River, apparently opposite the modern town of Green Cove Springs just northwest of Orangedale. Despite previous suggestions that Salamototo was located much farther to the south at the Rollestown site (8Pu64b) near Palatka (possibly the site of Antonico), several lines of evidence point to a much more northerly location.[18] Conclusive proof appears on at least two late-eighteenth-century Spanish maps, including the circa 1785 map detailing eastern Florida land holdings along the St. Johns River, which shows the name "Salamototo" situated at the mouth of a small creek well north of the site of Picolata, and within the tract of land entitled "royal lands [*realengo*] of the town of Salamototo." Using the map for locations of creeks known as "Bilia" (Trout Creek) and "Nicoloa" (Sixmile Creek) just south of Salamototo, and the mouth of the "Río Blanco" (literally "White River," but now called Black Creek) across the St. Johns to the north, it is possible to fix the location of mission San Diego de Salamototo at or near the community of Orangedale in St. Johns county. This precise location is additionally confirmed by a 1768 map by Joseph Elixio de la Puente, showing "Salamototo" on a sharp bend in the St. Johns River just north of the "R[ío] Nicoloa," which is itself situated just north of "Picalata," all three on the eastern bank of the river west of St. Augustine.[19]

Santa Rosa de Ivitanayo (circa 1682–94)

Santa Rosa de Ivitanayo was a short-lived mission intentionally established at a point roughly equidistant between the St. Johns River crossing at Salamototo and missions Santa Fé and San Francisco. Its location is almost certainly at or near the Blue Bead or Baldtree archaeological sites southeast of Hall Lake in southern Clay County, Florida.[20] Both of these sites have produced seventeenth-century Spanish and aboriginal artifacts and both are located immediately adjacent to the apparent course of the Camino Real. Furthermore, the "town of Vitanayo" is shown on the late-eighteenth-century Spanish land-grant map just south of a cluster of small lakes, the nearest of which (Hall Lake?) was called Lake of Vitanayo. The town is also indicated to be northeast of another lake—larger and elongated—shown on the map called "Challofare," probably corresponding to the ancestral Lake Grandin near the sixteenth-century town of Outina (also in this area).

San Francisco de Potano (1606–1705)

The site of this long-lived mission was most likely at the mission-period Fox Pond archaeological site (8Al272) northwest of present-day Gainesville in the area known as San Felasco hammock, certainly a corruption of San Francisco.[21] This location is consistent with stated distances of some twenty-five leagues from St. Augustine, three leagues from the La Chua hacienda at the Alachua sink, five leagues from Santa Fé I, and three to four leagues from Santa Fé II.[22] The principal town within the early-seventeenth-century remnants of the Potano chiefdom, San Francisco was originally only one of three *doctrinas* established in the local vicinity of Fox Pond, including Santa Ana and San Miguel one and one and one-half leagues distant, respectively.[23] The apparent one-league distance of Santa Ana from San Francisco at Fox Pond, and its probable location on a lake northwest of the La Chua hacienda that bore the name "Laguna de Santa Ana" well into the late eighteenth century,[24] makes it possible that Santa Ana was identical with the Moon Lake site (8Al327) south of Fox Pond.[25] Yet another outlying Potano satellite community at the Richardson site (8Al100) on Orange Lake ultimately became the *doctrina* of San Buenaventura, probably also known as Apalo.[26] Only the subordinate community at Santa Ana survived the first quarter of the seventeenth century, although it was ultimately fused with San Francisco about 1673. The remaining inhabitants of mission San Francisco may have relocated to an unidentified site half a league to the south after 1694 in consequence of soil exhaustion.[27] As the last surviving interior Timucuan mission west of the St. Johns River, mission San Francisco was finally abandoned in the spring of 1706 as a result of repeated English raids.

Santa Fé II, or Santo Thomás de Santa Fé (circa 1657–1703)

The Santa Fé de Teleco mission was evidently relocated from its original location at the Shealy site following the Timucuan rebellion of 1656, coinciding with the 1657 resettlement of Santa Fé by the cacique and inhabitants of the northern Arapaja mission and the concurrent political subordination of mission San Francisco de Potano within Santa Fé's local administrative jurisdiction. In his 1740 relation, Francisco de Castilla located the "new *ycapacha* [abandoned town]" of Santa Fé some one and a half leagues eastward from Santa Fé's "old *ycapacha*."[28] Camping at the site of Santa Fé II in 1716, Diego Peña confirmed Castilla's 1740 placement of this site exactly four leagues west of the lake of Amaca (Sunshine Lake) and furthermore noted that Santa Fé II was just two leagues from the trail's intersection with the river of Santa Fé (probably at the river sink).[29] Peña strayed from the main road past Santa Fé II, however (perhaps accidentally heading northwest toward Santa Fé I), covering three leagues instead of the normal two leagues from Santa Fé II directly to the river sink. Based on these distances, the undiscovered site of Santa Fé II was evidently located roughly in the vicinity of the modern-day community of Santa Fe, probably some two or three miles to the northwest on high ground adjacent to one of the small lakes or creeks in this area. The distance and direction of this relocation would also appear to be confirmed by a simultaneous decrease in the stated distance between missions Santa Fé and San Francisco (from five leagues to some three or four leagues). Apparently assimilating populations from the nearby missions of Santa Cruz and Santa Catalina in 1691, mission Santa Fé was itself aggregated to San Francisco to the south late in 1703.

Santa Fé de Teleco, or Santa Fé I (circa 1609–57)

The original site of mission Santa Fé de Teleco has been established through archaeological investigation to be at the Shealy archaeological site (8Al190) immediately west of the cluster of sinkhole lakes called Robinson Sinks near the present-day Santa Fe River, where early seventeenth-century Spanish and aboriginal artifacts are associated with the remnants of mission structures.[30] This location is consistent with the cited four-to-five-league distance between missions Santa Fé I and San Martín at the Fig Springs site to the northwest, and with the five-league distance to mission San Francisco de Potano prior to the 1656 rebellion.[31] Archaeological evidence confirms the abandonment of the original site of Santa Fé at the Shealy site during this period, indicated by historical documentation to have occurred during the closing years of Governor Rebolledo's term, when mission Santa Fé was repopulated by the inhabitants of the Arapaja mission from northern Yustaga.[32]

San Martín de Ayacutu (1608–circa late 1660s)

This important early mission was certainly located at the Fig Springs archaeological site (8Co1) on the east bank of the spring-fed Ichetucknee River. Extensive archaeological investigations at this site have confirmed the existence of both an extensive late prehistoric village and an early seventeenth-century mission compound.[33] The mission was said to be located some thirty-four leagues from St. Augustine in the 1655 list, and was thus four leagues distant from Santa Fé I and a total of nine leagues from San

Francisco de Potano.[34] In 1716 Diego Peña located the *ycapacha* of San Martín four leagues from his camp near the Santa Fe River sink, which itself was two leagues beyond the abandoned site of Santa Fé II.[35] Francisco de Castilla placed San Martín five leagues distant from the first *ycapacha* of Santa Fé (Santa Fé I, about a league northeast from the river sink). He additionally noted that San Martín had "lovely waters," corresponding to the location of the Fig Springs site along the clear, spring-fed waters of the present-day Ichetucknee River.[36] This important mission was repopulated by the inhabitants of Chamile from the northern Yustaga province after the 1656 Timucuan rebellion, but it was apparently abandoned during the mid-1660s following the arrest and long-term imprisonment of chief Lazaro after 1664. Its inhabitants may have relocated to form the new mission of Santa Catalina.

Santa Catalina (circa late 1660s–1691)

The location of this short-lived mission town has yet to be discovered, but detailed reanalysis of available documentary evidence indicates that it was approximately two to two and a half leagues distant from mission San Martín at the Fig Springs site along the postrebellion Camino Real. Established using unknown populations during the 1660s, Santa Catalina's proximity to San Martín and the fact that it appeared at about the same time as San Martín's abandonment suggests that it may have been the successor of that mission, the remaining inhabitants of which may have relocated from the original site at Fig Springs to a new more westerly location after the arrest of Chamile's cacique Lazaro. The earliest locational references to Santa Catalina occur during the mid-1670s, when the fall 1674 visitation of Bishop Gabriel Díaz Vara Calderón generated two detailed mission lists followed by another penned by Apalachee Lieutenant Juan Fernández de Florencia in the summer of 1675.[37] These three lists in combination with contextual evidence from later descriptions of this same region provide documentary evidence sufficient to project two probable locations for Santa Catalina.

During the 1674–75 period, Santa Catalina was situated between two occupied towns along the Camino Real—mission Santa Fé II to the east and San Agustín de Ajoica to the west. The more detailed lists of both Pedro de Palacios and Juan Fernández de Florencia agree that Santa Catalina was some nine leagues west of Santa Fé by road, providing support for dismissing visiting Bishop Díaz Vara Calderón's figure of twelve leagues (probably erroneously including the three-league travel distance from Santa Fé II to its off-road neighbor San Francisco). Given that mission Santa Fé was then located at its postrebellion site (Santa Fé II), known from the

1740 Castilla description to have been some one and a half leagues east of the original site of Santa Fé, it seems safe to conclude that Santa Catalina was situated roughly seven and a half leagues west of Santa Fé I.[38] Furthermore, both the 1655 Díez de la Calle list and the 1740 Castilla list place mission San Martín some four to five leagues west of Santa Fé I.[39] Using the more reliably accurate figure provided by Francisco de Castilla, we may subtract five leagues from the seven-and-a-half-league figure to arrive at a distance of just over two leagues between San Martín and Santa Catalina.

Now, given that San Martín was located at the Fig Springs site just below the headwaters of the Ichetucknee River, that Santa Fé I was located at the Shealy site just over five leagues to the east, and that Santa Fé II was thus located one and a half leagues east of that location, it would be expected that the bishop's 1674 visitation trek would have taken him just under seven leagues from Santa Fé II to the headwaters of the Ichetucknee River (near the then-abandoned site of San Martín), following the road across the old site of Santa Fé I to cross the Santa Fe River's land bridge and bearing northwest toward the headsprings of the Ichetucknee River. From there, just over two leagues would have brought the party to mission Santa Catalina. In fact, Pedro de Palacios's record of the bishop's visitation provides sound confirmation for this reconstruction of the route, for after departing Santa Fé on the morning of Wednesday, November 1, Palacios noted seven leagues of travel before the bishop's party camped for the night on the banks of a creek (*arroyo*). The following Thursday morning, the group traveled another two leagues beyond the creek to arrive at Santa Catalina for a siesta prior to traveling another three leagues farther on to Ajoica. The Ichetucknee River is in fact the one and only stream situated in the vicinity of seven leagues west of Santa Fé II by road, Thus, it must have been the arroyo mentioned by Palacios. Since mission San Martín had evidently been abandoned for perhaps ten years by this time, its location (like that of other abandoned missions along the Bishop's route) was not mentioned in his account.

The above discussion demonstrates the reasoning behind the conclusion that mission Santa Catalina was located between two and two and a half leagues by road west of San Martín at the Fig Springs site. Based on localized environmental conditions in this area, Santa Catalina is suspected to have been situated in one of two specific localities: (1) on the west bank of the Ichetucknee River at or very near its junction with the Santa Fé River, or (2) on one of the sinkhole lakes in the inter-riverine forest west of the Ichetucknee headsprings. In the former case, Santa Catalina would probably have been situated in roughly the same site indicated to be Weechatookamee Village (from which the name Ichetucknee derives) on the 1778

Purcell map.⁴⁰ In the latter case, Santa Catalina would have been situated somewhere in the northwest-to-southeast trending line of hills and sinkhole lakes west of the Ichetucknee River, in the area just north and south of a point roughly two miles east of the present-day community of Beachville. The Purcell map, in fact, shows a cluster of "remarkable rocky sprin[g]s 20 and 30 feet deep" in precisely this vicinity. The land in between both of these two localities seems unlikely for the site of a mission, comprising sandy pine barrens without substantial water sources.

The key to Santa Catalina's location (as well as that of its western neighbors San Agustín de Ajoica and Santa Cruz II) lies in the route of the postrebellion Camino Real and any spur trails leading to nearby mission towns between the Ichetucknee and Suwannee Rivers. Using the fixed locations discussed above (principally San Martín at Fig Springs and Santa Fé I at Shealy), postrebellion mission lists confirm that the straight-line distance between Fig Springs and the original Baptizing Spring location of San Juan de Guacara (San Juan I) is something on the order of nine leagues (supported by Luís Gerónimo de Oré's 1616 description of just eight leagues between San Martín and San Juan). The actual travel distance between these two sites on the late seventeenth-century Camino Real was closer to twelve to thirteen leagues (see fig. A.1). The former was the distance cited in 1740 by Francisco de Castilla, who additionally located a second abandoned mission site at the Suwannee River crossing (San Juan II based on other evidence) some two leagues west of San Juan I.⁴¹ In 1674, Bishop Díaz Vara Calderón apparently traveled a total of fourteen to fifteen leagues on his visitation route between the headwaters of the Ichetucknee River (at or near Fig Springs) and San Juan II (using both the bishop's list and the Palacios diary), confirming Castilla's fourteen-league travel distance between San Martín and San Juan II.⁴² Additionally, Capt. Juan Fernández de Florencia's thirteen-league distance between Santa Catalina and San Juan II backs up the bishop's secretary's fourteen- to fifteen-league calculation to the Ichetucknee's headsprings some two leagues beyond Santa Catalina.⁴³

Given, therefore, that the postrebellion Camino Real traversed some twelve to thirteen leagues between sites known to have been only nine leagues apart in straight-line distance, three possibilities exist: (1) the Camino Real swung well northward into the inter-riverine (and largely waterless) forest south of present-day Live Oak, Florida; (2) the road swung southward, closely following the main river corridor of the Ichetucknee, Santa Fe, and Suwannee Rivers; or (3) the road followed a somewhat indirect route between individual missions located both along and away from the Suwannee River and its tributaries. At present, none of these three alternatives can be definitively ruled out, although the latter two seem more likely than the first, if only for environmental reasons. Supporting the riverbank route, however, is the fact that a trail following the rivers as noted above would today traverse precisely between twelve and thirteen old Spanish leagues from the Fig Springs site to the Baptizing Spring site. If this were the case, the postrebellion Camino Real might have roughly followed the northern banks of the Ichetucknee/Santa Fe/Suwannee Rivers, winding southwest and then northwest before finally arriving at the Suwannee River crossing at Charles Ferry. Mission Santa Catalina would in this reconstruction be located at the mouth of the Ichetucknee River as proposed above. The remaining missions to the west would have been situated at other sites along the Suwannee River itself. If, however, Santa Catalina was located due west of Fig Springs in the uplands, the Camino Real might have subsequently turned southwest toward Ajoica on the Suwannee River, once again following its course upriver to Charles Ferry. Alternatively, the road might even have continued across the uplands north of the Suwannee, although appropriate sites for Ajoica and Santa Cruz II are largely lacking at the appropriate distances northeast of Baptizing Spring. Moreover, available evidence strongly suggests that Santa Cruz II was situated on the Suwannee River at or near Little River Springs, restricting possible alternatives for Ajoica and Santa Catalina.

A final clue was provided by Francisco de Castilla in his 1740 relation, where he specifically noted that both Santa Catalina (and presumably its aggregated neighbor Ajoica) and Santa Cruz were situated off to one or both sides of the primary Camino Real itself.[44] If we presume that the Camino Real at that time ran roughly parallel to the rivers, then it may have just bypassed the actual sites of these then-abandoned missions. Indeed, the fact that the bishop's 1674 route may have been as much as fifteen leagues between San Martín and San Juan II, described by Castilla as only fourteen leagues apart, might imply that the towns of Santa Catalina, Ajoica, and Santa Cruz II were just off the main road, perhaps following short side trails toward the riverbank or some other locale.[45] Nevertheless, until at least one of these late seventeenth-century mission sites is identified on the ground, any projections must be considered tentative. Based on all available evidence, however, the two localities described above seem to be the most likely for Santa Catalina. This mission, which was joined by aggregated populations from nearby Ajoica perhaps in the first half of 1675, seems to have been abandoned in the winter of 1690–91 as a result of disputes with resident friar Pedro de la Lastra.

San Agustín de Ajoica (circa 1657–75)

This apparently relocated mission town seems to have been the successor to San Agustín de Urihica, apparently also known as Niahica, which was moved far to the south of its original location following the Timucuan rebellion. Given its situation between two as yet undiscovered mission sites, however, the location of the short-lived community of Ajoica is extremely difficult to interpret. Documentary evidence from the 1674 visitation of Bishop Díaz Vara Calderón fixes Ajoica three leagues by road from mission Santa Catalina to the east, and between two and three leagues from the site of Santa Cruz II.[46] The route of the Camino Real in this area is unclear. Presuming, however, that Santa Cruz II was indeed located near Little River Springs, then Ajoica must have been located somewhere in an arc two to three leagues to the northeast, east, or southeast of that site. If Santa Catalina was located at the mouth of the Ichetucknee River, a three-league distance from this site would place Ajoica along the Suwannee River perhaps two to three miles south of Branford or somewhere in the uplands perhaps two miles north of Beachville. On the other hand, if Santa Catalina was located in the uplands east of Beachville, Ajoica might be located far to the north in the pine barrens several miles northwest of O'Brien, Florida, or might once again be located along the Suwannee south of Branford. Unfortunately, until Santa Catalina is located, no further precision is possible. Even then, however, the abandonment of this small community and its aggregation to Santa Catalina in 1675 suggests that archaeological deposits would be quite thin and thus quite difficult to discover.

Santa Cruz de Tarihica II (circa 1657–91)

This mission was evidently relocated from its original location at the Indian Pond archaeological site during the geographic transformation of Timucua administered by Governor Diego de Rebolledo following the 1656 rebellion. Using evidence from the two mission lists based on the 1674 visitation of Bishop Gabriel Díaz Vara Calderón as well as the 1675 list of Juan Fernández de Florencia, Santa Cruz II was situated two to three leagues west of the short-lived town of San Agustín de Ajoica and thus five to six leagues west of mission Santa Catalina by road.[47] At the same time, this mission was said to be seven to eight leagues east of San Juan II and thus five to six leagues east of San Juan I at the Baptizing Spring site. Presuming that the late seventeenth-century Camino Real ran roughly parallel to the Suwannee River itself in this vicinity (regardless of its course eastward to the Ichetucknee), the undiscovered site of this relocated mission town is strongly suspected to have been on the north bank of the Suwannee River, probably at or near Little River Springs some three miles northwest of present-day Branford, Florida.

The original southern branch of the prerebellion Camino Real followed just this same route between this location and Baptizing Spring. This conclusion is supported by the fact that the independent routes of the Timucuan rebellion-era Indians Juan Alejo and Antonio and the eighteenth-century Spaniard Diego Peña between San Martín and the river San Juan both crossed the spot called Calacala, apparently located near Royal Springs (upriver from Little River Springs), where the trail ran westward within sight of the Suwannee River for a short distance.[48] Furthermore, the 1778 Purcell map indicates that the primary trail running west between the headwaters of the Ichetucknee River and the Santa Fé I "old fields" first intersected the Suwannee River precisely in the vicinity of Little River Springs, correctly stated to be equidistant between these points, both of which were said to be eleven and a half miles distant.[49] Interestingly, from exactly this point a secondary trail ran southeast to Weechatookamee Village at the mouth of the Ichetucknee River, one of the possible locations for mission Santa Catalina. Like Santa Catalina, however, Santa Cruz II was eventually abandoned and aggregated to Santa Fé II in 1691.

San Juan de Guacara I (circa 1609–57)

This early mission was certainly located at the Baptizing Spring archaeological site (8Su65), where excavations have revealed the remains of an early seventeenth-century mission there.[50] Both Diego Peña and Francisco de Castilla made specific note of the abandoned site of San Juan two leagues east of the Suwannee River crossing at Charles Spring (San Juan II). Peña specifically noted that this was the "first *ycapacha*" of San Juan.[51] The 1778 Purcell map also noted the coincidence of a "cold spring" with an "old field" in a location just north of the river's course some six miles (just over two leagues) east from the "old field" at the Charles Spring crossing.[52] These comparatively clear indications are likewise supported by the eight-league direct distance between missions San Martín and San Juan de Guacara posited by Fray Luís Gerónimo de Oré during his 1616 visitation.[53] San Juan was moved two leagues to the west in the post-1656 transformations administered by Governor Diego de Rebolledo, and may also have been revitalized at that time using Timucuan populations from other areas.

San Juan de Guacara II (circa 1657–91)

The early mission of San Juan de Guacara was moved from its original location at Baptizing Spring some two leagues west to a site on the eastern bank of the modern Suwannee River at Charles Spring, where limited archaeological testing has confirmed the presence of seventeenth-century mission deposits there and just downriver (sites 8Su23 and 8Su67).[54] This relocation, probably taking place soon after the 1656 rebellion, was clearly intended to populate the point where the Camino Real crossed the river of San Juan de Guacara (the Suwannee), facilitating easy passage by canoe. This supposition is supported by statements from the 1670s in which not only was San Juan described as being situated on the banks of the river at its canoe crossing but also subjected to desertions by Indians, due to the "great amount of work they do in carrying the travellers."[55] The site of San Juan II was typically said to be located nine leagues by road from mission San Pedro I to the west (ranging from eight to ten leagues), and was noted to be seven to eight leagues west of Santa Cruz II.[56] Moreover, both Diego Peña and Francisco de Castilla noted an *ycapacha,* or abandoned town, at this location, said to be two leagues west of San Juan I. The Purcell map located an "old field" here as well.[57] San Juan II survived until August 30, 1691, when it was attacked and destroyed by Apalachicola Indians.

San Pedro I (circa 1623–91)

This mission was certainly located at site 8Md30 on the hill overlooking Sampala Lake to the northeast, where archaeological testing has revealed the presence of seventeenth-century Spanish and aboriginal artifacts, mission structures, and burials.[58] This conclusion is supported not only by the modern name Sampala (a corruption of San Pablo, from San Pedro y San Pablo) adjacent to San Pedro Bay, but also by a specific reference to the "Ruins of St. Pedro Fort" on the western side of this lake in the 1778 Purcell map.[59] As can be seen in figure A.1, a variety of late seventeenth-century mission lists and eighteenth-century descriptions place San Pedro I approximately nine leagues (ranging between eight and ten leagues) west of San Juan II along the primary southern Camino Real, and between one and a half and two and a half leagues east of Santa Elena I.[60] Following the establishment of a mission here after 1623, San Pedro remained in its original location until the early 1690s, when it was apparently relocated to the old site of Santa Elena de Machava after that mission was moved westward in the face of increasing raids by English-allied Indians. That San Pedro I was abandoned at that time and relocated to the site of Santa Elena I between 1689 and 1694 is indicated by a variety of lines of evidence, including not only the 1740 Castilla relation detailing the relative positions of the "old" and "new" *ycapachas* of San Pedro, but also the switch in the relative order of missions between these dates and the mention of an "old" site of San Pedro in the 1695 criminal proceedings against one of San Pedro's natives.[61]

Santa Elena de Machava I (circa 1620s–1691) / San Pedro II (circa 1691–1704)

The as yet undiscovered site of this important Yustagan mission was probably located on one of the hills along the course of the Camino Real some two leagues west of San Pedro I at Lake Sampala. The most likely site is the prominent hilltop approximately two miles west-northwest of present-day Moseley Hall, or on the neighboring isolated hill just to the west, where Santa Elena would have been located perhaps just north of the primary road. Santa Elena I was noted to be some one and a half to two leagues west of San Pedro I and three and a half to four leagues east of mission San Matheo in mission lists dating to 1675 and 1681.[62] The description of the "remains of a bridge and causeway" some four and a half miles (just under two Spanish leagues) west of San Pedro I on the 1778 Purcell map may suggest Spanish road improvements in the immediate vicinity of this mission site.[63] Comparative distances on the 1655 list suggest that Santa Elena was as much as four leagues west of San Pedro (sixty-four leagues as opposed to San Pedro's sixty leagues), but the subsequent placement of San Miguel de Asile at seventy-five leagues (eleven leagues from Santa Elena, and thus clearly too far) suggests that the list's author used estimated distances from St. Augustine (perhaps provided by resident friars) for the individual missions along this section of the 1655 visitation route.[64]

The relocation of Santa Elena to a site far to the west between 1689 and 1694 is confirmed by the abrupt appearance of mission Santa Elena between Asile and San Matheo in lists dating to the mid-to late 1690s, and by the 1740 description of an abandoned site for Santa Elena in precisely this vicinity.[65] The relocation of mission San Pedro to the then-abandoned site of Santa Elena I during this same time period is furthermore indicated by two early eighteenth-century Spanish accounts, which make note of a second site named San Pedro two to two and a half leagues west of San Pedro I (called the "woods" of San Pedro by Diego Peña and the "new *ycapacha*" of San Pedro by Francisco de Castilla), conforming to the earlier position of mission Santa Elena with respect to San Pedro.[66] The continued residence of Timucua's provincial lieutenant at this particular site after the departure of Santa Elena's inhabitants and the arrival of those from San Pedro is confirmed in the 1698 visitation of San Pedro II.[67] Mission San

Pedro evidently remained in this new location until its destruction in the summer of 1704 by English-allied Indians.

San Matheo de Tolapatafi (circa 1657–1704)

The precise location of this postrebellion mission convent, as well as its nearby neighbors San Miguel de Asile and Santa Elena II, remains somewhat difficult to sort out. Prior to the relocation of Santa Elena in the early 1690s, San Matheo was consistently stated to be some three and a half to four leagues west of Santa Elena de Machava (Santa Elena I), and two to three leagues east of Asile, which itself was some two leagues east of the first Apalachee mission of San Lorenzo de Ivitachuco.[68] Sometime around 1691, however, mission Santa Elena was apparently relocated far to the west of its original location and was placed at a point in between Asile and San Matheo along a standard visitation route. The only surviving distance measure for the location of Santa Elena II places it one league distant from mission Asile and less than a league from San Matheo in 1697, although these distances may have been underestimated.[69]

Using the predicted location of Santa Elena I described above and the presumed archaeological site of Ivitachuco (8Je100) just east of Lake Iamonia in Jefferson County,[70] the actual distance between these two sites along the probable path of the Camino Real is perhaps sixteen miles, converting to just more than six leagues at about two and one-sixth miles per league. Stated documentary distances between these sites sum to a total of eight leagues, however, suggesting that the road was not entirely straight or that distance estimates were individually skewed an average of 25 percent from actual distances (both of which may have been true). Between Ivitachuco and Santa Elena I there are two known archaeological sites with clear evidence for seventeenth-century mission period occupation. One, the Beatty site (8Md5), is located on a prominent hill east of the Aucilla River some nine miles (or about three and a half leagues) west of the probable location of Santa Elena I. The second (8Je106) is situated four miles (one and a half leagues) farther to the west on the western side of the Aucilla River. This latter site, which produced evidence for densely packed Christian Indian burials and a Spanish-style structure floor, is itself just over three miles (between one and one and a half leagues) east of Ivitachuco. Both intermediate sites have been proposed as possible candidates for the town of Asile.[71]

The recently discovered Castilla relation of 1740 provides important supplementary details regarding the relative placement of missions San Matheo and Asile, as well as their later neighbor Santa Elena II. Castilla traced the Camino Real from Ivitachuco eastward to the Asile (Aucilla) River, where he asserted that the Asile mission had been located on the bank (apparently on the western side) of the river itself, some three leagues distant from Ivitachuco.[72] Although Castilla may have been slightly in error regarding the precise placement of mission San Miguel de Asile on the riverbank, his distance measurements generally correspond to most earlier estimates. Following the ridge of clayey hills running east-southeast from the site of Ivitachuco, the riverbank is indeed located about a league farther east from 8Je106 (probably mission Asile), corresponding to Castilla's three-league estimate as opposed to the standard two-league stated distance between the Ivitachuco and Asile missions. From the Aucilla River, however, the reconstruction becomes somewhat more complicated.

Castilla asserted that the site of "Machaba" (presumably Santa Elena II) was located one league from the riverbank along the primary Camino Real, and that San Pedro II (Santa Elena I) was another four leagues to the east. Furthermore, he placed the site of mission San Matheo one league from "Machaba" on what seems to have been at that time a spur trail leading to the west across clayey lands. Based on these stated distances and directions, the Castilla account would tend to identify the Beatty site roughly a league east of the Aucilla River as the location of his "Machaba" (Santa Elena II), with San Matheo falling roughly a league to the northwest. San Matheo would thus have been located on one of two prominent, isolated hills located one and two miles east of the Aucilla River just south of present-day Lamont, Florida. This placement, indeed, would seem to fit the relative locations of missions identified on the 1697 list noted above. If the league distances stated on this 1697 list are somewhat underestimated in comparison to those of Francisco de Castilla (who additionally seems to have placed Asile too far east at the riverbank), then it is possible to place mission Asile in 1697 at site 8Je106, following the road east-southeast to the river crossing and on to Santa Elena II at the Beatty site roughly four miles distant (one and a half leagues at two and one-sixth miles per league), turning northwestward to the unidentified location of mission San Matheo perhaps two or three miles distant (about a league), before proceeding eastward either through Santa Elena II or bypassing it to the north and eventually arriving at San Pedro II some leagues away.

Two alternative solutions are presented here as possibilities, although neither seems likely. First, Francisco de Castilla might have confounded Santa Elena II ("Machaba") with San Matheo, making the substantial Beatty site San Matheo instead, and making the other undiscovered location Santa Elena II. This possibility might be confirmed were evidence to be found for only very minimal occupation dating to the period between 1691 and 1704 at the undiscovered site northwest of Beatty, and by long-term occupation (beginning in 1657 or even earlier) at Beatty itself. Even if this were found to be the case, however, Castilla might possibly have been correct if San Matheo had also been relocated at the same time as Santa Elena and San Pedro (circa 1691), with the immigrant residents of Santa Elena I actually taking up residence at the then-abandoned site of San Matheo (the Beatty site). This unlikely possibility would mean that San Matheo I became Santa Elena II and a previously undocumented San Matheo II was situated to its northwest. Unfortunately, archaeological evidence for such late and short-lived relocations may be impossible to extract, given that each and every one of these late sites may have been early *visitas,* or satellite communities, of the pre-1656 local chiefdom of Asile.

Nevertheless, based primarily on the verbatim text of the 1740 Castilla account, used in concert with other evidence from earlier mission lists and other documentary accounts, the placement of San Matheo one league northwest of the Beatty site, and the simultaneous identification of sites 8Je106 with Asile and 8Md5 (Beatty) with Santa Elena II, seems to represent the best-fit solution within the context of current archaeological knowledge. Future research should incorporate a broad-scale survey in this region in order to locate the one missing primary mission site (two of the three appear to have been discovered), as well as any outlying satellite communities in the immediate vicinity. San Matheo in particular should be at the center of a considerable cluster of small mission-period sites. Given current data, however, the undiscovered site of San Matheo itself seems most likely to be located on one of the hills described above, southeast of Lamont. Occupation at this site extended to 1704, when the mission was destroyed along with all of its neighbors.

Santa Elena de Machava II (circa 1691–1704)

As discussed above, based on existing documentary and archaeological evidence, the most likely location for this short-lived mission town is the Beatty site (8Md5), on a hilltop east of the Aucilla River. Although the proximity of this site to both San Matheo and Asile would tend to suggest that it was probably occupied prior to the establishment of Santa Elena II (perhaps as a subordinate community within the local Asile chiefdom), the 1740 Castilla relation leaves little doubt that his "Machaba" was identical with the Beatty site.[73] His placement of Machaba (Santa Elena II) one league from the west bank of the Aucilla River across clayey soils and four leagues west of San Pedro II across sandy soils, along with the location of San Matheo's abandoned site one league to the west of Machaba along a spur trail, is consistent with the location of 9Md5. These distances and locations roughly correspond to those presented for the route between missions noted on the 1697 list, which placed "Machaba" one league from Asile and less than a league from San Matheo, which itself was five leagues from San Pedro II (presuming these distances were somewhat underestimated using a longer perception of a league distance).[74] This mission was presumably destroyed along with San Pedro and San Matheo in the summer of 1704.

San Miguel de Asile (circa 1620s–1704)

This westernmost Yustagan mission was almost certainly located on the western side of the Aucilla River during the seventeenth-century mission period and probably at the seventeenth-century mission site 8Je106, as has been previously proposed.[75] Documentary accounts indicate that the border town of Asile was located between two and three leagues west of mission San Matheo and approximately two leagues from the Apalachee capital at San Lorenzo de Ivitachuco (9Je100).[76] Asile was also situated about half a league to the east of Governor Ruíz's short-lived wheat farm, located roughly equidistant between Asile and Ivitachuco. Although accounts from the 1540 expedition of Hernando de Soto clearly locate a town called Agile on the eastern side of the Aucilla River, which was said to be the boundary with the Apalachee province,[77] the seventeenth-century mission called San Miguel de Asile was apparently located on the opposite side of this river. Apart from the distance evidence noted above, the placement of Asile's principal mission town on the western side of the Aucilla River is also based on several subsidiary bits of evidence.

Perhaps the most compelling evidence is the sequence of events at the onset of the Timucuan rebellion of 1656. Interpreter Estéban Solana departed from Ivitachuco with the Timucuan warriors drafted by Governor Rebolledo. He arrived in San Pedro and was murdered either that same day or the following day, after which yet another Indian set out for Asile and ambushed soldier Bartolomé Pérez on his way to arrange for some corn for the departure of the Apalachee warriors. Significantly, on the day of the murders, Asile's resident friar Joseph Bamba arrived in Ivitachuco at 2 o'clock in the afternoon, riding a horse at high speed.[78] Given the speed with which the lone friar evidently made his way on horseback between Asile and Ivitachuco, the two missions must have been on the same side of the Aucilla River, unless there just happened to be a horse standing ready for him on the otherwise unoccupied western bank of the river, which seems unlikely with the apparent rarity of mounts on the frontier. Other more equivocal evidence dates to the 1647 Apalachee rebellion. Acting governor Francisco Menéndez Márquez (at the time in Ivitachuco) ordered squad leader Nicolás de Carmenatis to take command of half of his troops and Indian warriors and proceed through the town of Asile, which was on the road both squads had to return, and subsequently take the right fork of "the road that separates past the River of Vitachuco," eventually rejoining the governor's squad (which took the left fork) in mission San Pedro.[79] The wording of this order implies that the road from Ivitachuco passed through Asile on the western side of the Aucilla before dividing on the eastern side.

Notwithstanding Francisco de Castilla's placement of Asile on the western riverbank itself, San Miguel de Asile's location at the more elevated site of 9Je106, nearly a league from the Aucilla River, is supported not only by relative distances from Ivitachuco and the other Yustagan missions, but also by the fact that Asile never seems to have become a riverbank ferry town in the same sense as San Juan II and Salamototo on the Suwannee and St. Johns Rivers (both of which were admittedly wider than the Aucilla). Furthermore (and perhaps more significantly), Asile was said to be only about half a league from the seat of the Ruíz hacienda (circa 1646–52), which straddled the lands equidistant between Asile and the Ivitachuco mission, the site of which was also between half a league and one league west of the farm.[80] Given these distances, San Miguel was most likely to have been situated at site 8Je106, which is just slightly over three miles (actually less than one and a half leagues) in a straight line from Ivitachuco at 8Je100. The eventual discovery of the archaeological deposits of this Spanish farm, probably located on one of the level hilltops south of present-day Anderson Bay, might serve to confirm this conclusion.

Missions of the Northern Timucua Mission Province

Santa Cruz de Tarihica I (circa 1612–57)

This early mission was very probably located at the Indian Pond site (8Co229), where archaeological survey has revealed the remains of what appears to have been a substantial early-seventeenth-century Spanish mission distributed across the broad hilltop immediately north and northeast of Indian Pond some eight miles northwest of present-day Lake City, which is within the inter-riverine uplands between the Suwannee and Santa Fe River drainages.[81] The identification of this site as Tarihica is based primarily on the distances and relative order of missions presented in documentation generated during three distinct visitations. The first is that of Fray Luís Gerónimo de Oré, who in December of 1616 conducted individual visitations at the fledgling missions of San Martín, San Juan de Guacara, and Santa Cruz de Tarihica, each of which was said to be eight leagues from the other, in that order.[82] Given the secure locations of San Martín at Fig Springs and San Juan at Baptizing Spring, the Indian Pond site is the only large mission site located in a northwesterly direction from San Juan. Indeed, Fray Oré subsequently plunged northward from Tarihica into the hinterland behind the Okefenokee Swamp on his way to mission Santa Isabel de Utinahica near the forks of the Altamaha River in southern Georgia.[83]

Important supplementary evidence is provided by the 1656 route of Capt. Agustín Pérez de Villa Real and interpreter Estéban Solana on their ill-fated mission to deliver the order that sparked the Timucuan rebellion. Departing from mission San Martín, Pérez traveled next to mission Santa Cruz de Tarihica, then to mission Niahica, and finally to the far northern mission of Arapaja (along the present-day Alapaha River) after dispatching Solana westward to San Pedro from Niahica.[84] This evidence clearly locates Santa Cruz in a northerly direction from San Martín, not to the west past San Juan along the lower trail. Finally, the 1655 mission list provides an important clue. The visitor (Fray Pedro Chacón?) traveled from the northern Atlantic coastal missions of Guale and Mocama across the interior to mission Santiago de Oconi in the Okefenokee Swamp before proceeding to visit the northern constellation of missions within the Timucua mission province.[85] The first mission encountered was Santa Cruz, said to be located fifty-four leagues from St. Augustine and thus some twenty-four leagues farther into the western interior than the Oconi mission. This figure is roughly compatible with the travel distance between the Okefenokee and Indian Pond.[86] Perhaps more importantly, the route then proceeded another six leagues to mission San Agustín de Urihica before covering another ten leagues to arrive at the Arapaja mission. This sequence—Tarihica to Urihica to Arapaja—is remarkably similar to that of Agustín Pérez in 1656, who traveled from Tarihica to Niahica to Arapaja, incidentally suggesting equivalency between Urihica and Niahica.

These three sources, dating to 1616, 1655, and 1656, together make Indian Pond the best possible candidate for Santa Cruz. Beyond this evidence, there would seem to be no other viable alternative identification for this large early-seventeenth-century site. The date of Tarihica's relocation after the 1656 rebellion is furthermore confirmed by the apparent absence of late seventeenth-century artifacts at this and other outlying sites in this immediate vicinity.[87]

San Agustín de Urihica, or Niahica (circa 1620s?–1657)

The exact location of this undiscovered mission within the northern reaches of the broader Timucua mission province is quite difficult to identify based on documentary sources, principally because only the 1655 mission list and the 1656 Pérez route provide any clues as to its relative position. Furthermore, the direct equivalence of the missions named Urihica (pre-1656) and Niahica (1656–57) is only based on circumstantial evidence, although the persistence of the convent of San Agustín under yet another name—Ajohica—after 1657 implies some degree of continuity for the early Urihica mission. Apparently founded after 1616 (Fray Oré made no mention of it), and thus probably associated with the Yustaga regional chiefdom missionized after 1623, Urihica was evidently located six leagues by road from mission Santa Cruz and some ten leagues from the Arapaja mission in 1655.[88] Furthermore, during his 1656 visitation of all these missions, Capt. Agustín Pérez de Villa Real sent Estéban Solana ahead to San Pedro from the Niahica mission after traveling together from Santa Cruz, while he alone proceeded northward to the Arapaja mission.[89]

The persistence of established trail networks into the eighteenth and nineteenth centuries provides some assistance in locating seventeenth-century missions. In the case of mission San Agustín, this evidence suggests that Urihica was probably located along the primary northern Camino Real leading northwest from Santa Cruz (Indian Pond) toward the upper curve of the Suwannee River. Presuming that the primary trail crossed the Suwannee just below the mouth of the Alapaha River, heading west to cross the Withlacoochee before dropping to mission San Pedro, then Urihica would have been located somewhere west-northwest of Indian Pond. If the primary trail led across uplands through present-day Live Oak, Urihica might have been located either at Live Oak or possibly even at one of the known early-seventeenth-century archaeological sites located near Peacock Lake (such as sites 8Su29 or 8Su173).[90] If the 1655 list erroneously listed six leagues between Santa Cruz and San Agustín instead of the actual three to four leagues between Indian Pond and Peacock Lake, then the Peacock Lake site cluster might indeed be equated with the local chiefdom of Urihica/Niahica.

If, on the other hand, the sites at Peacock Lake were actually outliers to the important local chiefdom of Tarihica at Indian Pond, mission San Agustín de Urihica might have been located farther north, perhaps even on the southern side of the Suwannee River near present-day Suwannee Springs. It is even remotely possible that the road to Urihica originally crossed the Suwannee River due north of Indian Pond, in which case Urihica might be located in southern Hamilton County, Florida. The fact that Estéban Solana was sent west from Niahica while Agustín Pérez headed north to Arapaja nonetheless implies that Urihica/Niahica was on the southern side of the Suwannee, and that Solana followed the northern Camino Real west to cross the Suwannee much farther to the northwest or west.

Santa María de los Angeles de Arapaja (circa 1620s–1657)

This early mission was probably located along the present-day Alapaha River, the name of which almost certainly derives from the Arapaja mission. As discussed above, Arapaja seems to have been the northernmost Timucuan mission along the route from San Martín to Santa Cruz to San Agustín and finally to Santa María.[91] The 1655 list places it ten leagues from Urihica. Presuming this distance measurement is accurate, Arapaja could have been located as far north as about five miles north of present-day Statenville, Georgia (if Urihica was near Suwannee Springs), or as far south as the vicinity of Jennings, Florida, just below the Georgia state line (if Urihica was actually at Peacock Lake). The seventy-league estimate between St. Augustine and Arapaja was indicated in both the 1655 list and a 1630 description of the Florida frontier, although this distance is clearly too far.[92] The contemporaneous 1630 estimate of just thirty leagues between Arapaja and mission Santa Isabel de Utinahica at the forks of the Altamaha River would tend to favor the more northerly location, well within the present-day state of Georgia. As noted below, however, Arapaja might instead have been located somewhat to the west of the river by that name. Thus, it may have been situated in the cluster of archaeological sites near Twin Lakes and Lake Park, Georgia. Intensive archaeological survey along the Alapaha River itself should provide the answer. Arapaja's cacique Alonso Pastrana agreed to relocate his town and all its satellites far to the south after the 1656 rebellion, where he appears to have established a new community at Santa Fé II.

Santa Cruz de Cachipile (circa 1620s–1657)

The only source of evidence for the location of this little-known mission is the 1655 list, which places both Cachipile and the next mission in the list, San Ildefonso de Chamini (Chamile), at the same ten-league distance from Urihica as the Arapaja mission.[93] Given that Chamile was independently noted to have been located only four leagues from Santa Elena de Machava, apparently in a northerly direction, it seems likely that all three missions listed after San Agustín de Urihica—Arapaja, Cachipile, and Chamile—were broadly scattered in an arc roughly ten leagues north and west of Urihica. It is unclear whether or not the 1655 visitor (Fray Pedro Chacón?) actually visited each mission or simply recorded their approximate distances from Urihica. But, given the more or less secure locations of Arapaja on the Alapaha River and Chamile just north of present-day Hixtown Swamp, Cachipile might be predicted to lie somewhere in between, and very possibly in the cluster of sinkhole lakes just northeast of the Withlacoochee River near the present-day Georgia communities of Twin Lakes and Lake Park. Late prehistoric and possibly mission-period archaeological sites have recently been identified in this vicinity, including evidence for seventeenth-century Spanish artifacts.[94] It is of course possible that the Arapaja chiefdom and mission were actually located somewhat west of the present-day Alapaha River, making this cluster of archaeological sites equivalent to Arapaja, with Cachipile falling somewhat farther to the west in the vicinity of Cherry Lake in northern Florida. Only archaeological survey will clarify this complex situation. Cachipile was relocated in 1657 to the vicinity of mission San Martín, at that time governed by Chamile's chief Lazaro.

San Ildefonso de Chamile (circa 1620s–1657)

This early mission was located just four leagues from Santa Elena de Machava I. It was additionally noted on the 1655 list to be situated roughly at the same ten-league distance from mission San Agustín de Urihica as Arapaja and Cachipile.[95] Giving greatest emphasis to the stated distance from Machava, since this reference is supported by considerable testimony regarding Chamile's cacique Lazaro and his interaction with Sgt. Maj. Adrián de Cañizares at Machava, Chamile is postulated to have been located north of the immense Hixtown Swamp along the upper reaches of the Little Aucilla River, perhaps near Blue Sink or Johanan or Pine Lakes. Only archaeological survey in this little-known region will help clarify the exact site of this early seventeenth-century mission. Following the Timucuan rebellion of 1656, Chamile's cacique Lazaro was promoted to chief of mission San Martín, to which he agreed to move the inhabitants of his town in 1657.

San Francisco de Chuaquin (circa 1620s–1657)

As is the case with several of the missions above, the only direct source of evidence for the location of Chuaquin is the 1655 list, which places this mission between Chamile and San Pedro in the order of visitation and fixes its distance at sixty leagues from St. Augustine.[96] Since this distance is ten leagues less than those presented for the remote missions of Arapaja, Cachipile, and Chamile, and since Chuaquin is given the same sixty-league distance from St. Augustine as its neighbor San Pedro, located at the Sampala Lake site, the most likely location for San Francisco de Chuaquin is hypothesized to be along the lower Withlacoochee River and perhaps somewhere between present-day Blue Spring and the confluence with the Suwannee. This location would imply that the 1655 visitation route may have taken the visitor north from Urihica (along the primary northern Camino Real) along a spur trail to the distant mission of Arapaja, across the inter-riverine uplands to Cachipile and then Chamile, and finally back eastward perhaps ten leagues to the vicinity of the primary Camino Real where it crossed the Withlacoochee. Given the typically skewed sense of direction reflected in seventeenth-century descriptions of interior Spanish Florida,[97] Chuaquin may have been presumed to be roughly equidistant from St. Augustine with respect to Urihica, visited much earlier along the same road, since the visitor would have returned some ten leagues eastward from Chamile, which in turn was apparently presumed to be equidistant at seventy leagues with Cachipile and Arapaja. The subsequent placement of San Pedro at sixty leagues as well may have resulted from the fact that San Pedro was also connected to the southern Camino Real, which rejoined the northern branch just east of San Pedro. Thus, distances from this point onward may have reflected statements by resident friars using more accurate distances calculated through the southern Timucua missions of San Juan, San Martín, Santa Fé, and San Francisco.

One further clue supporting San Francisco de Chuaquin's placement along the primary northern Camino Real is the fact that its cacique joined the leaders of all other towns located on this northern branch (Santa Cruz and Niahica) in rebelling against Governor Rebolledo in 1656. Significantly, the only towns not involved in the Timucuan rebellion were precisely those three which were located on spur trails north and west of the northern Camino Real. As with all these northern missions, however, Chuaquin was relocated far to the south in 1657, taking up residence near San Martín along with Cachipile within the new local jurisdiction of Chamile's chief Lazaro.

Missions of the Upper St. Johns River Watershed

Antonico (1595– circa 1615)

The precise location for this early principal town of the Agua Dulce province is unclear from the documentary record. Based on the 1602 testimony of several witnesses who seem to have listed this province's towns in geographical order along the St. Johns River (principally Fray Blas de Montes), Antonico appears to have been situated roughly in the middle of the cluster of towns forming the Agua Dulce province, extending in north-south order from San Julian (Elano/Elanogue?) to Filache to Antonico to Calabay (Equale?) and finally to Enacape (Anacabila, apparently also known as

Nyaautina).[98] As late as 1684, a site called "las bocas de San Julian" was situated fifteen leagues south of St. Augustine. In 1602 several witnesses placed Antonico and the Agua Dulce (also Rio Dulce) province some eighteen to twenty leagues from St. Augustine.[99] Given the more secure location of San Antonio de Enacape at the Mount Royal site just north of Lake George, these measurements imply that Antonico was probably located somewhere between the mouth of the Oklawaha River and present-day Palatka, and possibly at or near the Rollestown site (8Pu64b), where local St. Johns series ceramics underlie a later San Marcos ceramic component (presumably related to the immigrant Yamassees who resettled several sites along the upper St. Johns River after 1679).[100] Antonico seems to have been abandoned not long after 1612.

San Antonio de Enacape (1595–late 1650s?)

The site of the Agua Dulce town of Enacape, initially named San Antón as a *visita* subordinate to the provincial capital at Antonico, was probably at the Mount Royal archaeological site just north of Lake George on the St. Johns River. Contemporaneous distance measurements from St. Augustine and other known missions are rare and occasionally conflicting, but the combined use of several late-eighteenth-century maps with mission lists from San Antonio's original Timucuan and subsequent Yamassee occupations provides important clues. In 1602, Fray Blas de Montes listed the Agua Dulce town of Anacabila (Enacape) as the southernmost of six riverine towns bordering the more distant Mayaca, far to the south; that same year, several soldiers appear to have given this town a similar placement, albeit under the name "Nyaautina" on account of the female chief.[101] Following San Antonio's rise to preeminence over Antonico as the provincial capital, Fray Luís Gerónimo de Oré gave the location of San Antonio some twenty leagues by canoe upriver from Tocoy.[102] The 1655 mission list specifies a twenty-league distance from St. Augustine as well, but recognizing that the author of this list (possibly Fray Pedro Chacón) seems to have compiled these distances based on summed distances along a visitation route, this figure may actually reflect only an additional thirteen leagues upriver from mission San Diego de Helaca at seven leagues from St. Augustine.[103] Later evidence dating to the Yamassee occupation at San Antonio places its distance at between sixteen and twenty leagues from St. Augustine.[104]

Important evidence for San Antonio's location is provided by the circa 1785 Spanish land grant map, which notes royal lands [*realengo*] in the "*rinconada* [corner] of San Antonio" on the east side of the large Lake of San Antonio where a river enters flowing in a northwesterly direction.[105]

The lake is distinguished by several islands clustered at the northern (downriver) end of the lake, which empties into the St. Johns River. Furthermore, one of the 1768 maps of Florida by Joseph Elixio de la Puente indicates an "Island of San Antonio" in a lake formed by a widening of the St. Johns River. Both of the maps show this island and lake north of Lake of Mayaca and Lake of Miami even farther to the south.[106]

This combined evidence implies that mission San Antonio de Enacape was located on the east side of the St. Johns River and very possibly at or near a significant lake with prominent islands. The only such site in this area currently known to have been occupied during the seventeenth-century mission period was the Mount Royal site (8Pu35), located just north of Lake George on the eastern side of the St. Johns. This conclusion has indeed been proposed by other researchers and probably represents the best fit for all currently available evidence.[107] Mission San Antonio survived until the post-Timucuan rebellion period, when its inhabitants seem to have relocated downriver to the newly established ferry town of San Diego de Salamototo. The abandoned site of this Timucuan mission was reoccupied by immigrant Yamassee Indians during the early 1680s.

San Blas de Avino (pre-1612–circa 1620s)

The site of this little-known early mission appears to have been somewhere along the middle to lower reaches of the Oklawaha River, where it formed part of a cluster of towns within the Acuera provincial designation. In 1627, the town of Avino was described along with Tucuru and Utiaca to be located in the interior some forty leagues, or four days travel, from St. Augustine.[108] As described by Governor Rojas y Borja, "the said villages are two leagues and one and a half league apart from one another," and were said to be located on "low land" and had "a river that floods them [*que los baña*]." Proposing these towns as the best location to grow hemp for making ropes, the governor anticipated the cultivation of an area of land "six leagues in length and a league and a half in width, and in some parts [only] a league." These details suggest that Avino and its two neighbors were clustered within a total distance of three and a half leagues (just over nine miles) along the river valley and were situated in an area of broad floodplain extending for more than fifteen miles.

Furthermore, Avino's relative proximity to mission San Antonio de Enacape was demonstrated in 1616, since its resident friar met Bishop Juan de las Cavezas Altamirano there during his trek into the Timucuan interior.[109] This fact, combined with Avino's apparent proximity to the Acuera capital (which would not be missionized until years after San Blas), suggests that its location was probably along the river between San Antonio and the more southerly Acuera missions. The residents of mission San Blas may have been relocated northward along with their neighbors in Utiaco and Tucuru during the mid-1620s to form the new mission known as San Diego de Helaca at the primary St. Johns River crossing.

San Luís de Eloquale (circa 1620s?–late 1650s?)

This mission was located just two leagues downriver from the Acuera mission of Santa Lucia along the Oklawaha River. As such, it was also said in 1655 to border with the Timucua province neighboring it to the north (more specifically the Potano district).[110] The origins of this mission are unclear. Although the cacique of Eloquale visited St. Augustine in 1597 with that of Tucuru (apparently just downriver near the Acuera mission of San Blas de Avino), Eloquale might nonetheless represent a relocated town from the sixteenth-century Ocale/Etocale chiefdom just to the west of this region. Regardless of its origins, however, San Luís was abandoned as a mission station after the 1656 rebellion, possibly coinciding with the relocation of its Christian inhabitants to Salamototo.

Santa Lucia de Acuera (circa 1620s–late 1650s?)

Mission Santa Lucia seems to have been established at the principal town within the Acuera chiefdom, almost certainly located along the Oklawaha River east-southeast of present-day Ocala, Florida.[111] The 1655 list located Santa Lucia some thirty-four leagues from St. Augustine, and a 1630 description of Florida's hinterland placed the "province of Santa Lucia" in the fifty-league stretch between St. Augustine and the Pojoy province centered just north of Tampa Bay.[112] Presuming that the thirty-four-league distance in the 1655 list was calculated based on the twenty-league distance given for San Antonio de Enacape downriver, then depending on whether the fourteen-league distance between San Antonio and Santa Lucia was based on river travel up the Oklawaha or on overland travel (which seems unlikely in this lacustrine area), Santa Lucia could be located anywhere between the vicinity of Lake Weir and Lake Griffin on the south and the area several miles downriver from the mouth of the Silver River/Silver Springs drainage on the north. This mission convent and its downriver neighbor, San Luís de Eloquale, were apparently abandoned by the Florida Franciscans soon after the 1656 Timucuan rebellion, perhaps as a part of a general relocation of Christian Acuera northward to the new Salamototo mission just west of St. Augustine.

Missions of the St. Marys/Satilla River Watersheds

Santiago de Oconi (circa 1620s–1656)

Long presumed to have been situated on or near Jekyll Island on the coast of Georgia based on its stated distance of thirty leagues from St. Augustine in 1655, and Juan Díez de la Calle's note that its location was on an island, the remote mission of Santiago de Oconi was actually located within the Okefenokee Swamp of southeastern Georgia.[113] The actual site of this mission has yet to be identified, but various clues suggest that it may have been situated on one of the large islands deep within the swamp, such as Floyds or Billys Island. Said in 1602 to be two days' travel from San Pedro and three days from San Juan del Puerto to the south, Oconi was further specified in 1646 to be twenty leagues from the nearest *doctrina* (presumably San Pedro), placing it securely within the heart of the Okefenokee.[114] Later descriptions of Santiago de Oconi on an island between two lakes, said to be extremely difficult to reach because of the "terrible swamp" surrounding it, confirm this placement.[115] The fact that people and corn from Oconi were to be shipped down the St. Marys River to the coast near San Pedro in 1656 implies that the island might have been near the headwaters of this Atlantic-draining river.[116] The mission was destroyed and abandoned in early 1656, when Governor Diego de Rebolledo evidently burned the town in an effort to forcibly relocate its inhabitants to Nombre de Dios, although eighteenth-century rumors suggested that other Christian Timucuan fugitives fled to Oconi after the 1702 Moore raid on St. Augustine.

San Lorenzo de Ibihica (circa 1620s–1656)

This interior mission was evidently located near mission Santiago de Oconi, to which it eventually seems to have become subject by the time of their destruction in early 1656. In 1602 the minor chiefdom called "Ybi" was said to be located on the mainland some fourteen leagues from mission San Pedro de Mocama on the southern end of Cumberland Island.[117] Like the deep interior chiefdoms of Timucua and Potano, Ibihica was at the same time said to be situated on the mainland (*tierra firme*, or firm ground) in an area "of good roads," where "the land promises fertility by being clayey and not sandy." Combining these three statements—clayey mainland soils, a fourteen-league distance from San Pedro, and proximity to the Okefenokee Swamp—with the fact that the Timucuan term *ibi* referred to water (lakes or rivers), the most probable location for San Lorenzo de Ibihica and its four satellite villages is along Trail Ridge directly inland from Cumberland Island. The location would be either on the easternmost margin of the Okefenokee Swamp or just over the ridge to the east along the middle courses of either the Satilla or St. Marys Rivers where they bend sharply northward and southward, respectively. The former possibility is considerably strengthened by the recent discovery of early seventeenth-century Spanish majolica and olive jar shards at the Martha Dowling North site (9Cr34) northeast of Folkston, Georgia.[118] The location of this site at a distance of roughly fifteen leagues from Cumberland Island makes it a strong candidate for Ibihica. San Lorenzo was probably a *visita of Santiago de Oconi in 1655, prior to its apparent destruction that winter.*

APPENDIX B

Translations of Selected Documents

Junta in San Pedro de Potohiriba, 1670

The documents below relate to internal Timucuan disputes between two noble lineages in the town of Santa Elena de Machava in the Yustaga province. These disputes seem to have begun in the early 1630s, when the cacique of Machava, named Lorenzo, died without a legitimate adult heir (his only sister had died during the birth of her only daughter, at that time a small child) and political leadership of the town was seized by a rival lineage. Nearly four decades later, the adult children of the only niece of the old cacique Lorenzo presented their case during the 1670 Spanish visitation of Timucua, and the acting representative of that rival lineage (the cacique Pedro Menéndez) was eventually deposed in favor of Benito, Lorenzo's legitimate heir according to Timucuan custom. The following petition by the new cacique Benito was made four years later, requesting royal confirmation of the results of the 1670 junta.[1] In the note of response penned on the original petition, the Council of the Indies ordered the dispatch of a royal *cédula* confirming Benito's claim and ordering the Florida governor to "do him justice, without giving occasion that they should come to complain."

> Señor Benito, principal Indian and *cacique* of the town of Santa Elena de Machava and its lands, and natural lord of them, in the provinces of Florida. He says that he is the legitimate son of Maria Magdalena, who was niece of Lorenço, legitimate *cacique* of the said town, and that being thus that on account of the death of his said mother and uncle, the said chiefdom [*cacicado*] pertained legitimately to him, [and that] since he and his brothers and sisters were very little, and being few, in times past [the chiefdom] was taken away from them by those of the lineage [*linage*] of Pedro Meléndez, who ultimately was *cacique* of the said town, treating them badly and possessing it until now injustly,

and without having any right to do so, and Captain and Sergeant Major Don Pedro Benedit Horruitiner, the lieutenant of the governor and captain general of those provinces, having gone to visit the [province] of Timuqua with order of the governor of [those provinces], the supplicant asked before him that the said chiefdom and its lands be restituted to him, by being the eldest of his brothers and sisters and the legitimate heir of the said Lorenzo, his uncle, and that the visitor having convened the said Pedro Meléndez, who was the *cacique* who possessed the [chiefdom], and many other *caciques*, principal Indians, and elders [*ancianos*] from different towns of that province, and having taken their statements, all uniformly declared that it was true that the said chiefdom of Machava and lordship [*señorio*] of its lands was of the said Benito and his brothers and sisters as legitimate heirs of the said *cacique* Lorenço, their uncle, from whom the ancestors of the said Pedro Meléndez violently took it away, and that in justice it ought to be restituted, and that many other principal Indians, old and young, said and confirmed the same. This being concluded by both sides by an *auto* that the said visitor Don Pedro Benedit Horruitiner provided on March 20 of the past year of 1670, he declared in the name of His Majesty that [the chiefdom] ought to be restituted to the said Benito as the principal heir (in the concourse of his brothers and sisters [*en concurso de sus hermanos*]) of the said Lorenço, his uncle, and with effect he restored the said chiefdom of Santa Elena de Machava and its lands with all its rights to him, and gave him possession of it, and made his *principales* who found themselves present and the rest of his vassals render him obedience, and having tranquilly and peacefully done so, the said visitor confirmed it in the name of His Majesty in virtue of the faculty that the governor of Florida gave him in order to visit the said province of Timucua, and attentive that the said Pedro Meléndez remained deprived of this chiefdom, he likewise provided that during his lifetime a field should be sown for him in the said town of Machava, his house and corncrib [*garita*] should be repaired for him, and they should be made anew when there was need, as if he were *cacique*, and the said Benito promised it thus as is all on record by the copy of the *autos* that he presents with this [petition], and so that there are no lawsuits or obstacles placed against him in this with time, he supplicates to Your Majesty that, in view of the justice that attends him, and by being the legitimate heir of the said Lorenço, his uncle, the *auto* provided by the said visitor on the aforementioned day of March 20, 1670 should be approved, and the possession of the said chiefdom of the town of Santa Elena de Machava and the lordship of its lands that he gave him in virtue of it in the name of Your Majesty, so that in no time should the said Pedro Meléndez or his heirs disturb him in the possession of it, nor should they disturb those who, after his days, legitimately inherit the said chiefdom, commanding with all precision to the present governor, and he who might be [governor] of the said provinces of Florida, and to the rest of its officials, to protect them in this without permitting nor giving occasion that they should receive any offense with any pretext, nor that he or his heirs should be divested of the said chiefdom until they have been heard in justice in the Council, and from this he [Benito] will receive mercy.

Copy of the junta that was made about the chiefdom of the town of Santa Elena de Machava in the village of San Pedro de Potohiriba that was generally made by Don Pedro Benedit Horruytiner, commissioned judge, year of 1670.

In the town of San Pedro de Potohiriba on the twentieth of March, sixteen seventy, before the señor Captain and Sergeant Major Don Pedro Benedit Horruitiner, lieutenant of the governor and captain general and visitor of these provinces, there appeared Benito and Gregorio, and they said that they and Juan Camacho, Santiago Pasqua, Joseph Alonso, and María de Salaz[ar], and María Lorença, their sisters, are children of María Magdalena, and their said mother was the daughter of a legitimate sister of Lorenço, legitimate *cacique* of Machava, and that on account of their [lineage] being few [in number], those of the lineage [*linaje*] of Pedro Meléndez, who at the present is the principal *cacique* of the said town of Sancta Helena de Machava, took it away from them and treated them badly with all violence in times past, and up to now they have possessed [the chiefdom], and they [Benito and Gregorio] asked that it be restored to the said Benito by being the oldest of his brothers, attentive to being the legitimate heir of the said *cacique* Lorenço, his uncle. And this petition being heard by His Grace, in order to proceed with all justification, he called to his presence the said *cacique* of Machava and his *principales,* and the *caciques* of this said town [of San Pedro] and of San Matheo, and many other *principales,* and in the presence of all of them the said Benito and Gregorio repeated their demand, which was explained by Juan Bautista de la Cruz, interpreter, with the aid of Diego Salvador and Joseph de Aispiolea, likewise interpreters. Their petition being ordered by His Grace, the said *cacique* Pedro Meléndez responded that it was true that they were the lands of the said *cacique* Lorenço, but that they had not taken them away from him, but that his [Lorenço's] predecessors had given them to his [Pedro Meléndez's], in which faith they had possessed them. The same was said by Manuel, an old principal Indian of the said town of Machava, and about this case they had many conferences, which although they might conclude today, the twentieth, they began to negotiate three days ago, and in all of them they have conferred in open meetings [*junta abierta*] before His Grace, and on account of not having agreed among themselves, nor having given a means of agreement, it resulted that each one of those present should state the right of each [side] in accordance with God and their consciences. His Grace made them explain this, and required them on behalf of His Majesty to state what they know so that each one of them might be sheltered in the justice that they might have. And all in the said meeting having understood, Francisco Martín El Calbo, *cacique* of Ybiuro, said that in his conscience he knows that the chiefdom of Machava and its land are of Benito and his brothers and sisters, as the legitimate heirs of the said *cacique* Lorenço, his uncle, which were violently taken away from him by the predecessors of the said Pedro Meléndez, who possesses it today, and that in justice they ought to restore them to the above stated [Benito and his brothers and sisters], and that all the land will feel the same if they wish to state the truth, and he swore before God and a cross in order to free his conscience, and that in this he was not proceeding with passion, but rather in conformity with [justice]. And Manuel, *cacique* of Ybichua, confirmed the same under the said oath with specific words, and in this conformity each one of them did the same for themselves: Pedro, *cacique* of this said town; Francisco, *cacique* of the [town] of San Matheo de Tolapatafa; Francisco Alonso, *cacique* of San Juan Ebanjelista de Arapaxa; Matheo, *cacique* of San Francisco de Arapaxa; Antonio, *cacique* of San Antonio de Arapaxa; Francisco Bernavé, *cacique* of San Juan de Arapaxa; Baltasar, *cacique* of San Pablo; Francisco, old *hinija* of San Pedro; Clemente, *principal* of San Pedro; Bernardino, *principal* of San Pedro; Pablo, *hinija* of Machava; Marcos, *principal* of San Pedro; Pedro, *principal* of San Pedro; Francisco Bernavé, *principal* of San Matheo; and many other old and young men [*viejos y mosos*], confirming the same, and His Grace hearing them, he asked the stated Benito and Gregorio for what cause they had not asked for their justice until now, presuming that [the Spaniards] had come to visit this province, or [why had they not] come to the presidio to the presence of the señor governor. They responded that they had not done it in any visitation because they were young men, and that they had not witnessed the visitation with clarity like now, and as they are alone, they have never let them go to the presidio to ask for their justice, and although they have written many letters, all of them have been seized by their opposition, for which reasons neither the said Pedro Meléndez nor anyone else responded, [and] their grandmother, sister of the said *cacique* Lorenço, died in childbirth when the said María Magdalena, their mother, was born, and as she was a girl and alone, neither she nor them nor their brothers and sisters were able to ask until now that they are men, and doing so is in order to recover what is legitimately theirs, and regarding what the said *cacique* Pedro Meléndez and Manuel, his *principal,* say about their [Benito and Gregorio] ancestors having given the lands to theirs, there is no more proof than their saying so, and that nevertheless they could not give them up with the chiefdom while having heirs. And His Grace commanded the said Pedro Meléndez and his stated principal to respond to this, and they responded and alleged the possession, and that it was true that they were the lands of the said *cacique* Lorenço, the uncle of the above stated, and they gave no more answer, and His Grace again asked all those named above who were present and the rest if they had to say anything new in this case, and all said that what they had said was true, and that the said Benito, by being the eldest of his brothers named above was the legitimate *cacique* and lord of the said lands of Machava, and although His Grace admonished them to negotiate among themselves some final settlement to resolve whether the chiefdom and its lands belonged to the said Benito in accordance with justice, they did not wish to cede anything regarding his right. And having seen what was said on one side and the other, he was declaring and declared in the name of His Majesty that they ought to restore it to the said Benito, as the principal heir, with the concurrence of his brothers and sisters, of the said Lorenço, his uncle, and he restored the said chiefdom of Santa Helena de Machava and its land with all his rights, and as such he was commanding and commanded that he be seated in the principal *barbacoa* of this council house of San Pedro with the permission of the said principal *cacique* Pedro, who conceded it, so that the *principales* of the said village and chiefdom of Machava who are present and the rest of their vassals should give him [Benito] lifelong obedience, as they are obligated, which was done, and His Grace confirmed it in the name of His Majesty, in virtue of the faculty conceded to him by the commission of the señor governor and captain general, which is at the head of the autos of visitation. And likewise, attentive that the said Pedro Meléndez is deprived of the said chiefdom, it was agreed that during the days of his life a field [*savana*] would be sown for him in the town of Machava, and that his house and granary [*garita*] would be maintained and made anew when it might be necessary, [all] as if he were *cacique*, without there being any lack in this, and the said *cacique* Benito promised it thus, without permitting the contrary. And His Grace represented to him the obligations that he has on account of being *cacique*. In the first place, the prompt obedience that he owes to the orders of the señores governors in service of His Majesty, as the vassals that they were, and to the patronage [*patrocinio*] and protection of his vassals, and not to consent to anything that might pertain to public scandals and sins, and for their conservation, the government that he ought to have in cultivating the land for the abundance of their sustenance, a means for the conservation of the towns. And with this the said meeting concluded, and Benito, *principal* of Machava, signed it with His Grace, and Diego Salvador, named interpreter, and the rest did not sign on account of not knowing how. I swear. Pedro Benedit Horruitiner. Benito. Diego Salvador. Before me, Geronimo Rejidor, named notary. Amended—Joseph—valid.

I, Adjutant Alonso Solana, public and governmental notary of this city and provinces of St. Augustine, Florida, made, corrected, and reconciled this transcription of the original *autos* made by Sergeant Major Don Pedro Benedit Horuitiner, judge commissary for its visitation, and it is certain and true, as passed before Adjutant Gerónimo Rejidor, named notary, and so that it is on record at the petition of Benito and Gregorio of the town of Macha[va], I give the present in St. Augustine, Florida on the fourteenth of August, sixteen seventy-four.

I make my sign in true testimony.
Alonso Solana
Public and Governmental Notary

1682 Report by the Royal Officials

The letter below was penned in response to a royal *cédula* dated August 5, 1681, in which the king of Spain ordered a general census of Spanish Florida, including Spaniards and Indians. Their response is of considerable

198 / Appendix B

significance to Florida historians, since in it they confirmed that no official lists or rolls of Indians in the mission provinces were maintained by the secular officials of St. Augustine, since Florida was a nontributary colony (and thus had no need for precise counts of individual Indians). Nevertheless, the following document also reveals that a registry *was* maintained of the assigned posts of each Franciscan friar, presumably because annual rations and supplies for each friar were issued from the royal warehouses in St. Augustine as a part of the colony's overall expenses. Consequently, the following information was probably extracted from lists of such mission assignments in the Florida *contaduría,* or accounting records.

The primary importance of this relation, however, lies in the fact that not only did the royal officials list the active Franciscan missions in 1682 but also those that had been abandoned during the previous forty years, further noting the destiny of the inhabitants of these abandoned missions in most cases. Whether or not this figure of forty years suggests they consulted a similar record of Franciscan assignments in 1642 is unclear, but the list of missions that were active at that time but subsequently abandoned seems accurate, implying that the list is based on sound information. Discovered only recently, this 1682 relation essentially confirms the previously reconstructed pattern of mission abandonment and aggregation described in this book and in other, earlier publications.[2]

> The official judges of the royal coffers of these provinces of Florida, Captains Don Antonio Menéndez Márquez, accountant, and Francisco de la Rocha, treasurer and quartermaster, in fulfillment of a royal *cédula* from His Majesty, its date on the fifth of August of sixteen eighty-one, in which he is served to command that he be given a count and individual report of the places [*lugares*] that there are in these provinces, and the number of Spaniards and Indians that there are in them, we say that in the royal accounting office at our charge, there do not end up any lists, rolls [*padrónes*], or regulatory codes [*aranzeles*] of the number of the said Indians, with respect to those of these provinces not being tributary, for which reason there is no account of them. They can only inform His Majesty that by the sites [*asientos*] of the religious missionaries who find themselves in this conversion, it seems that in the province of Apalache there are the following villages of Indians: Vitachuco, Ayubale, Santa Cruz, Tomole, La Tama, San Luis, Yscambe, Bacuqua, Patali, Ocuya, Oconi, Azpalaga, Chacatos, and the Chines, without any Spaniards living or residing in them, only in the said village of San Luis the infantry that serves there in garrison, who are alternatively moved; and in the province of Ustaca

and Timucua there are the following villages of the said Indians: Asile, Machava, San Matheo, San Pedro, Tary, Guacara, Ajoyca, Santa Fee, San Francisco, Vitanayo, and Salamototo; and in the provinces of Guale and Mocama there are the following: Tholomato, San Juan, Santa María, San Phelipe, San Pedro, Guadaquini, Colon, Asaho, and Zapala, all of Christian Indians except the three of Santa María, San Pedro, and Colon; and although forty years ago there were many more villages to be found, as there were in the said province of Timucua: Arapaha, San Martín, Cachipile, Chamile, Pachala, Niahica, and Choaquine, these find themselves depopulated, and their inhabitants aggregated to the villages of the said province, and in the [province] of Ybinihiute all [the villages] find themselves depopulated, which were San Luis, Santa Lucia, San Antonio, and Mayaca, and part of their inhabitants find themselves in the said [village] of Zalamatoto, and the other part in their settlements [*rancherías*] in the woods; and in the province of Guale there find themselves depopulated Santo Ache, Tupiqui, Santa Ysabel, Oconi, Santo Domingo, San Juan, and Santa Catalina, which in the entrance of the English enemy the year of sixteen eighty in it, by being the frontier, it withdrew to the said [village] of Zapala, as likewise the inhabitants of the others find themselves; and in the said time and years, there find themselves newly settled and made in the said provinces the stated villages in the [province] of Apalachee: La Tama, Chines, and Chacatos; and in that of Timucua, those of Guacara and Vitanaio, which is what we can inform to His Majesty for the reasons that we state and the news that we have, and so that it is on record in virtue of the said royal *cédula* and *auto* of the señor Governor Don Juan Márquez Cabrera, who is [governor] for His Majesty of these provinces, we give the present in St. Augustine, Florida, on the second of October, sixteen eighty-two. Don Antonio Menéndez Márquez. Francisco de la Rocha.

1740 Francisco de Castilla Relation

The relation below, presented in both draft and final versions, was composed as a part of a longer proposal to the Spanish crown made in 1740 by St. Augustine's public and governmental notary Francisco de Castilla.[3] In this package, Castilla proposed that the most fertile lands of old Spanish Florida, at that time largely unoccupied, should be granted as estates, along with noble titles, in order to more effectively attract settlers. Although at least portions of a distinct copy of Castilla's proposal have been seen by modern researchers,[4] the original proposal, and more specifically the two drafts of his detailed description of the missions along the Camino Real, does not seem to have been used, and thus is translated in full below.

During the summer of 1739, Francisco de Castilla had carried out extensive historical investigations in both the governmental and Franciscan archives of St. Augustine, selecting and transcribing a large number of sixteenth-, seventeenth-, and eighteenth-century documents for inclusion in a package being assembled by Gov. Don Manuel de Montiano for submission to the king. This package was designed to demonstrate the historical and legal claim that Spain held to the territory of the new English colony of Georgia, and has been recently published in its entirety.[5] Perhaps as a direct consequence of this research, Castilla presumably had direct access to a considerable amount of documentary information regarding the seventeenth-century missions of Spanish Florida. Consequently, the following accounts should probably be viewed with a considerable degree of confidence, since Castilla may have been the most knowledgeable "historian" of Spanish Florida alive at the time he composed these texts. Since the wording and contents of each version is different (in some cases significantly), both versions are presented for comparative purposes.

[draft version]
St. Augustine, Florida, January 6, 1740
News of the Terrain of the Provinces of Apalache and Florida

The entrance of Apalachee has in the lower tides 16 palms of water, and in high [tides] 18 and 20, until entering in the backwater, which has four and 5 *brazas* of depth, and only the south wind can disturb the vessels that are within it, because on the other sides the hill [*montaña*], sand banks [*bajos*], and reefs shelter it. From the backwater to the fort there is one long league in distance, and a regular sloop [*valandra*] can enter up to it half-loaded, but a medium-sized [sloop] can do so [fully] loaded.

From the fort of Apalache, following the road from the provinces of Cabeta, capital of the towns of the Uchices and other nations, comes forth a sand bank [*bajio*] that is 500 paces long. Its beginning is inundated with the tides to the space of a rifle shot [*tiro de fusil*], and the rest is only flooded when there are storms. This [part] that is inundated with them [storms] produces splendid fodder for all animals. Then follow sandy pine woods subject to flooding, good for cattle, up to the *chicasa* [*chicasa* means town] of the Chacatos, which is six leagues from the fort of Apalachee. From there to San Luis there is one league of clayey, hilly agricultural land [*tierra de labor barrosa, montuossa*], with hills [*montañas*] and good watering places [*aguadas*], and from San Luis up to the river of Chacatos and the mouth of [the river] Pedernales there are twelve leagues of lands like those in Spain, and they continue upriver on both sides, and if one attends to the road that goes to the provinces, it is an admiration of clayey and extremely fertile agricultural land, with lovely waters and leafy groves of trees [*frondossas arboledas*], although there are some bad crossings in stream gullies [*arroyos barrancosos*]. By this road there were one hundred leagues from San Marcos to Cabeta, and ninety-four of them are agricultural lands like the best of Europe, which run from the aforementioned *chicasa* or town of Chacatos up to Cabeta, and by the river there are more than 140 because the meanders are many and extensive. The groves of trees on the said road and river are deciduous oaks [*robles*], live oaks [*encinas*], chestnuts, walnuts with bitter nuts [*nogales de nuez amarga*], and others, and many Castilian canes [*cañas de Castilla*]. If one goes from San Luis to look for the first town [*primer pueblo*] of the provinces of Apalache, or Cabeta, which is Vitachuco, they are all agricultural lands that can sustain a kingdom with wheat.

Following the Road that comes from Apalachee to Florida.

From the fort of San Marcos to Vitachuco by the road that comes to Florida there are seven leagues of low and boggy pine woods [*pinares bagios y senagossos*], good for cattle. Vitachuco was the first town of the province of Apalachee when it was dominated by us, and from it up to the river of Acile there are three leagues of splendid agricultural lands, and at the bank of the river there was another town of the same name as the river, which was [a town] of Timucuan Indians. From Acile to Machaba, a town of the same nation, there is one league of land of the same quality. To the west of this town there was another of the same nation named San Matheo, and all those environs are clayey agricultural lands with many walnuts and deciduous oaks, and from Azile to San Matheo there is one league. I mean, and from Machaba to San Matheo. From Machaba to San Pedro run four leagues of sandy pine woods, good for cattle. This town of San Pedro has clayey agricultural land, and this same quality of land runs for two and a half leagues distance up to the old *chicasa* of the same San Pedro, and on part of these lands more than 500 Christian Indians from Timucua cultivated. From the old *chicasa* of San Pedro to the river of Guacara there are nine leagues of sandy pine woods that produce lovely pastures for cattle. On the river itself, on this side, there is a *chicasa* that has one league of clayey agricultural land. From there to the *chicasa* of San Juan there are two leagues distance of clayey land, and this *chicasa* of San Juan had one league of land that were cultivated, and outside of this it is surrounded on all sides by hills on lands of the same quality. From there to the *chicasa* of San Martín run twelve leagues of sterile pine woods, and the aforementioned *chicasa* of San Martín has a little less than one league of agricultural land of the same quality, and lovely waters. From there run five leages of sterile pine woods up to the old *chicasa* of Santa Fé, which has a league and a half of agricultural land. From there to the new *chicasa* of Santa Fé runs a league and a half of fertile pine woods on clayey lands with small stones, which can be cultivated without hindrance. From there to the lake of Amaca there are four leagues of pine woods, fertile for cattle. This lake has lovely and permanent waters with a creek [*arroyo*] and groves of trees where one could make a large hacienda, as there was, and it was the seat of a splendid herd [*hato*] of cattle. From the said lake up to the banks of the river of Picalata run fourteen leagues of fertile pine woods with pastures and watering places for haciendas of cattle.

From the river of Picalata to Florida there are seven leagues of pine lands and groves [*bariales*] with many waters suitable for raising livestock. In all these pine woods it is known with infallibility that there are many pieces of woods with deciduous oaks, live oaks, and fields [*faxinales*], which are suitable for agricultural lands, and in all the area of Florida there is an abundance of lands that were cultivated in other times, and with the exception of the Island of Santa Anastacia, which is where the quarries are, farmers could establish themselves in all the rest of the country, because there is an immensity of lands, called *sabanas,* that are suitable for a diversity of agriculture.

As is known, on one and the other side of the road that comes from Apalache, there were other known *chicasas,* which were San Francisco, Santa Catarina, Tarihica, Abozaya, and La Chua, and it is also said that there were many others that have not been cleared, nor has there been need to do so.

Above I said that the first town of the province of Apalachee was Vitachuco, and now I say that in the environs of those areas there were other towns, which were Ayubale, Capole, Aspalaga, Patale, Bacucua, Tomole, La Tama, and San Luis, which were in the space of eight leagues of lands so fertile and abundant that many Europeans have esteemed them as their best at least. And apart from the said towns there were others named Escambe, Ocuya, and Ocone, of Apalachee Indians, the Chacatos, the Ocatasas, and the Tabasas.

There was harvested wheat, barley, corn, broad beans [*habas*], small beans [*frijol*], garbanzos, peas [*arbejas*], sugar cane, tobacco, muscatel grape, mulberries, figs, strawberries, walnuts [*nuezes dulces*], chestnuts, pomegranates, quince, peaches, and other good fruits, and flowers like roses, carnations, lilies, irises, rosemary, marjoram, and jasmine.

The cattle and horses are corpulent and of good circumstances. They always remain stout, because in the summer the wild basil [*poleo*] is extremely abundant, and the Castilian cane, from the leaves of which they sustain themselves well in winter, because it never withers, and there is so much that it cannot be weighed.

Don Francisco de Castilla

[final version]
News of the Most Fertile Lands of the Provinces of Apalachee and Florida

The entrance of Apalachee has sixteen palms of water in the ordinary tides, and in high [tides] eighteen and twenty, until entering in the backwater [*poza*], which has four and five palms of depth, and only the south wind can disturb the vessels that are within it, because on the other sides it is sheltered by the mountain [*montaña*], sand banks [*vajos*], and reefs. From this backwater to the fort of San Marcos there is one league of distance through the channel [*caño*] or arm of the sea that penetrates up to there, and through it a sloop [*valandra*] of regular capacity can enter half-loaded, and a small sloop entirely [loaded].

From the fort of San Marcos de Apalache, following the road from the provinces of Caveta, capital of the towns of the Uchises and other nations, there is a sand bank [*vagio*] that is five hundred paces in length. The beginning of this sand bank is inundated with the tides up to the distance of the shot of a rifle [*fusil*], and the rest is only flooded when there are storms, and it always produces splendid fodder for all animals. Then follow six leagues of pine woods [*pinares*] up to the *chicasa* of the Chacatos, and these woods are sandy and subject to flooding, but they serve for haciendas of cattle, because they have watering places [*abrebaderos*] and produce lovely pastures [*pastos*]. From the Chacatos to San Luis there is one league, and it is clayey agricultural land [*tierra de labor barrosa*] with many hillocks [*lomas*] and watering places [*aguadas*]. This road from the provinces, until arriving at the river called [the river] of the Chacatos and the mouth of the [river of] Pedernales, which is twelve leagues distant from San

Luis and eighteen from San Marcos, is all agricultural land, and [the lands] are likewise all upriver on one side and the other. If one looks to the other road with comes from Sabacola el Viejo, twelve leagues distant from San Luis, where Chilacaliche was settled, one will find that they are agricultural lands like those of Spain up to Caveta, all with good waters and leafy groves of trees [*frondosas arboledas*], although there are some bad crossings in stream gullies [*arroyos varrancosos*].

By this road that passes through Sabacola el Viejo, there are a little more or less than one hundred leagues from the fort of San Marcos to Caveta, ninety-four of them extremely fertile for agriculture, which run from the aforementioned *chicasa* or town of Chacatos up to Caveta, and by the river of Chacatos or the mouth of the [river] Pedernales there are more than one hundred and forty due to the many turns that the river makes. The groves of the aforementioned road and river are oaks [*robles*], live oaks [*encinas*], chestnuts, walnuts of bitter nuts [*nogales de nuez amarga*], and others, and many Castilian canes [*cañas de Castilla*] one both sides of the river and in the creeks. From San Luis to the beginning of the provinces of Apalache or Caveta, or to their first town [*primer pueblo*], which is Vitachuco, everything is agricultural land on all sides, and looking in a northeasterly direction, there is much agricultural land of hillocks [*lomas*] and hills [*montes*], which is where there were other towns and many haciendas. From San Luis to the river and mouth of Pedernales one goes to the northwest. By the road from Sabacola el Viejo toward the provinces one goes always to the north and northwest, all with splendid lands. In sum, those provinces are a remedy for our Spain, and there have been those who have exalted them more.

Beginning the road that comes from Apalachee to Florida, from San Marcos to Vitachuco there are seven leagues of pine woods, low [*vagios*] and boggy [*zenagosos*], where only cattle can be raised. The aforementioned Vitachuco was the first town of the Province of Apalachee. From it to the river of Asile there are three leagues of agricultural land. From Asile to Machaba there is one league of agricultural land. To the west of this same town there was another called San Matheo at a distance of one league, all agricultural land, clayey, compact [*prietas*], and with many walnuts and oaks. From Machaba to San Pedro there are four leagues of sandy pine woods [*pinares arenosos*] that only serve for raising cattle. From San Pedro to the old *chicasa* of the same name there are two and a half leagues of good clayey agricultural land which in part was occupied by Indians, and more than five hundred men cultivated them. From the old *chicasa* of

San Pedro to the river of Guacara there are nine leagues of sandy pine woods that produce good pastures and serve for haciendas of cattle. On the same river of Guacara on this side there is a *chicasa* that has a league round about of clayey agricultural land. From there to the *chicasa* of San Juan there are two leagues of pine woods with good clayey land for agriculture. This *chicasa* of San Juan also has a league of cleared [*desmontada*] agricultural land round about [*en contorno*], and on all its borders there are hilly [*montuosas*] lands of the same quality. From there to the *chicasa* of San Martín run twelve leagues of pine woods that are sterile. This *chicasa* has a little less than one league of agricultural land, and lovely waters. From there to the old *chicasa* of Santa Fé there are five leagues of useless pine woods. This old *chicasa* of Santa Fé has a league and a half of agricultural land round about. From there to the new *chicasa* of Santa Fé runs a league and a half of fertile pine woods which can be cultivated, because they are on clayey lands with small stones [*pedregales menudos*] that cannot hinder agriculture, and the stated new *chicasa* of Santa Fé has close to a league of agricultural land round about, and thick groves of trees on all its borders with the same quality of land. From there to the lake of Amaca run four leagues of fertile pine woods for cattle. The said lake has lovely permanent waters with a creek [*arroyo*] and groves of trees where one could make a good plantation, as there was, since in the neighborhood of this lake a great hacienda of cattle endured much time. From there to the river of Picalata run fourteen leagues of very fertile pine woods, with pastures and watering places for haciendas of cattle. From the river of Picalata to Florida there are seven leagues of pine woods, many waters, and good pastures, suitable for raising livestock. Within these pine woods it is known with certainty that there are various pieces of woods of deciduous oak, live oak, and fields [*faxinales*] that are suitable for agricultural lands, and in all the area of Florida there is an abundance of lands that were cultivated in other times, and with the exception of the Island of Santa Anastasia, which is where the quarries are, farmers could be established throughout the rest of the country. And to the sides of the road that comes from Apalache to this city there are other known *chicasas,* which are San Francisco, Santa Catharina, Tarihica, Abozaya, and La Chua.

I already said above that the principal town of the province of Apalache was Vitachuco, and now I ought to express that to the east followed Ayubale, Capole, Aspalaga, Patale, Bacucua, Tomole, La Tama, San Luis, all of which were within the space of eight leagues of extremely fertile lands. Apart from these there were other towns named

Escambe, Ocuya, and Ocone, of Apalachee Indians, the Chacatos, the Ocotazas, and Tabazas. Wheat was harvested at a hundred to one, barley, corn, broad beans [*habas*], small beans [*frixol*], garbanzos, peas [*guisantes*], sugar cane, tobacco, muscatel grapes, mulberries, figs, strawberries, walnuts [*nuezes dulzes*], chestnuts, pomegranates, quince, peaches, and other good fruits, and of flowers, roses, carnations, lilies, irises, rosemary, marjoram, jasmine, and others.

The cattle and horses are corpulent, and of good circumstances. They always remain stout in winter and in summer. The wild basil [*poleo*] is extremely abundant, and the stands of Castilian cane, from the leaves of which they sustain themselves in winter, because it never dries out, and because there is so much that it cannot be weighed. St. Augustine, Florida, January 6, 1740.

Notes

Chapter 1: Demographic Collapse

1. See, for example, discussions by Hann 1996, 257–65, and Milanich 1996.
2. López 1602; Oré 1936, 114.
3. Ocaña 1635.
4. See relative population figures provided by Fernández de Florencia 1675; Riço 1681; Ebelino de Compostela 1689.
5. Horruytiner 1670; see chapter 7.
6. Castilla 1740.
7. Dobyns 1983. See also Hann 1996, 260, for a critical review of Dobyns's "parity principle."
8. Alonso de Jesús 1633; Oré 1936, 116. See also Hann 1988a, 160–64.
9. López 1602.
10. Ocaña 1635.
11. Montes 1602; Davila 1606.
12. Milanich 1996.
13. Peñaranda 1608; Pareja et al. 1617b; Alonso de Jesús 1630c; Ocaña 1635.
14. Alonso de Jesús 1633; Díez de la Calle 1659.
15. Fernández de Florencia 1675; Arcos 1675; Fernández de Florencia 1681; Riço 1681; Fuentes 1681.
16. E.g., Milner 1980; Dobyns 1983; Smith 1987; Ramenofsky 1987; Larsen et al. 1990; Larsen 1993.
17. Pareja et al. 1617b.
18. Ocaña 1635.
19. Ibid.
20. Bushnell 1978, 419; Moral et al. 1673b; Moreno Ponce de León 1651.
21. Menéndez Márquez 1660.
22. Rebolledo 1655a, 1655b.
23. Menéndez et al. 1657; Rebolledo 1657g.
24. Aranguiz y Cotes 1659c.
25. Larsen 1993, 340–41.
26. Hoshower and Milanich 1993, 227, 235.
27. Rebolledo 1654a.

28. Gómez de Engraba 1657a.
29. Alonso de Jesús 1630a.
30. Prado 1654a.
31. Spanish Crown 1651.
32. E.g., Spanish Crown 1651; Rebolledo 1657a, 1658a.
33. Ruff and Larsen 1990; Fresia et al. 1990; Larsen 1993.
34. Hoshower and Milanich 1993; Larsen 1993; Hutchinson and Larsen 1990.
35. See, for example, Timucuan criminal cases in Hann 1992a; 1993b, 276–93.
36. E.g., Worth 1995c, 15–55.
37. Ybarra 1608.
38. Díaz de Badajoz 1630.
39. Fernández de Olivera 1612.
40. See Hann 1991, 9–12.
41. Trevijano 1643; Horruytiner 1639a.
42. Oré 1936, 121; Horruytiner 1635.
43. Calvo 1630.
44. Ocaña 1635. This particular passage of the Ocaña account may be erroneous. It probably describes the missionization of Apalachee itself in 1633.
45. Horruytiner 1638b. By 1674, at least some Amacanos were living with the Chine and Pacara Indians south of Apalachee; see Fernández de Florencia 1674.
46. Horruytiner 1640; Vega Castro y Pardo 1639.
47. See Hudson 1990, 26–29, 90–91. At least one Chisca woman apparently had a son Juan Fernández de Diosale by a Chacato husband in the Florida panhandle during the 1590s, possibly indicating an early presence there; see Hann 1993b, 31–76.
48. Cañisares y Osorio 1635. Chichimeco was a generic term for such groups until the appearance of the Rechahecrians/Westo after 1659; see Worth 1995c, 15–18. Despite the use of Chisca interpreters for several captured Chichimeco, in at least one documented case, Hann 1996, 238–39, there seems to be no concrete evidence for any direct ancestral relationship between the Chisca and the post–1659 Chichimeco/Westo. This is particularly indicated by the clear evidence for the early and sustained Chisca presence in peninsular Florida discussed below, as well as the documented warfare between the two groups during which the Chisca captured their first two firearms from the Chichimeco before 1676; see Hann 1993b, 61.
49. Vega Castro y Pardo 1639.
50. See Hann 1988a, 16–19.
51. Menéndez Márquez 1647.
52. Ruíz de Salazar Vallecilla 1650.
53. Ibid., 1651.
54. Argüelles et al. 1678.
55. Ruíz de Salazar Vallecilla 1651.
56. Argüelles et al. 1678.

57. Ponce de León 1651a, 1651b.
58. Ponce de León 1651a.
59. Russell et al. 1990, 45–48.
60. Menéndez et al. 1657.
61. Ruíz de Salazar Vallecilla 1646.
62. Santiago 1658.
63. Ruíz de Salazar Vallecilla 1648b.
64. Florencia 1670.
65. Guerra y Vega 1665d.
66. Ruíz de Salazar Vallecilla 1646; Alcayde de Córdoba 1660.
67. Manuel 1651.
68. E.g., Pérez 1646.

Chapter 2: Repopulating Timucua

1. Pareja et al. 1617a.
2. Oré 1936, 118.
3. Pareja et al. 1617a.
4. Leturiondo 1678. See translation in Hann 1993b, 132, 135.
5. See discussion in Worth 1995c, 9–13.
6. Worth 1995c, 47–50, 105–27.
7. Márquez 1606.
8. Peñaranda 1608; Dávila 1606.
9. Rojas y Borja 1627b.
10. Santiago 1658.
11. Rojas y Borja 1627a.
12. Ruíz de Salazar Vallecilla 1648b.
13. Ibid.
14. Menéndez Márquez and Rocha 1682.
15. Ibid.; Alejo 1660; Pasqua 1660; Cruz 1660; see Hann 1993a regarding the Mayaca.
16. Fernández de Florencia 1670.
17. Menéndez Márquez and Horruytiner 1647b.
18. Rebolledo 1655a.
19. Ruíz de Salazar Vallecilla 1646.
20. Ibid., 1648a.
21. Ibid., 1648b.
22. Fernández de Florencia 1670.
23. Menéndez Márquez and Horruytiner 1647b.
24. See Worth 1995c, 19–22, 35.
25. Ruíz de Salazar Vallecilla 1650, 1651.
26. Ponce de León 1651a, 1651b; see Hann 1988b.
27. Cruz 1660.
28. See discussions in Weisman 1992, 124–40, 188–205; Worth 1992, 171–85; Hann 1996, 231–36; and Milanich 1996.

29. E.g., Deagan 1990, 303–7; 1993, 92–101; Russo 1992.
30. Worth 1995c, 9–55.

Chapter 3: The Timucuan Rebellion

1. Spanish Crown 1653.
2. Gómez de Engraba 1657b.
3. Prado 1654a, 1654b.
4. Rebolledo 1654a.
5. Council of the Indies 1657a, 1657c; Ranjel 1660.
6. See, for example, comments by Fray Alonso de Jesus 1630b regarding the lack of progress in conversion in this area.
7. Council of the Indies 1657a.
8. E.g., Sotomayor 1660; Rocha 1660; Hernández 1660; Entonado 1660.
9. Horruytiner 1660a.
10. Alcayde de Cordoba 1660.
11. Pérez de Villa Real 1660.
12. Menéndez Márquez 1660.
13. Ibid.
14. Rocha 1660.
15. This crucial line was burned, but the date seems certain, since Rebolledo administered only the 1655 and 1656 drafts prior to the rebellion.
16. Menéndez Márquez 1660.
17. Calderón 1660.
18. Menéndez et al. 1657.
19. Rebolledo 1655a.
20. Ibid., 1656a.
21. Alcayde de Cordoba 1660.
22. Ibid.
23. Rebolledo 1656b.
24. Alcayde de Cordoba 1660.
25. Spanish Crown 1655.
26. Rebolledo 1657b.
27. Ibid.
28. Argüelles 1660a.
29. Ponce de León 1660; Pérez de Villa Real 1660; Argüelles 1660a.
30. Puerta 1660; Argüelles 1660a.
31. Rebolledo 1657b; Prado 1657; Rios 1657; Cigarroa 1657; Horruytiner 1657a; Puerta 1660.
32. Ponce de León 1660; Argüelles 1660a; Hernández 1660.
33. Reyes 1660.
34. Menéndez Márquez 1660; Entonado 1660.
35. San Antonio et al. 1657; Puerta 1660; Santiago 1660; Pérez de Villa Real 1660.
36. Rebolledo 1657b; San Antonio et al. 1657.

37. Rebolledo 1656c, 1656d.
38. Menéndez et al. 1657.
39. Rebolledo 1656e.
40. Bernal 1660.
41. Pérez de Villa Real 1660.
42. Ibid.; Gómez de Engraba 1657b.
43. Alejo 1660.
44. San Antonio et al. 1657.
45. Prado 1660; Menéndez Márquez 1660.
46. San Antonio et al. 1657; Argüelles 1660a; Menéndez Márquez 1660.
47. Argüelles 1660a; Alejo 1660.
48. Prado 1660; Menéndez Márquez 1660.
49. San Antonio et al. 1657.
50. Alejo 1660.
51. San Antonio et al. 1657.
52. Alejo 1660.
53. Monzón 1660; Sotomayor 1660; San Antonio et al. 1657. But see also Hann 1996, 208–9.
54. Alejo 1660.
55. Cruz 1660; Bernal 1660.
56. Argüelles 1660a.
57. Díez de la Calle 1659.
58. Menéndez et al. 1657.
59. Cruz 1660; Bernal 1660.
60. Monzón 1660.
61. Pérez de Villa Real 1660.
62. Ibid.; Rocha 1660.
63. Alejo 1660.
64. Sotomayor 1660; Calderón 1660; Cruz 1660.
65. Sotomayor 1660.
66. Pérez de Villa Real 1660.
67. López de Gabira 1660.
68. Puerta 1660; Monzón 1660.
69. Alejo 1660.
70. Peña 1717. The Timucuan name Calacala literally refers to two "cuts" or deaths, thus might possibly have been given to this particular spot in recognition of the two murders here in 1656; Granberry 1993, 121.
71. López de Gabira 1660; Argüelles 1660a; Alejo 1660.
72. Alejo 1660.
73. San Antonio et al. 1657.
74. Puerta 1660.
75. Ponce de León 1660; Puerta 1660; Monzón 1660; Calderón 1660.
76. Rocha 1660; López de Gabira 1660; Puerta 1660; Calderón 1660; Menéndez Márquez 1660.

77. Argüelles 1660a; Pasqua 1660.
78. Puerta 1660; Rocha 1660.
79. Rocha 1660; Menéndez Márquez 1660.
80. Calderón 1660; Menéndez Márquez 1660; Romo de Uriza 1660; Puerta 1660.
81. San Antonio et al. 1657.

Chapter 4: The Pacification of Timucua

1. Puerta 1660; Calderón 1660; Monzón 1660.
2. Hernández 1660; Ponce de León 1660; Rocha 1660; Calderón 1660.
3. Argüelles 1660a.
4. Pérez de Villa Real 1660.
5. Calderón 1660; Texeda 1660.
6. Argüelles et al. 1678.
7. Argüelles 1660a; Texeda 1660.
8. Calderón 1660.
9. San Antonio et al. 1657.
10. Pasqua 1660.
11. Manuel 1651.
12. Calderón 1660.
13. Rocha 1660.
14. San Antonio et al. 1657.
15. Pedrosa 1660.
16. Rebolledo 1656f.
17. Menéndez et al. 1657.
18. Pérez de Villa Real 1660.
19. Sánchez de Uriza 1660; Santiago 1660; Argüelles 1660b.
20. Sánchez de Uriza 1660; Santiago 1660.
21. Menéndez et al. 1657.
22. Rebolledo 1656g.
23. Pedrosa 1660; Monzón 1660; Sotomayor 1660; Rocha 1660; Calderón 1660; Menéndez Márquez 1660.
24. Rebolledo 1657c; 1657d.
25. Argüelles 1660a; Entonado 1660.
26. Sotomayor 1660; Calderón 1660; Menéndez Márquez 1660; Entonado 1660.
27. Pedrosa 1660; Calderón 1660.
28. Monzón 1660; Sotomayor 1660; Calderón 1660.
29. Cruz 1660; Sotomayor 1660.
30. Argüelles 1660a; Sotomayor 1660; Menéndez Márquez 1660; Entonado 1660; Monzón 1660; Calderón 1660.
31. Cruz 1660.
32. Ibid.
33. Sotomayor 1660; Sánchez de Uriza 1660.

34. Cruz 1660.
35. Entonado 1660; Argüelles 1660a.
36. Cruz 1660.
37. Sotomayor 1660; Entonado 1660.
38. Pedrosa 1660; Sotomayor 1660; Calderón 1660; Cruz 1660; Rocha 1660.
39. Monzón 1660; Sotomayor 1660; Rocha 1660; Calderón 1660; Menéndez Márquez 1660; Cruz 1660; Entonado 1660.
40. Pedrosa 1660; Monzón 1660; Sotomayor 1660; Rocha 1660; Calderón 1660; Menéndez Márquez 1660; Entonado 1660; Cruz 1660.
41. Cruz 1660; Calderón 1660.
42. Argüelles 1660a; Cruz 1660.
43. Argüelles 1660a; Cruz 1660; Calderón 1660.
44. Argüelles 1660a; Calderón 1660; Menéndez Márquez 1660; Entonado 1660; Cruz 1660.
45. Pedrosa 1660; Monzón 1660; Sotomayor 1660; Cruz 1660.
46. Pedrosa 1660; Argüelles 1660a; Monzón 1660; Calderón 1660; Menéndez Márquez 1660; Entonado 1660; Cruz 1660.
47. Argüelles 1660a; Monzón 1660; Sotomayor 1660; Rocha 1660; Calderón 1660; Menéndez Márquez 1660; Entonado 1660; Cruz 1660.
48. Pedrosa 1660; Argüelles 1660a; Monzón 1660; Sotomayor 1660; Rocha 1660; Calderón 1660; Menéndez Márquez 1660; Entonado 1660; Cruz 1660.
49. Pérez de Villa Real 1660; Argüelles 1660a; Rocha 1660; Calderón 1660; Cruz 1660.
50. Argüelles 1660a.
51. Rebolledo 1656g.
52. Pearson 1983, 261; Gannon 1965, 58.
53. Argüelles 1660a; Sotomayor 1660; Rocha 1660; Calderón 1660; Menéndez Márquez 1660; Entonado 1660; Cruz 1660.
54. Ibid.
55. Despite Juan Moreno y Segobia's 1660 search of the house of Cañizares's widow, Juana de Mendoza, where Sotomayor 1660 believed the case to remain, Cañizares's executor Manuel Gómez 1660 reported that the papers were in the Apalachee garrison with Andrés Pérez.
56. Pedrosa 1660; Argüelles 1660a; Monzón 1660; Sotomayor 1660; Rocha 1660; Calderón 1660; Menéndez Márquez 1660; Entonado 1660; Cruz 1660.
57. Pérez de Villa Real 1660; Monzón 1660; Sotomayor 1660; Calderón 1660; Menéndez Márquez 1660; Entonado 1660.
58. Pedrosa 1660; Argüelles 1660a.
59. Monzón 1660; Pedrosa 1660; Entonado 1660; Cruz 1660.
60. Argüelles 1660a; Sánchez de Urisa 1660; Pedrosa 1660.
61. Monzón 1660; Entonado 1660; Cruz 1660; Calderón 1660; Pérez de Villa Real 1660; Menéndez Márquez 1660.
62. Calderón 1660; Cruz 1660; Argüelles 1660a.
63. Ponce de León 1660.

64. Bernal 1660; Rebolledo 1657a; Pérez de Villa Real 1660.
65. Moreno y Segovia 1657; Ponce de Leon 1660.
66. Heras 1657b.
67. Puerta 1660; Argüelles 1660a; Entonado 1660.
68. Argüelles 1660a; Sotomayor 1660; Calderón 1660.
69. Rebolledo 1657g noted that the case had already been dispatched before October 18, 1657, and on May 7, 1660, Royal Secretary Juan Díez de la Calle (1660) was informed in writing that this bound trial record was in Madrid in the possession of Don Luís de Valdivia, the *relator* of the Ruíz *residencia* papers from which the trial record is now missing.
70. Bernal 1660.
71. Rebolledo 1657e.
72. Calderón 1660.
73. Ranjel 1660; Alejo 1660.
74. Ponce de León 1660.
75. Herrera, López, y Mesa 1660b.
76. Rebolledo 1657j.

Chapter 5: The Transformation of Timucua

1. See discussion by Pearson 1983 and Hann 1986a.
2. Rebolledo 1657a; Gómez 1660.
3. Rebolledo 1657a.
4. Rebolledo 1657a. See also Hann 1986a, 84.
5. Rebolledo 1657j; see below.
6. Rebolledo 1657a; Argüelles, Sánchez de Uriza, et al. 1678. See translation of visitation by Hann 1986a.
7. Rebolledo 1657a.
8. See also comments by Hann 1996, 225.
9. Argüelles, Sánchez de Uriza, et al. 1678; Horruytiner 1670.
10. Rebolledo 1657j.
11. Ibid., 1657a.
12. Pérez de Villa Real 1660.
13. Calderón 1660.
14. Ibid.
15. Gómez de Engraba 1657b.
16. E.g., Puerta 1660; Pérez de Villa Real 1660; Rocha 1660; Sotomayor 1660; Ponce de León 1660.
17. E.g., Díaz Vara Calderón 1675; Fernández de Florencia 1675; Riço 1681. See also appendix A.
18. Rebolledo 1657a. The Rangel 1993, 266–67, account of the Soto expedition not only states that Agile was a subject of Apalachee, but also that it was located on the eastern side of the river of Ivitachuco presumably the Aucilla.
19. Rebolledo 1658d.
20. See Rebolledo 1657c, 1657d, 1657g. See also Hann 1996, 225.

21. Manuel 1651.
22. Rebolledo 1657a.
23. Horruytiner 1670.
24. Argüelles 1660a; Calderón 1660; Cruz 1660.
25. Rebolledo 1657a.
26. See also my earlier comments in this regard in Worth 1992, 301, and Milanich 1995, 179–83.
27. Rebolledo 1657a.
28. Ibid., 1657f; San Antonio et al. 1657.
29. Moreno y Segovia 1657.
30. Pérez de Villa Real 1657.
31. González 1657; Estevez de Carmenatis 1657; Florencia 1657.
32. Ebelino de Compostela 1689.
33. Menéndez Márquez and Rocha 1682. Despite my earlier suggestion (Worth 1995c, 185) that southward migration from the coastal Timucuan area might have accounted for Salamototo's 1736 grouping within the "province of Mocama," this 1682 document confirms other evidence that Salamototo was actually populated with people from the south along the upper St. Johns watershed.
34. See Deagan 1978, 106, and Hann 1996, 86, regarding their earlier placement of Salamototo at the Rollestown archaeological site in Putnam County far to the south.
35. See references to Helaca's "geraca" location in documents translated by Hann 1992a, 454, 464.
36. Pacheco y Salgado 1660.
37. E.g., Díez de la Calle 1659; Díaz Vara Calderón 1675. See also Hann 1996, 248.
38. Castilla 1740; see appendix A.
39. See Johnson 1991, 298; 1993, 142–43.
40. Perete et al. 1676; Ebelino de Compostela 1689; see also Márquez Cabrera 1680.
41. Leturiondo 1685; see Worth 1995c, 107, 111.
42. Compare Díez de la Calle 1659 with later lists such as those in Díaz Vara Calderón 1675; Fernández de Florencia 1675; Riço 1681; and Menéndez Márquez and Florencia 1697.
43. E.g., Oré 1936; Díez de la Calle 1659.
44. Florencia 1670.
45. E.g., Díaz Vara Calderón 1675; Palacios 1675.
46. E.g., Puerta 1660.
47. See Milanich 1995, 181.
48. E.g., Díaz Vara Calderón 1675; Palacios 1675; Fernández de Florencia 1675; Riço 1681; Castilla 1740.
49. Castilla 1740; Rebolledo 1658a; Alcayde de Cordoba 1660; Fernández de Florencia 1670.
50. Díez de la Calle 1659; Pérez de Villa Real 1660.

51. Díaz Vara Calderón 1675; Palacios 1675; Leturiondo 1678.
52. See Fernández de Florencia 1675 and Castilla 1740 regarding the location of this town on the riverbank.
53. See Loucks 1979, 1993; Worth 1992, 312; Milanich 1995, 180–81; Hann 1996, 180.
54. Menéndez Márquez and Rocha 1682.
55. Rebolledo 1657a.
56. Pacheco y Salgado 1660.
57. Reyes 1660.
58. Heras 1657a; San Antonio et al. 1657.

Chapter 6: Implementation and Resistance

1. Rebolledo 1657j; Herrera, López, y Mesa 1660a. As correctly surmised by Hann 1996, 226, my earlier estimate of 1658 for Lieutenant Alcayde's placement was too conservative; see Worth 1992, 299.
2. The Franciscans claimed that Timucua had no lieutenant as late as September 1657; see San Antonio et al. 1657, translated in Hann 1993b, 25.
3. Alcayde de Cordoba 1660.
4. Rebolledo 1657j.
5. Monzón 1660.
6. Cañizares y Osorio 1657a, 1657b; Puerta 1657.
7. Santiago 1660.
8. Puerta 1657.
9. Menéndez Márquez 1660.
10. San Antonio et al. 1657.
11. Council of the Indies 1657b.
12. San Antonio et al. 1657.
13. Cañizares y Osorio 1657a, 1657b.
14. Cañizares y Osorio 1657b.
15. Puerta 1657.
16. Cañizares y Osorio 1657c.
17. Rebolledo 1657i.
18. Ibid., 1657b.
19. San Antonio et al. 1657; see translation by Hann 1993b, 11–12.
20. Rebolledo 1657f.
21. Gómez 1660; Cañizares y Osorio 1669; see Cañizares y Osorio 1657c.
22. Rebolledo 1658a.
23. Ibid., 1658d.
24. Salvador 1658.
25. Gómez 1658.
26. Aranguiz y Cotes 1659b, 1659c, 1659d. See also Worth 1995, 17.
27. Worth 1995c, 15–22, 27, 30–32.
28. Aranguiz y Cotes 1659d.
29. Ibid., 1659a.

30. Argüelles, Sánchez de Uriza, et al. 1678.
31. Fernández de Florencia 1670.
32. Ranjel 1660.
33. Monzón 1660; Alcayde de Cordoba 1660; Cruz 1660.
34. Menéndez Márquez and Rocha 1682.
35. Hann 1996, 227, however, concludes that Rebolledo's policy "failed, particularly in the phase launched by Rebolledo" in large part based on Lieutenant Juan Fernández de Florencia's 1659 commission to continue the repopulation of the eastern towns in Timucua, begun earlier by Martín Alcayde de Cordoba.
36. Medina et al. 1662.

Chapter 7: Late Seventeenth-Century Timucua

1. Menéndez Márquez and Rocha 1682.
2. Guerra y Vega 1668; translation in Worth 1995c, 78–79.
3. Ponce de León 1664a.
4. Menéndez Márquez 1667a; see also Menéndez Márquez 1667b.
5. Menéndez Márquez and Rocha 1682.
6. Ríos Enríquez 1690a.
7. Argüelles 1660a.
8. Worth 1995c, 18–20.
9. Guerra y Vega 1665f.
10. Ibid., 1665d.
11. See Hann 1992a, 459.
12. Guerra y Vega 1665g.
13. Argüelles, Sánchez de Uriza, et al. 1678.
14. Guerra y Vega 1673.
15. Horruytiner 1670.
16. See Benito 1674 and subsequent comments by the fiscal and council.
17. Leturiondo 1677.
18. Guerra y Vega 1666a.
19. Fernández de Florencia 1675; Riço 1681; Ebelino de Compostela 1689.
20. Leturiondo 1678; Cárdenas 1681; Ayala Escobar 1698.
21. E.g., Rodríguez Tisnado 1685; Gómez 1685; Herrera 1688.
22. See, for example, Hann 1988a, 200.
23. Leturiondo 1678.
24. Fuentes 1681; see Worth 1995c, 100–103.
25. Leturiondo 1678. The final phrase of the original manuscript reads, "porque sentian andar de unas partes a otras," which might also be translated, "because they regretted walking from some places to others." See also fragmentary transcription with translations in Hann 1993a, 134–38.
26. Leturiondo 1678.
27. Florencia 1695; Ayala Escobar 1698; Hann 1996, 300.
28. Díaz Vara Calderón 1675; Palacios 1675; Fernández de Florencia 1675.
29. Leturiondo 1678.

30. Márquez Cabrera 1680.
31. Horruytiner 1670.
32. Menéndez Márquez and Rocha 1682; Solana 1683.
33. Zuñiga y Cerda 1700; Anonymous 1785?; see also Arnade 1961.
34. Leturiondo 1678.
35. Florencia 1695.
36. Ibid.; Xaen 1703.
37. Leturiondo 1685; Florencia 1695.
38. Zuñiga y Cerda 1700; see Florencia 1695 regarding the locations of these and other Apalachee ranches.
39. Castilla 1740.
40. For an overview of the formation of the Yamassee confederacy in the context of Chichimeco raids north of Guale, see discussion in Worth 1995c, 15–30.
41. See Hann 1993a, 122–25.
42. Barreda 1680 in Worth 1995c, 94–97; Márquez Cabrera 1680.
43. Zamora 1991, 306.
44. Cardenas 1681a, 1681b; Riço 1681.
45. Hann 1993a, 124; Bushnell 1994, 165. For details on the Yamassee towns to which they moved, see Fuentes 1681, translated in Worth 1995c, 100–103.
46. Menéndez Márquez and Rocha 1682.
47. Solana 1683; Ebelino de Compostela 1689.
48. Hann 1993a, 125–32.
49. Fernández de Florencia 1681; Riço 1681; Fuentes 1681. See full translation of Guale and Mocama portion in Worth 1995c, 100–103.
50. See Worth 1995c, 27.
51. Palacios 1675; Díaz Vara Calderón 1675.
52. Hann 1991, 23–27; 1992a, 471.
53. Hita Salazar 1680; translation in Worth 1995c, 85–86.
54. Hita Salazar 1678; translation in Hann 1992a, 471.
55. Solana 1688. Don Thomás was accused with several others of "cooperating in the crime of sodomy."
56. Menéndez Márquez and Rocha 1682.
57. For details on this complex process, see Worth 1995c, 9–55.

Chapter 8: The Destruction of Timucua

1. See Hann 1996, 272–74; Worth 1995c, 45–46, 167; Bushnell 1994, 167.
2. See Livingston 1686; translation in Worth 1995c, 152–53.
3. Leturiondo 1685; translation in Worth 1995c, 122.
4. Ebelino de Compostela 1689.
5. Ríos Enríquez 1690a, 1690b, 1691; see Hann 1996, 266–67.
6. Rodrigo de Ortega 1736; translation in Worth 1995, 183–85.
7. Florencia 1695; Menéndez Márquez and Florencia 1697; Ayala Escobar 1698.

8. See Johnson 1991, 298; 1993, 142–43.
9. See Hann 1996, 265–66.
10. Quiroga y Losada 1697.
11. Florencia 1695. See full translation by Hann 1993b, 196–219, and also Hann 1996, 277–82.
12. Quiroga y Losada 1697.
13. Menéndez Márquez and Florencia 1697; Ayala Escobar 1698.
14. Zuñiga y Cerda 1702. See also Hann 1996, 293–94.
15. See Swanton 1922, 120–21 and Hann 1988a, 233–34; 1996, 294.
16. Arnade 1959, 14–22; Crane 1981, 75–77; Bushnell 1994, 190–92; Worth 1995c, 50; Hann 1996, 291–93.
17. Xaen 1703.
18. See Hann 1996, 295.
19. For a detailed overview and analysis of available documentary evidence for these raids, see Hann 1988a, 264–83.
20. Zuñiga y Cerda 1704a; Junta de Guerra 1705.
21. Zuñiga y Cerda 1704b.
22. See Hann 1996, 298–302.

Chapter 9: Remnants

1. Florencia 1706.
2. Córcoles y Martínez 1706; Hita Salazar 1707.
3. Córcoles y Martínez 1711.
4. Anjurgo 1711; Uriza 1711.
5. Ayala Escobar 1698; Romo de Uriza 1701.
6. Hann 1989; Crane 1981, 162–86; Swanton 1922, 97–103; Green 1991, 32–37.
7. Primo de Ribera 1717.
8. Benavides 1726.
9. Castillo 1728.
10. Arredondo 1736.
11. Morales et al. 1735; Ojitos 1736.
12. See Hann 1996, 322–23.
13. García de Solís 1754.
14. See Hann 1996, 323–25.
15. Arredondo 1736.
16. See Gold 1969.
17. Gelabert et al. 1764.
18. Lyon 1992c.
19. See Milanich 1996.
20. Anjurgo 1711.
21. Lyon 1992c.
22. Elixio de la Puente 1768a.

Appendix A: Mission Locations

1. Distance data extracted from direct visitation or travel records appear in at least Oré 1936; Díaz Vara Calderón 1675; Palacios 1675; Riço 1681; Peña 1717; and probably Díez de la Calle 1659. Secondary reconstructions include Menéndez Márquez and Florencia 1697 and Castilla 1740. The list by Fernández de Florencia 1675 may have resulted from records generated during the little-known visitation of Domingo de Leturiondo to Apalachee and Timucua beginning on October 12, 1674; see Leturiondo 1677.
2. Solana 1683; see reproductions in Chatelain 1941; Worth 1995c, 38; and Hann 1996, 270.
3. Anonymous 1785(?). See Arnade 1961 for reproduced portions of this much larger map.
4. Moncrief 1764.
5. Elixio de la Puente 1768a, 1768b; Anonymous 1785?; Purcell 1778; see Boyd 1938 for small-scale photographic reproductions of the entire 1778 Purcell map.
6. See, for example, the many historical maps used by Johnson 1991 and Milanich and Hudson 1993 in their reconstructions of the 1539 Hernando de Soto route.
7. Díez de la Calle 1659, 68–69; Oré 1936. The commonly used transcript of the 1655 list in Serrano y Sanz 1912, 132–33, is out of order, poorly transcribed, and otherwise severely flawed (including a nonexistent mission called Coaba), despite the fact that the source was correctly cited to be page 69 in the first volume of Díez de la Calle's 1659 book; see also comments in Hann 1988a, 28–30; 1996, 189–91.
8. See service summary in the service record of Juan's son Francisco Díez de la Calle y Madrigal 1678. Juan's father Juan Fernández de Madrigal also served fifty-six years in the same office, as noted in correspondence of the Junta de Guerra 1663.
9. See comments in Worth 1992, 70, 77.
10. Rebolledo 1657a, 1658c; see translations in Hann 1986a and Worth 1995c, 13–14.
11. Rebolledo 1657b.
12. See also Hann 1990, 451.
13. Davila 1606.
14. Oré 1936.
15. Hita Salazar 1678; see translation in Hann 1992a, 454.
16. See visitation of Bentura González's hacienda called Piquilaco in the nearby mission of Salamototo in Florencia 1695; translation in Hann 1993b, 210. Although Sastre 1995 provides a sound overview of the forts at Picolata and Pupo during the 1730s and later, her assertion that they were established prior to 1706 is certainly erroneous, presumably confounding the late seventeenth-century garrison at the Salamototo mission with the eighteenth-century forts built several leagues to the south (see below).

17. Díez de la Calle 1659.
18. See Deagan 1978, 106; Hann 1990, 503; 1996, 86.
19. Anonymous 1685?; Elixio de la Puente 1768a.
20. Johnson 1991, 89–91, 209.
21. Symes and Stephens 1965.
22. Díez de la Calle 1659; Pedroso 1660; Díaz Vara Calderón 1675; Fernández de Florencia 1675; Riço 1681; Menéndez Márquez and Florencia 1697.
23. Oré 1936, 113; Leturiondo 1678.
24. Anonymous 1785?
25. See Johnson 1991, 346–47.
26. Milanich 1972; see Worth 1992, 29, 55–56, 74, and Worth, *The Timucuan Chiefdoms of Spanish Florida*, vol. 1, chap 4.
27. Florencia 1695; see chapter 7.
28. Castilla 1740.
29. Peña 1717.
30. Johnson 1991, 1993.
31. Díez de la Calle 1659; Peña 1717; Castilla 1740.
32. See Johnson 1991, 298; 1993, 142–43 and Milanich 1995, 183.
33. Weisman 1992; Hoshower and Milanich 1993; Worth 1990, n.d.
34. Díez de la Calle 1659.
35. Peña 1717.
36. Castilla 1740.
37. Díaz Vara Calderón 1675; Palacios 1675; Fernández de Florencia 1675.
38. Castilla 1740.
39. Díez de la Calle 1659.
40. Purcell 1778.
41. Castilla 1740.
42. Díaz Vara Calderón 1675; Palacios 1675.
43. Fernández de Florencia 1675.
44. Castilla 1740.
45. Díaz Vara Calderón 1675.
46. Ibid.; Palacios 1675.
47. Díaz Vara Calderón 1675; Palacios 1675; Fernández de Florencia 1675.
48. Alejo 1660; Peña 1717.
49. Purcell 1778.
50. Loucks 1979, 1993; see also Milanich 1995, 180–81.
51. Peña 1717; Castilla 1740.
52. Purcell 1778.
53. Oré 1936.
54. See Hann 1990, 462; Milanich 1995, 180–82; and Johnson 1991, 355–56.
55. Díaz Vara Calderón 1675; Fernández de Florencia 1675; Leturiondo 1678.
56. Díaz Vara Calderón 1675; Fernández de Florencia 1675; Riço 1681; Peña 1717; Castilla 1740.
57. Peña 1717; Castilla 1740; Purcell 1778.

58. Jerald Milanich, personal communication, 1996.
59. Purcell 1778.
60. Díaz Vara Calderón 1675; Fernández de Florencia 1675; Riço 1681; Peña 1717; Castilla 1740.
61. Castilla 1740; Ebelino de Compostela 1689; Florencia 1695; Menéndez Márquez and Florencia 1697; García 1695, translated in Hann 1993b, 281.
62. Díaz Vara Calderón 1675; Fernández de Florencia 1675; Riço 1681.
63. Purcell 1778.
64. Díez de la Calle 1659.
65. Florencia 1695; Menéndez Márquez and Florencia 1697; Ayala Escobar 1698; Castilla 1740.
66. Peña 1717; Castilla 1740.
67. Ayala Escobar 1698.
68. Díaz Vara Calderón 1675; Florencia 1675; Riço 1681.
69. Menéndez Márquez and Florencia 1697.
70. See Jones and Shapiro 1991. The Ivitachuco mission seems to have been relocated at least some distance prior to 1650, but this "new" location is presumed to be the Lake Iamonia site; see Hann 1988a, 28.
71. See Goggin 1952; Milanich and Hudson 1993, 166; Milanich 1995, 209; Jones and Shapiro 1991, 501; and my own earlier placement of Asile in Worth 1992, 51–52.
72. Castilla 1740.
73. Ibid.
74. Menéndez Márquez and Florencia 1697.
75. See Jones and Shapiro 1991, 501.
76. Díaz Vara Calderón 1675; Fernández de Florencia 1675; Riço 1681; Peña 1717; Castilla 1740.
77. See Milanich and Hudson 1993, 166–67, 211–14.
78. Pérez de Villa Real 1660.
79. Menéndez Márquez 1647.
80. Ibid.; Pérez de Villa Real 1652; Horruytiner 1657b.
81. Johnson 1991, 168–79, 356–57; see Milanich 1995, 181–82.
82. Oré 1936, 122.
83. See Worth 1992, 75–77; 1993, 34–37.
84. Pérez de Villa Real 1660.
85. Díez de la Calle 1659.
86. See Worth 1992, 78.
87. See discussion by Milanich 1995, 179–83.
88. Oré 1936; Díez de la Calle 1659.
89. Pérez de Villa Real 1660.
90. See Johnson 1991, 357–58, and Milanich 1995, 181–82.
91. Díez de la Calle 1659; Pérez de Villa Real 1660.
92. Díez de la Calle 1659; Fernández de San Agustín 1630. Hann 1990, 470, originally placed it within the Altamaha River drainage based on this distance.

93. Díez de la Calle 1659.
94. Smith and Worth 1994; Marvin Smith, personal communication, 1995.
95. Díez de la Calle 1659; Argüelles 1660a.
96. Díez de la Calle 1659.
97. See Worth 1992, 77; 1993, 30.
98. Montes 1602; Sánchez Sáez de Mercado 1602; Cruz 1602.
99. Fernández de Ecija 1602; González de la Torre 1602; Cruz 1602.
100. This site has long been interpreted as Salamototo; see Deagan 1978, 106; Hann 1990, 503; 1996, 86.
101. Montes 1602; Sánchez Sáez de Mercado 1602; Cruz 1602.
102. Davila 1606; Oré 1936, 120.
103. Díez de la Calle 1659.
104. Menéndez Márquez and Florencia 1697; Márquez Cabrera 1680; see also Milanich and Hudson 1993, 197.
105. Anonymous 1785?
106. Elixio de la Puente 1768a.
107. Goggin 1952; Hann 1990, 439, 506.
108. Rojas y Borja 1627a.
109. Oré 1936, 120.
110. Díez de la Calle 1659; Alejo 1660.
111. See Milanich and Hudson 1993, 96–98.
112. Díez de la Calle 1659; Fernández de San Agustín 1630. Pojoy's precise location is portrayed on the circa 1785 Spanish map of Tampa Bay; see Anonymous 1785?
113. Díez de la Calle 1659. See Lanning 1935 and Hann 1990, 463–64, regarding its earlier Jekyll Island placement and Worth 1992, 156, 183, for the reinterpretation of its location in the Okefenokee.
114. Pareja 1602; Ruíz de Salazar Vallecilla 1646.
115. Díez de la Calle 1659; Alcayde de Cordoba 1660; Elixio de la Puente 1768a.
116. Rebolledo 1656b.
117. López 1602.
118. Weisman et al. 1997.

Appendix B: Translations of Selected Documents

1. Horruytiner 1670; Benito 1674.
2. Menéndez Márquez and Rocha 1682; see Worth 1992 regarding resettlement in Timucua, and Worth 1995c regarding Guale and Mocama.
3. Castilla 1740.
4. E.g., Hann 1988a, 68. Hann's source was apparently a copy in the Stetson Collection at the P. K. Yonge Library of Florida History in Gainesville, made from Santo Domingo *legajo* 2565, whereas the package used for this translation was in SD 2584. The fact that Castilla's name was listed as Don Juan suggests that the Stetson copy may have been flawed.
5. Worth 1995c.

Bibliography

Abbreviations

AGI   Archivo General de Indias (Seville)
BN   Biblioteca Nacional (Madrid)
CD   Contaduría
CT   Contratación
EC   Escribanía de Cámara
IG   Indiferente General
MEX   Audiencia de Mexico
PAT   Patronato Real
SD   Audiencia de Santo Domingo

Primary Sources

Aguilar, Pedro de. 1585. Testimony against Fray Alonso de Reynoso, January 23, 1585. AGI SD 146. Photostat in the Mary Letitia Ross Collection, Georgia Department of Archives and History, Atlanta.

Alas, Alonso de las. 1602. Certification provided to Fernando de Valdés, September 15, 1602. In Valdes 1602.

Alcantarilla, Luís de. 1602. Testimony, September 5, 1602. In Valdes 1602.

Alcayde de Cordoba, Martín. 1649. Summary of service record, March 9, 1649. AGI IG 113, no. 100.

———. 1660. Testimony, May 2, 1660. In Ranjel 1660.

Alejo, Juan. 1660. Testimony, May 17, 1660. In Ranjel 1660.

Alonso de Jesús, Francisco. 1630a. Letter to the king, March 2, 1630. AGI SD 235.

———. 1630b. Petition to Governor Don Luís de Rojas y Borja, April. In Rojas y Borja 1630.

———. 1630c. Memorial, October. AGI MEX 302. Full translation in Hann 1993c.

———. 1633. Letter to the king, January 12, 1633. AGI SD 27b.

Alvarez de Castrillón, Pedro. 1597. Certification of expenses to Indian caciques between August 2 and September 14, 1597. AGI SD 231.

Angiano, Carlos de. 1663. Certification regarding the state of Guale, April 6, 1663. AGI SD 2584. Translation in Worth 1995c, 92–93.

Anjurgo, Alonso de. 1711. Census of Santo Thomas de Santa Fee, alias Esperanza, and Salamototo, January 13, 1711. In Córcoles y Martínez 1711.

Anonymous. 1785(?). Spanish map of part of East Florida, a portion of the inland parts of East Florida, and the Bahia de Tampa. Crown Collection of colonial maps in the British Public Records Office, ser. 3, Florida, no. 126–31. Photostats in the P. K. Yonge Library of Florida History, Gainesville.

Aranguiz y Cotes, Alonso de. 1659a. Order to Matheo Pacheco y Salgado, September 18, 1659. Transcription in Pacheco y Salgado 1698.

———. 1659b. *Auto* and accord concerning the expansion of the Apalachee garrison, October 1659. In Aranguiz y Cotes 1659d.

———. 1659c. Letter to the king, November 1, 1659. AGI SD 852.

———. 1659d. Letter to the king, November 9, 1659. AGI SD 839.

———. 1660. Order to Sebastián Rodríguez, May 10, 1660. Original in Lara 1663.

———. 1661a. Order to Nicolás Estévez de Carmenatis, January 19, 1661. In Estévez de Carmenatis 1680.

———. 1661b. Order to Sebastián Rodríguez, June 25, 1661. Original in Lara 1663.

———. 1662. Order to Antonio de Argüelles, October 8, 1662. Transcription in Argüelles 1663.

———. 1663. Order to Antonio de Argüelles, January 23, 1663. Transcription in Argüelles 1663.

———. 1664. Sentences in posthumous residencia, 1664. AGI EC 1191.

Arcos, Pedro de. 1675. Report on the missions of Guale and Mocama, 1675. AGI SD 839.

Argüelles, Alonso de. 1660a. Testimony, May 2, 1660. In Ranjel 1660.

———. 1660b. Testimony, May 11, 1660. In Ranjel 1660.

———. 1660c. Testimony, late May, 1660. In Ranjel 1660.

———. 1663. Petition and service record, 1663. AGI SD 23.

———. 1678. Visitation of Guale and Mocama, December 1677–January 1678. AGI EC 156B. Translation in Hann 1993b, 83–95.

Argüelles, Antonio de, Francisco González de Villa García, Francisco García de la Vera, Nicolás Estévez de Carmenatis, Salvador de Cigarroa, Francisco de la Rocha, and Juan Sánchez de Uriza. 1678. Certification of the service of Juan Bauptista Terraza, October 20, 1678. AGI SD 234.

Argüelles, Antonio de, Juan Sánchez de Uriza, Domingo de Leturiondo, and Francisco de la Rocha. 1678. Certification of the service of Matheo Luís de Florencia, November 10, 1678. Paraphrased in Florencia 1679.

Argüelles, Bartolomé de. 1598. Letter to the king, August 3, 1598. AGI SD 229.

Arredondo, Antonio de. 1736. State of the Indians who are at the devotion of the presidio of St. Augustine, Florida, with separation of towns able to take up arms, November 27, 1736. AGI SD 2591. Uncited transcription in Swanton 1922, 104–6.

———. 1737. Plan of the city of St. Augustine, Florida, and its environs (with census), May 15, 1737. AGI SD 2592.

Ayala Escobar, Juan de. 1698. Visitation of Timucua and Apalachee, January–February 1698. AGI EC 157A.

———. 1717. Letter to the king with attached census, April 18, 1717. AGI SD 843.

Barreda, Jacinto de. 1680. Patent concerning the death of Fray Sebastián Martínez, 1679–80. AGI SD 2584. Translated in Worth 1995c:94–97.
Beltrán de Santa Cruz, Pedro. 1655. Summary of audit for accounts of Treasurer Francisco Menéndez Márquez, November 20, 1655. AGI SD 233.
Benavides, Antonio de. 1726. Visitation and census of Florida missions, December 2–11, 1726. AGI SD 866. Translated in Hann 1991: 363–68.
———. Letter to the King, April 21, 1738. AGI SD 265.
Benito, *cacique* of Machava. 1674. Petition to the king, 1674. AGI SD 234.
Bernal, Clemente. 1660. Testimony, May 16, 1660. In Ranjel 1660.
Bernaldo de Quirós, Thomás. 1584. Petition and service record, June 20, 1584 (date in council). AGI SD 125. Translation by Eugene Lyon.
Biana, Luís de. 1660. Testimony, May 20, 1660. In Ranjel 1660.
Calderón, Manuel. 1660. Testimony, May 7, 1660. In Ranjel 1660.
Calvo, Juan. 1630. Testimony, April. In Rojas y Borja 1630.
Campaña, Juan Bauptista. 1663. Certification regarding the state of Guale, April 14, 1663. AGI SD 2584. Translation in Worth 1995c, 94.
Cañizares y Osorio, Adrián de. 1635. Petition and service record, 1635. AGI SD 233.
———. 1657a. Letter to Governor Rebolledo, May 8, 1657. Transcription in Rebolledo 1657a.
———. 1657b. Letter to Governor Rebolledo, May 21, 1657. Transcription in Rebolledo 1657a.
———. 1657c. Letter to Governor Rebolledo, July 18, 1657. Transcription in Rebolledo 1657a.
Cañizares y Osorio, Francisco de. 1669. Petition and service record of Adrián de Cañizares y Osorio, 1669. AGI SD 233.
Cañizares y Osorio, Petronela de. 1635. Petition and service record of Pedro Alvarez de Godón, March 20, 1635. AGI SD 21.
Cárdenas, Joseph de. 1681. Publication of the residencia of Governor Manuel de Cendoya in Timucua, April 3–13, 1681. AGI EC 155C.
———. 1682. Publication of the residencia of Governor Pablo de Hita Salazar in Timucua, December 23, 1681–January 1, 1682. AGI EC 155C.
Castilla, Francisco de. 1740. Proposal to the king, 1740. AGI SD 2584.
Castillo, Joseph del. 1728. Census of Nombre de Dios and aggregated town of Timuca, February 12, 1728. In Valdéz 1728.
Cendoya, Manuel de. 1673. Order to Diego Díaz Mexia, January 24, 1673. AGI SD 2584. Translation in Worth 1995c:186–87.
Cigarroa, Salvador de. 1657. Testimony, April 13, 1657. In Rebolledo 1657b.
Córcoles y Martínez, Francisco de. 1706. Letter to the king, September 30, 1706. AGI SD 858.
———. 1711. Letter to the king with attached census, April 9, 1711. AGI SD 843.
Council of the Indies. 1657a. Consultation to the king of Spain, June 15, 1657. AGI SD 6. Translation in Hann 1986a, 130–35.
———. 1657b. Consultation to the king of Spain, July 6, 1657. AGI SD 6.

———. 1657c. Consultation to the king of Spain, July 7, 1657. AGI SD 6. Translation in Hann 1986a, 135–38.
Cruz, Juan de la. 1602. Testimony, September 5, 1602. In Valdes 1602.
Cruz, Juan Bauptista de la. 1660. Testimony, May 13, 1660. In Ranjel 1660.
Davila, Diego. 1606. Relation of the visitation of Bishop Juan de las Cavezas Altamirano, June 26, 1606. AGI SD 235.
Díaz, Francisco. 1612. Register of shipment sent from La Palma to Florida in *Nuestra Señora del Rosario*, April 14, 1612. AGI CT 1453.
Díaz de Badajoz, Alonso. 1630. Testimony, April. In Rojas y Borja 1630.
Díaz Vara Calderón, Gabriel. 1675. Relation of what is discovered in all the district of Florida and specification of the natives of each part and their inclinations, 1675. AGI SD 151.
Díez de la Calle, Juan. 1659. Noticias sacras i reales de los dos ymperios de las Indias occidentales de la Nueva España. BN, MSS 3023, 3024.
———. 1660. Letter to Diego de Zavate, May 7, 1960, with reply. AGI SD 839.
Díez de la Calle y Madrigal, Francisco. 1678. Summary of service record (with summary of service of Father Juan), August 1, 1678. AGI IG 203, no. 93.
Domínguez, Juan. 1670. Military service record, November 20, 1670. AGI IG 119, no. 143.
Ebelino de Compostela, Diego. 1689. Letter to the king, September 28, 1689. AGI SD 151.
Elixio de la Puente, Juan Joseph. 1768a. Plan of the Provinces of Florida, 1768. Servicio Geographico e Histórico del Ejército, Madrid.
———. 1768b. New Description of the Eastern and Western Coast of the Province of Florida, 1768. Servicio Geographico e Histórico del Ejército, Madrid.
Elvas, Gentleman of. 1993. True relation of the hardships suffered by Governor Hernando de Soto and certain Portuguese gentlemen during the discovery of the province of Florida. In *The DeSoto Chronicles: The Expedition of Hernando de Soto to North America in 1539–1543*, translated by James Alexander Robertson and edited by Lawrence A. Clayton, Vernon James Knight Jr., and Edward C. Moore, 19–219. Tuscaloosa: Univ. of Alabama Press.
Entonado, Bartolomé. 1660. Testimony, May 10, 1660. In Ranjel 1660.
Espinosa, Eugenio de. 1633. Sentences for *residencia*, 1633. AGI EC 1188.
Estévez de Carmenatis, Nicolás. 1657. Testimony, October 1657. In Rebolledo 1657f.
———. 1660. Testimony, April 1660. In Ranjel 1660.
———. 1680. Petition and service record, June 22, 1680. AGI IG 128, no. 124.
Fernández de Cendrera, Francisco. 1616a. Audit of Florida situado accounts between November 25, 1611, and August 26, 1613. AGI CD 956.
———. 1616b. Audit of Florida situado accounts between August 6, 1613, and October 20, 1616. AGI CD 955.
Fernández de Ecija, Francisco. 1602. Testimony, September 4, 1602. In Valdes 1602.
———. 1605. Testimony, June 23, 1606. In Márquez 1606.

Fernández de Florencia, Juan. 1670. Summary of petition and service record, July 31, 1670. AGI SD 233.

———. 1674. Certification regarding the establishment of San Pedro de los Chines, April 28, 1674. AGI SD 235. Translated in Hann 1993, 74–75.

———. 1675. Report on the missions of Apalachee and Timucua, July 15, 1675. AGI SD 839.

———. 1681. Census of Apalachee, May 27, 1681. Transcription in BN, MS 300.

Fernández de Olivera, Juan. 1612. Letter to the king, October 13, 1612. AGI SD 229.

Fernández de San Agustín, Juan. 1630. Testimony, April. In Rojas y Borja 1630. Relevant section translated in Worth 1992, 68–69.

Fernández Turel, Marcos. 1633. Summary of service record, January 13, 1633. AGI SD 233.

Florencia, Francisco de. 1706. Petition and investigation, May 19–26, 1706. AGI SD 853.

Florencia, Joachín de. 1695. Visitation of Apalachee and Timucua, November 1694–January 1695. AGI EC 157A. Translation in Hann 1993b, 152–219.

Florencia, Matheo Luís de. 1679. Summary of petition and service record, November 10, 1679. AGI IG 203.

Florencia, Matheo Luís de, and Adrián de Cañizares y Osorio. 1652. Certification regarding the hacienda of Asile, March 15, 1652. In Horruytiner 1652.

Florencia, Patricio de. 1657. Testimony, October 16, 1657. In Rebolledo 1657f.

Florencia, Pedro de. 1670. Summary of petition and service record, July 26, 1670. AGI SD 233.

Fuentes, Francisco de. 1681. Census of Guale and Mocama, July 1, 1681. Transcription in BN, MS 300. Translation in Worth 1995c, 100–103.

García, Andrés. 1695. Criminal case against Santiago, native of San Pedro, February–September 1695. Appended to Florencia 1695. AGI EC 157A. Translation in Hann 1993b, 276–96.

García de Capilla, Bartolomé. 1630. Testimony, April 1630. In Rojas y Borja 1630.

García de la Vera, Alonso. 1601. Conversation between the cacique of Potano and Governor Méndez de Canço, March 13, 1601. AGI SD 232. Translated in Worth 1992, 40–41.

García de la Vera, Francisco. 1645. Testimony during the residencia of Governor Damián de Vega, Castro, y Pardo, 1645. AGI EC 155A.

García de Solís, Fulgencio. 1754. Auto regarding the new regulations by the Viceroy of New Spain for Florida, June 15, 1754. AGI SD 2226.

Gelabert, Joseph Antonio, Justis de Santa Ana, Juan Estévan de la Peña, and Juan Joseph Elixio de la Puente. 1764. Review of the filiation of Indians lodged in the villa of Guanabacoa, having come from the presidio of St. Augustine, Florida, April 10, 1764. AGI SD 2574.

Gómez, Manuel. 1658. Testimony, September 25, 1658. In Rebolledo 1658d.

———. 1660. Testimony, May 15, 1660. In Ranjel 1660.

———. 1685. Letter to Governor Juan Márquez Cabrera, November 12, 1685. Transcription in AGI SD 839.

Gómez de Engraba, Juan. 1657a. Letter to Francisco Martínez, March 13, 1657. AGI SD 225. Translation in Hann 1986a, 127–28.

———. 1657b. Letter to Francisco Martínez, April 4, 1657. AGI SD 225. Translation in Hann 1986, 128–29.

González, Domingo. 1657. Testimony, October 1657. In Rebolledo 1657f.

González de la Torre, Juan. 1602. Testimony, September 1602. In Valdes 1602.

Guadalupe, Juan de. 1628. Transcription of congregation list, January 8, 1628. AGI SD 2584. Translation in Worth 1995c, 67–68.

Güemes y Horcasitas, Juan Francisco. 1739. Letter to the King, May 21, 1739. AGI SD 866. Corrected using original census dated December 31, 1738 in AGI SD 867.

Guerra y Vega, Francisco de. 1665a. Order to Ventura González, January 15, 1665. Summary in Moreno y Segobia 1671.

———. 1665b. Order to Pedro de Florencia, January 16, 1665. Summary in Florencia 1670.

———. 1665c. Order to Bartolomé Sánchez de Entonado, January 17, 1665. Transcription in AGI SD 2584. Translation in Worth 1995c, 71–72.

———. 1665d. Order to Ysidro de Reynoso, April 18, 1665. Original in Reynoso 1669.

———. 1665e. Order to Manuel Gómez, June 27, 1665. Summary in Moreno y Segobia 1671.

———. 1665f. Order to Francisco Sánchez, November 17, 1665. Summary in Moreno y Segobia 1671.

———. 1665g. Order to Manuel de Torres, December 22, 1665. Summary in Moreno y Segobia 1671.

———. 1666a. Order to Thomás Menéndez Márquez, January 24, 1666. Summary in Menéndez Márquez 1681.

———. 1666b. Order to Manuel Ponce de León, January 24, 1666. Summary in Moreno y Segobia 1671.

———. 1666c. Order to Alonso de Alvarez, February 1, 1666. Transcription in AGI SD 2584. Translation in Worth 1995c, 74–75.

———. 1666d. Order to Juan Domínguez, February 15, 1666. Summary in Moreno y Segobia 1671.

———. 1667a. Order to Francisco de Aispiolea, January 10, 1667. Transcription in AGI SD 2584. Translation in Worth 1995c, 81–82.

———. 1667b. Order to Pedro de Florencia, January 10, 1667. Summary in Florencia 1670.

———. 1668a. Order to Nicolás Estévez de Carmenatis, January 12, 1668. In Estévez de Carmenatis 1680.

———. 1668b. Order to Juan Domínguez, January 21, 1668. Transcription in AGI SD 2584. Translation in Worth 1995c, 78–79.

———. 1669. Order to Francisco de Aispiolea, January 16, 1669. Transcription in AGI SD 2584. Translation in Worth 1995c, 80–81.

———. 1670. Order to Nicolás Estévez de Carmenatis, January 26, 1670. In Estévez de Carmenatis (1680).

———. 1673. Certification regarding the service and numbers of repartimiento laborers, October 20, 1673. AGI SD 235.
Heras, Sanctos de las. 1657a. Certification regarding the number of friars in service, June 26, 1657. AGI SD 6.
———. 1657b. Certification regarding expenses during Governor Rebolledo's visitation of Apalachee and Timucua, October 12, 1657. In Rebolledo 1657f.
Heras, Sanctos de las, and Domingo de Leturiondo. 1658. Relation of tithes, May 31, 1658. AGI SD 229.
Hernández, Diego. 1660. Testimony, May 8, 1660. In Ranjel 1660.
Hernández de Biedma, Luys. 1993. Relation of the island of Florida. In *The DeSoto Chronicles: The Expedition of Hernando de Soto to North America in 1539–1543*, translated by John E. Worth and edited by Lawrence A. Clayton, Vernon James Knight Jr., and Edward C. Moore. Tuscaloosa: Univ. of Alabama Press.
Herrera, Juan de. 1688. Certification regarding publication in Santa Fé of the general autos of the residencia of Governor Juan Márquez Cabrera, September 8, 1688. AGI EC 156A.
Herrera, López, y Mesa, Antonio de. 1649. Petition and relation of services, May 11, 1649. AGI IG 114, no. 23.
———. 1660a. Certification regarding gubernatorial lieutenants of Diego de Rebolledo, April 24, 1660. In Ranjel 1660.
———. 1660b. Certification regarding royal slaves, forced laborers, carpenters, and oxen, June 8, 1660. In Ranjel 1660.
Hita Salazar, Gerónimo Fernando de. 1680. Summary of service record, November 6, 1680. AGI IG 128, no. 120.
Hita Salazar, Pablo de. 1676. Order to Nicolás Estévez de Carmenatis II, October 21, 1676. In Estévez de Carmenatis 1680.
———. 1678. Criminal case against Calesa, August 12–November 20, 1678. AGI EC 156A. Translation in Hann 1992a.
———. 1680. Order to Lorenzo Joseph de León, July 22, 1680. Translation in Worth 1995c, 85–86.
———. 1707. Publication of the residencia of Governor Zuñiga y Cerda in the mission villages, January 13–14, 1707. AGI SD 858.
Horruytiner, Luís. 1633a. Letter to the king, November 15, 1633. AGI SD 233.
———. 1633b. Order to Antonio de Herrera, López, y Mesa, December 6, 1633. Transcription in Herrera, López, y Mesa 1649.
———. 1635. Order to Sebastián Rodríguez, June 2, 1635. Transcription in Rodríguez 1639.
———. 1636. Order to Juan Gómez Navarro, January 27, 1636. Transcription in recipient's service record, AGI SD 232.
———. 1637. Letter to the king, June 24, 1637. AGI SD 225.
———. 1638a. Certification of the service of Sebastián Rodríguez, September 12, 1638. Transcription in Rodríguez 1639.
———. 1638b. Order to Antonio de Herrera, López, y Mesa, November 3, 1638. Transcription in Herrera, López, y Mesa 1649.

———. 1639a. Certification of the service of Nicolás Estévez de Carmenatis, February 16, 1639. Transcription in Estévez de Carmenatis 1680.
———. 1639b. Certification of the service of Antonio de Herrera, López, y Mesa, March 8, 1639. Transcription in Herrera, López, y Mesa 1649.
———. 1640. Relation of services, March 12, 1640 (council). AGI IG 111, no. 239.
Horruytiner, Pedro Benedit. 1652. Investigation regarding the hacienda of Asile, March. In Rebolledo 1657i.
———. 1657a. Testimony, April 13, 1657. In Rebolledo 1657b.
———. 1657b. Letter to the king, November 10, 1657. AGI SD 233.
———. 1657c. Response to residencia charges, 1657. In Rebolledo 1657h.
———. 1660a. Testimony, May 18, 1660. In Ranjel 1660.
———. 1660b. Complaint and demand against Governor Diego de Rebolledo, June 6, 1660. In Ranjel 1660.
———. 1670. Record of the junta held in San Pedro de Potohiriba, March 20, 1674. In Benito 1674.
Horruytiner, Pedro Benedit, Matheo Luís de Florencia, and Adrián de Cañizares y Osorio. 1652. Agreement regarding the delivery of the Asile hacienda to the Franciscans, March 16, 1652. In Horruytiner 1652.
Junco, María de. 1605. Petition concerning the service of Juan Ramírez de Contreras, October 1605. AGI SD 24.
Junta de Guerra. 1663. Notes regarding service of Francisco Díez de la Calle, May 29, 1663. AGI IG 1876.
———. 1705. Summary of letter September 15, 1704, letter from Governor Zuñiga y Cerda, July 14, 1705. AGI SD 852.
Lara, Juan de. 1606. Testimony, June 23, 1606. In Márquez 1606.
Lara, María de. 1663. Petition and service record of Sebastián Rodríguez, 1663. AGI SD 233.
Leturiondo, Domingo de. 1677. Summary of service record and petition, November 16, 1677. AGI IG 127, no. 91.
———. 1678. Visitation of Apalachee and Timucua, December 1677–January 1678. AGI EC 156B. Translation in Hann 1993b, 95–142.
———. 1685. Visitation of Guale and Mocama, December 1685. AGI SD 2584. Translation in Worth 1995c, 106–22.
Livingston, John. 1686. Testimony, September 23, 1686. AGI SD 2584. Translation in Worth 1995c:152–53.
López, Baltasár. 1602. Declaration, September 15, 1602. AGI SD 235.
López de Gabira, Bartolomé. 1660. Testimony, April 1660. In Ranjel 1660.
Manuel, cacique of Asile. 1651. Letter to Governor Don Pedro Benedit Horruytiner, December 9, 1651. Translated from the Timucuan language by Fray Alonso Escudero. AGI EC 155b.
Márquez, Gaspar. 1606. Petition to the king, June 23, 1606. AGI SD 232.
Márquez Cabrera, Juan. 1680. Letter to the king, December 6, 1680. AGI SD 226.
Marrón, Francisco de. 1596. Letter to the king, January 23, 1596. AGI SD 235.

Medina, Juan de. 1651. Letter to Governor Horruytiner, December 29, 1651. In Horruytiner 1652.

Medina, Juan de, Sebastián Martínez, Gaspar de Ribota, Francisco de San Antonio, Antonio de la Cruz, Alonso Escudero, and Joseph Bamba. 1662. Letter to the king, December 21, 1662. AGI SD 235.

Melgar, Manuel de. 1672. Report to the Council of the Indies regarding the Florida missions, December 31, 1672. AGI SD 864.

Méndez de Canço, Gonzalo. 1597. Certification of expenses to Indians, July 28, 1597. In Morgado 1597.

———. 1598a. Investigation and relation of expedition against the Guale rebels, January 12, 1598. In Méndez de Canço 1598b.

———. 1598b. Letter to the king, February 23, 1598. AGI SD 224.

———. 1598c. Investigation regarding the rescue of Fray Francisco de Avila and criminal case against the Indian Lúcas of Tupiqui, July 1–29, 1598. AGI PAT 19, R 28.

———. 1602. Letter to the king, September 22, 1602. AGI SD 224.

Menéndez, Don Alonso, Don Francisco de Ybarra, Don Juan de Zapala, Bernabé de Aluste, and Don Thomás de Yor. 1657. Letter to the king, September 16, 1657. AGI SD 235.

Menéndez Márquez, Antonio. 1660. Testimony, May 9, 1660. In Ranjel 1660.

———. 1673. Summary of service record, March 20, 1673. AGI IG 124, no. 21.

———. 1675. Certification regarding royal cédula of November 20, 1641, providing for yearly supplies for each friar, June 5, 1675. AGI SD 235.

Menéndez Márquez, Antonio, and Francisco de Rocha. 1682. Certification regarding past and present Florida missions, October 2, 1682. Transcription in BN, MS 300, 356–61f.

Menéndez Márquez, Francisco. 1647. Order to Nicolás Estévez de Carmenatis, June 9, 1647. In Estévez de Carmenatis 1680.

———. 1648. Letter to the king, February 8, 1648. AGI SD 229.

Menéndez Márquez, Francisco, and Pedro Benedit Horruytiner. 1647a. Letter to the king, March 18, 1647. AGI SD 229.

———. 1647b. Order to Nicolás Estévez de Carmenatis, November 5, 1647. In Estévez de Carmenatis 1680.

Menéndez Márquez, Juan. 1602. Certification provided to Fernando de Valdés, September 13, 1602. AGI SD 2533.

———. 1652. Testimony, March 1652. In Horruytiner 1652.

———. 1667a. Letter to the king, January 25, 1667. AGI SD 229.

———. 1667b. Letter to the king, September 12, 1667. AGI SD 229.

———. 1675. Summary of service record, March 8, 1675. AGI IG 125, no. 22.

Menéndez Márquez, Juan, and Alonso de las Alas. 1595. Letter to the king, December 13, 1595. AGI SD 229.

Menéndez Márquez, Juan, Alonso de las Alas, and Alonso Sancho Sáez de Mercado. 1605. Certification regarding the fruits of the land, December 24, 1605. AGI SD 232.

Menéndez Márquez, Pedro. 1588. Letter to the king, July 17, 1588. AGI SD 224. Photostat in Mary Letitia Ross Collection, Georgia Department of Archives and History, Atlanta.

———. 1593. Relation, August 23, 1593. AGI PAT 260. Photostat in Mary Letitia Ross Collection, Georgia Department of Archives and History, Atlanta.

Menéndez Márquez, Thomás. 1681. Summary of service record, March 12, 1681. AGI IG 129, no. 100.

———. 1697. Certification regarding corn deposits during term of Governor Laureano de Torres, March 8, 1697. AGI SD 228, R 1, no. 46.

Menéndez Márquez, Thomás, and Joachín de Florencia. 1697. Certification regarding Florida missions and friars, April 15, 1697. AGI SD 230.

Menéndez de Posada, Alonso. 1647. Petition to the king, 1647. AGI SD 229.

Moncrief, James. 1764. Map of part of East Florida from St. Johns River to Bay of Mosquitos, showing names of proprietors of estates. Drawn from the original plan of John Gordons, Esquire, given to Governor Grant. Crown Collection of colonial maps in the British Public Records Office, Florida, no. 54–57. Photostats in the P. K. Yonge Library of Florida History, Gainesville.

Montes, Blas de. 1601. Petition regarding Fray Baltasár López, June 1601. AGI SD 224.

———. 1602. Letter to the king, September 16, 1602. AGI SD 232.

Montiano, Manuel de. 1738. Letter to the King, June 4, 1738. AGI SD 865.

Monzón, Francisco de. 1660. Testimony, May 4, 1660. In Ranjel 1660.

Moral, Alonso del, Sebastián Martínez, Martín Lasso, Roque Domínguez, Francisco de San Joseph, Juan Bauptista Campaña, and Juan de Pajua. 1673a. Memorial and testimony of all the missionaries who presently find themselves in the province of Santa Elena de la Florida, their native lands, ages, years of habit, exercise, and offices that they have had and have in the last 40 years. Photostat of original in the Mary Letitia Ross Collection, Georgia Department of Archives and History, Atlanta.

———. 1673b. Authentic memorial of the missionaries who have been provincial ministers in the province of Santa Elena de la Florida in the last forty years. Photostat of original in the Mary Letitia Ross Collection, Georgia Department of Archives and History, Atlanta.

Moral, Alonso del, Bernardo de Santa María, Miguel Garçon, Pedro Vázquez, Francisco de San Joseph, and Martín Lasso. 1657. Letter to Governor Rebolledo, May 10, 1657. Transcription in San Antonio et al. 1657.

Morales, Pedro, Antonio Navarro, Pedro del Corral, Ignacio Venegas, Francisco Gutiérrez, Joseph de Flores Rubio, Gabriel de Llerena. 1735. Chapter list [Latin], September 17, 1735. AGI SD 867.

Moreno, Juan. 1673. Summary of letter to the king, April 18, 1673. AGI SD 235.

Moreno Ponce de León, Pedro. 1651. Petition to the king, September 7, 1651. AGI SD 235.

Moreno y Segovia, Juan. 1657. Testimony, October 16, 1657. In Rebolledo 1657f.

———. 1660. Certification regarding the Cañizares case, April 30, 1660. In Ranjel 1660.
———. 1671. Summaries of orders relating to good treatment of the Indians issued during the term of Governor Guerra y Vega, August 13, 1671. AGI EC 155C.
Morgado, Francisco. 1597. Certification of expenses to Indian caciques between June 8 and July 27, 1597. AGI SD 231.
Muñoz de Oñate, María. 1654. Petition and service record of Martín de Cuevas, May 17, 1654. AGI IG 1876.
Ocaña, Francisco de. 1635. Relación acerca del presente feliz estado de las Indias Occidentales en la appostólica administración de los Santos Sacramentos y Combersión de los Indios por los Religiossos de nuestro seraphico Padre San Francisco. Hasta el año de 1635. Transcribed in Pou y Martí 1927a, 1927b.
Ojitos, Manuel. 1736. Census of convents and missionaries of the province of Santa Elena de la Florida, their age, quality, and ministries in which they occupy themselves, October 17, 1736. AGI SD 867.
Oré, Luís Gerónimo de. 1936. *Relación Histórica de la Florida, escrita en el siglo XVII*, edited by Atanasio López. Madrid: Imprenta de Romona Velasco.
Pacheco y Salgado, Lucía and María. 1698. Petition and service record for Matheo Pacheco y Salgado, 1698. AGI SD 848.
Pacheco y Salgado, Matheo. 1660. Testimony, May 5, 1660. In Ranjel 1660.
Palacios, Pedro de. 1675. Report on the visitation of Florida by Bishop Gabriel Díaz Vara Calderón, 1675. Partial transcription in the Mary Letitia Ross Collection, Georgia Department of Archives and History, Atlanta.
Pareja, Francisco. 1602. Declaration, September 14, 1602. AGI SD 235.
———. 1612. *Catechismo en Lenua Castellana y Timuquana, en el Qual Se Contiene Lo Que Se les Puede Enseñar a los Adultos Que An de Ser Baptizados*. Mexico: Press of the Widow of Pedro Balli.
———. 1614. *Arte y Pronunciación en Lengua Timuquana y Castellana*. Mexico: Imprenta de Juan Ruíz. Transcription in Adam and Vinson 1886.
———. 1616. Relation composed for Fray Luís Gerónimo de Oré, 1616. Transcibed in Oré 1936, 108–12.
Pareja, Francisco, and Alonso de Peñaranda. 1607. Letter to the king, November 20, 1607. AGI SD 224.
Pareja, Francisco, Alonso de Peñaranda, Alonso Serrano, Juan Bauptista de Capilla, and Bartolomé Romero. 1608. Letter to the king, January 11, 1608. AGI SD 235.
Pareja, Francisco, Lorenzo Martínez, Pedro Ruíz, Alonso de Pesquera, Juan de la Cruz, Francisco Alonso de Jesús, Bartolomé Romero. 1617a. Letter to the king, January 14, 1617. AGI SD 235.
———. 1617b. Letter to the king, January 17, 1617. AGI SD 235.
Pasqua, Francisco. 1660. Testimony, May 17, 1660. In Ranjel 1660.
Pastrana, Alonso de. 1605. Testimony, October 16, 1605. In Junco 1605.
Pedrosa, Salvador de. 1660. Testimony, April, 1660. In Ranjel 1660.
Peña, Diego. 1717. Diary of 1716 expedition. AGI SD 843.

Peñaranda, Alonso de. 1608. Letter to the king, January 1608. AGI SD 224.
Perete, Francisco, Sebastián Martínez, Francisco Maillo, Blas de Robles, Pedro de Luna, and Domingo Padura. 1676. Chapter list [Latin], April 25, 1676. Photostat from the Buckingham Smith Papers, New York Historical Society, in the Mary Letitia Ross Collection, Georgia Department of Archives and History, Atlanta.
Pérez, Andrés. 1674. Certification regarding the establishment of San Carlos and San Nicolás de los Chacatos, June 23, 1674. AGI SD 235. Translation in Hann 1993b, 75.
Pérez, Francisco. 1646. Petition to the king, 1646. AGI SD 235.
Pérez de Villa Real, Agustín. 1652. Testimony, March 1652. In Horruytiner 1652.
———. 1657. Testimony, October 1657. In Rebolledo 1657f.
———. 1660. Testimony, April 30, 1660. In Ranjel 1660.
Pesquera, Alonso de. 1623. Petition to the king, July 12, 1623. AGI SD 26.
Pesquera, Alonso de, Gregorio de Movilla, Francisco Pareja, Alonso Ortíz, Estéban de San Andrés, and Francisco Fernández. 1621. Letter to the king, September 1, 1621. In Pesquera 1623.
Ponce de León, Nicolás I. 1637. Certification of the service of Pedro de Aispiolea, June 27, 1637. AGI SD 232.
———. 1651a. Order to Antonio de Argüelles, May 17, 1651. In Argüelles 1663.
———. 1651b. Order to Antonio de Argüelles, June 20, 1651. In Argüelles 1663.
———. 1651c. Letter to the king, September 20, 1651. AGI SD 233.
Ponce de León, Nicolás I, and Salvador de Cigarroa. 1651. Record of the purchase of the hacienda of Asile, September 5, 1651. In Ponce de León 1651c.
Ponce de León, Nicolás II. 1660. Testimony, April 26, 1660. In Ranjel 1660.
———. 1664a. Order to Antonio Menéndez Márquez, March 24, 1664. Paraphrased in Menéndez Márquez 1673.
———. 1664b. Order to Gonzalo Hernández, March 26, 1664. AGI SD 23, no. 9.
———. 1664c. Certification of the service of Matheo Luís de Florencia, June 10, 1664. Paraphrased in Florencia 1679.
Prado, Joseph de. 1654a. Petition to Governor Rebolledo, December 23, 1654. Transcription in Prado 1654b.
———. 1654b. Letter to the king, December 30, 1654. AGI SD 229.
———. 1657. Testimony, April 13, 1657. In Rebolledo 1657b.
———. 1660. Testimony, April 1660. In Ranjel 1660.
Primo de Ribera, Joseph. 1717. Census of mission inhabitants, April 1717. In Ayala Escobar 1717.
Puerta, Pedro de la. 1657. Letter to Governor Rebolledo, July 12, 1657. Transcription in Rebolledo 1657a.
———. 1660. Testimony, April 1660. In Ranjel 1660.
Pueyo, Juan de. 1695. Visitation of Guale and Mocama, January–February 1695. AGI EC 157A. Translation in Hann 1993b, 220–48.
Pulido, Blas. 1722. Auto in chapter, October 5, 1722. AGI SD 842.
Purcell, Joseph. 1778. A map of the road from Pensacola in West Florida to St. Augustine in East Florida. Crown Collection of colonial maps in the British Public

Records Office, ser. 3, Florida, no. 108–15. Reduced-size photostats in the P. K. Yonge Library of Florida History, Gainesville. Full-size photostats in the Hargrett Rare Book and Manuscript Collection, University of Georgia Libraries, Athens.

Quiroga y Losada, Diego de. 1687. Letter to the king, December 20, 1687. AGI PAT 241, R. 17.

———. 1688. Letter to the king, April 1, 1688. AGI SD 839.

———. 1692. Letter to the king, April 16, 1692. AGI SD 227B, R 1, no. 91.

———. 1697. Letter to the king, October 9, 1697 (date in council). AGI SD 839.

Ramírez, Francisco, Juan de Cueva, and Francisco Menéndez Márquez. 1627. Letter to the king, January 30, 1627. AGI SD 229.

Ranjel, Diego. 1660. Residencia of Governor Don Diego de Rebolledo, April–May 1660. AGI CD 963, 964.

Rangel, Rodrigo. 1993. Account of the northern conquest and discovery of Hernando de Soto. In *The DeSoto Chronicles: The Expedition of Hernando de Soto to North America in 1539–1543*, translated by John E. Worth and edited by Lawrence A. Clayton, Vernon James Knight Jr., and Edward C. Moore. Tuscaloosa: Univ. of Alabama Press.

Rebolledo, Diego de. 1654a. Provision regarding the Indian fund, July 24, 1654. Transcription in Prado 1654b.

———. 1654b. Instruction to Antonio de Sartucha, November 8, 1654. Transcribed in Rebolledo 1657a.

———. 1655a. Order to Antonio de Argüelles, March 10, 1655. In Argüelles 1663.

———. 1655b. Letter to the king, October 24, 1655. AGI SD 852.

———. 1656a. Order to Juan Domínguez, January 12, 1656. Original in Domínguez 1670.

———. 1656b. Order to Juan Domínguez, February 15, 1656. Original in Domínguez 1670.

———. 1656c. Order to Agustín Pérez de Villa Real, April 19, 1656. Transcription in Rebolledo 1657b.

———. 1656d. Order to Nicolás Fernández de Goyas, April 20, 1656. Transcription in Rebolledo 1657b. Translation in Worth 1995c.

———. 1656e. Letter to Antonio de Sartucha, April 20, 1656. Original in Ranjel 1660.

———. 1656f. Order to Matheo Pacheco y Salgado, July 11, 1656. Transcription in Pacheco y Salgado 1698.

———. 1656g. Order and instruction to Adrián de Cañizares y Osorio, September 4, 1656. Transcription in Ranjel 1660.

———. 1657a. Visitation of Apalachee and Timucua, January–February 1657. Transcription in Rebolledo 1657h. Full translation in Hann 1986a.

———. 1657b. Auto concerning the meeting at Tolomato, April, 1657. Transcription in Ranjel 1660.

———. 1657c. Letter to the Florida Franciscans, June 4, 1657. Transcription in San Antonio et al. 1657.

———. 1657d. Letter to the Florida Franciscans, August 5, 1657. Transcription in Rebolledo 1657a.

———. 1657e. Letter to the king, September 18, 1657. AGI SD 839.

———. 1657f. *Auto* concerning gubernatorial term, October. Original in Ranjel 1660.

———. 1657g. Letter to the king, October 18, 1657. AGI SD 839.

———. 1657h. Residencia of Governors Ruíz, Ponce de León, and Horruytiner. AGI EC 155b.

———. 1657i. Order to Juan Domínguez, December 21, 1657. Original in Domínguez 1670.

———. 1658a. General order concerning the towns of the Camino Real, January 23, 1658. Transcription in Ranjel 1660.

———. 1658b. Order to Matheo Pacheco y Salgado, February 7, 1658. In Pacheco y Salgado 1698.

———. 1658c. Commission to Nicolás Estévez de Carmenatis, May 10, 1658. Transcription in Estévez de Carmenatis 1680.

———. 1658d. Auto concerning the provincial lieutenants of Apalachee and Timucua, September–November 1658. Transcription in Ranjel 1660.

Redondo Villegas, Pedro de. 1602a. Audit of Florida warehouse accounts between 1595 and 1597. AGI CD 947.

———. 1602b. Audit of Florida warehouse accounts between 1597 and 1601. AGI CD 956.

———. 1602c. Audit of Florida warehouse accounts between 1601 and 1602. AGI CD 950.

Rexidor, Antonio. 1735. Certification regarding Florida, March 2, 1735. AGI SD 867.

Reyes, Jacinto de los. 1660. Testimony, May 9, 1660. In Ranjel 1660.

Reyes, Gaspar de los. 1687. Certification regarding 1687 Indian fund expenses, December 31, 1687. AGI EC 157A.

Reynoso, Ysidro de. 1669. Petition and service record, 1669. AGI SD 233.

Riço, Manuel. 1681. Census of Timucua, July 14, 1681. Transcription in BN, MS 300.

Ríos, Diego de los. 1657. Testimony, April 13, 1657. In Rebolledo 1657b.

Ríos Enríquez, Dionicio de los. 1690a. Transcription of letter to Governor Diego de Quiroga y Losada, September 2, 1690. AGI SD 227B, R 1, no. 97.

———. 1690b. Transcription of letter to Governor Diego de Quiroga y Losada, November 29, 1690. AGI SD 227B, R 1, no. 97.

———. 1691. Transcription of letter to Governor Diego de Quiroga y Losada, January 11, 1691. AGI SD 227B, R 1, no. 97.

Rocha, Francisco de la. 1660. Testimony, May 6, 1660. In Ranjel 1660.

———. 1679. Summary of service record, November 13, 1679. AGI IG 135, no. 108.

Rodrigo de Ortega, Luís. 1736. Certification regarding past and present provinces of Florida, November 27, 1736. AGI SD 2584. Translation in Worth 1995c: 183–85.

Rodríguez, Sebastián. 1639. Petition and service record, January 18, 1639 (date in Junta). AGI SD 233.

———. 1647. Petition and service record, 1647. AGI SD 233.

Rodríguez Tisnado, Juan. 1685. Letter to Governor Juan Márquez Cabrera, March 16, 1685. AGI SD 839.

Rojas y Borja, Luís de. 1627a. Letter to the king, February 13, 1627. Translation in the Mary Letitia Ross Collection, Georgia Department of Archives and History, Atlanta (original document no longer in cited legajo).

———. 1627b. Auto regarding the *cacica* of San Juan del Puerto, August 18, 1627. AGI SD 232.

———. 1628. Letter to the king, February 29, 1628 (date in council). AGI SD 225.

———. 1630. Investigation regarding the petition of Fray Francisco Alonso de Jesús, April. Transcribed for the residencia of Governor Ruíz de Salazar Vallecilla, October 17, 1657. AGI EC 155b.

Romo de Uriza, Francisco. 1660. Testimony, May 17, 1660. In Ranjel 1660.

———. 1701. Letter to Governor Zuñiga y Cerda, August 18, 1701. AGI SD 858.

Ruíz, Pedro. 1602. Declaration, September 16, 1602. AGI SD 235.

———. 1610. Relation of items needed for the Franciscans in Florida, June 15, 1610. AGI CT 5544.

Ruíz de Salazar Vallecilla, Benito. 1645a. Letter to the king, April 16, 1645. AGI SD 225.

———. 1645b. Order to Sebastián Rodríguez, September 30, 1645. Transcribed in Rodríguez 1647.

———. 1646. Order to Antonio de Argüelles, January 27, 1646. In Argüelles 1663.

———. 1647. Letter to the king, May 22, 1647. AGI SD 229.

———. 1648a. Order to Juan Domínguez, April 18, 1648. In Domínguez 1670.

———. 1648b. Order to Nicolás Estévez de Carmenatis, July 5, 1648. In Estévez de Carmenatis 1680.

———. 1648c. Order to Juan Domínguez, July 20, 1648. In Domínguez 1670.

———. 1648d. Order to Nicolás Estévez de Carmenatis, October 6, 1648. In Estévez de Carmenatis 1680.

———. 1650. Order to Nicolás Estévez de Carmenatis, April 15, 1650. In Estévez de Carmenatis 1680.

———. 1651. Order to Nicolás Estévez de Carmenatis, April 24, 1651. In Estévez de Carmenatis 1680.

Salamanca, Juan de. 1658. Letter to the king, November 1, 1658. AGI SD 229.

Salinas, Juan de, Francisco Ramírez, Juan de Cueva, Francisco Menéndez Márquez. 1623. Accord regarding the petition of Fray Alonso de Pesquera, July 12, 1623. In Pesquera 1623.

Salvador, Diego. 1658. Testimony, September 25, 1658. In Rebolledo 1658d.

San Antonio, Francisco de, Juan de Medina, Sebastián Martínez, Jacinto Domínguez, Alonso del Moral, Juan Caldera. 1657. Letter to the king, September 10, 1657. AGI SD 235. Full translation from Woodbury Lowery transcript in Hann 1993b.

Sánchez de Uriza, Juan. 1660. Testimony, April 28, 1660. In Ranjel 1660.
Sánchez Judrero, Juan. 1608. Petition and service record. AGI SD 232.
Sánchez Sáez de Mercado, Alonso. 1602. Testimony, September 6, 1602. In Valdés 1602.
San Martín, Pedro de. 1635. Summary of service record, October 15, 1635. AGI SD 233.
Santiago, mico of Tolomato. 1658. Letter to the king, March 21, 1658. AGI SD 233.
Santiago, Phelipe de. 1660. Testimony, April 26, 1660. In Ranjel 1660.
Solana, Alonso. 1660. Testimony, May 12, 1660. In Ranjel 1660.
———. 1683. Map of the island of Florida. AGI SD 226. Reproduced in Worth 1995c:38 and Hann 1996:270.
———. 1688. Summaries of all criminal cases fulminated by Governor Márquez Cabrera, September 4, 1688. AGI EC 156A.
Sotomayor, Andrés de. 1616. Factor's account, records for credits and disbursements of corn, 1611–1616. AGI SD 958.
Sotomayor, Juan Joseph de. 1660. Testimony, May 1660. In Ranjel 1660.
Spanish Crown. 1615. Cédula to the royal officials of Florida, November 21, 1615. Transcription in Ranjel 1660.
———. 1651. Cédula to the royal officials of Florida, December 5, 1651. Partial transcription in Prado 1654b.
———. 1653. Title of governor and captain general of Florida to Diego de Rebolledo, March 24, 1653. AGI SD 2539.
———. 1655. Cédula to Governor Rebolledo, November 16, 1655. Transcription in Rebolledo 1657b.
Texeda, Pedro. 1660. Testimony, May 14, 1660. In Ranjel 1660.
Torres, Juan de. 1739. Census of converted Indians, March 6, 1739. AGI SD 867.
Trevijano, Diego de. 1643. Summary of service record, September 14, 1643. AGI IG 112, no. 51.
Trevino Guillamas, Juan. 1616. Order to Pedro Alvarez de Godón, April 17, 1616. Transcribed in Petronela de Cañizares y Osorio (1635).
Uriza, Manuel de. 1711. Census of Nombre de Dios, January 1711. In Córcoles y Martínez 1711.
Valdés, Fernando de. 1602. Investigation regarding the presidio of Florida, September 1602. AGI SD 2533.
Valdéz, Gerónimo. 1728. Autos regarding the state of the Florida missions, including census, September 20, 1728 (date of transcript). AGI SD 2226.
Vega Castro y Pardo, Damián de. 1639. Letter to the king, April 8, 1639. AGI SD 225.
———. 1640. Commission to Antonio de Herrera, López, y Mesa, August 27, 1640. In Herrera, López, y Mesa 1649.
———. 1643a. Letter to the king, July 9, 1643. AGI SD 225.
———. 1643b. Order to Nicolás Estévez de Carmenatis, September 23, 1643. In Estévez de Carmenatis 1680.
Vermejo, Pedro. 1602. Declaration, September 14, 1602. AGI SD 235.

Xaen, Diego de. 1703. Investigation regarding murder charges against the slave Juan Francisco, July 18–August 11, 1703. In Zuñiga y Cerda 1703.
Ybarra, Pedro de. 1605a. Summary of letter to the king, July 1605. AGI SD 224.
———. 1605b. Letter to Pedro de Bermejo, December 13, 1605. Transcription in AGI SD 232.
———. 1608. Letter to the king, August 22, 1608. AGI SD 224.
Zuñiga y Cerda, Joseph de. 1700. Investigation and order regarding Florida haciendas, November 29, 1700. AGI SD 858.
———. 1702. Letter to the king, September 30, 1702. AGI SD 858.
———. 1703. Criminal case against Juan Francisco, *moreno* slave of Captain Don Francisco Romo de Urisa about having killed an Apalachee Indian, July 21–November 27, 1703. AGI SD 858.
———. 1704a. Letter to the king, September 15, 1704. AGI SD 852. Translation in Boyd et al. 1951.
———. 1704b. Letter to the king, October 6, 1704. AGI SD 858.

Secondary Sources

Adam, Lucien, and Julien Vinson. 1886. *Arte de la Lengua Timuquana, compuesto por el Padre Francisco Pareja*. Paris: Bibliotheque Linguistique Americaine.
Anderson, David G. 1994. *The Savannah River chiefdoms: Political change in the late prehistoric southeast*. Tuscaloosa: Univ. of Alabama Press.
Arnade, Charles W. 1959. *The seige of St. Augustine in 1702*. Gainesville: Univ. of Florida Press.
———. 1961. Cattle raising in Spanish Florida, 1513–1763. *Agricultural History* 35:116–24.
Baker, Henry A. 1993. Spanish ranching and the Alachua Sink site: A preliminary report. *The Florida Anthropologist* 46(2):82–100.
Boyd, Mark F. 1937. The expedition of Marcos Delgado from Apalachee to the Upper Creek country in 1686. *Florida Historical Quarterly* 16(1):2–32.
———. 1938. Map of the road from Pensacola to St. Augustine, 1778. *Florida Historical Quarterly* 17:1–23.
Boyd, Mark F., Hale G. Smith, and John W. Griffin. 1951. *Here they once stood: The tragic end of the Apalachee missions*. Gainesville: Univ. of Florida Press.
Bushnell, Amy Turner. 1978. The Menéndez Márquez cattle barony at La Chua and the determinants of economic expansion in seventeenth-century Florida. *Florida Historical Quarterly* 56(4):407–31.
———. 1981. *The King's coffer: Proprietors of the Spanish Florida treasury, 1565–1702*. Gainesville: Univ. of Florida Press.
———. 1989. Ruling "the Republic of Indians" in seventeenth-century Florida. In *Powhatan's mantle: Indians in the colonial southeast*, 134–50, edited by Peter H. Wood, Gregory A. Waselkov, and M. Thomas Hatley. Lincoln: Univ. of Nebraska Press.
———. 1994. *Situado and sabana: Spain's support system for the presidio and

mission provinces of Florida. Anthropological papers of the American Museum of Natural History, no. 74.
Carder, Nanny. 1989. Faunal remains from Mixon's Hammock, Okefenokee Swamp. *Southeastern Archaeology* 8(1):19–30.
Chatelain, Verne E. 1941. *The defenses of Spanish Florida, 1565 to 1763*. Publication 511. Washington: Carnegie Institute of Washington.
Crane, Verner W. 1981. *The Southern frontier, 1670–1732.* New York: W. W. Norton & Company.
Deagan, Kathleen A. 1978. Cultures in transition: Fusion and assimilation among the eastern Timucua. In *Tacachale: Essays on the Indians of Florida and Southeastern Georgia during the historic period,* 89–119, edited by Jerald Milanich and Samuel Proctor. Gainesville: Univ. of Florida Press.
———. 1985. Spanish-Indian interaction in sixteenth-century Florida and Hispaniola. In *Cultures in contact: The impact of European contacts on Native American cultural institutions, a.d. 1000–1800,* 281–313, edited by William W. Fitzhugh. Washington, D.C.: Smithsonian Institution Press.
———. 1990. Accommodation and resistance: The process and impact of Spanish colonization in the Southeast. In *Columbian consequences: Archaeological and historical perspectives on the Spanish borderlands east,* 297–314, edited by David Hurst Thomas. Washington, D.C.: Smithsonian Institution Press.
———. 1993. St. Augustine and the mission frontier. In *The Spanish missions of La Florida,* 87–110, edited by Bonnie G. McEwan. Gainesville: Univ. Press of Florida.
DePratter, Chester B. 1983. *Late prehistoric and early historic chiefdoms in the Southeastern United States.* Ph.D. diss., Department of Anthropology, University of Georgia.
Dobyns, Henry F. 1983. *Their number became thinned: Native population dynamics in Eastern North America.* Knoxville: Univ. of Tennessee Press.
Earle, Timothy K. 1987. Chiefdoms in archaeological and ethnohistorical perspective. *Annual Review of Anthropology* 16:279–308.
———. 1989. The evolution of chiefdoms. *Current Anthropology* 30:84–88.
———, ed. 1991. *Chiefdoms: Power, economy, and ideology.* Cambridge: Cambridge Univ. Press.
Foster, George M. 1953. Cofradía and Compadrazgo in Spain and Spanish America. *Southwestern Journal of Anthropology* 9(1):1–28.
Fresia, Anne E., Christopher B. Ruff, and Clark Spencer Larsen. 1990. Temporal decline in bilateral asymmetry of the upper limb on the Georgia coast. In *The archaeology of mission Santa Catalina de Guale: 2. Biocultural interpretations of a population in transition,* 121–32, edited by Clark Spencer Larsen. New York: Anthropological papers of the American Museum of Natural History, no. 68.
Fried, Morton H. 1967. *The evolution of political society.* New York: Random House.
Galloway, Patricia, ed. 1989. *The Southeastern ceremonial complex: Artifacts and analysis, the cottonlandia conference.* Lincoln: Univ. of Nebraska Press.

Gannon, Michael V. 1965. *The cross in the sand: The early Catholic church in Florida, 1513–1870*. Gainesville: Univ. of Florida Press.

García, Sebastián. 1988. La evangelización de América en la legislación general de la Orden franciscana en el siglo XVI. In *Actas del II Congreso Internacional sobre Los Franciscanos en el Nuevo Mundo (Siglo XVI)*. Madrid: Editorial Deimos.

———. 1991. América en la legislación franciscana del siglo XVII. In *Actas del III Congreso Internacional sobre Los Franciscanos en el Nuevo Mundo (Siglo XVII)*. Madrid: Editorial Deimos.

———. 1993. América en la legislación general de la Orden franciscana, siglo XVIII. In *Actas del IV Congreso Internacional sobre Los Franciscanos en el Nuevo Mundo (Siglo XVIII)*. Madrid: Editorial Deimos.

Geiger, Maynard. 1937. *The Franciscan conquest of Florida, 1573–1618*. Washington, D.C.: The Catholic Univ. of America.

———. 1940. *Biographical dictionary of the Franciscans in Spanish Florida and Cuba (1528–1841)*. Paterson, N.J.: St. Anthony Guild Press.

Goggin, John M. 1952. *Space and time perspectives in northern St. Johns archeology, Florida*. New Haven: Yale University Publications in anthropology, no. 47.

Gold, Robert L. 1969. *Borderland empires in transition: The triple-nation transfer of Florida*. Carbondale: Southern Illinois Univ. Press.

Gómez Canedo, Lino. 1983. Franciscans in the Americas: A comprehensive view. In *Franciscan presence in the Americas: Essays on the activities of the Franciscan friars in the Americas, 1492–1900*. Potomac, Md.: Academy of American Franciscan History.

Granberry, Julian. 1993. *A grammar and dictionary of the Timucua language*. Tuscaloosa: Univ. of Alabama Press.

Green, William. 1991. The search for Altamaha: The archaeology and ethnohistory of an early 18th-century Yamasee Indian town. Master's thesis, Department of Anthropology, University of South Carolina, Columbia.

Hally, David J. 1992. Platform mound construcion and the instability of Mississippian chiefdoms. Paper presented at the Southeastern Archaeological Conference, Little Rock, October 22.

———. 1993. The territorial size of Mississippian chiefdoms. In *Archaeology of Eastern North America: Papers in honor of Stephen Williams*, 143–68, edited by James B. Stoltman. Mississippi Department of Archives and History, Archaeological Report 25.

Hally, David J., Marvin T. Smith, and James B. Langford Jr. 1990. The archaeological reality of de Soto's coosa. In *Columbian consequences: Archaeological and historical perspectives on the Spanish borderlands east*, 121–38, edited by David Hurst Thomas. Washington: Smithsonian Institution Press.

Hann, John H. 1986a. Translation of Governor Rebolledo's 1657 visitation of three Florida provinces and related documents. *Florida Archaeology* 2:81–145.

———. 1986b. Church furnishings, sacred vessels, and vestments held by the missions of Florida: Translations of two inventories. *Florida Archaeology* 2:147–64.

———. 1986c. Demographic patterns and changes in mid-seventeenth-century Timucua and Apalachee. *Florida Historical Quarterly* 64:371–92.

———. 1988a. *Apalachee: The land between the rivers*. Gainesville: Univ. of Florida Press.

———. 1988b. Florida's terra incognita: West Florida's natives in the sixteenth and seventeenth century. *The Florida Anthropologist* 41(1):61–107.

———. 1989. St. Augustine's fallout from the Yamassee war. *Florida Historical Quarterly* 68:180–200.

———. 1990. Summary guide to Spanish Florida missions and visitas with churches in the sixteenth and seventeenth centuries. *The Americas* 46:417–513.

———. 1991. *Missions to the Calusa*. Gainesville: Univ. of Florida Press.

———. 1992a. Heathen Acuera, murder, and a Potano cimarrona: The St. Johns River and the Alachua Prairie in the 1670s. *Florida Historical Quarterly* 70:451–74.

———. 1992b. Political leadership among the natives of Spanish Florida. *Florida Historical Quarterly* 71(2):188–208.

———. 1993a. The Mayaca and Jororo and missions to them. In *The Spanish missions of La Florida,* 111–140, edited by Bonnie G. McEwan. Gainesville: Univ. Press of Florida.

———. 1993b. Visitations and revolts in Florida, 1656–1695. *Florida Archaeology* 7.

———. 1993c. 1630 memorial of Fray Francisco Alonso de Jesús on Spanish Florida's missions and natives. *The Americas* 50(1):85–105.

———. 1996. *A history of the Timucua Indians and missions*. Gainesville: Univ. Press of Florida.

Hernández Aparicio, Pilar. 1991. Estadisticas Franciscanas del S. XVII. In *Actas del III Congreso Internacional sobre Los Franciscanos en el Nuevo Mundo (Siglo XVII),* 555–91. Madrid: Editorial Deimos.

Hoffman, Paul E. 1994. Narváez and Cabeza de Vaca in Florida. In *The forgotten centuries: Indians and Europeans in the American South, 1521–1704,* 50–73, edited by Charles Hudson and Carmen Chaves Tesser. Athens: Univ. of Georgia Press.

Hoshower, Lisa M., and Jerald T. Milanich. 1993. Excavations in the Fig Springs mission burial area. In *The Spanish missions of La Florida,* 217–43, edited by Bonnie G. McEwan. Gainesville: Univ. Press of Florida.

Hudson, Charles. 1976. *The Southeastern Indians*. Knoxville: Univ. of Tennessee Press.

———. 1990. *The Juan Pardo expeditions: Exploration of the Carolinas and Tennessee, 1566–1568*. Washington, D.C.: Smithsonian Institution Press.

Hutchinson, Dale L., and Clark Spencer Larsen. Stress and lifeway change: The evidence from enamel hypoplasias. In *The archaeology of mission Santa Catalina de Guale: 2. Biocultural interpretations of a population in transition,* 50–65, edited by Clark Spencer Larsen. New York: Anthropological papers of the American Museum of Natural History, no. 68.

Jefferies, Richard W. 1994. The Swift Creek site and Woodland platform mounds in the Southeastern United States. In *Ocmulgee archaeology, 1936–1986,* 71–83, edited David J. Hally. Athens: Univ. of Georgia Press.

Johnson, Allen W., and Timothy K. Earle. 1987. *The evolution of human societies.* Stanford: Stanford Univ. Press.

Johnson, Kenneth W. 1991. *The Utina and the Potano peoples of northern Florida: Changing settlement systems in the Spanish colonial period.* Ph.D. diss., Department of Anthropology, University of Florida, Gainesville.

———. 1993. Mission Santa Fé de Toloca. In *The Spanish Missions of La Florida,* 141–64, edited by Bonnie G. McEwan. Gainesville: University Press of Florida.

Johnson, Kenneth W., and Bruce C. Nelson. 1990. The Utina: Seriations and chronology. *The Florida Anthropologist* 43(1):48–62.

Jones, Grant D. 1978. The ethnohistory of the Guale coast through 1684. In *The anthropology of St. Caterines Island: 1. Natural and cultural history,* 178–210, edited by David Hurst Thomas, Grant D. Jones, Roger S. Durham, and Clark Spencer Larsen. New York: Anthropological papers of the American Museum of Natural History 55(2).

Jones, B. Calvin, and Gary N. Shapiro. 1990. Nine mission sites in Apalachee. In *Columbian consequences: Archaeological and historical perspectives on the Spanish borderlands east,* 491–509, edited by David Hurst Thomas. Washington: Smithsonian Institution Press.

Keegan, Gregory Joseph, and Leandro Tormo Sanz. 1957. Experiencia misionera en la Florida (Siglos XVI y XVII). Madrid: Talleres Graficos Jura.

Knight, Vernon James, Jr. 1985. *Tukabatchee: Archaeological investigations at an historic creek town, Elmore County, Alabama, 1984.* Tuscaloosa: Report of Investigations 45, Office of Archaeological Research, University of Alabama.

———. 1986. The institutional organization of Mississippian religion. *American Antiquity* 51:675–87.

———. 1990. Social organization and the evolution of hierarchy in Southeastern chiefdoms. *Journal of Anthropological Research* 46(1):1–23.

Landers, Jane. 1992. Africans in the land of Ayllón: The exploration and settlement of the Southeast. In *Columbus and the land of Ayllón: The exploration and settlement of the Southeast,* 105–23, edited by Jeannine Cook. Darien, Ga.: The Darien News.

Lanning, John Tate. 1935. *The Spanish missions of Georgia.* Chapel Hill: Univ. of North Carolina Press.

Larsen, Clark Spencer. 1993. On the frontier of contact: Mission bioarchaeology in la Florida. In *The Spanish missions of La Florida,* 322–56, edited by Bonnie G. McEwan. Gainesville: Univ. Press of Florida.

———, ed. 1990. *The Archaeology of mission Santa Catalina de Guale: 2. Biocultural interpretations of a population in transition.* New York: Anthropological papers of the American Museum of Natural History, no. 68.

Larsen, Clark Spencer, Margaret J. Shoeninger, Dale L. Hutchinson, Katherine F. Russell, and Christopher B. Ruff. 1990. Beyond demographic collapse: Biological adaptation and change in native populations of la Florida. In *Columbian consequences: Archaeological and historical perspectives on the Spanish borderlands east,* 409–28, edited by David Hurst Thomas. Washington: Smithsonian Institution Press.

Larson, Lewis H., Jr. 1972. Functional considerations of warfare in the Southeast during the Mississippian period. *American Antiquity* 37:383–92.

———. 1980. *Aboriginal subsistence technology on the Southeastern coastal plain during the historic period.* Gainesville: Univ. Press of Florida.

Loucks, Lana Jill. 1979. *Political and economic interactions between Spaniards and Indians: Archaeological and ethnohistorical perspectives of the mission system in Florida.* Ph.D. diss., Department of Anthropology, University of Florida, Gainesville.

———. 1993. Spanish-Indian interaction on the Florida missions: The archaeology of Baptizing Spring (1983 article published posthumously). In *The Spanish missions of La Florida,* 193–216, edited by Bonnie G. McEwan. Gainesville: Univ. Press of Florida.

Lyon, Eugene. 1976. *The enterprise of Florida: Pedro Menéndez de Avilés and the Spanish conquest of 1565–1568.* Gainesville: Univ. Press of Florida.

———. 1992a. The failure of the Guale and Orista mission: 1572–1575. In *Columbus and the land of Ayllón: The exploration and settlement of the Southeast,* 89–104, edited by Jeannine Cook. Darien, Ga.: The Darien News.

———. 1992b. Richer than we thought: The material culture of sixteenth-century St. Augustine. *El Escribano* 29:1–117.

———. 1992c. Cuban church records examined in June 1992. Manuscript copy in possession of the author.

Matter, Robert Allen. 1972. *The Spanish missions of Florida: The friars versus the governors in the "Golden Age," 1606–1690.* Ph.D. diss., University of Washington.

———. 1973. Economic basis of the seventeenth-century Florida missions. *Florida Historical Quarterly* 52(1):18–38.

McAlister, Lyle N. 1984. *Spain and Portugal in the New World, 1492–1700.* Minneapolis: Univ. of Minnesota Press.

Milanich, Jerald T. 1971a. The Alachua tradition of north-central Florida. *Contributions of the Florida State Museum, Anthropology and History,* no. 17. Gainesville.

———. 1971b. Surface information from the presumed site of the San Pedro de Mocamo mission. *Conference on Historic Site Archaeology Papers* 5:114–21.

———. 1972. Excavations at the Richardson site, Alachua County, Florida: An early 17th century Potano Indian village (with notes on Potano culture change). *Bureau of Historic Sites and Properties Bulletin* 2:35–61.

———. 1994. *Archaeology of precolumbian Florida.* Gainesville: Univ. Press of Florida.

———. 1995. *Florida Indians and the invasion from Europe.* Gainesville: Univ. Press of Florida.

———. 1996. *The Timucua.* Oxford: Blackwell Publishers.

Milanich, Jerald T., and Charles Hudson. 1993. *Hernando de Soto and the Indians of Florida.* Gainesville: Univ. Press of Florida.

Milanich, Jerald T., and William C. Sturtevant. 1972. *Francisco Pareja's 1613 confessionario: A documentary source for Timucuan ethnography.* Tallahassee: Division of Archives, History, and Records Management, Florida Department of State.

Milner, George G. 1980. Epidemic disease in the postcontact Southeast: A reappraisal. *Midcontinental Journal of Archaeology* 5:39–56.

Mitchem, Jeffrey M. 1993. Beads and pendants from San Luis de Talimali: Inferences from varying contexts. In *The Spanish missions of La Florida,* 399–417, edited by Bonnie G. McEwan. Gainesville: Univ. Press of Florida.

Newsom, Lee. n.d. Ethnobotanical analysis for the Fig Springs site, 1990 excavations. In Worth n.d.

Payne, Claudine. 1982. Farmsteads and districts: A model of Fort Walton settlement patterns in the Tallahassee Hills. Paper presented at the Southeastern Archaeological Conference, Memphis.

Pearson, Fred Lamar, Jr. 1983. Timucuan rebellion of 1656: The Rebolledo investigation and the civil-religious controversy. *Florida Historical Quarterly* 61(3):260–80.

Peebles, Christopher S. 1978. Determinants of settlement size and location in the Moundville phase. In *Mississippian settlement patterns,* 369–416, edited by Bruce D. Smith. New York: Academic Press.

Pou y Martí, José María. 1927a. Estado de la orden Franciscana y de sus misiones en América y extremo Oriente en el año de 1635 [part 1]. *Archivo Ibero-Americano* 27:196–227.

———. 1927b. Estado de la orden Franciscana y de sus misiones en América y extremo Oriente en el año de 1635 [part 2]. *Archivo Ibero-Americano* 28:43–92.

Quitmyer, Irvy R. n.d. Zooarchaeological analysis for the Fig Springs site, 1990 excavations. In Worth n.d.a.

Ramenofsky, Ann F. 1987. *The vectors of death: The archaeology of European contact.* Albuquerque: Univ. of New Mexico Press.

Real Acadèmia Española. 1737. Diccionario de la lengua Castellana. Facsimile published as *Diccionario de autoridades,* 1990. Madrid: Editorial Gredos.

Reitz, Elizabeth J. 1993. Evidence for animal use at the missions of Spanish Florida. In *The Spanish missions of La Florida,* 376–98, edited by Bonnie G. McEwan. Gainesville: Univ. Press of Florida.

Reitz, Elizabeth J., and C. Margaret Scarry. 1985. *Reconstructing historic subsistence with an example from sixteenth-century Spanish Florida.* Society for Historical Archaeology special publication no. 3.

Ruff, Christopher B., and Clark Spencer Larsen. 1990. Postcranial biomechanical adaptations to subsistence strategy changes on the Georgia coast. In *The Archaeology of mission Santa Catalina de Guale: 2. Biocultural interpretations of a population in transition,* 94–120, edited by Clark Spencer Larsen. New York: Anthropological papers of the American Museum of Natural History, no. 68.

Russell, Katherine F., Inui Choi, and Clark Spencer Larsen. 1990. The paleode-mography of Santa Catalina de Guale. In *The archaeology of mission Santa Catalina de Guale: 2. Biocultural interpretations of a population in transition,* 36–49, edited by Clark Spencer Larsen. New York: Anthropological papers of the American Museum of Natural History, no. 68.

Russo, Michael. 1992. Chronologies and cultures of the St. Marys region of northeast Florida and southeast Georgia. *The Florida Anthropologist* 45(2):107–26.

Sastre, Cécile-Marie. 1995. Picolata on the St. Johns: A preliminary study. *El Escribano* 32:25–64.

Saunders, Rebecca. 1990. Ideal and innovation: Spanish mission architecture in the Southeast. In *Columbian consequences: archaeological and historical perspectives on the Spanish borderlands east,* 527–42, edited by David Hurst Thomas. Washington: Smithsonian Institution Press.

Scarry, John F. 1994. The Apalachee chiefdom: A Mississippian society on the fringe of the Mississippian world. In *The forgotten centuries: Indians and Europeans in the American South, 1521–1704,* 156–78, edited by Charles Hudson and Carmen Chaves Tesser. Athens: Univ. of Georgia Press.

Seaberg, Lillian M. 1955. The Zetrouer site: Indian and Spanish in central Florida. Master's thesis, Department of Anthropology, University of Florida, Gainesville.

Serrano y Sanz, Manuel. 1912. *Documentos históricos de la Florida y la Luisiana, siglos XVI al XVIII.* Madrid: Libraria General de Victoriano Suárez.

Service, Elman R. 1971. *Primitive social organization: An evolutionary perspective.* 2d ed. New York: Random House.

Shapiro, Gary N., and John H. Hann. 1990. The documentary image of the council houses of Spanish Florida tested by excavations at the mission of San Luis de Talimali. In *Columbian consequences: Archaeological and historical perspectives on the Spanish borderlands east,* 511–26, edited by David Hurst Thomas. Washington, D.C.: Smithsonian Institution Press.

Sluiter, Engel. 1985. *The Florida situado: Quantifying the first eighty years, 1571–1651.* Research publications of the P. K. Yonge Library of Florida History, no. 1. Gainesville: University of Florida Libraries.

Smith, Bruce D. 1978. Variation in Mississippian settlement patterns. In *Mississippian Settlement Patterns,* 479–503, edited by Bruce D. Smith. New York: Academic Press.

———. 1984. Mississippian expansion: Tracing the historical development of an explanatory model. *Southeastern Archaeology* 3(1):13–32.

Smith, Marvin T. 1987. *Archaeology of Aboriginal culture change in the interior Southeast: Depopulation during the early historic period.* Gainesville: Univ. of Florida Press.

Smith, Marvin T., and John E. Worth. 1994. Spanish Missions of the Northern Timucua Province. Paper presented at the Southeastern Archaeological Conference, Lexington, November 9–12.

Steponaitis, Vincas P. 1978. Location theory and complex chiefdoms: A Mississippian example. In *Mississippian settlement patterns,* 417–53, edited by Bruce D. Smith. New York: Academic Press.

Swanton, John R. 1922. *Early history of the Creek Indians and their neighbors.* Bureau of American Ethnology Bulletin 73. Washington, D.C.: Government Printing Office.

Symes, M. I., and M. E. Stephens. 1965. A272: The Fox Pond site. *The Florida Anthropologist* 18:65–76.

Thomas, David Hurst, Jr. 1990. The Spanish missions of La Florida: An overview. In *Columbian consequences: Archaeological and historical perspectives on the Spanish borderlands east,* 357–97, edited by David Hurst Thomas. Washington, D.C.: Smithsonian Institution Press.

———. 1993. The archaeology of mission Santa Catalina de Guale: Our first 15 years. In *The Spanish missions of La Florida,* 1–34, edited by Bonnie G. McEwan. Gainesville: Univ. Press of Florida.

Vernon, Richard, and Ann S. Cordell. 1993. A distributional and technological study of Apalachee colono-ware from San Luis de Talimali. In *The Spanish missions of La Florida,* 418–41, edited by Bonnie G. McEwan. Gainesville: Univ. Press of Florida.

Weisman, Brent Richards. 1992. *Excavations on the Franciscan frontier: Archaeology at the Fig Springs mission.* Gainesville: Univ. Press of Florida.

Weisman, Russell M., S. Dwight Kirkland, and John E. Worth. 1997. An archaeological reconnaissance of the proposed Trail Ridge mine, Charlton County, Georgia. Report submitted to Golder Associates, Inc.

Widmer, Randolph J. 1988. *The evolution of the Calusa: A nonagricultural chiefdom on the southwest Florida coast.* Tuscaloosa: Univ. of Alabama Press.

———. 1994. The structure of Southeastern chiefdoms. In *The forgotten centuries: Indians and Europeans in the American South, 1521–1704,* 125–55, edited by Charles Hudson and Carmen Chaves Tesser. Athens: Univ. of Georgia Press.

Williams, Mark, and Marvin T. Smith. 1989. Power and migration. Paper presented at the Southeastern Archaeological Conference, Tampa, November 8–11, 1989.

Worth, John E. 1990. Archaeology in the Timucua mission province: 1990 excavations at Fig Springs (8Co1), South End Village. Paper presented at the Southeastern Archaeological Conference, Mobile, November 7–10.

———. 1992. *The Timucuan missions of Spanish Florida and the rebellion of 1656.* Ph.D. diss., Department of Anthropology, University of Florida, Gainesville.

———. 1993. Prelude to abandonment: The interior provinces of early 17th-century Georgia. *Early Georgia* 21(1):24–58.

———. 1994. Late Spanish military expeditions in the interior Southeast, 1597–1628. In *The forgotten centuries: Indians and Europeans in the American South, 1521–1704,* 104–22, edited by Charles Hudson and Carmen Chaves Tesser. Athens: Univ. of Georgia Press.

———. 1995a. Fontaneda revisited: Five descriptions of sixteenth-century Florida. *Florida Historical Quarterly* 73(3):339–52.

———. 1995b. The early 17th-century locations of Tama and Utinahica. Appendix A to *Historic Indian period archaeology of the Georgia coastal plain* by Chad O. Braley, 59–A8. Georgia Archaeological Research Design Paper No. 10.

———. 1995c. *The struggle for the Georgia coast: An eighteenth-century Spanish retrospective on Guale and Mocama*. Anthropological papers of the American Museum of Natural History, no. 75.

———. n.d. Prehistory in the Timucua mission province: Archaeological investigations at Ichetucknee Springs State Park, 1990. Draft report in possession of the author.

Zamora, Hermenegido. 1991. Contenido Franciscano de los libros registro del archivo general de Indias, 1651–1700. In *Actas del III congreso internacional sobre los Franciscanos en el nuevo mundo (siglo XVII)*, 183–322. Madrid: Editorial Deimos.

Index

Abosaya, Apalachee settlement at, 132, 146, 203, 206; refugees in St. Augustine, 147, 148
accounting records, Spanish, 40, 198
Achito, town of, 144. *See also* Hitchiti
acorns, 142
Acuera, province of, 23, 25, 31, 32, 35, 36, 37, 55, 100, 121, 130, 133, 135, 159, 162, 189, 190; population of, 7–8
Agile, town of, 180. *See also* Asile; San Miguel de Asile
aggregation, settlement, 2, 11, 27–29, 30, 35, 90, 93, 95, 96, 104, 115, 127, 128, 138, 140–41, 144, 146
agriculture, 1, 48
Agua Dulce, province of, 32, 37, 159, 187, 188; population of, 3
Ais, settlement of near St. Augustine, 148
Ais, province of, 41, 42
Aispiolea, Joseph de, 194
Ajoica, mission of, 114, 120, 121, 125, 131, 170, 172, 173; aggregation to Santa Catalina, 29, 103, 128; location of, 98, 161; establishment of, 103. *See also* Lúcas, cacique; San Agustín de Ajoica; San Agustín de Urihica; Santa Catalina de Ajoica
Alachua sink, 167
Alapaha River, 54, 182, 183, 184, 185
Alcayde de Cordoba, Martín, 23, 42, 103, 106, 107, 108, 111, 114, 131

Alejo, Juan, Indian from Acuera, 55, 56, 61, 62, 63, 86, 174
Alexo, cacique of Santa María (under Tarihica), 91
Alisa, town of, 121, 135
Alonso, cacique of Salamototo, 148, 149
Alonso de Jesús, Francisco, 14
Altamaha, cacique of the Yamassees, 140
Altamaha River, 182, 184
Amaca, lake of, 132, 168, 202, 205
Amacano Indians, 18, 135, 136
amber, 39, 41, 42
Amelia Island, 144
Anacabila, town of, 187, 188. *See also* Enacape
anchors, ship, 41
Anderson Bay, 181
Angel, Juan, 136
Antonico, province of, 8, 32; population of, 7
Antonico, town of, 166, 188; location of, 187
Antonio, cacique (under San Matheo), 129, 130
Antonio, cacique of San Antonio de Arapaja, 130, 195
Antonio, cacique of Santa Fé (under San Matheo), 91
Antonio, son of cacique Lazaro of Chamile, 55, 56, 62, 63, 174

Apalachee, province of, 1, 9, 12, 14, 16, 18, 22, 24, 26, 33, 35, 36, 37, 38, 41, 43, 44, 50, 55, 59, 61, 62, 64, 68, 69, 72, 74, 75, 79, 80, 81, 82, 83, 84, 85, 90, 97, 101, 105, 107, 108, 111, 112, 115, 118, 126, 129, 135, 139, 142, 146, 151, 152, 155, 162, 177, 180, 200, 201, 202, 203, 204, 206; population of, 6, 134, 136, 148; 1647 rebellion, 19, 20, 34, 65, 71, 181; laborers from, 51, 67, 70, 73, 122; garrison in, 54, 60, 65, 88, 89, 106, 109, 110, 113, 145, 199; annexation of Asile, 94–95, 96, 123; haciendas in, 130, 132; destruction of, 132, 145
Apalachicola, province of, 18, 41, 140, 144
Apalo, town of, 167. *See also* San Buenaventura, mission of (in Potano)
Appalachian Mountains, 19
Aramuqua, settlement at, 84
Aranguiz y Cotes, Alonso de, 12, 112, 113, 115, 119, 122
Arapaja, chiefdom of, 96, 124, 185. *See also* Santa María de los Angeles de Arapaja
archaeological record, 2, 36, 101, 102, 103, 104, 141, 159, 166, 167, 168, 169, 173, 174, 175, 178, 179, 180, 182, 184, 185, 187; bioarchaeology, 12–13, 15–16, 21
archives, Spanish, 157, 200
Argüelles, Alonso de, 20, 47, 57, 82, 84, 85
Argüelles, Antonio de, 44, 131
Arias, Juan, 136
Arredondo, Antonio de, 151
arrows, 52, 72
Arucatesa, Juan, cacique of Santo Thomás de Santa Fé, 149, 150, 151
Asile, chiefdom of, 96, 179, 180. *See also* San Miguel de Asile
Asile, River of, 67, 178, 201, 205
assimilation, of chiefdoms, 38, 57, 59, 87, 117, 157
atiqui, 51. *See also* interpreters
Atlantic Ocean, 1, 7, 12, 22, 41, 130, 157, 182, 190
Aucilla River, 67, 69, 94, 95, 96, 123, 142, 143, 177, 178, 180, 181
autonomy, of Timucuan chiefdoms, 39, 45

Avino, town of, 31, 189. *See also* San Blas de Avino
axes, iron/steel, 20, 130
Ayachin, site of, 152
Ayacuto, chiefdom of. *See* Timucua, province of
Ayala, Antonio de, cacique of Nuestra Señora de la Candelaria de la Tamaja, 150
Ayala, Bartolomé de, 136
Ayala Escobar, Juan de, 143
Ayeheriva, forest of, 120
Ayepacano, town of, 76. *See also* Santa Catalina de Ayepacano
Ayubale, war of, 145

Bahama Channel, 46
Baldtree site, 166
Baltasar, cacique of San Pablo (in Yustaga), 195
Bamba, Joseph, 60, 69, 110, 181
baptism, 6, 15, 36
Baptizing Spring site, 103, 104, 171, 172, 174, 175, 182
barbacoa, 81, 196
Beachville, 171, 173
beads, rosary, 157
Beatty site, 177, 178, 179, 180
bells, mission, 134
Bellamy Road, 98
Benito, heir/cacique of Machava, 122, 123, 192, 193, 194, 195, 196, 197
Bernabé, cacique of San Pablo (under San Matheo), 91
Bernal, Clemente, cacique of San Juan del Puerto, 85, 86
Bernardino, *principal* of San Pedro de Potohiriba, 195
Biblioteca Nacionál, 162
Bilia, creek of, 166
Billys Island, 190
Biro Zebano, town of, 121
Bishop of Santiago de Cuba, 124, 135
Black Creek, 166
Blanco, Francisco, 136
Blue Bead site, 166
Blue Hole, 75
Blue Sink, 186

Blue Spring, 186
bows, 52, 72
Branford, 103, 173, 174
Bravo, Gregorio, 95
burden bearers, Indian, 1, 25, 50, 58, 78, 89, 111, 116; stresses of, 13–16, 29

Cabale. *See* Cavale
cacica, 53, 77, 80, 81, 91, 103, 128
cacicado, 119, 192. *See also* chiefdoms
cacique, 17, 18, 20, 21, 24, 26, 27, 30, 31, 33, 34, 37, 39, 40, 41, 42, 43, 44, 45, 49, 51, 52, 53, 55, 56, 57, 58, 59, 61, 64, 67, 69, 70, 71, 72, 73, 74, 75, 76, 78, 79, 80, 81, 82, 83, 84, 85, 86, 87, 88, 89, 90, 91, 92, 94, 95, 96, 99, 106, 107, 108, 109, 110, 111, 112, 118, 119, 123, 127, 137, 140, 145, 147, 149, 150, 155, 186, 192, 194, 197; -*mayor*, 135
caciquillo, 43, 93, 129
Calabay, town of, 187
Calacala, site of, 62; location of, 53, 174
Calderón, Manuel, 94
Calesa, Indian from Acuera, 121
Calusa, province of, 138
Camino Real, 1, 2, 5, 25, 30, 32, 33, 34, 35, 37, 38, 53, 58, 69, 70, 71, 75, 79, 85, 87, 89, 90, 93, 94, 95, 96, 97, 98, 99, 100, 101, 102, 103, 104, 105, 111, 114, 115, 116, 117, 118, 119, 120, 124, 128–29, 131, 132, 140, 143, 159, 160, 166, 167, 169, 170, 171, 172, 174, 175, 176, 177, 178, 182, 186, 187, 200; and factions within the Timucuan rebellion, 76, 78
Campaña, Juan Bauptista, 137
Cañizares y Osorio, Adrián de, 19, 23, 42, 74, 75, 78, 79, 80, 81, 82, 83, 84, 85, 88, 92, 106, 109, 110, 111, 185
cannons, 41, 66
canoes, 17, 18, 29, 31, 44, 104, 113, 126, 175
Cape Canaveral, 41
captain, rank of, 55, 128
Cárdenas, Alonso de, 45, 46
Cárdenas, Joseph de, 126
Caribbean Sea, 45
Carlos, cacique of, 17

Carlos, town of (Piaja), 151
Carolina, 16, 139, 144, 145, 149
Cartagena, 39
Castilla, Francisco de, 5, 103, 132, 168, 169, 170, 171, 172, 174, 175, 176, 177, 178, 179, 180, 181; 1740 relation of, 200–206
Castillo de San Marcos, 56, 86, 113, 140. *See also* fortifications, Spanish
catechesis, 35
cattle, 64, 131, 132, 133, 142, 201, 202, 203, 204, 205, 206
Cavale, Juan Alonso, Timucua Indian, 156
Cavale, Pedro, Timucua Indian, 156
Caveta, town of, 200, 203, 204
Cavezas Altamirano, Juan de las, 30, 165, 189
census, mission, 124, 133, 134–35, 136–37, 156, 198
ceramics: Lamar-related, 36; Suwannee Valley, 36; Alachua, 36; Altamaha/San Marcos, 36, 187; Savannah, 37; St. Johns, 37, 187; majolica, 191; olive jar, 191
Chacato, province of, 18
Chacatos, River of, 201, 204
Chacón, Pedro, 48, 94, 162, 182, 185, 188; 1655 visitation route of, 162–65
Challofare, lake of, 167
Chamile, chiefdom of, 92. *See also* San Ildefonso de Chamile
chapters, Franciscan. *See* Franciscan chapters
Charles Ferry, 172
Charles Spring, 103, 104, 174, 175
Charles Town, 140
Chatuache. *See* San Diego de Satuache
Cherry Lake, 185
chicasa, 201, 202, 203, 204, 205
Chichimeco Indians, 19, 113, 120, 121, 133, 137. *See also* Chisca Indians
chiefs: as administrative intermediaries, 39; as military leaders, 49–50; privileges of, 50, 59, 123, 127, 193, 197; usurpation of, 92, 96, 122–23, 192–97; ownership of lands, 99, 192–97; house of, 120, 123, 193, 197
chiefdoms, 133, 192, 193, 196; Timucuan, 1, 2, 4, 6, 8, 9, 10, 13, 29, 32, 36, 37,

38, 39, 45, 49, 63, 87, 97, 105, 117, 124, 135, 138; local, 3, 4, 5, 6, 7, 8, 27, 29, 38, 78, 90, 92, 97, 105, 117; population of, 3–4; simple, 6; regional, 78, 97
Chilacaliche, cacique of Sabacola, 204
Chiluca/Chiluque. *See* Mocama
Chiquito, mission of, 153; location of, 154. *See also* Nombre de Dios Chiquito
Chisca, 16th-century province of, 19
Chisca Indians, 18–21, 34–35, 71, 75; caciques and *principales* of, 34
churches, mission, 120, 134, 140, 143
cimarrones, 2, 22, 25, 26, 27, 33, 35, 44, 121, 157. *See also* fugitives, Indian
Clay County, 166
Clemente, *principal* of San Pedro de Potohiriba, 195
clothing: for friars, 17; as gifts to chiefs, 40, 73
Coastal Plain, 117
Cofa, mission of, 17, 18, 30
Cofa, River of, 17
colonial system, 1, 2, 26, 27, 37, 38, 45, 47, 49, 57, 58, 59, 65, 87, 92, 104, 139
comisario visitador, 48, 162. *See also* visitations
communities, 7, 15, 22, 24, 26, 27, 29, 93, 97, 127; number of in local chiefdoms, 3–4
compounds, mission, 27
congregación, 27, 29, 35, 105. *See also* aggregation, settlement
contact, European, 2, 3, 8, 10, 11
convento, 93, 95, 100, 133, 134, 155
convents, Franciscan: mission, 1, 4, 5, 25, 68, 101, 108, 109, 117, 140, 143, 145, 153, 177, 190; of St. Augustine, 48, 152, 163; of Cuba, 152
Corcoles y Martínez, Francisco de, 146
corn, 25, 42, 45, 47, 49, 50, 52, 55, 59, 60, 62, 130, 181, 190; production in missions, 1; purchase of from missions, 51, 73, 112, 118
Costa, La, mission of, 148, 153; location of, 154. *See also* San Antonio de las Costas
Cotocochuni, province of, 5. *See also* Yustaga

council houses, 57, 60, 61, 80, 83, 84, 85, 89, 90, 120, 122, 145, 196
Council of the Indies, 40, 116, 162, 192, 194
couriers, Indian, 56, 104, 129
Creeks, Lower, 144. *See also* Apalachicola
crops, 44, 48, 68
crossings, river, 2, 19, 24, 30, 31, 33, 104, 126
Cruz, Alonso de la, cacique of Santa Catalina de Guale, 150
Cruz, Antonio de la, 111, 112
Cruz, Francisco de la, 137
Cruz, Juan Bauptista de la, 78, 79, 81, 83, 85, 93, 135, 138, 194
Cuba, 46, 47, 48, 156, 158
Cuellar, Antonio del, 11
Culiparca, María Rosa, Yamassee Indian, 156
Cumberland Island, 191
cutlasses, 140

dances, Indian, 68, 89
definitors, Franciscan, 85, 113
demography. *See* population
depopulation. *See* population, collapse
Díaz de Badajoz, Alonso, 17
Díaz de León, Juan, 138
Díaz Vara Calderón, Gabriel, 119, 128, 169, 170, 171, 173, 174
Díez de la Calle, Juan, 94, 162, 165, 170, 190
Diego, cacique of San Pedro, 52, 53, 54, 55, 56, 57, 60, 61, 63, 76, 77, 81, 86, 88, 92
Diminiyuti. *See* Ibiniuti
Dionicio, cacique of San Lorenzo (under Santa Elena), 91, 96
Dionicio, cacique of Santa Elena de Machava, 76, 77, 80, 81, 86, 92, 96, 123
diseases, European, 1, 2, 5, 10–13, 15, 26, 28, 33, 44, 57, 58, 114, 115, 151; plague (*peste*), 12, 43; smallpox (*viruela*), 12
doctrina, 4, 14, 20, 33, 94, 120, 127, 163, 167, 190
Domingo, cacique of San Agustín (under San Matheo), 91

Domingo, cacique of San Francisco de Potano, 90, 91
Domínguez, Juan, 23, 33, 44, 108

Ebb, 79
Ebelino de Compostela, Diego, 100, 101, 140
Elano[gue], town of, 187
Elixio de la Puente, Juan Joseph, 157, 160, 166, 188
Eloquale, town and cacique of, 189. *See also* San Luís de Eloquale
Enacape, town of, 187, 188. *See also* San Antonio de Enacape
England, 45, 46
English, aggression by, 45–49, 66, 74, 101, 113, 121, 124, 138, 139, 140–46, 147, 199
environment, of Timucuan area, 5
epidemics. *See* diseases
Equale, town of, 187
Escamaçu, province of, 26
Escudero, Alonso, 55, 56, 57, 58, 59, 65, 109, 111
Esperanza, site of, 152
Estevez de Carmenatis, Nicolás, 20, 32, 181
Europe, 46, 201

Fernández de Florencia, Juan, 23, 32, 33, 44, 45, 114, 128, 169, 170, 171, 174
Fernández de Olivera, Juan, 17, 18
ferries, Indian, 23, 30, 33, 101, 111, 117, 131, 181, 188; stresses of, 126–27, 175. *See also* crossings, river
fields, agricultural: Spanish-owned, 44, 50, 51; mission, 48, 50, 72, 130; chief's, 123, 127, 197
Fig Springs site, 13, 168, 169, 170, 171, 172, 182
Filache, town of, 187
firearms, 50–51, 52, 71, 113, 136, 137; arquebuses, 41, 72, 73, 75, 80; muskets, 41, 139; shotguns, 140; rifles, 200
firewood, 80
fleets: English, 46, 48, 67, 110; Spanish, 46
Flint River, 144
Florencia, Francisco de, 147
Florencia, Joachín de, 142, 143

Florencia, Matheo Luís de, 90, 92, 113, 122
Florencia, Pedro de, 23, 24, 102
Florida, Spanish, 1, 2, 3, 7, 10, 11, 13, 20, 22, 24, 26, 31, 34, 35, 37, 38, 39, 46, 47, 56, 57, 59, 65, 74, 75, 87, 97, 98, 105, 108, 116, 117, 121, 124, 130, 132, 133, 138, 144, 157, 160, 186, 194, 198, 200; surrender to English, 156, 158
Florida, state of, 19, 35, 127, 142, 158, 185
Floyds Island, 190
Folkston, 191
fortifications, Spanish: in St. Augustine, 41, 46, 47, 48, 49, 66, 71, 144, 147; in Apalachee, 88, 112, 200, 201; in Timucua, 144, 146, 165
fortifications, Timucuan, during Timucuan rebellion, 69–72, 74, 76, 78, 79, 80, 81, 82, 83, 86, 92
Fox Pond, 167
Fox Pond site, 167
Franciscan chapters, 10, 11, 28, 84, 101, 112, 113, 115, 152
Franciscan expeditions, 133
Franciscan provincial minister, 12, 48, 55, 108, 109, 113
Francisco, cacique of Cachipile, 77, 81, 91
Francisco, cacique of San Diego (under San Mateo), 91
Francisco, cacique of San Francisco (under San Mateo), 91
Francisco, cacique of San Joseph (under San Martín?), 108
Francisco, cacique of San Matheo de Tolapatafi, 195
Francisco, cacique of Santa Lucia (under San Mateo), 91
Francisco, cacique of Utiaco, 31, 33
Francisco, old *iniha* of San Pedro de Potohiriba, 195
Francisco, Timucua/Yamassee Indian, 157
Francisco Alonso, cacique of San Juan Evangelista de Arapaja, 195
Francisco Alonso, cacique of San Miguel (under San Matheo), 91

Francisco Alonso, cacique of San Pablo (under Arapaja/Santa Fé), 90, 91
Francisco Bernabé, cacique of San Juan de Arapaja, 195
Francisco Bernabé, *principal* of San Matheo de Tolapatafi, 195
Francisco Luís, cacique of San Luis de Inhayca, 109
Francisco Martín, cacique of Tolomato, 150
Francisco Martín El Calvo, cacique of Ybiuro, 195
Francisco, Bartolomé, 61, 66, 67, 128, 129
French colonists, 16th-century, 7
friars, Franciscan, 4, 7, 11, 14, 18, 22, 26, 28, 29, 38, 48, 49, 55, 56, 63, 67, 68, 78, 83, 84, 88, 89, 94, 95, 98, 104, 105, 109, 110, 112, 113, 116, 118, 120, 129, 130, 133, 141, 144, 152, 176, 186, 189, 198; exempted from murder during Timucuan rebellion, 60, 64, 65; murders of, 65
frigates, 47
fugitives, Indian, 2, 10, 12, 15, 19, 22–26, 27, 33, 34, 37, 43, 58, 95, 100, 102, 105, 114, 115, 116, 117, 120, 121, 122, 127, 142

Gainesville, 132, 167
galleons, Spanish, 46
games, Indian, 89
García, Andrés, 126
García, Francisco, 137
García Martín Xinija, Antonio, executed Indian, 86. *See also* Antonio, son of Lazaro of Chamile
García de la Vera, Francisco, 47, 52
garrisons, provincial, 1, 54, 60, 65, 88, 89, 106, 109, 110, 113, 121–22, 126, 133, 144, 145, 199
Garzón de los Cobos, Miguel, 110, 113
Gaspar, cacique of Asile, 77, 91, 95
gasto de indios, 40. *See also* Indian fund
gender, and the labor system, 15, 58
Georgia, English colony of, 157, 200
Georgia, state of, 31, 117, 127, 133, 182, 184, 185, 190, 191
Gerónimo, Indian from Tabasco, 53, 62, 66

gifts, distribution of: to chiefs, 39, 40, 41, 43, 57, 73; to Indians, 40
godfather, 60
Gómez, Manuel, 111, 112
Gómez de Engraba, Juan, 14, 54, 94
González, Bentura, 132, 142
Gordons, John
governor, aboriginal office of, 91
governor and captain-general of Florida, 12, 15, 21, 24, 28, 40, 50, 56, 59, 192, 194; royal title to, 39; *residencias* of, 41, 47, 52, 69, 74, 83, 85, 86, 93, 94, 104, 106, 108, 110, 114, 119, 147
Grandin, Lake, 167
Green Cove Springs, 166
Gregorio, brother of heir/cacique of Machava, 194, 196, 197
Guale, province of, 9, 12, 15, 16, 20, 21, 22, 23, 24, 26, 29, 31, 34, 35, 36, 37, 43, 44, 50, 58, 72, 73, 75, 108, 113, 120, 127, 133, 138, 139, 144, 151, 152, 156, 162, 182, 199; laborers from, 51, 122; 1597 rebellion, 65; population of, 134, 137, 148
Guanabacoa, 156
Guerra y Vega, Francisco de, 120, 121, 122
Gulf of Mexico, 1, 17, 18, 138
gunpowder, 46

haciendas, 144; La Chua, 20, 42, 59, 62, 63, 64, 66, 68, 75, 82, 85, 86, 102, 121, 130, 131, 132, 142, 144, 146, 160, 203, 206; location of La Chua, 53, 76, 167; Asile, 51, 95, 180, 181; late 17th-century, 128, 130–33; Santa Cruz, 131, 142, 144; Santa Catalina/Chicharro, 132, 144; San Joseph de Puibeta, 132, 142; Piquilaco/Picolata, 132, 142, 165; La Rosa del Diablo, 132; Acuitasique, 132; Abosaya, 132; Ablosuro, 132; Amaca, 132, 202, 205; Tocoy, 165
Hall Lake, 166, 167
Hamilton County, 184
hamlets, 134
hardtack, 14, 72
hatchets, 15, 60, 61, 83
Havana, 41, 46, 47, 52, 75, 104, 138, 156

headman, 89, 92, 93
hemp, 31
hereditary leadership: in Timucuan chiefdoms, 39, 59; persistence despite depopulation, 127; dispute over, 192–97
Hernández, Matheo, 104
Herrera, Lopez, y Mesa, Antonio de, 18
Heva, Diego, cacique of Santa Catalina de Ayepacano/San Pedro de Potohiriba, 75, 77, 82, 83, 84, 91, 92, 111, 112, 115
Hinachuba, Patricio de, cacique of Ivitachuco, 145, 146
Hiriba, Francisco, *mandador* of Lazaro of Chamile, 76, 78, 79, 80, 82, 84
Hita Salazar, Antonio de, 131–32, 142
Hita Salazar, Pablo de, 129, 131, 135, 138
Hitchiti, town of, 144
Hixtown Swamp, 185, 186
hoes, iron, 20, 41
holatama, 92
Horruytiner, Luis, 18, 41
Horruytiner, Pedro Benedit, 24, 34, 41, 42, 122, 193, 194, 197
horses, 52, 60, 64, 108, 181, 203, 206
houses, Indian, 28, 44; of chief, 120

Ibihica, province of, 8, 37; population of, 3, 6
Ibiniuti, province of, 12, 18, 25, 26, 33, 35, 36, 37, 43, 44, 55, 78, 117, 138, 199; Chisca Indians in, 20, 34; emergence of, 32
Ichetucknee River, 169, 173, 174; headspring, 75, 120, 170, 171, 172
immigration. *See reducción*
Indians: Apalachee, 8, 61, 68, 71, 73, 75, 79, 82, 111, 142; mission, 13, 15, 16, 21, 74, 112, 144, 149, 150, 151, 203, 206; Guale/Ybaja, 15, 73, 150; Christian, 16, 17, 18, 19, 20, 21, 26, 35, 134, 178; Pohoy, 18; Amacano, 18, 135, 136; Timucuan, 25, 57, 60, 78, 87, 142, 144, 148, 150, 155, 157; Florida, 119, 156; Acuera, 121, 142; Chacato, 135, 136, 144, 145, 203, 206; Chine, 135, 136; Pacara, 135, 136; Colon, 137; Ayapaja, 142; Apalachicola, 144, 175; Chachise,
149, 150; Casapuia/Cosapuya, 150, 151; Chasta, 150; Macapira, 151; Costa, 151; Piaja, 151; Ocatasa, 203, 206; Tabasa, 203, 206
Indian fund, 39, 40; control over distribution, 39–42
Indian Pond, 182, 183, 184
Indian Pond site, 102, 182, 183
Indies, 45
infantry, Spanish, 44, 47, 48, 49, 50, 67, 70, 71, 72, 74, 75, 78, 79, 108, 121, 129, 199. *See also* soldiers
infrastructure of Spanish Florida, 27
iniha, 67
interpreters, 81, 83, 85; Timucuan, 36, 42, 58, 78, 85, 111, 194, 197; Spanish, 51, 60, 78, 180, 194
iron, 41
Ivitanayo, woods of, 129, 130, 131. *See also* Santa Rosa de Ivitanayo

Jabajica, cacique of Acuera, 135
Jacán, 113. *See also* Virginia
Jamaica, 45
Jefferson County, 177
Jekyll Island, 190
Jennings, 184
Jiménez, Diego, 132
Jororo, province of, 134
Joseph Alonso, brother of heir/cacique of Machava, 194
Jospo, Yamassee cacique, 150
Juan Alonso, cacique of Nombre de Dios, 149, 150. *See also* Alonso, cacique of Salamototo
Juan Bauptista, cacique of San Francisco, 64, 76, 77, 82, 85, 86
Juan Bauptista, cacique of San Juan (under Arapaja/Santa Fé), 90, 91
Juan Bauptista Xiriva, executed Indian, 86
Juan Camacho, brother of heir/cacique of Machava, 194
Juan Ebangelista, cacique of San Lúcas (under Asile), 69, 76, 77, 81, 86, 93, 94, 95
Juan Joseph, Timucua/Yamassee Indian, 157
Junta de Guerra, 162

258 / Index

jurisdictions: Franciscan, 4, 27; chiefly, 34, 35–36, 42, 58, 69, 77, 90, 91, 93, 94, 95, 113, 123, 129, 141; disputes over, 38, 56, 57, 59, 63, 108–10, 112; military, 39, 41, 117

Kendall Creek, 101
kinship, 28; between chiefs, 95

labor, 31, 50, 59, 71, 102, 116; pools of, 1; stresses of, 13–16, 29; as chiefly tribute, 123
labor draft. See *repartimiento*
labor system. See *repartimiento*
laborers, Indian, 1, 14, 21, 47, 50, 57, 70, 73, 111, 127; forced, 86, 87; on Spanish haciendas, 142
Lagne Chapqui, cacique of Pocosapa, 150
lakes, 75, 120, 132, 157, 167, 168, 171, 185, 188, 190
Lake City, 182
Lake George, 32, 187, 188
Lake Griffin, 190
Lake Iamonia, 177
Lake Park, 184, 185
Lake Weir, 190
Lamont, 178, 179
lands, royal, 131
languages, 28; Timucuan, 25, 26, 29, 32, 62, 120, 150, 157; Guale/Ybaja, 136, 150; Yamassee, 136, 150; Apalachee, 150; Mayaca, 150; Casapuia, 150; Chasta, 150
Lastra, Pedro de la, 141, 173
launches, 17
Lazaro, cacique of Chamile/San Martín, 55, 76, 77, 78, 79, 80, 81, 82, 86, 87, 91, 92, 93, 99, 100, 107, 108, 110, 114, 118, 119, 120, 135, 169, 185, 187
Lem, Juan de, 136
León, Lorenzo Joseph de, 131
Leturiondo, Domingo de, 123, 126, 127, 129, 131
lieutenants to the governor: of Apalachee, 43, 51, 60, 88, 106, 109, 110, 111, 113, 128, 169; of Timucua, 69, 103, 106, 113, 114, 120, 124, 126, 130, 133, 138, 140, 141, 143, 144, 145, 177, 192, 193; as interim governor, 85; provincial, 111, 112; of Guale, 144
literacy, among mission Indians, 62
Little Aucilla River, 186
Little River springs, 103, 172, 173, 174
Live Oak, 172, 183, 184
Lorenzo, cacique of Chuaquin, 91
Lorenzo, cacique of Machava, 122, 192, 193, 194, 195, 196
Lorenzo, Indian from Helaca, 32
Lorenzo, Indian from Santa Fé, 62
Lorenzo, *mandador* of San Martín, 62
Lúcas, cacique of Ajoica, 128, 131
Lúcas, cacique of Asile, 91
Lúcas, cacique of San Lúcas (under San Matheo), 91
Lucia, *cacica* of Niahica, 91, 103
Luís, Don, cacique of Ivitachuco, 41, 70, 73, 75, 94, 95; heir of, 67; *iniha* of, 67

Macaríz, mission of, 149, 151, 153; location of, 154. See also Nombre de Dios
Machava, chiefdom of, 122. See also Santa Elena de Machava
Madrid, 162
mandador, 76, 78, 79, 82
Manuel, cacique of Asile, 26, 95
Manuel, cacique of Ybichua, 195
Manuel, old *principal* of Machava, 195, 196
maps, 130, 132, 134, 157, 160, 166, 167, 171, 174, 175, 176, 187, 188
Marcos, cacique of the Ocochunos, 141
Marcos, *principal* of San Pedro de Potohiriba, 195
María, *cacica* of San Juan Ebangelista, 77, 80, 81
María Jacoba, Indian fugitive from Potano, 121
María de Jesús, *cacica* of San Francisco de Potano, 128, 129
María Lorenza, sister of heir/cacique of Machava, 194
María Magdalena, heir of Machava, 192, 194, 196

Index / 259

María de Salazar, sister of heir/cacique of Machava, 194
Márquez, Pedro, cacique of Tocoy/San Sebastián, 30
Márquez Cabrera, Juan, 133, 138, 199
marriage, Indian, 21, 32, 149
Martha Dowling North site, 191
Martín, cacique of San Pedro de Aqualiro, 91
Martín, governor of Tari, 91. *See also* Santa Cruz de Tarihica II
Martínez, Sebastián, 113
Martínez de Sala, Simón, 137
Martorel, Miguel, 136
Marzela, *cacica* of Santa Ana (in Potano), 128, 129
Mass, 142
material culture, changes in, 36–37
Matheo, cacique of San Francisco de Arapaja
matrilineages, 50, 95; chiefly, 29, 92, 96, 122, 124; noble, 59, 92, 127; disputes between, 192–97
Mayaca, Lake of, 188
Mayaca, province of, 20, 22, 23, 32, 37, 157, 162, 188
Medina, Juan de, 48, 55
Medina, Thomás de, cacique of Santa Fé II, 128, 135, 138
Meléndez, María, *cacica* of Santa Ana (under San Pedro de Potohiriba), 91
Meléndez, Pedro, cacique of Santa Elena de Machava, 91, 92, 96, 122, 123, 192, 193, 194, 195, 196, 197
Mendoza, Manuel de, 145
Menéndez, Juan, interpreter from Nombre de Dios, 42
Menéndez, Lúcas, cacique of San Martín, 38, 42, 43, 45, 52, 53, 54, 55, 56, 57, 58, 59, 60, 61, 62, 63, 64, 65, 66, 75, 76, 77, 82, 83, 84, 86, 88, 92, 99, 135
Menéndez Márquez, Antonio, 42, 43, 75, 84, 104, 118, 119, 198, 199
Menéndez Márquez, Francisco I, 19, 34, 42, 60, 131, 181
Menéndez Márquez, Francisco II, 131
Menéndez Márquez, Juan, 42, 60, 62, 63, 64, 66, 75, 79, 84, 119

Menéndez Márquez, Thomás, 131, 132, 133, 142
Mercado, Juan de, 136
Miami, Lake of, 188
Miguel, cacique of San Francisco de Potano, 128, 138, 142, 146, 148
Milanich, Jerald, 8
militia, Indian, 55, 67, 71, 89, 110; activation of, 48–50, 52, 57, 59; ranks within, 128
mico, 24, 72
missions, 51, 88, 122, 134, 138, 159, 160, 198, 200
mission provinces, 89; emergence of, 37
missionaries, 20, 28, 35, 58, 64, 100, 104, 109, 113, 118, 129, 141, 198. *See also* friars, Franciscan
missionization, 36, 37
Mobile, 145
Mocama, province of, 9, 12, 22, 24, 29, 31, 34, 36, 37, 85, 86, 127, 133, 139, 144, 149, 151, 152, 155, 156, 182, 199; population of, 134, 137, 148
Mocoso, town of, 36
Molina, *cacica* of San Juan de Guacara, 77, 81, 90, 104
Moloa, town of, 35
Moncrief, James, 160
Montano, Juan, 46, 47
Montes, Blas de, 187, 188
Montiano, Manuel de, 200
Monzon, Francisco de, 84
Moon Lake site, 167
Moore, James, 144, 145, 157, 191
Moreno y Segovia, Juan, 85, 90, 99
Moral, Alonso del, 110
Moseley Hall, 79, 176
Mount Royal site, 187, 188
Moze, site of, 152
Muelle, El, site of, 152
munitions, 46, 113
murders, 71; of Christian Indians, 19, 20, 21; during Timucuan rebellion, 36, 38, 53, 56, 59, 60, 61, 62, 63, 64, 66, 74, 82, 83, 85; of African slaves, 53, 64, 82, 146; of friars, 65, 145; of Apalachee Indians, 132, 144, 145; of Spanish soldiers, 145

Namo, Timucuan name for Juan Bauptista de la Cruz, 78
Namo, town of, 43, 77; cacique of, 77, 81
Napufai, town of, 20
nayoa of La Chua, 132
New Spain, 46, 48, 162
New World, 10, 46
Niahica, mission of, 91, 115, 173, 182, 187, 199; location of, 53, 76, 183–84; *cacica* of, 53, 77, 81; relocation of, 98, 103. *See also* San Agustín de Urihica; Lucia, *cacica*
Nicoloa, creek of, 166
Nocoroco, town of, 20
Nombre de Dios, mission of, 24, 30, 42, 44, 45, 147, 148, 149, 150, 151, 153, 155, 156, 162, 191; location of, 98, 143, 154. *See also* Macaríz; Juan Sánchez, cacique
Nombre de Dios Chiquito, mission/site of, 152, 153
noroco, 52, 81, 83; definition of, 61
North Carolina, state of, 19
notaries, 75, 83, 85, 86, 90, 94, 114, 197
Nuestra Señora de la Asunción, church of (in Cuba), 156
Nuestra Señora de la Asumpción, mission of, 153. *See also* San Juan del Puerto de Palica
Nuestra Señora de la Candelaria de la Tama[ja], mission of, 136, 199, 203, 206; refugees in St. Augustine, 150. *See also* Antonio de Ayala, cacique
Nuestra Señora de la Concepción de Ayubale, mission of, 136, 145, 163, 199, 203, 206
Nuestra Señora de la Concepción de Pocotalaca, mission of, 153. *See also* Pocotalaca
Nuestra Señora de los Dolores, mission of, 149, 150
Nuestra Señora de Guadalupe de Tolomato, mission of, 24, 48, 49, 50, 163, 199; establishment of, 31; location of, 98, 143; refugees in St. Augustine, 152, 153. *See also* Tolomato
Nuestra Señora de la Leche, mission of, 155. *See also* Nombre de Dios

Nuestra Señora del Monte, frigate, 47
Nuestra Señora del Rosario de Abosaya, mission of, 150, 152. *See also* Pedro Osunaca, cacique
Nuestra Señora del Rosario de la Punta, mission of, 153
Nyaautina, town of, 187, 188. *See also* Enacape

O'Brien, 173
Ocala, 190
Ocale, province of, 7, 189
Ocaña, Francisco de, 6, 11
Ocochunos Indians, 141. *See also* Marcos, cacique
Ocon, Juan de, 136
Oconi, Lake of, 157. *See also* Okefenokee Swamp
Oconi, province of, 7, 8, 11, 12, 25, 26, 37, 45, 57, 157; population of, 3, 6. *See also* Santiago de Oconi
Ocute, Alonso, Yamassee cacique, 150
Okefenokee Swamp, 22, 25, 26, 45, 157, 162, 182, 190, 191
Oklawaha River, 7, 31, 162, 187, 189, 190
Orange Lake, 167
Orangedale, 101, 166
Oré, Luís Gerónimo de, 28, 160, 165, 171, 175, 182, 183, 188
Oria, Francisco de, 41
Osuna, Juan de, 53, 63
Osunaca, Pedro, cacique of Nuestra Señora del Rosario de Abosaya, 150
out-migration, 1, 10, 20, 22–26, 32–34, 115, 121, 127
Outina, province of, 7, 8
Outina, town of, 167
Oyubel, town of, 113. *See also* Pedro Miguel, cacique

Pablo, *iniha* of Santa Elena de Machava, 195
Pachala, town of, 76, 77, 80, 96, 115, 199; cacique of, 77
Pacheco y Salgedo, Matheo, 72
padres de provincia, Franciscan, 113
Palacios, Pedro, 128, 135, 170, 171
Palatka, 166, 187

Palica, mission of, 153, 155, 156; location of, 154. *See also* San Buenaventura de Palica; San Juan del Puerto de Palica
palisade, Timucuan. *See* fortifications, Timucuan
Palmo, 165
Pardo, Juan, 19
Parga, Juan de, 145
Pasqua, Juan, Timucuan Indian, 64, 86
Pastrana, cacique of Arapaja, 54, 77, 81, 93
Pastrana, Alonso, cacique of Arapaja/Santa Fé, 90, 91, 93, 99, 135, 185. *See also* Pastrana, cacique of Arapaja
Paynes Prairie, 132
Peacock Lake, 184
pearls, 157
Pedernales, River of, 201, 204
Pedro, cacique of San Pablo (in Yustaga), 77, 81
Pedro, cacique of San Pedro de Potohiriba, 195, 197
Pedro, *principal* of San Pedro de Potohiriba, 195
Pedro Miguel, cacique of Oyubel, 113
Peña, Diego, 168, 169, 174, 175, 177
Pensacola, 145, 146, 160
Pérez, Andrés, 126
Pérez, Bartolomé, 53, 60, 61, 66, 82, 83, 181
Pérez de Villa Real, Agustín, 51, 52, 54, 55, 56, 57, 60, 61, 62, 63, 64, 66, 67, 84, 85, 93, 99, 111, 112, 131, 182, 183, 184; route to deliver 1656 order, 53
Peru, 28
Picolata, River of, 202, 206
Picolata, site of, 101, 132, 166
Pilijiriba, site of, 144
Piliuco, town of, 121. *See also* Piriaco
Pine Lake, 186
pirates, 139
Piriaco, town of, 121. *See also* Piliuco
Pocosapa, mission of, 150. *See also* Lagne Chapqui, cacique
Pocotalaca, mission of, 150, 153, 155; location of, 154. *See also* Francisco Yaquisca, cacique; San Antonio de Pocotalaca
Pohoy, cacique of, 17, 18
Pohoy, province of, 17, 18, 149, 151, 190

Ponce de León, Nicolás I, 12
Ponce de León, Nicolás II, 118, 119
Population: pre-European, 2, 3, 8; ca. 1600, 3–8; collapse, 1–26, 27, 28, 29, 30, 32, 37, 38, 43, 45, 51, 58, 69, 105, 124, 126, 139, 148; differential distribution of, 5, 70, 97, 105, 124; density, 5; rate of depopulation, 10; reduction in growth, 10, 21–22; Spanish efforts to counter depopulation, 27–37, 97, 99, 105, 106, 118; "backflow" of, 35–37; of individual Timucuan missions, 126; 1681 census of, 134–36, 137–38; of refugee missions, 148, 150, 151, 152, 153
ports: in St. Augustine, 1, 45, 46; in Apalachee, 75, 200, 203
Potano, province of, 5, 8, 11, 17, 18, 23, 29, 36, 37, 70, 121, 127, 130, 146, 162, 167, 189, 191; population of, 3
power, chiefly, 16; erosion of, 39, 50, 58, 59
Prado, Joseph de, 14, 15, 39, 40, 48
prehistory, 37, 71, 158, 169, 185
Prieto, Martín, 17
principales, 34, 49, 52, 55, 58, 59, 62, 67, 71, 81, 88, 89, 118, 127, 128, 147, 193, 194, 197
prisoners, Indian, 56, 82, 83; executions of, 83, 86, 138. *See also* laborers, forced
provincial minister. *See* Franciscan provincial minister
Puerta, Pedro de la, 108, 110, 111
Pueyo, Juan de, 132, 142
Puje, Juan, Timucuan Indian, 156
Pulilica, landing at, 130
Punta, La, mission of, 153, 155; location of, 154. *See also* Nuestra Señora del Rosario de la Punta
Pupo, site of, 101, 165
Purcell, Joseph, 160, 171, 174, 175, 176

Quiñones, Bartolomé de, 134
Quiroga y Losada, Diego de, 141, 142

raiding, 1, 10, 16–21, 34–35, 75, 121; English-sponsored, 16, 21, 101, 113, 120, 121, 138, 139, 140–46, 151, 157, 176
rancherías, 138, 147

ranches. *See* haciendas
Ranjel, Diego, 114
rations: for Indian laborers, 13, 14; for visiting Indians, 39, 43, 57; for sick Indians, 40
rebellions. *See* Apalachee, Guale, Timucuan rebellion
Rebolledo, Diego de, 12, 13, 14, 36, 37, 38, 46, 47, 48, 49, 50, 51, 52, 53, 54, 55, 56, 57, 58, 59, 60, 61, 62, 63, 65, 66, 67, 68, 70, 72, 73, 74, 75, 78, 83, 84, 85, 86, 87, 88, 89, 90, 91, 92, 93, 94, 95, 96, 97, 98, 99, 100, 101, 102, 103, 104, 105, 106, 107, 108, 109, 110, 111, 112, 114, 115, 116, 117, 118, 123, 124, 135, 166, 168, 173, 175, 187, 191; early gubernatorial term of, 39–45
reducción, 2, 19, 27, 28, 34–35, 105
reformados, 72, 74, 113
Rejidor, Gerónimo, 197
relocation, settlement, 2, 5, 27, 30–32, 35, 37, 44, 105, 119, 143; under Governor Rebolledo, 87, 89, 92, 93, 96, 97–105, 115
rendering of obedience, reaffirmation during visits to St. Augustine, 39, 40, 41, 42
repartimiento labor system, 1, 10, 12, 22, 24, 26, 29, 33, 44, 47, 50, 59, 64, 67, 70, 71, 75, 78, 89, 111, 116, 117, 123, 130, 134; stresses of, 13–16, 25, 37; abuses in, 21, 58; draft quotas for, 43, 51, 122
Republic of Indians, 38, 59
Republic of Spaniards, 38, 59
reserve officers, Spanish. *See re-formados*
residencias. *See* governor and captain general of Spanish Florida
Reynoso, Ysidro de, 23, 121
Richardson site, 167
Riço, Francisco, cacique of Santa Fé II, 138, 141, 146, 148, 156
Riço, Manuel, 133, 138, 156
Rio Blanco, 166
Ríos Enríquez, Diego de los, 120, 140, 141
rivers, 1, 31, 46, 104, 172, 189
roads, 11, 13, 14, 19, 25, 49, 84, 90, 97, 98, 102, 103, 160, 176, 183, 184, 191, 200, 201, 206; way stations along, 1, 2, 38, 97, 105; construction of, 101, 130; maintenance of, 104
Rocha, Francisco de la, 23, 104, 198, 199
Robinson Sinks, 168
Rodríguez de Cartaya, Juan, 17
Rojas y Borja, Luis de, 18, 31, 50, 165, 189
Romo, Juan, cacique of San Joseph de Jororo, 150
Romo de Uriza, Francisco, 132, 144
Rollestown site, 166, 187
royal officials of Florida, 85, 113, 115, 129, 134, 138, 143, 198
Royal Springs, 62, 174
Rueda, Francisco de, 114
Ruíz, Benito, cacique of Santa Cruz de Tarihica, 43, 53, 54, 76, 77, 81, 86, 88
Ruíz de Cañizares, Juan, 144
Ruíz Maroto, Juan, 85
Ruíz de Salazar Vallecilla, Benito, 12, 14, 20, 22, 26, 33, 85, 95, 110, 180, 181

Sabacola el Viejo, mission of, 204
sacristan, Franciscan office, 57, 62
St. Augustine, 1, 13, 14, 19, 24, 30, 34, 35, 36, 37, 38, 39, 41, 42, 43, 44, 45, 50, 51, 54, 56, 57, 59, 60, 61, 62, 63, 64, 65, 66, 67, 68, 70, 71, 73, 74, 75, 84, 85, 86, 87, 90, 97, 101, 105, 109, 110, 112, 113, 121, 130, 131, 138, 139, 140, 144, 146, 147, 148, 149, 151, 152, 154, 155, 157, 160, 162, 165, 167, 169, 176, 182, 184, 186, 187, 188, 189, 190, 191, 197, 198, 199, 200, 206; presidio of, 29, 46, 47, 48, 49, 52, 55, 72, 99, 108, 114, 196
St. Johns County, 166
St. Johns River, 7, 8, 18, 19, 20, 24, 25, 30, 31, 32, 33, 34, 35, 43, 70, 100, 101, 113, 117, 121, 122, 130, 131, 132, 133, 135, 144, 157, 159, 160, 166, 167, 181, 187, 188, 189
St. Marys River, 45, 190, 191
Salamototo, creek of, 101, 166
Salamototo, River of, 129

Salinas, Joseph, 132
Salinas, Juan de, 19
Salvador, Diego, 36, 78, 81, 83, 85, 111, 112, 194, 197
Sampala Lake, 175, 176
Sampala Lake site, 186
San Agustín, town of (under San Matheo), 91. *See also* Domingo, cacique
San Agustín de Ajoica, mission of, 103, 106, 120, 128, 140, 170, 171, 174, 183; location of, 173. *See also* Ajoica
San Agustín de Urihica, mission of, 53, 163, 173, 183, 185, 186; relocation of, 98, 103; location of, 183–84. *See also* Ajoica, Niahica
San Antonio, Francisco de, 108
San Antonio, Island of, 188
San Antonio, Lake of, 188
San Antonio, mission of (Cosapuya), 151
San Antonio, mission of (Yamassee), 151
San Antonio de Arapaja, town of, 130. *See also* Antonio, cacique
San Antonio de Bacuqua, mission of, 136, 199, 203, 206
San Antonio de Enacape, mission of, 7, 25, 32, 33, 162, 163, 189, 190, 199; abandonment of, 100; royal lands reserved for, 131, 188; Yamassee Indians in, 133–34, 135, 188; location of, 164, 187–88
San Antonio de la Costa, mission of, 151, 152, 153
San Antonio de Pocotalaca, mission of, 152. *See also* Pocotalaca
San Antonio de la Tama, mission of, 152, 155
San Blas de Avino, mission of, 7, 30, 31; location of, 189
San Buenaventura, mission of (in Potano), 4; location of, 167
San Buenaventura de Guadalquini, mission of, 101, 137, 163, 199
San Buenaventura de Palica, mission of, 149, 150, 151, 152. *See also* Juan Ximénez, cacique
San Carlos de los Chacatos, mission of, 136, 199, 201, 204

San Cosme y San Damián de Cupiaca, mission of, 163; location of, 164
San Damián de Escambé, mission of, 136, 145, 199, 203, 206
San Diego, mission of (Yamassee), 151
San Diego, town of (under San Matheo), 91. *See also* Francisco, cacique
San Diego de Helaca, mission of, 23, 24, 33, 34, 35, 36, 37, 70–71, 101, 163, 188; establishment of, 30–32, 165, 189; relocation of, 100, 166; location of, 164, 165–66
San Diego de Salamototo, mission of, 24, 32, 102, 111, 117, 124, 125, 127, 129, 132, 134, 138, 142, 144, 157, 165, 181, 188, 189, 190, 199; location of, 98, 143, 161, 166; establishment of, 100–101, 166; garrison post at, 113, 121–22, 133; population of, 126; royal lands reserved for, 131, 166; aggregation of, San Francisco/Santa Fé, 146; retreat to St. Augustine, 146; refugees in St. Augustine, 147, 148, 149, 150. *See also* Alonso, cacique
San Diego de Satuache, mission of, 137, 162, 163, 199; location of, 164
San Felasco hammock, 167
San Francisco, town of (under San Matheo), 91, 124. *See also* Francisco, cacique
San Francisco de Chuaquin, mission of, 92, 111, 115, 163, 199; location of, 53, 76, 164, 186–87; cacique of, 77, 81; relocation of, 99, 100, 106, 187. *See also* Lorenzo, cacique
San Francisco de los Corrales, Padre, mission of, 152
San Francisco de Oconi, mission of, 136, 163, 199, 203, 206
San Francisco de Potano, mission of, 4, 24, 25, 29, 42, 52, 64, 77, 85, 86, 91, 92, 93, 101, 102, 103, 106, 111, 114, 121, 125, 131, 142, 156, 163, 166, 168, 169, 170, 186, 199, 203, 206; location of, 53, 76, 98, 143, 164, 167; population of, 126, 136; aggregation of Santa Ana, 127–28, 129, 167; aggregation of Santa

Fé II, 144; aggregation to Salamototo, 146; refugees in St. Augustine, 147, 148, 149. *See also* Juan Bauptista, cacique; Domingo, cacique; María de Jesús, *cacica;* Miguel, cacique

San Ildefonso de Chamile, mission of, 55, 77, 78, 80, 81, 91, 93, 107, 108, 111, 115, 163, 199; location of, 53, 76, 164, 185–86; relocation of, 99, 100, 106, 169, 186, 187. *See also* Lazaro, cacique

San Joseph, town of (under Santa Elena de Machava), 91. *See also* Sebastián, cacique

San Joseph, town of (under San Martín?), 108. *See also* Francisco, cacique

San Joseph, Francisco de, 136

San Joseph, Marçelo de, 136

San Joseph de Jororo, mission of, 150. *See also* Juan Romo, cacique

San Joseph de Ocuya, mission of, 136, 163, 199, 203, 206

San Joseph de Sapala, mission of, 137, 163, 199; refugees in St. Augustine, 151

San Juan, mission of (Apalachee/Yamassee), 151

San Juan, town of (under Arapaja/Santa Fé), 91, 123. *See also* Juan Bauptista, cacique

San Juan de Aspalaga, mission of, 136, 163, 199, 203, 206

San Juan Ebangelista, town of, 69, 77, 79, 80. *See also* María, *cacica*

San Juan de Guacara, mission of, 77, 90, 97, 142, 171, 182, 186, 202, 205; location of, 53, 76, 161, 174–75; relocation of, 103–4, 175. *See also* Molina, *cacica*

San Juan de Guacara II, mission of, 90, 102, 111, 114, 124, 125, 171, 172, 174, 176, 181, 199, 202, 205; location of, 98, 161, 175; establishment of, 103–4, 106; population of, 126, 136; destruction of, 141, 175

San Juan de Guacara, River of, 62, 84, 174, 175, 202, 205

San Juan del Puerto, mission of, 24, 85, 137, 144, 163, 190, 199; location of, 98, 143; refugees in St. Augustine, 148, 149; survival of conventual name, 152, 155

San Juan del Puerto de Palica, mission of, 153. *See also* San Buenaventura de Palica

San Julian, town of, 187

San Lorenzo, town of (under Santa Elena), 91, 92, 96; cacique of, 77, 81. *See also* Dionicio, cacique

San Lorenzo de Ibihica, mission of: destruction of, 44–45, 117; location of, 191

San Lorenzo de Ivitachuco, mission of, 19, 41, 52, 54, 60, 61, 65, 67, 68, 69, 70, 72, 75, 78, 79, 83, 84, 94, 95, 136, 143, 145, 146, 163, 177, 178, 180, 181, 199, 200, 203, 204, 205; location of, 53, 76; trial of Timucuan caciques in, 85–87; survival of conventual name, 152, 155. *See also* Patricio de Hinachuba, cacique

San Lúcas, town of (under Asile), 77, 92, 93, 94, 95. *See also* Juan Ebangelista, cacique

San Lúcas, town of (under San Matheo), 91. *See also* Lúcas, cacique

San Luís de Eloquale, mission of, 7, 32, 163, 190, 199; abandonment of, 100, 189; location of, 189

San Luís de Inhayca, mission of, 88, 89, 106, 109, 110–11, 163. *See also* Francisco Luís, cacique

San Luís de Talimali, mission of, 126, 134, 136, 145, 199, 201, 203, 204, 206; refugees in St. Augustine, 148, 151, 152; survival of conventual name, 152, 155

San Luís de la Tama, mission of, 152

San Marcos de Apalachee, fort of, 201, 203, 204, 205. *See also* fortifications, Spanish

San Martín, Pedro de, 23

San Martín, River of, 130

San Martín de Ayacuto, mission of, 4, 13, 42, 52, 56, 58, 62, 68, 69, 75, 77, 79, 84, 91, 92, 93, 96, 97, 99, 100, 102, 103, 106, 107, 108, 111, 114, 115, 163, 168, 170, 171, 172, 174, 175, 182, 184, 185, 186, 187, 199, 202, 205; location of, 53, 76, 161, 164, 169; abandonment of, 118–20, 135. *See also* Lúcas Menéndez, cacique; Lazaro, cacique

San Martín de Tomole, mission of, 136, 163, 199, 203, 206

San Matheo, town of (under San Matheo de Tolapatafi), 91. *See also* Santiago, cacique
San Matheo de Tolapatafi, mission of, 91, 123, 124, 125, 129, 130, 142, 176, 180, 194, 199, 201, 202, 205; establishment of, 93–96; location of, 98, 143, 161, 177–79; population of, 126, 137; destruction of, 145. *See also* Francisco, cacique; Sebastián, cacique
San Miguel, mission of (in Potano), 4, 167
San Miguel, town of (under San Matheo), 91. *See also* Francisco Alonso, cacique
San Miguel de Asile, mission of, 26, 60, 61, 69, 77, 83, 84, 86, 91, 93, 94, 95, 96, 109, 117, 123, 125, 142, 163, 176, 177, 178, 179, 199, 201, 202, 205; location of, 53, 76, 98, 143, 161, 164, 180–81; population of, 126, 137. *See also* Gaspar, cacique
San Nicolás de Casapuyas, mission of, 153; location of, 154
San Pablo, town of (under Arapaja/Santa Fé), 91. *See also* Francisco Alonso, cacique
San Pablo, town of (under San Matheo), 91. *See also* Bernabé, cacique
San Pablo, town of (under San Pedro), 77. *See also* Pedro, cacique
San Pedro, province of, 23
San Pedro de Aqualiro, town of, 91. *See also* Martín, cacique
San Pedro Bay, 67, 175
San Pedro de Medellín de los Chines, mission of, 136, 199
San Pedro de Mocama, mission of, 45, 134, 137, 162, 163, 190, 191, 199; location of, 164
San Pedro de Potohiriba, mission of, 19, 52, 54, 55, 60, 61, 62, 63, 69, 77, 84, 89, 90, 91, 92, 94, 96, 97, 103, 104, 109, 111, 112, 115, 125, 129, 148, 163, 182, 183, 186, 199, 202, 205; location of, 53, 76, 98, 161, 164, 175–76, 181; meeting held before Timucuan rebellion in, 57, 68, 86; 1670 junta at, 122–24, 192–97; population of, 126,

137; relocation of, 126, 142, 176, 177. *See also* Diego, cacique; Diego Heva, cacique; Pedro, cacique
San Pedro de Potohiriba II, mission of, 125, 178, 179, 180, 202, 205; establishment of, 142; location of, 143, 161, 176–77; destruction of, 145, 177; survival of conventual name, 152, 155; refugees in St. Augustine, 155
San Pedro y San Pablo de Patale, mission of, 136, 165, 199, 203, 206
San Phelipe de Alave, mission of, 163
San Phelipe II, mission of, 134, 137, 199
San Phelipe III, mission of, 144; location of, 143
San Salvador de Mayaca, mission of, 163, 199; abandonment of, 100; Yamassee Indians in, 133–34, 135; location of, 164
San Sebastián, mission of, 30
San Simón/Colon, mission of, 199
Sánchez, Francisco, 104, 120
Sánchez, Juan, cacique of Nombre de Dios, 155
Santa Ana, lake of, 167
Santa Ana, mission of (in Potano), 4, 25, 85, 121; aggregation to San Francisco, 29, 127–28, 129, 167; cacique of, 77, 81; location of, 167. *See also* Marzela, *cacica*
Santa Ana, town of (under San Pedro de Potohiriba), 91. *See also* María Meléndez, *cacica*
Santa Anastacia, Island of, 202, 206
Santa Catalina, mission of (in Timucua), 29, 103, 124, 125, 131, 134, 136, 174; possible locations of, 98, 161, 169–73; establishment of, 119–20, 135, 169; aggregation of Ajoica, 128, 173. *See also* Santa Catalina de Ajoica
Santa Catalina de Ajoica, mission of, 199, 203, 206; population of, 126; aggregation of Santa Catalina and Ajoica, 128; Yamassee assault on, 140; aggregation to Santa Fé II, 141, 168, 174
Santa Catalina de Ayepacano, town of, 76, 77, 84, 92. *See also* Diego Heva, cacique
Santa Catalina de Guale, mission of, 21, 137, 163, 199; refugees in St. Augustine,

148, 150, 151, 152; survival of conventual name, 152, 155. See also Alonso de la Cruz, cacique
Santa Clara de Tupiqui I, mission of, 199
Santa Clara de Tupiqui II, mission of, 137
Santa Clara de Tupiqui III, mission of, 144; location of, 143
Santa Cruz de Cachipile, mission of, 77, 92, 111, 115, 163, 186, 199; location of, 53, 76, 164, 185; relocation of, 99, 100, 106, 185, 187. See also Francisco, cacique
Santa Cruz de Capole, mission of, 203, 206
Santa Cruz de Guadalquini, mission of, 101
Santa Cruz de San Buenaventura de Guadalquini, mission of, 101
Santa Cruz de Tarihica, mission of, 4, 11, 20, 77, 163, 184; location of, 53, 76, 164, 182–83; relocation of, 98, 102–3, 173, 183
Santa Cruz de Tarihica II, mission of, 91, 92, 118, 120, 125, 140, 171, 172, 175, 199, 203, 206; location of, 98, 161, 173–74; establishment of, 102–3, 173; population of, 126, 136; aggregation to Santa Fé II, 141, 168. See also Martín, governor
Santa Cruz de Ychutafum, mission of, 136, 199
Santa Elena de la Florida, Franciscan province of, 152
Santa Elena de Machava, mission of, 54, 55, 60, 65, 68, 69, 71, 77, 78, 79, 83, 86, 91, 92, 93, 94, 96, 110, 125, 129, 163, 178, 179, 185, 199; location of, 53, 76, 98, 161, 176–77; meeting in council house with Timucuan rebels, 80–82; dispute over chiefdom, 122–24, 192–97; population of, 126, 137; relocation of, 126, 142, 176–77. See also Dionicio, cacique; Pedro Meléndez, cacique
Santa Elena de Machava II, mission of, 125, 179, 201, 202, 205; establishment of, 142, 176–77, 178; location of, 143, 161, 180; destruction of, 145

Santa Fe, modern community of, 168
Santa Fé, River of, 168
Santa Fé, town of (under San Matheo), 91. See also Antonio, cacique
Santa Fé de Teleco, mission of, 20, 24, 52, 62, 96, 141, 163, 169, 170, 171, 174, 186, 202, 205; location of, 53, 76, 161, 167, 168; cacique of, 64, 77, 82, 85; relocation of, 101–2
Santa Fé II, mission of, 90, 91, 93, 96, 100, 103, 111, 113, 114, 123, 124, 125, 129, 131, 140, 142, 146, 156, 166, 169, 170, 199, 202, 205; location of, 98, 143, 161, 167–68; establishment of, 101–2, 106, 167, 185; population of, 126, 136; cacique of, 130; as new provincial capital, 135; aggregation of Santa Catalina/Santa Cruz, 141, 168; Apalachicola assault, 144; aggregation to San Francisco, 144, 168; refugees in St. Augustine, 147, 148, 149, 151, 155. See also Alonso Pastrana, cacique; Thomás de Medina, cacique; Francisco Riço, cacique
Santa Fe River, 102, 103, 120, 168, 169, 170, 171, 172, 182
Santa Isabel de Utinahica, mission of, 182, 184, 199
Santa Lucia, province of, 190. See also Acuera
Santa Lucia, town of (under San Matheo), 91. See also Francisco, cacique
Santa Lucia de Acuera, mission of, 7, 32, 33, 35, 55, 163, 189, 199; abandonment of, 100, 190; location of, 164, 190
Santa María, town of (under Tarihica), 91. See also Alexo, cacique
Santa María de los Angeles de Arapaja, mission of, 5, 54, 77, 80, 90, 91, 93, 103, 111, 115, 123, 163, 182, 183, 186, 199; location of, 53, 76, 164, 184–85; relocation of, 99, 100, 101, 106, 167, 168, 185. See also Pastrana, cacique; Alonso Pastrana, cacique
Santa María de Galves de Pansacola, mission of, 152, 155
Santa María de Sena, mission of, 134, 137, 144, 199; location of, 98, 143; Guale refugees in St. Augustine, 147

Santa Rosa de Ivitanayo, mission of, 104, 125, 132, 134, 199; population of, 126; establishment of, 128–30, 131, 166; abandonment of, 142; location of, 166–67
Santiago, cacique of San Matheo (under San Matheo de Tolapatafi), 91
Santiago de Oconi, mission of, 11, 22, 26, 33, 35, 162, 163, 182, 199; destruction of, 44–45, 117, 191; location of, 164, 190–91
Santiago Pasqua, brother of heir/cacique of Machava, 194
Santo Domingo de Asajo, mission of, 137, 199
Santo Domingo de Chiquito, mission of, 153. *See also* Nombre de Dios Chiquito
Santo Domingo de Talaje, mission of, 113, 120, 163, 199
Santo Thomás de Santa Fé, mission of, 101; refugees in St. Augustine, 148, 152, 155, 156; survival of conventual name, 152, 155. *See also* Juan Arucatesa, cacique; Santa Fé II
Santos, Domingo, 137
Sartucha, Antonio de, 51, 52, 54, 60, 65, 66, 67, 75
Satilla River, 191
Savannah River, 120
scalping, 61, 62, 63, 83
Sebastián, cacique of San Joseph (under Santa Elena), 91
Sebastián, cacique of San Matheo de Tolapatafi, 91
Seminole Indians, 158
sergeant major, rank of, 55, 74, 128
settlement system: in Timucuan chiefdoms, 3; transformation of following Timucuan rebellion, 38
Seven Years' War, 156
Seville, 12
Shealy site, 141, 167, 168, 170, 171
ships, 24, 46, 51, 75, 95, 140. *See also* frigates; sloops
shipping, 1
Silver River, 190
Silver Springs, 190

Sixmile Creek, 166
slaves, African, 20, 53, 64, 82, 132, 146
slaves, Indian, 16, 21, 113, 120, 133, 139, 140, 145; rumored intent of Governor Rebolledo, 56, 58, 59, 64, 67, 70, 86
sloops, 200, 203
soil, arable, in Timucua mission province, 5
Solana, Alonso, 130, 134, 160, 197
Solana, Estéban, 42, 51, 52, 53, 54, 55, 57, 60, 61, 62, 66, 180–81, 182, 183, 184
soldiers, Spanish, 11, 14, 15, 18, 19, 21, 25, 34, 38, 43, 46, 49, 56, 58, 60, 64, 65, 66, 68, 70, 72, 78, 79, 80, 81, 83, 84, 89, 102, 104, 109, 126, 128, 129, 135, 144, 188; officers, 20, 48, 55, 67, 74, 75, 85, 106, 111, 112, 113, 118, 122, 130
Soto, Hernando de, 97, 180
Sotomayor, Juan Joseph de, 75, 83
South Carolina, state of, 133
Spain, 64, 85, 109, 110, 156, 198, 200, 201, 204, 205
Spanish crown, 11, 13, 14, 15, 17, 19, 21, 24, 28, 40, 44, 45, 46, 51, 58, 61, 63, 66, 72, 73, 81, 86, 99, 106, 108, 110, 111, 112, 114, 115, 116, 119, 138, 157, 193, 194, 195, 196, 197, 198, 199, 200
Statenville, 184
Stuart, George, 160
Stuart's Town, 140
Suárez, Nicolás, 128, 131
Sunshine Lake, 132, 168
Suwannee River, 17, 18, 54, 62, 93, 97, 103, 104, 130, 171, 172, 173, 174, 175, 181, 182, 183, 184, 186
Suwannee Springs, 184
swamps, 25, 190
swords, 41

Tabasco, province of (Mexico), 62
Tama, province of, 26
Tampa Bay, 17, 18, 190
Tarihica, chiefdom of, 184; population of, 3
Terraza, Juan Bauptista, 20, 67

Timucua, province of, 8, 9, 11, 14, 15, 17, 18, 19, 22, 23, 29, 34, 36, 37, 51, 58, 75, 88, 113, 114, 123, 191, 199; population of, 3, 5

Timucua, mission province of, 2, 9, 12, 16, 17, 20, 22, 26, 33, 35, 36, 37, 38, 39, 45, 47, 50, 56, 57, 60, 61, 62, 64, 67, 68, 69, 70, 71, 72, 73, 74, 75, 78, 80, 82, 83, 86, 87, 88, 109, 113, 120, 121, 122, 127, 130, 135, 138, 141, 143, 144, 145, 146, 159, 160, 162, 182, 183, 189; laborers from, 51; population of, 58, 134, 136, 148; political restructure of following Timucuan rebellion, 89–96, 106, 115; geographical restructure of following Timucuan rebellion, 97–105, 106, 107, 111, 112, 115, 116, 117, 124, 166, 173; garrison in, 126, 140; refugees in St. Augustine, 147–56

Timucuan rebellion, 2, 25, 27, 30, 36, 37, 38–87, 89, 90, 91, 92, 93, 94, 95, 96, 97, 99, 100, 104, 105, 107, 109, 110, 111, 112, 114, 117, 123, 127, 133, 135, 162, 166, 167, 168, 169, 173, 175, 180–81, 182, 183, 185, 186, 187, 188, 190

tithes, 132

Tocobaga, province of, 17

Tocoi, modern town of, 30, 165. *See also* Tocoy

Tocoy, town/mission of, 4, 7, 8, 24, 30, 35, 188; location of, 165

Tolapatafi, town of, 95. *See also* San Matheo de Tolapatafi

Toledo, 41

Toledo, Francisco de, Viceroy of Peru, 28

Tolomato, mission of (in Georgia), 31. *See also* Nuestra Señora de Guadalupe de Tolomato

Tolomato, mission of (at St. Augustine), 147, 148, 150, 151, 152, 153, 155, 156; location of, 154. *See also* Francisco Martín, cacique; Nuestra Señora de Guadalupe de Tolomato

Tolomato River, 24

tools, iron, 40, 41

Torres, Manuel de, 122

towns, 1, 2, 17, 21, 27, 29, 30, 35, 38, 57, 72, 82, 87, 90, 97, 105, 108, 116, 127, 130, 133, 141

trade, 89; in amber, 39, 41, 42; in deerskins, 41

Trade, House of, 162

trade goods, as barter, 41, 102

Trail Ridge, 191

transportation: 2, 12, 13, 23, 24, 25, 27, 31, 33, 36, 37, 38, 58, 78, 97, 98, 104, 105, 107, 114, 129; maritime, 1, 51; pack animals for, 14

Trebejo, Francisco, 12

Trevijano, Diego de, 23

Trout Creek, 166

Tucuru, town of, 31; cacique of, 189

turkeys, 52

Twin Lakes, 184, 185

Uchise Indians, 141, 200, 203

Umanes, Manuel, 79

Urrutia, José de, 56

Utiaca, town of, 31, 32, 35, 189

Valverde, Miguel de, 136

Vásquez, Francisco, 53, 62, 66

Vega, Francisco de, 136

Vega, Castro, y Pardo, Damián de, 19, 34, 50

Viceroy of New Spain, 46, 162

Villa Real, Juan Miguel de, 133

villages, 2, 20, 28, 71, 74, 79, 82, 93, 97, 104, 107, 116, 120, 133, 134, 138, 143, 159

Virginia, 16, 113

visita, 179, 187, 191

visitations, 29, 102, 124, 159, 177; by Fray Luís Gerónimo de Oré, 28, 160, 165, 175; by Bishop Juan de las Cavezas Altamirano, 30, 165, 189; by Juan Fernández de Florencia, 32, 33; by Governor Diego de Rebolledo, 86, 88–91, 92, 93, 94, 95, 96, 98, 99, 103, 104, 106, 109, 110, 123; by Fray Pedro Chacón, 94, 162, 164, 176, 182, 185, 186, 188; by Domingo de Leturiondo, 104, 126, 127, 129, 131, 140; by Fray Francisco de San Antonio, 108; by Bishop Gabriel Díaz Vara Calderón, 119, 128, 135, 169, 170,

171, 172, 173, 174; by Pedro Benedit Horruytiner, 122, 192–97; by Joachín de Florencia, 142; by Juan de Ayala Escobar, 143
Vitanayo, Lake of, 167. *See also* Ivitanayo

warehouses, Royal, 13, 40, 47, 49, 198
warfare, 5; between Apalachee and Timucua/Yustaga, 6, 16; between Pohoy and Amacano, 18
warriors, 48, 49, 50, 51, 52, 54, 71, 72, 73, 79, 82, 113, 140, 144, 153, 181
water, limited availability of, 120
Weechatookamee Village, 171, 174
Westo Indians, 133. *See also* Chichimeco Indians
wheat, 42, 47, 180, 203, 206
wine, 14
Withlacoochee River (Florida), 7
Withlacoochee River (Georgia/Florida), 183, 185, 186
wolves, 15
wood, 48, 66

Xaen, Diego de, 144
Ximénez, Juan, cacique of San Buenaventura de Palica, 150

Yamassee Indians, 9, 34, 133, 134, 135, 137, 140, 141, 145, 149, 150, 151, 152, 155, 156, 187, 188. *See also* Altamaha, cacique
Yamassee War, 149
Yaquisca, Francisco, cacique of Pocotalaca, 150
Ybaja. *See* Guale
Ybarra, Pedro de, 17
Ybichua, town of, 123
Ybiuro, town of, 123
ycapacha, 168, 169, 174, 175, 176, 177; definition of, 141
Yguaja. *See* Guale
Yucatan, province of, 46, 48
Yustaga, province of, 8, 9, 19, 23, 29, 36, 37, 51, 52, 54, 55, 58, 60, 67, 69, 70, 75, 76, 88, 90, 92, 93, 95, 96, 98, 99, 100, 104, 105, 109, 113, 114, 122, 123, 124, 126, 129, 135, 142, 145, 145, 147, 148, 155, 159, 162, 168, 169, 176, 180, 181, 183, 192, 199; population of, 5

Zuñiga y Cerda, Joseph de, 147

John E. Worth is associate professor of anthropology at the University of West Florida. He is the editor and translator of *Discovering Florida: First-Contact Narratives from Spanish Expeditions along the Lower Gulf Coast.*

Ripley P. Bullen Series
Florida Museum of Natural History

Tacachale: Essays on the Indians of Florida and Southeastern Georgia during the Historic Period, edited by Jerald T. Milanich and Samuel Proctor (1978)
Aboriginal Subsistence Technology on the Southeastern Coastal Plain during the Late Prehistoric Period, by Lewis H. Larson (1980)
Cemochechobee: Archaeology of a Mississippian Ceremonial Center on the Chattahoochee River, by Frank T. Schnell, Vernon J. Knight Jr., and Gail S. Schnell (1981)
Fort Center: An Archaeological Site in the Lake Okeechobee Basin, by William H. Sears, with contributions by Elsie O'R. Sears and Karl T. Steinen (1982)
Perspectives on Gulf Coast Prehistory, edited by Dave D. Davis (1984)
Archaeology of Aboriginal Culture Change in the Interior Southeast: Depopulation during the Early Historic Period, by Marvin T. Smith (1987)
Apalachee: The Land between the Rivers, by John H. Hann (1988)
Key Marco's Buried Treasure: Archaeology and Adventure in the Nineteenth Century, by Marion Spjut Gilliland (1989)
First Encounters: Spanish Explorations in the Caribbean and the United States, 1492–1570, edited by Jerald T. Milanich and Susan Milbrath (1989)
Missions to the Calusa, edited and translated by John H. Hann, with an introduction by William H. Marquardt (1991)
Excavations on the Franciscan Frontier: Archaeology at the Fig Springs Mission, by Brent Richards Weisman (1992)
The People Who Discovered Columbus: The Prehistory of the Bahamas, by William F. Keegan (1992)
Hernando de Soto and the Indians of Florida, by Jerald T. Milanich and Charles Hudson (1992)
Foraging and Farming in the Eastern Woodlands, edited by C. Margaret Scarry (1993)
Puerto Real: The Archaeology of a Sixteenth-Century Spanish Town in Hispaniola, edited by Kathleen Deagan (1995)
Political Structure and Change in the Prehistoric Southeastern United States, edited by John F. Scarry (1996)
Bioarchaeology of Native American Adaptation in the Spanish Borderlands, edited by Brenda J. Baker and Lisa Kealhofer (1996)
A History of the Timucua Indians and Missions, by John H. Hann (1996)
Archaeology of the Mid-Holocene Southeast, edited by Kenneth E. Sassaman and David G. Anderson (1996)
The Indigenous People of the Caribbean, edited by Samuel M. Wilson (1997; first paperback edition, 1999)
Hernando de Soto among the Apalachee: The Archaeology of the First Winter Encampment, by Charles R. Ewen and John H. Hann (1998)
The Timucuan Chiefdoms of Spanish Florida, by John E. Worth: vol. 1, *Assimilation*; vol. 2, *Resistance and Destruction* (1998; first paperback edition, 2020)
Ancient Earthen Enclosures of the Eastern Woodlands, edited by Robert C. Mainfort Jr. and Lynne P. Sullivan (1998)
An Environmental History of Northeast Florida, by James J. Miller (1998)
Precolumbian Architecture in Eastern North America, by William N. Morgan (1999)
Archaeology of Colonial Pensacola, edited by Judith A. Bense (1999)
Grit-Tempered: Early Women Archaeologists in the Southeastern United States, edited by Nancy Marie White, Lynne P. Sullivan, and Rochelle A. Marrinan (1999; first paperback edition, 2001)
Coosa: The Rise and Fall of a Southeastern Mississippian Chiefdom, by Marvin T. Smith (2000)
Religion, Power, and Politics in Colonial St. Augustine, by Robert L. Kapitzke (2001)
Bioarchaeology of Spanish Florida: The Impact of Colonialism, edited by Clark Spencer Larsen (2001)
Archaeological Studies of Gender in the Southeastern United States, edited by Jane M. Eastman and Christopher B. Rodning (2001)
The Archaeology of Traditions: Agency and History Before and After Columbus, edited by Timothy R. Pauketat (2001)

Foraging, Farming, and Coastal Biocultural Adaptation in Late Prehistoric North Carolina, by Dale L. Hutchinson (2002)
Windover: Multidisciplinary Investigations of an Early Archaic Florida Cemetery, edited by Glen H. Doran (2002)
Archaeology of the Everglades, by John W. Griffin (2002; first paperback edition, 2017)
Pioneer in Space and Time: John Mann Goggin and the Development of Florida Archaeology, by Brent Richards Weisman (2002)
Indians of Central and South Florida, 1513–1763, by John H. Hann (2003)
Presidio Santa María de Galve: A Struggle for Survival in Colonial Spanish Pensacola, edited by Judith A. Bense (2003)
Bioarchaeology of the Florida Gulf Coast: Adaptation, Conflict, and Change, by Dale L. Hutchinson (2004; first paperback edition, 2020)
The Myth of Syphilis: The Natural History of Treponematosis in North America, edited by Mary Lucas Powell and Della Collins Cook (2005)
The Florida Journals of Frank Hamilton Cushing, edited by Phyllis E. Kolianos and Brent R. Weisman (2005)
The Lost Florida Manuscript of Frank Hamilton Cushing, edited by Phyllis E. Kolianos and Brent R. Weisman (2005)
The Native American World Beyond Apalachee: West Florida and the Chattahoochee Valley, by John H. Hann (2006)
Tatham Mound and the Bioarchaeology of European Contact: Disease and Depopulation in Central Gulf Coast Florida, by Dale L. Hutchinson (2007)
Taíno Indian Myth and Practice: The Arrival of the Stranger King, by William F. Keegan (2007)
An Archaeology of Black Markets: Local Ceramics and Economies in Eighteenth-Century Jamaica, by Mark W. Hauser (2008; first paperback edition, 2013)
Mississippian Mortuary Practices: Beyond Hierarchy and the Representationist Perspective, edited by Lynne P. Sullivan and Robert C. Mainfort Jr. (2010; first paperback edition, 2012)
Bioarchaeology of Ethnogenesis in the Colonial Southeast, by Christopher M. Stojanowski (2010; first paperback edition, 2013)
French Colonial Archaeology in the Southeast and Caribbean, edited by Kenneth G. Kelly and Meredith D. Hardy (2011; first paperback edition, 2015)
Late Prehistoric Florida: Archaeology at the Edge of the Mississippian World, edited by Keith Ashley and Nancy Marie White (2012; first paperback edition, 2015)
Early and Middle Woodland Landscapes of the Southeast, edited by Alice P. Wright and Edward R. Henry (2013; first paperback edition, 2019)
Trends and Traditions in Southeastern Zooarchaeology, edited by Tanya M. Peres (2014)
New Histories of Pre-Columbian Florida, edited by Neill J. Wallis and Asa R. Randall (2014; first paperback edition, 2016)
Discovering Florida: First-Contact Narratives from Spanish Expeditions along the Lower Gulf Coast, edited and translated by John E. Worth (2014; first paperback edition, 2016)
Constructing Histories: Archaic Freshwater Shell Mounds and Social Landscapes of the St. Johns River, Florida, by Asa R. Randall (2015)
Archaeology of Early Colonial Interaction at El Chorro de Maíta, Cuba, by Roberto Valcárcel Rojas (2016)
Fort San Juan and the Limits of Empire: Colonialism and Household Practice at the Berry Site, edited by Robin A. Beck, Christopher B. Rodning, and David G. Moore (2016)
Rethinking Moundville and Its Hinterland, edited by Vincas P. Steponaitis and C. Margaret Scarry (2016; first paperback edition, 2019)
Gathering at Silver Glen: Community and History in Late Archaic Florida, by Zackary I. Gilmore (2016)
Paleoindian Societies of the Coastal Southeast, by James S. Dunbar (2016; first paperback edition, 2019)
Cuban Archaeology in the Caribbean, edited by Ivan Roksandic (2016)
Handbook of Ceramic Animal Symbols in the Ancient Lesser Antilles, by Lawrence Waldron (2016)
Archaeologies of Slavery and Freedom in the Caribbean: Exploring the Spaces in Between, edited by Lynsey A. Bates, John M. Chenoweth, and James A. Delle (2016; first paperback edition, 2018)

Setting the Table: Ceramics, Dining, and Cultural Exchange in Andalucía and La Florida, by Kathryn L. Ness (2017)
Simplicity, Equality, and Slavery: An Archaeology of Quakerism in the British Virgin Islands, 1740–1780, by John M. Chenoweth (2017)
Fit for War: Sustenance and Order in the Mid-Eighteenth-Century Catawba Nation, by Mary Elizabeth Fitts (2017)
Water from Stone: Archaeology and Conservation at Florida's Springs, by Jason O'Donoughue (2017)
Mississippian Beginnings, edited by Gregory D. Wilson (2017; first paperback edition, 2019)
Harney Flats: A Florida Paleoindian Site, by I. Randolph Daniel Jr. and Michael Wisenbaker (2017)
Honoring Ancestors in Sacred Space: The Archaeology of an Eighteenth-Century African-Bahamian Cemetery, by Grace Turner (2017)
Investigating the Ordinary: Everyday Matters in Southeast Archaeology, edited by Sarah E. Price and Philip J. Carr (2018)
New Histories of Village Life at Crystal River, by Thomas J. Pluckhahn and Victor D. Thompson (2018)
Early Human Life on the Southeastern Coastal Plain, edited by Albert C. Goodyear and Christopher R. Moore (2018)
The Archaeology of Villages in Eastern North America, edited by Jennifer Birch and Victor D. Thompson (2018)
The Cumberland River Archaic of Middle Tennessee, edited by Tanya M. Peres and Aaron Deter-Wolf (2019)
Pre-Columbian Art of the Caribbean, by Lawrence Waldron (2019)
Iconography and Wetsite Archaeology of Florida's Watery Realms, edited by Ryan Wheeler and Joanna Ostapkowicz (2019)
New Directions in the Search for the First Floridians, edited by David K. Thulman and Ervan G. Garrison (2019)
Archaeology of Domestic Landscapes of the Enslaved in the Caribbean, edited by James A. Delle and Elizabeth C. Clay (2019)
Cahokia in Context: Hegemony and Diaspora, edited by Charles H. McNutt and Ryan M. Parish (2020)
Bears: Archaeological and Ethnohistorical Perspectives in Native Eastern North America, edited by Heather A. Lapham and Gregory A. Waselkov (2020)
Contact, Colonialism, and Native Communities in the Southeastern United States, edited by Edmond A. Boudreaux III, Maureen Meyers, and Jay K. Johnson (2020)
An Archaeology and History of a Caribbean Sugar Plantation on Antigua, edited by Georgia L. Fox (2020)
Modeling Entradas: Sixteenth-Century Assemblages in North America, edited by Clay Mathers (2020)
Archaeology in Dominica: Everyday Ecologies and Economies at Morne Patate, edited by Mark W. Hauser and Diane Wallman (2020)
The Historical Turn in Southeastern Archaeology, edited by Robbie Ethridge and Eric E. Bowne (2020)

www.ingramcontent.com/pod-product-compliance
Lightning Source LLC
Chambersburg PA
CBHW052329010526
44270CB00038B/1870